GREAT NEED OVER THE WATER

GREAT NEED OVER THE WATER

The Letters of Theresa Huntington Ziegler, Missionary to Turkey, 1898–1905

Edited and with an Introduction
and Commentary
by

Stina Katchadourian

Gomidas Institute
Ann Arbor, Michigan

Photo Credits:
The photographs on pages 55–60 have been reproduced by permission of the Ellsworth Huntington Papers, Manuscripts and Archives, Yale University Library. The photographs on pages 183–88 and 311–14 have been reproduced by permission of the Houghton Library, Harvard University. The maps on page ix are courtesy of the Gomidas Institute.

Published by Taderon Press, P. O. Box 2735, Reading RG4 8GF, England, by arrangement with the Gomidas Institute

Printed in the United States of America
05 04 03 02 01 00 995 4 3 2 1

ISBN 0-9535191-0-4

For comments and inquiries please contact:
Gomidas Institute Books
PO Box 208
Princeton, New Jersey 08542

Email: books@gomidas.org

Table of Contents

Illustrations

Acknowledgements

Many benevolent spirits have sustained this project from its inception to its completion. My profound thanks to Caroline Ziegler Peck, her sister, Miriam Ziegler Wilson, and their sister-in-law, Frances Lewis Ziegler, who found Theresa Huntington Ziegler's letters and undertook the considerable task of arranging them in chronological order. All of them also generously shared their memories of Theresa Huntington Ziegler with me. My thanks also go to family members Mary Fletcher Hunt and Alice Huntington Allen, who added their written recollections. Helen Rice of Omaha, the daughter of the last President of Euphrates College, Henry Riggs, offered me both hospitality as well as a glimpse into her private family archives. To all, my sincere thanks.

Financial support for this book came from three sources: Mrs. Helen Bing gave an initial grant and a crucial push to get started, and in addition, provided funds to support the publication. She has truly been this project's angel, and I am profoundly grateful. I am deeply indebted as well to Mrs. Joyce Stein of the Philibosian Foundation, and the Armenian Missionary Association of America (AMAA). Their generous grants enabled me to consult archives on the East Coast.

Many others also provided valuable help along the way: my husband Herant Katchadourian, who read the manuscript at an early stage and offered important suggestions; Risa Goldberg, who with a keen eye and a sense of order put all Theresa Huntington's letters on disk. My thanks also to Bitte Boucht, Poppy Berghem, and Marilyn Yalom of the Institute for Research on Women and Gender at Stanford for reading the manuscript and for their insights. Lia and Bill Poorvu and Sanford and Ingrid Gifford of Cambridge, Massachusetts have my warmest thanks for extending to me their hospitality while I worked at the Houghton library at Harvard.

To the archivists at the Houghton Library, Harvard, my heartfelt thanks for patiently fetching file after file as I followed the paper traces of the various people connected to the missionary work at Harpoot. Likewise, their colleagues at the Yale library provided assistance for a glimpse into the files of Professor Ellsworth Huntington, Theresa's brother. My thanks as well to the Wellesley College Archives and the Wellesley College Alumni Association for information about Theresa Huntington when she was a student there.

I am grateful to professor Richard Hovannisian of UCLA for suggesting the Gomidas Institute as a publisher. Last, but not least, it has been a pleasure and a privilege to work with Ara Sarafian, whose historical insights and editorial expertise have helped guide this book into its final shape.

Stanford, 10.5.98
Stina Katchadourian

Introduction

Miss Frearson. Miss Blake. Like two lighthouses, these two American missionary women towered over the girlhood of Efronia, my Armenian mother-in-law, as she was growing up in the Ottoman empire in the last decade of the 19th century. While working on a book about my mother-in-law, I sought for more information about these women, who seemed to have lost none of their power as role models and inspiration for her well into her old age. The Houghton Library at Harvard houses one of the largest and most significant collections of primary source materials on the American Protestant missionary enterprise, and that is where I conducted my search. Would the archives yield any information about the Misses Frearson and Blake? Would they shed some light on the extraordinary impact they had on the young Efronia?

No such luck. Yes, there was a brief mention of their names in a file but that was all. No tantalizing letters in their hand, no first-hand accounts of that young girl, my future mother-in-law, who evidently had been the favorite of her missionary teachers from kindergarten all through high-school.

But once in that vast forest of documents which is the Archives of the American Board of Commissioners for Foreign Missions, I decided to take a few side trips. The possibilities were vast: the ABCFM Archives include well over half a million items, many of them in manuscript form. There are letters, diaries, obituaries, minutes from meetings, annual reports; histories of mission stations and the schools and hospitals and orphanages and vocational schools that they founded and ran all over the world; detailed financial accounts from the mission stations; population figures; reports of the political situation; thousands of photographs and daguerreotypes of missionary men and women, in groups or alone: stern-looking and calm in the pictures taken when they left their home country as young men and women; and photographs with a lifetime of service under harsh conditions etched on their faces after they returned.

Not only missionary work is discussed in these papers. Missionaries, in many parts of the world, were often doing double duty as on the scene observers of the country in which they were working: with their passion for knowledge typical of the times, they recorded information about flora and fauna, geographical features, political conditions and native customs in the regions where they lived. The churches that sent them out were looking for almost superhuman versatility in their recruits. One article states that "The London Missionary Society, in 1823, lists the following qualifications for a missionary to an 'uncivilized' nation: facility in languages, acquaintance with most popular sciences, knowledge of the 'mechanical arts,' including agriculture, carpentry, and handicrafts, some skill in medicine and surgery, teaching ability, an intimate knowledge of human nature, a prudent, patient, and persevering mind, and genuine religion—all this at the age of twenty-one."[1]

Browsing in the Ottoman Empire records of the American Board of Commissioners for Foreign Missions that afternoon, I came across a file containing a dozen letters written by a young woman. Her name was Theresa Huntington. She was writing from Harpoot, a town in the foothills of the Taurus Mountains in Eastern Anatolia. It seemed there had been a four-year college in Harpoot at one time, by the name of Euphrates College. Theresa had been a teacher there.

The first letter was dated March 16, 1899. It was addressed to 'Miss Lord'. The handwriting, neat and forceful, seemed to fly over the page in excitement:

> I want to take you with me to the Sunday school for the Mangaran or Grammar School girls. We must go down a slippery, dirty hill, and scatter the chickens assembled about the rude door, before we can enter. Just inside the doorway are the shelves filled with shoes; coarse, shapeless, flat shoes, which flop, flop from the heels of the wearers. We, too, must carefully remove our overshoes. All the girls will rise, when they see us, and will regard us with shy, but very observing eyes. Deeroohee, the head of the school, poor, faithful, misshapen girl, will offer us some of the few chairs and stools which the room contains. It is a dingy, low room, on the floor are strips of coarse carpet of village make, and on the walls are a repulsive crucifix and some paraphernalia of the Gregorian Church, for this room we rent from them, and their services are held here. However, we see, too upon the walls, some large, bright Sunday School lesson pictures, which were sent to us from America.
>
> The children sing heartily, though their voices are somewhat shrill. At lesson-time the teachers, most of whom are our college girls, sit on low benches, while the class gather about them on the floor.

1. Mary Walker, *Harvard Library Bulletin*, Vol. VI, 1952, Harvard University Library publication.

> Such big, bright, eyes as these girls have! and such quick, eager answers they give! You will wish that you could hear such choruses in answer to questions that you put to your own American Sunday School class. Most of these girls learn from three to twenty or even more verses every Sunday. The knowledge which the older girls have of the Bible often fairly alarms me. When we rise to go, some little girl will scamper for our over-shoes, and if we happen to smile our thanks will be sure to duck her head down into her apron or cover her face with her shawl in giggling confusion.

Who was this writer with her lively style and her eye for the telling detail? I read on: in letter after letter, mainly addressed to "My Dear Friends of the Norfolk and Pilgrim Branch,"—a ladies missionary auxiliary—Theresa Huntington made her world in Harpoot come alive. But why had she left her family and made this commitment for several years in that God-forsaken place? What had that experience really been like for her? What had happened to the people and to the community to which she had devoted all those years?

There is a ledger on a shelf in the library, listing the names of the missionaries who were sent out to various parts of the world. I looked up the Eastern Turkey Mission, and found Theresa Huntington's name. In miniscule handwriting someone had written down the barest profile of this young woman:

"Theresa Lyman Huntington, b. Galesbury, Ill., May 21, 1875. Prof. relig. Milton, Mass 1896—Wellesley College—left NY Sept. 10, 1898, arr. Harpoot Nov. 15. Arr. Boston Sept. 1905,- released July 3, 1906."

There was one more piece of information in this cryptic life summary: Theresa had married a Mr. Charles Ziegler and settled in Waban, Mass., a small community just outside Boston.

Theresa was a Congregational missionary. If she had settled in Waban, as the ledger claimed, then chances were she had joined a Congregational church there. The next morning, which was a Saturday and my last in Cambridge, I decided to call the operator and ask for the phone numbers of any Congregational churches in Waban. I was given two numbers and called the first one. An elderly woman answered the phone. I explained my errand. I had read the letters of a certain Theresa Huntington written while she was a missionary in Turkey. I wanted to find out what happened to her after she returned. Might there have been, at some point in time, a member of that congregation by the name of Theresa Huntington Ziegler?

There was a long silence at the other end of the line. Then the woman said: "She was my mother."

Caroline Ziegler Peck and I met for a cup of coffee. Carol, in her mid-eighties and Theresa's oldest child, turned out to be a vivacious, small woman with a keen mind and a wry sense of humor; one of the first female graduates of Union Theological Seminary in New York, who for years had lived in the greater Boston area and worked with dyslexic children. Her memories of her mother were warm and admiring and were recounted to me in the same precise and detailed language that I found in Theresa's letters from Harpoot. The meeting left me even more intrigued with Theresa Huntington. After I returned to California, I wrote Carol Peck and asked her whether she knew about any other letters or articles written by her mother. She replied:

"Whether a careful examination of family papers will bring valuable material to light is a question. All of this is in large cartons in the basement of the vacation home of my brother's widow in New Hampshire. I doubt that we will find any articles by her, but there may be letters of real interest. Time will tell."

The next fall, Mrs. Peck called me. "I think you'll be pleased," she said. "Rummaging through the attic of the summer house, we found boxes and boxes of letters written by my mother from Harpoot to her family that none of us had ever seen. I have arranged them in chronological order and made copies of them and I'll be glad to send them to you. I think you'll find them interesting."

Theresa Huntington's letters from the town of Harpoot in the eastern part of the Ottoman empire where she spent an uninterrupted stretch of seven years, constitute the core of this book. Through these letters—written mostly by candle-light in her small room in Harpoot at the end of a long day's work—we not only get a rich insight into the daily lives of the Ottoman Armenians, townspeople and villagers alike, but also glimpses of their holidays and celebrations, their social customs and traditions. In addition, Theresa Huntington gives us an insider's portrait of a missionary community and its relationship to Armenians and Turks during the perilous times of Sultan Abdul Hamid II. She writes about the people who preceded her at Harpoot, about those who were there with her, and about what motivated them to do what they were doing. She describes their holidays and their work, what they read in their free time, what games they played, how they dressed. She describes, in mouth-watering detail, what they ate; she describes their illnesses and their social mores, their friendships and loves, their hopes and their fears.

Many of these missionaries figure in the ABCFM Archives and in other published sources. It was thus possible to add to the picture Theresa gives us of them in her letters, and this I have tried to do. Some of these men and women really deserve books of their own. At the very least, Theresa's letters demanded that I give them space in this one.

Theresa's stint as a missionary came at the height of the women's foreign mission movement in the United States. Like other women's organizations, this movement had its roots in the aftermath of the Civil War. Women had been drawn out of their homes and into active participation in their communities in support of the war effort. Once they had discovered their strengths and organizing skills, many women were ready to be active in their communities in the service of social causes. One of these was the missionary movement, drawing well educated, middle class churchgoing women into an activism that aimed at spreading the blessings of American womanhood to "women and children in heathen lands." On the premises that the well-being of society hinged on the education of women, and that the best way to democracy was through a Christian way of life, women had founded their own missionary organizations parallel to those run by men. Theresa was a Congregationalist; she always made sure to point out that she had been sent to Turkey by the Congregational Woman's Board of Missions, founded in Boston in 1868.

Through the prism of Theresa's letters, I have tried to present a picture of the Harpoot missionary station as a whole, beginning before the time she arrived and following its dramatic history until it was forced to close its doors. The Harpoot Station was in many ways typical of so many of the Protestant missionary stations throughout the Ottoman Empire. It was founded with the same high hopes and lived through the same crushingly hard times. The timing of Theresa Huntington's work in Harpoot is of great interest: she arrives there just a couple of years after a major massacre of the Armenians, under Sultan Abdul Hamid II in 1894-96. She leaves just a few years before the First World War, when the Armenian Genocide was to end the Armenian presence in their traditional homeland for ever. Many books have focused on these two massacres; the period between them has received less attention.

Finally, Theresa's letters also present us with a portrait of a young woman and her family in late nineteenth-century New England. I grew very fond of Theresa reading her letters. She was an honest and intelligent woman who approached her frequently gruelling years in Harpoot with courage, high spirits and a keen sense of humour. She did nothing to hide her tenderness toward her parents and her brothers and sisters in her letters. Unfortunately, we do not have the letters that the members of the Huntington family wrote to her: her father, who was a Congregational minister; her mother, and her three brothers and two sisters. But Theresa addresses herself to each of them in turn in her "family letters" with a warmth, a love, and an immediacy that belies her geographical distance to them and which may make us think again, in this time of instant communication, about what 'keeping in touch' really means.

MAPS

OTTOMAN EMPIRE IN ASIA MINOR CIRCA 1900

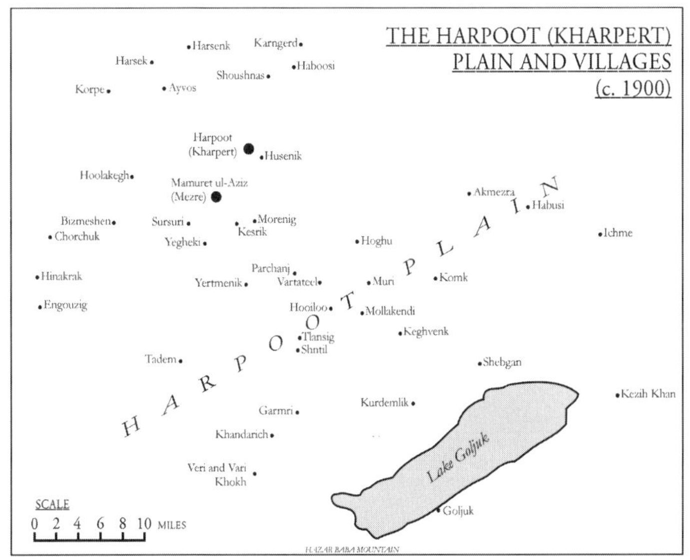

Chapter One: The Man God Has Meant for Me Will Find Me in Turkey

The Rev. Henry Huntington and his wife Mary were hardly surprised when Theresa announced that she was going abroad as a missionary. They had raised her in a home that from the time she was old enough to remember had always been filled with meetings of ladies' missionary societies and talk of all the work that needed to be done in "heathen lands." As their six children were growing up, Mrs. Huntington herself was actively involved in supporting overseas missionary work and the Rev. Huntington often showed them articles from the *Missionary Herald* and *The Congregationalist* and *Light and Life for Women* with descriptions of the lives of missionaries in far-off mission stations.

They knew, too, that Theresa was particularly well-suited for the work. She was energetic and robust. She had a winning way about her and her religious beliefs were sound and strong. They knew something else as well: once Theresa had made up her mind, she was going to do what she was going to do.

Still, they were hoping she would not venture out. Their reluctance to have her go, even under ordinary circumstances, would have been understandable. She wanted to go to a place in the interior of the Ottoman Empire to which there were no decent roads. Letters from this place would take several weeks to reach them and sometimes would not make it through at all. There would be no furlough for the next seven years. Many women missionaries of their acquaintance had made this their life's work and would return only for brief periods over their entire lifetimes. When the Huntingtons saw these returning missionaries again, it would be during visits to the Walker Missionary Home in nearby Auburndale, where years of gruelling work and ill health would clearly show on their faces and bodies. Some never returned. The Rev. Huntington and his wife knew that if Theresa decided to leave, they might very well be asked to make the ultimate sacrifice for missionary work.

As if all this was not enough, the year 1898 was no ordinary year for a missionary to set out for the Ottoman empire. Most of the work there was being done among the Armenians, an ancient Christian minority in a Moslem country whose minority existence had always been precarious. Between 1894 and 1896, the year Theresa graduated from Wellesley college, a series of massacres of the Armenians had swept the empire. Decades of missionary work had been wiped out, mission stations lay in ruins, and thousands of Armenian orphans roamed the towns and villages in search of food and shelter. People were raising serious questions about the wisdom of missionary work there: should the missionaries be allowed to continue working in the Ottoman empire? Would it be possible to guarantee their safety in the future if such a disaster should happen again?

To add to their burdens, the Rev. and his wife already had one child to worry about over the waters: their eldest son, Ellsworth. Just a year younger than Theresa, he had to pass on Harvard for financial reasons and instead went to Beloit College in Wisconsin where his maternal aunt, Theresa Gaytes, helped him with room and board. Ellsworth graduated from this small liberal arts school—"The Yale of the West"—near the top of his class with a strong concentration in the sciences and an urge to travel to "some part of the world where everything is different." His chance came in late September, 1897, when he received an offer from the President of the American Board of Commissioners for Foreign Missions in Boston, James Barton, to become the assistant to the President of Euphrates College in Harpoot in eastern Turkey. To this budding young scientist of limitless enthusiasm and curiously, who later would be a Professor of Geography at Yale, eastern Turkey sounded like a geographical and archaeological paradise. Ellsworth sailed for Harpoot in 1897, only one year after the last wave of massacres and arrived in the town on the Upper Euphrates river in late November. The ailing President of the college, Dr. Caleb Gates, wrote to the Trustees: "Mr. Huntington arrived on Thanksgiving Day, and we gave thanks! Our first impressions are very favorable. He is quiet, dignified, self-possessed, full of resources and earnest. He rode twelve hours on Thanksgiving Day, and in the evening asked what his work would be on the morrow. I take to this young man."

Ellsworth was twenty-one years old when he arrived in Harpoot. His two older sisters, Cornelia (or Kindie, as she is sometimes called in Theresa's letters) and Theresa, had wholeheartedly supported his going and tried to shore up the worried parents. Cornelia herself, optimistic and warm-hearted but always somewhat frail, had very much wanted to follow Ellsworth to Harpoot, but was afraid her health would not be able to take the strain of missionary work.

But Theresa was a different story: although she was an English major at Wellesley, she was robust and athletic. She rowed first boat on the Wellesley crew; she took courses in Practical Gymnastics at the Harvard Summer School; she seemed never to be walking, always running. She spent the two years after graduation teaching high school in Milton, in the Departments of Physical Culture and the Department of English, feeling vaguely dissatisfied.

In 1896, she wrote from Milton to her brother Ellsworth:

> I feel five or six years older than when I began to teach. My work isn't wholly satisfactory. I don't believe it is what I can do best. I don't know now whether I don't love it because I don't do it well, or whether I don't do better because I don't love it. It shows me my weaknesses with terrible distinctness. I am not systematic; I am lazy, and I put off things. It is an awful thing to know the right, and not to do it. I read a fine bit in the "Outlook" the other day. It was poetry and the concluding lines were: They fail and they alone/who have not striven. Now you know something about me. As to looks, I am 'plain'—like the rhinoceros, and I am growing somewhat severe and vinegary a la schoolmarm of fiction.

This overly critical reference to her looks—Theresa had fine, regular features, a beautiful complexion and expressive, dark eyes—is a reference to her brother's descriptions of girls he had met and looked at in a way that did not please Theresa:

> Don't be afraid to tell about the pretty girls you like. I won't jeer. It is only when you size up a girl almost entirely by her looks that I object. The question always seems to be: Is a girl pretty? We don't talk that stuff and say 'handsome men.' We don't care much how they look, if we like other things about them. I don't know what made me think of saying that just now, but I think boys always do talk that way, and I don't like it.

Theresa's little sermon to her brother may have been dictated by a certain amount of envy: there were very few interesting young men in her own circles just then:

> I meet about three young men in the daily course of my life—Mr. Chaddock who is very talkative and friendly and sometimes gives me a ride home from meeting behind his little trotter; Mr. McCulley who shakes hands pleasantly and is silent; and Mr. Clapp, who nods "Good Morning" and stalks on, his hands thrust deep into his trouser's pockets, his head sunk between his shoulders, his eyes perusing the ground.

But there is another strain in the correspondence between brother and sister, based on religion. At this point, Theresa was far from clear about what she believed, but we can see on what basis she would later decide to go out as a missionary:

> I don't practise all I believe, but I do think that the living means more and more to me, and the theology and creed less. I still believe Christ is the Son of God and I trust that I always shall. His life is a pattern for us and it seems to me more and more possible of imitation in every way. I do believe that the humble, fearless, righteous life of Christ means everything and that men as years go by will grow more like him and that social reform will come through men who are selfless and full of love, as He was. The trouble is that we are all afraid to follow.

We don't know just when Theresa first made inquiries to the Woman's Board of Missions, an organization parallel to the American Board and set up specifically with the aim of educating and evangelizing among women, but the following letter from her brother who by this time was working in Harpoot shows that she clearly had given the question of going to Turkey a great deal of thought:

> Harpoot, Turkey
> June 5, 1898
>
> Dear Sister,
>
> Your letter of May 8 was received last Thursday, June 2, and of course interested me very much. By the time this reaches you, you will probably have decided for or against coming to Harpoot this year, but perhaps if you do not come now you may come later. Anyhow I will write as good an answer as I can to your letter. Most of what you say for or against coming seems to be perfectly true. The question of money troubles me sometimes. I feel as though I ought to help the family at home more or less, but in order to get fitted out for coming here I had to run somewhat into debt and it will take a year to get that paid up and perhaps a little more. However, after Jan. 1899 my salary will be more than I need and I can spare $100 a year I think. You see I get $400 while those who are regular missionaries get only $300. I do not think that is important, however, because I think the Lord shows what he wants us to do and if it is something which does not furnish as much money as is needed, He will provide some other way of sending it. I am well

aware that many people call that idea folly but it is scriptural and "The wisdom of this world is foolishness with God." 1 Cor. 3:19.

As for preparation, you are as well prepared as most of the missionaries in Turkey and have had two years of excellent experience. Of course it would be an advantage, not to be despised, if you had a musical and kindergarten training. The case stands like this: Miss Daniels and Miss Barnum have all they can do and more and Miss Seymour helps by teaching about three classes. Mr. Barnum is 71 years old and has had a great many experiences of the kind that wear a man out. Last summer he completely broke down, although he has been quite well this winter. He gets tired very easily and Mrs. B. also is doing more than she can bear. It stands to reason that they can only stay here a few years longer at most and they may go in a year. When they leave Harpoot Miss Emma will have to go too because they both rely on her all the time, and Miss Seymour will go with them. She has been here twenty years without visiting America and is 67 years old so that she will not return and there is no knowing how soon Miss Barnum will come back or even whether she will come. So you see that in a year perhaps and anyway in two or three years Miss Daniels will be left alone. Miss Bush has her touring work and ought not to be called on for much help in the school, although she sometimes helps in a pinch like these few weeks now when Miss Barnum is at Erzroom. What is needed is someone who can come this fall and get the language before Miss D. is left alone. Afterward another lady is needed but in the present condition of the Board's finances it is doubtful how soon we can have her.

As for music you know as much about it theoretically as Miss Barnum who teaches now and you can sing but not play as well. If you came, could you not practise and study an hour or two every day while you are learning the language and just devote yourself to those two things? You know a good deal about kindergarten methods, I think, and if you could spend the month of July studying in a summer school you could learn a great deal. You would have to have someone else get your outfit ready. Mr. Gates does not start till August and no doubt would wait for you until at least the middle if the month. Dr. B. cannot get to Constantinople before Oct. 1 as far as we can see now, although he may change his plans.

The question of health need not trouble you at all. This is a very good climate after one gets used to it. It is necessary to become acclimated and during the first year one somehow wants a lot of sleep, and because of the unsanitary condition of the city there is some malaria here as well as on the coast. All our ladies keep in very good health unless they overwork. Miss Bush is a little bit of a thing, very slight and frail and weighing only 85 pounds but she travels all over and lives in all sorts of uncomfortable and unhealthy places and yet she is almost always well.

Of course you will have to live in a house without a furnace but I do not think you will find that very hard. Most winters are not as cold as last winter and if you take a little care of your fire you can be warm all the time. I did not take much care of mine last winter but I did not suffer any. For instance I almost never started it in the morning but left that for the servant to do while we were at breakfast. The girls' school is now in a very ill-adapted and inadequate building so that you would not live there until we have a new building. For the present you would live in one of the new houses which will be well-built and comfortable. You and I might live in the same house in the story below where Miss Bush and Miss Seymour live or you and Miss Newnham, the English lady who is coming, may live together somewhere else. First we will find out what Miss N. is like. She has started and is in Smyrna or Constantinople now, waiting for an escort and she will probably have to come with Dr. Ussher unless she is so anxious to come with a lady that she decides to wait for Mrs. Gates. We expect her with Dr. Ussher.

If you come, there will be eight of us who will not belong to either of the two regular families and no one knows where we will board. If Mrs. Browne comes it will leave seven of us to be divided among three families.

A great deal of your work will be teaching but you will have to help Miss Daniels in making all sorts of plans, and to run a Christian Endeavor society, teach some of the teachers and be ready to give counsel or help to any teacher or scholar, in part to help give the school a stiff backbone.

I know the Lord will not let you come if this is not the right place and we have a right to tell Him to guide because He has promised. We do wrong every time we are anxious about the future. It is just like saying to God, "I am not sure that you tell the truth." To be sure I do not live up to this but that is because I have not entirely put off the old man, and God *is* teaching me. I don't think I am fit to be here but we must go where we are called and do all we can. One ought to do everything from a sheer love of souls but such a feeling is a growth, not a sudden acquisition. I am becoming impressed with the absolute necessity of more careful Bible study. I spend a little time every morning—15 or 20 minutes or so—and an hour or two on Sunday, but that is not enough. Hereafter I must have more at any cost. I am going to get up a little earlier and as I can't wake myself up I shall ask the Lord to do it and He will.

It is good that you have so many openings for next year, but I really think Turkey will be your choice, and Miss Daniels seems to be convinced of it too. It is an odd thing that as long ago as last February she said she believed you would come here, in fact the very first time she spoke of it to me she said that she thought her idea was from the Lord.

One thing more, sister; I know that neither Miss Daniels or I or anyone else can guess what the Lord wants you to do and if you think that we are mistaken, say so and stay in America or go wherever the Lord tell *you* that He wants you.

This note has grown to serious dimensions. Don't laugh at the poor way in which I have expressed my meaning.

Most lovingly, your brother,
Ellsworth Huntington

Unbeknownst to Ellsworth, Theresa had already secured some letters of recommendation and her application process was under way. "I know of no young lady more eminently fitting, both by nature and by grace, for Christian work, than Miss Huntington," wrote Mary Waterman of Gorham, Maine. "She has spent her life in a home, the whole atmosphere of which is that of a Christian consecration, she has had a thorough and careful education, her personality is peculiarly attractive and winning." "I have known her from her babyhood and consider her particularly well-qualified for the work she is contemplating," wrote the Reverend C. M. Daniels of Norfolk, Mass. "Intellectually brought up in an atmosphere of books and study and refined culture, with the advantages of academic and college education, she has made the best of these opportunities and is intelligent, bright, fond of study and has the command of mental resources which only thorough training gives. She also has a cheerfulness and elasticity of spirit and sympathy for others which seem to one important qualifications for missionary service."

To this, Theresa added her own words:

My father and mother both came from New England ancestry, and practically all my life has been spent in New England. I was born in Galesburg, Ill., May 21, 1875, being the third child of six, all of whom are living. In 1877 we came to Gorham, Maine, where my father was the pastor of the Congregational Church until 1881. I studied in the public schools, in Gorham, Maine, and Milton, Mass., preparing for college in the high school of the latter town. In 1892 I entered Wellesley College where I took a regular 4 year course. I have also had some private lessons in gymnastic work, and in the summer of -97 took the course in Practical Gymnastics at the Harvard Summer School.

There is now no duty at home which prevents me from going, and God has spoken to me so plainly through my brother and the missionaries now at Harpoot, that I do not dare to disobey Him. The need and sadness of those who are without Christ has lately begun to be a burden upon my breast.

If there is a touch of defensiveness in the opening of the last paragraph, it is explained in this letter to her beloved aunt Theresa Gaytes in Wisconsin:

Milton, Mass.

Dear Aunt Theresa,

Your note made me feel sad, too, at first, but I can't help feeling that I have done the right thing in deciding to go to Turkey, hard as it is to leave my home-people and my home-land. I know that there is work to do in the United States, but here will always be, till the millennium, and there is oh, so much more work to be done in foreign countries.

What you said about homes, and a mother's work, almost made me laugh, just because I agree with you so thoroughly, and yet its application to me seemed so funny. I believe that Mamma would like best to have me marry, but imagine me, with that great need over the water, staying at home waiting for a possible husband because I think I could make a happy home. If God wants me to marry (which I very much doubt) the man He has meant for me will find me in Turkey. I don't believe, however, that there are more than half a dozen unmarried American men in that country. Somehow this subject amuses me a little.

Dear Auntie, I do thank you for praying for me. No one knows how much I need it, and Mamma and Pappa need it,—they feel so badly to have me go. It makes my heart ache a little because so many people whom I love, don't want me to go, or at least, have no joy in my going. The teachers at Harpoot are over-worked and are in great need of help which I can give, and Ellsworth won't be so much alone, when I am there. When I think of those things, I am happy.

With much love to Herbert,

Very affectionately,
Theresa L. Huntington.
August 26th, 1898

In the face of this determination and Theresa's sense of a higher calling, there was little her parents could do to persuade her to stay. Three weeks after writing this letter to her aunt, Theresa sits in her stateroom on board the freight steamer SS Winifreda and writes the first of her letters to her family.

Chapter Two: The Atlantic, and a Long Train Ride

SS Winifreda
American Transport Line
September 10, 1898
Monday, Sept. 2, at 2:45

My very dear family,

A clear air, clouds large and fleecy, the water a glorious deep blue, very opaque. This morning there was hardly a white-cap visible. This afternoon it is a little rougher. No one has been sick today. A little flock of stormy petrels follows in our wake. One I saw shimmering over the water before the bow, I wish I could make out their color and markings. I am disappointed that it is not rougher; or rather that the waves are not higher in mid-ocean. I should like to see one day which the sailors call rough.

Wed., Sept. 14

We are rolling and pitching gloriously just now—about 9:15 P.M. I sway back and forth as I write, curled up on the broad seat which runs the length of my stateroom.

Yesterday nothing exciting happened, except that we had venison instead of grouse for dinner, and rice au jus, instead of rice au something else. Meals seem to be important functions on shipboard. We made a run of 318 miles yesterday, as we did also the day before and today. At this rate we shan't make our 3,800 miles in ten days, because at first we went more slowly. Miss Ellsworth, Miss Bushnell and I are reading Kipling's "Soldiers Three" aloud. Cornelia will appreciate what Mulvaney says about "the shuparfluous necessity of sleep." Her books, by the way, are a god-send. Nobody else had anything at all light, and I only regret that I didn't take the third one. Isn't it queer that Mrs. Browne has a copy of "With Fire & Sword" exactly like mine?

Fri., Sept. 16

Yesterday was an interesting day. I was awakened at about 5 o'clock by a comb and whiskbroom which alighted on my berth in quick succession. Then my trunk began to skate back and forth, and gradually, shoes, books, letters etc. joined in the scrimmage. There was a constant, long roll from side to side (Pitching, by the way, is the motion from end to end). I had to stand with one foot braced against my trunk, while I dressed. It was very droll to see the people get into the dining room that morning. Some sidled in, hanging onto railings and chairs. Others tried to be dignified and deliberate, only to find themselves suddenly rushing posthaste toward the tables. The trays were on the table, as they were the day before. At one point in the meal we rolled so that nobody could eat. In the central partition of the tables, oranges, rolls, china and silver were all piled together, sliding back and forth. Some people were hanging onto their water cups and holding them out over the table to prevent them from spilling. The waiters were almost standing on their heads and everybody was leaning back and laughing immoderately. I never saw anything much more amusing than the waiters steering around a corner with their hands full on a rough day. Where other people hang on, they lean at an angle. They lean sideways too and keep on walking in the most ludicrous way. After breakfast, we went on deck. The water magnificent. The waves piled up higher than the deck when we were in the trough. It somehow seemed to me like winter weather. The air was clear and cold (49°), and the clouds had a peculiar wintry look. They were broken and ragged. Off and on during the day little rain squalls broke over us, and passed quickly away. There was a beautiful rainbow in the morning which lasted an hour or more. In fact we are constantly having rainbows. Just now at 5 P.M., as I sit on the deck writing I can see the lower end of one against the clouds. Overhead it is clear blue sky, and there has been no rain for an hour or two. Yesterday I had two drenchings—one partial and one thorough. The first time, I was in my stateroom with my back toward the port-hole which was open. Suddenly the water poured in over my neck and shoulders, splashing all the large objects in the room more or less. Later in the morning I had been standing on the lower deck on the sheltered side, where most everybody was. I wanted Miss Lord to see the rainbow on the other side and started across the end. The ship was tipped so that I had to climb at first, then it rolled over the other way and just as I reached the end of

> the deck, a great wave met me and completely enveloped me for an instant. I turned to run back just as the boat swung over, and slid and skipped back to my starting point with the water running along with me up to my ankles. Just as I reached the corner I sat down in all the brine. Mrs. Browne and several other people were standing there and of course got their feet wet. All my clothing was more or less wet. Mamma may be glad to know that I had on my old brown skirt and winter jacket. Nothing was much injured. The waves were remarkable all day. Mrs. Browne had never seen them so high before, and the officers told us that such a sea was very unusual. We had met the tail-end of a storm.

Already, hidden behind all this wind-blown excitement, is another strand in Theresa's letters she never tries to conceal during her seven years in Turkey: "love more than tongue can tell" for her family. Theresa knew enough about the lives of missionaries not to discount the possibility that she might have left her family for a very long time, maybe even for good. Packed into her steamer trunk were bunches of letters from various family members, to be opened at designated dates and in designated places, and small packages of candy and books. "Did I speak of Papa's beautiful letter which I read last Sunday?" "To-day we ate Ruth's candy." "Mamma's funny, frivolous book will be good for us all. Thank you, my dear mother." "I was very glad to receive Mamma's and Cornelia's letters, which were handed to me last night."

Theresa's "Papa," Henry Strong Huntington, was born in New York City in 1836, and was a 1857 graduate of Yale College. From there, he went on to Andover Theological Seminary and in 1870 married Mary Lawrence from Ellsworth, Maine. In 1863, the Huntingtons settled in Galesburg, Illinois where their first three children were born: Cornelia (1872), Theresa (1875) and Ellsworth (1876). When Theresa was two years old, the family moved to the parsonage of Gorham, Maine where the Rev. Huntington became the minister of the Congregational Church. Three more children were born in Gorham: George (1878), Henry (Harry in the letters, 1881), and Ruth (1882). At the time Theresa left for Turkey, Cornelia, who had preceded her at Wellesley, was twenty-six and living at home; Ellsworth was eagerly waiting for her in Turkey; George was a sophomore at Williams; Harry and Ruth were attending the local public high school in Milton.

Theresa grew up at a time when very few people had telephones at home; electricity was just being introduced; trolleys were appearing for the first time in some cities; cars were the playthings of a wealthy few. The pace of life was slow, and the atmosphere of the Huntington home devoutly Christian. "We always had a blessing at meals," wrote Harry, "and after breakfast we sat down together in the back parlor for prayers. Each morning we read a chapter from the Bible, each of us who had reached the age where he could read, reading two verses in turn in the circle. Then we sang a hymn; then all knelt down in front of his chair while father led us in prayer." Theresa never forgot this aspect of her upbringing: years later as a mother, she held strictly to rules that seemed to belong to a puritan era: no loud talk, work or play on Sundays, only quiet reading. No make-up, no short hair, no shaving of legs for her daughters.

There was another aspect of the Huntington household typical of the times: the tremendous enthusiasm for facts and learning. Just as the world was full of souls thirsting to be filled with the light of religion, so it was filled with blank spots on the map that needed to be described, charted, measured. Ellsworth spent most of his life as an explorer and geographer doing just that. And Theresa, at home and later at Wellesley, had developed a strong belief in her own capabilities as a woman and an urge to teach and inform:

> SS Winifreda
> American Transport Line
> September 10, 1898
>
> My very dear family,
>
> We sailed at nine from New York. The Winifreda is a freight steamer, carrying now some 300 head of cattle and 89 horses, which all together weigh about 10 tons. We have also 1000 slaughtered cattle on board, packed below in a temperature of 10°. We travel at the rate of 14 or 15 miles a hour. Now some 80 miles lie between us and New York.
>
> The distance from the lowest of the 3 decks down to the bottom of the vessel is 40 ft. and here the freight is kept. Most of this information Harold and I gleaned from one of the men who cares for the cattle. We two, H. and I went on a tour of investigation this afternoon, after which we played a game.
>
> To return to this morning, the pilot climbed down the ladder with his bundle of letters, when we were off Sandy Hook, at half-past ten. At the same time the flags were run down. I spent a large part of the morning in making a list of the contents of my trunk, for the special convenience of the Turks, and in making my stateroom cozy. I have an outside stateroom all to myself. Miss Lord and Miss Bushnell are opposite, and Mrs. Browne and Harold next to them.
>
> There are 32 passengers on board—about half the number for which there are accommodations. We have breakfast at 8:30, lun-

> cheon at one and dinner at 6:30. At eleven the deck steward will bring you beef tea and crackers or fruit, if you want any. The table is good on the whole—a great many kinds of meat, and very few vegetables.
>
> In the stern of the vessel is the log which records the distance we sail every 24 hours. We are sailing now north of east, toward the Banks of Newfoundland, instead of going directly toward London. Yesterday we met or passed four ocean vessels in the afternoon—all at a distance. Today I have seen only two—one a steamer of this line bound westward, and a large schooner sailing north-west. After all, the Winifreda does belong to the Atlantic Transport Line. The Wilson & Turners-Leyland Company was bought by the former line some six months ago. This steamer cost about 120,000 dollars.

Theresa's fellow passengers don't always measure up. Theresa was a severe critic of character and her standards were high:

> I had a little conversation with Mr. Lane, the consul. This is the first time he has crossed the ocean. To me he seems astonishingly ignorant of the land and people to which he goes. I rather suspect that he sympathizes with the Turks in the recent troubles....Yesterday evening we spent in the music room, for the first time. I am disappointed in the passengers. I thought there would be some delightful people among them....Mr. Baker is a loquacious, self-admiring, half-educated man whom I blush to own as a countryman.

Theresa spent most of her time on board the Winifreda with the missionary party bound for Turkey. Mrs. Browne and her eight year old son Harold and Miss Laura Ellsworth were also bound for Harpoot and the Misses Lord and Bushnell were going to Erzroom, also in the so-called Eastern Turkey Mission.

Nine days later, little Harold Browne excitedly announced that the English coast had been sighted:

> Monday, Sept. 19th, 1898
>
> This morning nothing of special interest happened. I spent most of my time in letter-writing. Between 12 and 1 o'clock, Harold came running into the music room where we had spread out our papers, to announce that a lighthouse was in sight. It was difficult to make out at first because it looked merely like a little

white line against the sky. In less than an hour we were passing the Scilly Islands, at a distance of about six miles. They are low and rounded. From far off they remind me of the islands in Boston Harbor. At five minutes of four by my watch I saw the coast of England—Land's End. From that time till six o'clock I couldn't keep my eyes off the land. We were passing along the Cornwall coast—a rough dangerous shore. There are high cliffs here, and beautiful rolling lands farther inland. At least, so it looks from the water. With the glass (which has been, by the way, a great pleasure) we could see plainly the hedge-rows running between the fields, and some large square brick houses, which even from this distance have a peculiarly English look. We have seen four or five light-houses. An English lady, who had spent part of one summer on this very coast told me a good deal about it and pointed out some interesting places. We have seen numerous fishing-boats—almost all with sails painted black, as well as some ocean vessels, just going out of the channel. There is a great deal to tell, but it is late and I am sleepy.

I shall send a letter to Mamma by the pilot-boat and probably mail this in London. I don't know which will reach you sooner. I may add something to this tomorrow, but after that there won't be such full letters from me, or such trifling ones, for I shall have less time. I suppose that tomorrow's paper will say that the Winifreda has been sighted, because we have run up our signals for two different stations. The clouds have hung low today. It has been chilly and we have had intermittent rainstorms.

London, Wed morning.

It is hard to take my thoughts back to the water. All yesterday afternoon we passed along an interesting coast. Folkston, Brighton, Dover, Deal, Ramsgate, Margate. We saw the white chalk cliffs, signal stations, coast guards, lighthouses and cosy towns, smuggled down by the shore. With the glass we could even make out trees and some beautiful summer houses, rather residences. I have seen my first castle—Dover Castle. It rises up nobly from the cliffs, close to the water. It was built about 1160, and is used now by the gov't for soldiers. Near the mouth of the Thames we came upon queer craft with reddish-brown sails. Pleasure boats, lowing steamers began to shoot by us, for we went slowly. At two different times we took pilots on board. Dinner was served at 4.30. About 6 o'clock when we were between Tillbury and Gravesend, our tender came alongside. Then the baggage jam began, and we didn't leave the steamer till about 8. One of my trunks—the steamer trunk—was opened and looked through very hastily. Only one other trunk belonging to the party was opened. The usual questions about cigars, perfumery etc. were asked, of course. From Tillbury to London is an hour's journey by rail. You should have seen us stagger when we reached firm land. More in Mamma's letter.

Most lovingly,
Theresa L. Huntington

Theresa was delighted to be in London—so much so that she found it necessary to include this preamble in one of her letters:

Dear Papa,

I really feel as if you ought to be careful to whom you read this letter or what parts you read, for I think that many people wouldn't understand how I who have gone to Turkey, as a missionary, should be gadding about London, seeing the sights. Of course, I know you'll say, they would be glad to have me have this pleasure, but still they won't look at it quite right. I wish you would please consider this seriously. There will be plenty of letters which you can read later.

Lovingly,
Theresa

Gadding about London she was:

Yesterday the man came with the "luggage" at about 11.30 and afterward we went out to the post office, a block away and then strolled about till luncheon time. The other half of our party took a ride on the top of a bus. Miss Hazen left for Oxford at noon, and all of us except Miss Lord spent the greater part of the afternoon in shopping, buying almost everything at Shoolbred's on Tottenham Court Road, not far from here. This is a large department concern, on a smaller scale and much more roomy and composed than Whites. I bought two pairs of driving gloves at four shillings, sixpence, $1.08. Miss Ellsworth bought exactly the same glove (the same make and color) in America for $1.90. I bought also a large and excellent pair of scissors for 1s and a good-sized bottle of ammonia for 6 d. Ribbon cost more than in the U.S., but most things were cheaper. It was droll to see how soon the clerks recognized us as Americans and made references to "the States." I can handle English money fairly easily now. We spent the evening in writing and planning for today.

The difference between London and New York, e.g. is most marked and yet it depends upon so many details that it is hard to sum up the causes. Speaking superficially, you are aware that you are meeting one race and nation instead of a conglomeration of Jews, Italians, Irish, Americans etc. and the people move about quietly.

There seems to be little confusion in the streets, but it is a perilous thing to cross them, for no cabman or driver holds up for you—at least he does so rarely. I and all of us have had to run for our lives several times today. The men wear silk hats, very generally, and rather long coats; most of the little children, even those of the poor, wear the short, half-stockings. The women—well if our American voices are loud, their hats are. Their ugly clothing, especially their poor taste in hats is to me very noticeable. A great many two-wheeled vehicles of all sorts are used, the general appearance of many wagons and carriages being different from ours. Quantities of tricycles with boxes behind or pushcarts are used to deliver goods—bread, vegetables, dry goods, etc. I haven't seen yet (with just one exception) an ill-fed, over-driven horse. They all seem sleek and contented. I don't understand the cab system. Somehow the element of grab is lacking in it. There is a dignity about it. It is amazing and inexplicable to me to see the long row of cabs, chiefly two-wheelers (hansons) lined up in the middle of many streets specially at corners and crossings are little oases, consisting of a raised pavement and a few posts, for poor travellers scrambling from one side of the street to the other. Also in the middle of several streets (They call them roads a great deal) I have seen diminutive fire engine houses, with long ladders reaching up behind, exposed to the elements.

We have come upon some very tenacious beggars. Speaking generally now, of guides, ports, policemen etc, it is astonishing to me that I ever can find it so hard to understand anyone who speaks the English tongue. The uneducated people have a peculiar accent, the sound t being made very prominent. By the way, the people, all of them say tuppence and ha-penny. The weather has been pleasant during our stay, though the atmosphere is always hazy. This is not the time of year for fogs. I could write on and on about the trifling peculiarities of London, but I shall never get to our sight-seeing if I do. Already the city and people begin to seem familiar—at least this portion of the city, and it is harder to tell you my first impressions.

After London, the missionary party boarded the Orient express train for Constantinople and from Vienna the family received the following report:

Vienna, Sept. 28, 1898

I did not have time to finish this letter in London, and now I can't write again till we reach Constantinople, when I'll try to tell of these same things more fully. Omitting detail, we "did" the Tower with some thoroughness, saw the English troops drill, and later visited Tower Hill. We spent a short time in a small and very old church—All-Hallows Barking Church. The guide said that John Quincy Adams, "the president of America," was married there. Then, because it was too late to take a boat up the Thames to the Houses of Parliament, as we had planned, we went to St. Paul's, where a service was held at four o'clock, which I enjoyed greatly—that is, from the sight-seer's point of view. Part of us climbed by I don't know how many steps, up to the dome, and tested the whispering gallery. We also went outside the dome, and revelled in a fresh breeze. It was too hazy for the view to be at all extensive. One can't describe the impression which such a building makes upon him (or her).

On Friday I filled up much of the morning with errands. In the afternoon, we visited the Royal Mews (stables) at Buckminster, and saw the Queen's carriage horses, riding horses, the 8 cream-colored horses used upon state occasions by her, the 8 coal-black ones used by the Prince of Wales, the state coaches, gorgeous in gold, and the royal coat of arms, the coronation coach—a great carved, gilded affair, made for George the Third (?), the state harnesses of red and gold, and various other interesting things which I can't tell about at eleven o'clock at night. After leaving the stables we took two hansons (which are amazingly cheap) and saw swell-dom—Hyde Park, Rotten Row, the Duke of Wellington's mansion, and the houses of numerous nobles and dignitaries, including the U.S. ambassador. We were finally landed at the British Museum, where I saw possibly a 1000th of what there is to see. This fraction included the Elgin marbles, the originals of the well-know busts of Homer, the young Augustus, Julius Caesar, and I don't know how many more which I can't stop to name. Aside from the time spent in looking at statuary, I occupied myself in examining old books and parchments and signatures of kings and queens and poets.

[...]

We left the city at about 8.30 P.M. on Monday, taking the steamer from Queenboro! The passage across the channel was unusually smooth, and none of us were sea-sick. We took our train at Flushing at 5.20, reaching Cologne about noon. To me the cathedral is most beautiful from *without.* Inside, the atmosphere is musty and the doors and floors dirty. Grand as the arches and columns are, and beautiful as the light is falling through the colored glass upon the gray stone, I could not help thinking more of the people who worshipped there and what it meant to them. Everywhere there were tawdry gilded virgins or cheap shrines, great crucifixes, which were almost repulsive, dirty holy water and tallow candles. The cathedral is glorious as long as you look up. We three girls strolled about the city a little and amused ourselves by trying to talk German. I just can't describe all I saw—the swaggering soldiers in gorgeous uniforms, which after all did not in this respect outstrip the English military dress, the droll school-boys with satchels on their backs. That evening we saw the Rhine by moonlight from our car windows. A wonderful, misty sight it was—one which I would not have missed, but was almost too sleepy to wholly appreciate, at the last. We could make out several ruined castles and long stretches of vineyard very plainly.

We had expected to change cars at two and again at five in the night, but between twelve and one when we had bundled up somewhat and rolled over to sleep (We were all asleep) a guard opened the door suddenly as we reached Frankfort and told us we must change there. We tumbled out, Miss Lord with a veil tied over her head and I with some things bunched up in my rug like an emigrant, and ran off after a porter who carried the bags. He led us down under the tracks, where some of the crowd lost sight of him and went running about like a flock of bewildered goats. Finally he shoved us into a new train and banged the door. These guards have been very good about helping us to change cars. Of course, we converse under difficulties and of course, a fee is expected. At two we changed again, but not at five.

Our luggage was examined at Passau, on the Austrian frontier, rather superficially and we had to pay exorbitantly for some crackers in tin boxes and some canned meat. The cracker boxes we had opened long before and the crackers were half gone. Here too, we changed cars again, as we did also at 5.15. This afternoon we had some lovely views of the Danube from the car windows.

Dear Mamma,

I hope my two letters from Vienna reached you. I was afraid that one of them was a little overweight.

It is hard to write letters in these days because I have so much to tell. We left Vienna Thursday morning early and took a through train to Constantinople, spending the next two nights on the train. Of course it was tiresome but we are resting delightfully now. We bought in London two baskets and enough food to last us till yesterday, but in addition to this we bought bread at Cologne and Vienna and after leaving the latter city, made frequent rushes out of the train at stopping places to buy drinking water and grapes. We passed through some beautiful mountains—the foothills of the Balkan Mountains. The scenery all through Bulgaria was very fine, but grew tamer and more level as we reached Romania. We passed through Belgrade at about eleven Thursday night. Mrs. Browne and Miss Bushnell stayed in the train by the stuff, while the rest of us went out to open the trunks for inspection. We were disappointed to find that they had not left Vienna. We ought to have them by tomorrow. We did have a funny time at Belgrade. Of course we had to talk German, as we had for two days already, but here there were as many officers and porters in dirty uniforms crowing about and gesticulating that it was bewildering. One took our receipt and carried it off. Then a higher official demanded it and there was a great melée till it was found. Meanwhile time was flying and when we reached the platform again, the train was going out of the station. Miss Lord started off on a trot, both us after her but we were headed off by somebody who shouted that the train was coming back, as it eventually did. Our hand luggage was examined some six times, but not at all at Constantinople. We must have given our tickets to be punched or to have slips torn but twenty times. It was an interesting experience to pass from civilization to semi-civilization, to see the houses become smaller and dirtier till we came to mud huts in Servia and Bulgaria. Here in the latter countries, we saw shepherds wearing sheep skin cloaks.

In order to have this letter go immediately I must skip a great deal and tell you that our train reached Constantinople at about 7.30 on Saturday morning. Mr. Peet and Mrs. Stapleton met us. We went directly to the Bible House, where we were given some breakfast. Dr. Gates came in while we were eating, and likewise Dr. Herrick and Dr. Dwight. Mrs. Browne and Harold went with Dr. H. and we were assigned to Dr. Dwight, who lives on the Bosphorus several miles from Stamboul, close to Robert College. We went to the service at the college on Sunday. The two daughters with whom Ellsworth travelled are here now.

I will write again very soon

With much love,

Theresa (L. Huntington)

Chapter Three: Arrival in Constantinople and the Scope of the Work

So far, Theresa's journey had proceeded without a hitch. Three weeks after sailing from Boston, she and the rest of the missionary party arrived in Constantinople. Theresa and Laura Ellsworth were invited to stay with one of the missionary families, the Dwights, in the village of Roumeli Hissar on the most narrow stretch of the Bosphorus just outside the city. They did not intend to stay more than a couple of days—just long enough to meet the people at Bible House, the center of American Board work in Turkey—and clear the formalities for going into the interior. But there was a problem: their arrival coincided with the visit to Constantinople of the German Emperor Wilhelm II and his Empress. All official business came to a standstill while Abdul Hamid II entertained his political ally in true imperial splendor. Theresa may not have been aware of the sumptuous banquets in the Yildiz palace, eaten on "bejewelled gold plates from Paris."[1] Travel to the interior was stopped. Sultan Abdul Hamid II wanted to make sure no revolutionaries could reach the capital from the provinces, and this meant that the missionaries could not get the necessary travel permits, the tezkerehs. Theresa would have to stay in Constantinople for another three weeks:

> Dear family,
>
> Our tezkerehs are still being held back. There was a slight chance that they might be issued Monday, so we all prepared ourselves to start, and waited with our baggage at the Bible House for some hours—until about 2.30 when it became evident that there was no more hope for that day. A Greek steamer for the Black Sea waited for us an hour or two. Indeed, last week a French steamer, at Dr. Gates' request, waited a whole day. You understand that this matter has to be pushed by our consul, Mr. Dickinson, with Bible House men to urge him, and dragomen, etc. to communicate between Mr. D. and the Turkish officials. The word which came Monday afternoon was that the Sultan hadn't even considered the

1. Lord Kinross, *The Ottoman Centuries. The Rise and Fall of the Turkish Empire.* New York: Morrow Quill Paperbacks, 1977, p. 566.

> tezkerehs. There have been so many Americans recently in Constantinople that the government has become suspicious. In Bebek and Hissar officials have been recently to several houses, to ask whether the occupants were Americans or English, saying that if they were English, it didn't matter. They didn't go to the Dwights because they knew that they were American. They have also asked at the Bible House for a list of all the Americans who have recently come. This latter request has been made before.
>
> Today the German Emperor came. If the south wind had been stronger, he would have been obliged to land at Bebek, and we should have seen him, but as it was, we only heard the roar of the cannon, saluting the German ruler, with German powder, which has not yet been paid for and probably never will be.

Theresa's comment refers to the disastrous state of Ottoman affairs. Even before Sultan Abdul Hamid's ascension to the throne in 1876, the Ottoman state had been in decline for more than a century. Financial mismanagement and extravagance on the part of the Sultan were compounded by pressures from abroad, both economic and military, on the part of the Great Powers. Many of the nationalities within the wide empire, in North Africa and the Balkans, had become independent or autonomous. The Ottoman empire was looking more and more like "the sick man of Europe" every day.

Theresa seldom makes more than oblique references to Sultan Abdul Hamid II. She had to be circumspect: mail was being censored and the Sultan was well known for his extreme suspiciousness. In addition, she knew that her family was as aware as she was of the Sultan's misdeeds: the atrocities he had perpetrated on the Armenians of the Ottoman empire, among whom she was going to work, had been well covered in American papers. The *Missionary Herald* had published several articles on the massacres themselves as well as the arduous work of reconstruction that followed. Theresa came prepared to view the Ottoman Sultan with a jaundiced eye.

Yet to those rare Westerners who got invited to attend his weekly Selamliks—the lavish ceremony that accompanied the Sultan's going to the Mosque on Fridays—or for those who got the even rarer invitation to an audience or a dinner, Sultan Abdul Hamid did not lack a certain charm. Slight of build and with eyes that seemed to notice everything, he could impress his guests with a genuine love of music and sometimes treated them to four-handed piano playing with his sons. He took pride in his vast library, he was in favor of educating women, and he supported archaeological work and kept in close touch with the news from various excavations. His vast gardens at the marble Yildiz Palace were a marvel of landscape design. His well-kept stables contained horses that inspired envy in visiting British dignitaries.

By the time Theresa arrived in Constantinople, the Sultan seldom ventured outside this magical world. He rarely had time: he trusted no one to make any decisions on any matter, however insignificant. Once, for example, an English ship was found to be anchored perilously close to an underwater reef. The permission to move the buoy a few feet had to be given by the Sultan. So, too, was the case with Teresa's tezkerehs: the matter needed the personal attention of the Sultan.

Bebek, Con'ple
October 22, 1898,

Mamma dear,

You are asleep just now at three o'clock in the morning. It is about ten here, and I am sitting in Mrs. Green's very pretty guestroom and writing till church time. Nobody knows when we are going to Harpoot. It may be Wednesday, and it may be next week. The English consul is having just the same trouble about tezkerehs for his country men. Mr. Strauss' blood is up, and he means to say some plain things to the Sultan if nothing is done before he interviews him next Friday. We are not sure whether all our communications have gone to the Sultan, or whether they have stopped with some under-official. The German Emperor left yesterday. We were coming up the Bosphorus from the Bridge just as he started, and were in the midst of all the booming. The *Hohen-Zollern* and *Hertha* arc bcautiful vcssels. I am sorry not to have had a glimpse of His Majesty, but I'm nevertheless glad to have him go. One afternoon he sailed up the Bosphorus and on his way back in the evening, stopped off Bebek and dined in his yacht. We saw nothing of this because it was late and dark when it happened, but we did see some of the beautiful illuminations along the shore. The Turks use candles for these—thousands of them enclosed in clear glass (not clean glass).

In Theresa's Constantinople it was not the Yildiz Palace that stood at the center; it was Bible House, the administrative center of all Protestant missionary activity in Turkey since the inception of the work in 1831. In the central office at Bible House sat the widely respected Mr. William Peet, the American Board Treasurer and link between all the missionaries in the Ottoman empire and the Ottoman government. In 1898, the American Board of Commissioners for Foreign Missions—organized in 1810 by Congregationalists—had been in the Ottoman empire for nearly eighty years. From the vantage point of the turn of the century, the journey of the newly arrived missionaries had been easy:

> "Today a trip to Turkey is a simple matter," writes a contemporary observer. "If any of you ever go out as missionaries you can sail any day of the week to Europe to take the Oriental Express straight through to Constantinople or journey on luxurious ships through the Mediterranean past Italy and Greece, up the Dardanelles and the Sea of Marmora to the 'Queen City.' But it was an immense and dangerous task upon which our first missionaries entered in 1819. They were commissioned by the Board to undertake a mission to Bible Lands. Little was then known about the Moslem problem or the great land of Armenia. The missionaries were to survey from the 'heights of Zion' the homes of 40,000,000 souls scattered over 2,000,000 square miles of territory in all the lands of Bible story from Egypt to the Euphrates. Like the spies of old they were to pass through the land and to decide how best they might carry the message of Christ to Jews, Pagans, Moslems and to the Oriental Churches.[2]

The journeys of exploration by intrepid missionaries disguised as native merchants into the interior of the Ottoman empire were followed by an early missionary settlement in Constantinople itself, starting in the 1820'ies.

"It was no accident which led the founder of the Board...to turn an eager eye to the lands of the Bible," wrote the Rev. Judson Smith in 1896.[3] "This region of the earth is central, not by arbitrary choice, but by the nature of things. Here three great continents meet; hence go out the natural highways of travel and trade and imperial power. The faith that holds these regions is heir-presumptive to the religious throne of the world."

The first efforts of the missionaries, who arrived in Turkey in the 1820'ies, met with modest success. They soon discovered that they could make very little headway among the Jews and that apostasy from Islam was punishable by death. In the 1830'ies, they turned instead toward "revitalizing" what they regarded as the stagnated Christianity of the Eastern Churches, especially the old Armenian Apostolic Church. Founded in the 4th century A.D., the Ar-

---

2. David Brewer Eddy, *What Next in Turkey: Glimpses of the American Board's Work in the Near East.* Boston: The Taylor Press, 1913, p. 57.
3. *Missionary Herald,* 1896, p. 443.

menian Apostolic Church had played a vital role in preserving the national identity of the Armenians through their long history, and the Church soon viewed the attention of the missionaries with a great deal of suspicion.

But until 1846, the work of the missionaries proceeded as planned. Their activities of educational work and translation of the Bible into modern Armenian and Armeno-Turkish was accomplished thanks to ground breaking work by linguists like Dr. Elias Riggs, grandfather of the last President of Euphrates College in Harpoot. In a history of Near East Protestant missions, Julius Richer describes this extraordinary man:

> Elias Riggs was a reticent, retiring student, whose companions were his books, and whose chief delight was the acquiring of ancient and modern languages. He was a complete master of Greek, Armenian and Bulgarian; he studied the dead languages of the Near East, Hebrew and Chaldaic, Syriac and Coptic; he understood most of the living languages of Europe and Western Asia, at least well enough to be able to read their literature without any trouble. He had a gift for exact philological investigation, and was deeply interested in all questions connected with the study of languages. With all this scientific endowment, he was a man possessed of a steady determination to devote these talents to the service of the Christian churches of the Orient, by providing them with good Protestant literature in languages understood by the common people. His work was devoted to the three great Oriental Churches, the Greek, the Bulgarian, and the Armenian. He wrote many of the tracts and school-books that were necessary to the mission of their church and educational work. He assisted in the production of the magazines which the missionaries published, though he did not edit them himself. He translated and composed many hymns for the church services. Above all else, he devoted himself to the translation of the Bible with all his mind and heart. This work of his predilection was characterized by painful exactitude, patient research, sincere fidelity and a wonderfully consistent style. With equal intentness he strove to gain for himself a clear understanding of a passage and then to present it in words and phrases that would be at once understood by the simplest mind. His two complete versions, in Armenian and Bulgarian, are regarded by experts as masterpieces of translation.[4]

4. Julius Richter, *A History of Protestant Missions in the Near East.* 1910, repr. New York: AMS Press, 1970, p. 109.

This educational and literary activity, however, with its ultimate aim of teaching the people to read their Bible themselves in the spirit of democratic Protestantism, went against the grain of the old Armenian Apostolic church and its hierarchical structure. The threat was double-edged: to the Apostolic clergy, the activities of the Protestants not only looked like a threat to their position, but by extension, like a threat to the only institution that held the scattered Armenian community together: the ancient church itself.

The Church now lashed out at the converts. The ultimate weapon of the Armenian Patriarch in Constantinople was the power of excommunication, and he used it freely. Richter writes: "The churches in the metropolis, and in all the districts in which the Protestants had exercised any influence, resounded with the anathemas of excommunication. Parents were commanded to disown their children, employers to dismiss Protestant labourers. Protestants were forced to pay their debts at once, without any mercy; no baker nor butcher was to sell them anything; they were to be shunned like the plague."[5]

This is the background to the critical (and sometimes slightly condescending) tone in Theresa Huntington's letters when she talks about "the Gregorians." The situation came to a head, and eventually—with British pressure on the Patriarch—resulted in a firman (declaration) from the Sultan in 1847 which granted the Protestants the status of a separate religious community or millet. Although the missionaries, and the Armenians they converted to Protestantism, were still being harassed, specially in the provinces where catcalls of 'prote, prote' (which also means leper in Turkish) often followed them, they were now free to expand their activities. And this they did with a vengeance, to the point where in 1910 more than one third of all the missionaries of the American Board were working in Turkey and the field had grown so large that it was necessary to divide it into four different missions. In 1910, Henry Riggs, the grandson of Elias Riggs who like his own father was born in Turkey, wrote this overview of the work in Turkey:

> The Turkey "missions" were organized as four independent missions—a plan made necessary by the difficulties of travel and communication in an undeveloped country fifteen hundred miles long and five hundred wide. The European Turkey Mission—later called the Balkan Mission—in 1910 *was* European Turkey, including Macedonia and Albania, plus a large part of southern Bulgaria, already quite independent of Turkey. Its stations were Kortcha and Elbasan in Albania, Salonika and Monastir in Macedonia, and

---

5. Henry Riggs, "The Turkey Missions in 1910." Unpublished manuscript, Houghton Library, Harvard University.

Samokov and Philippopolis in Bulgaria. In all of this mission the Turks were a small minority.

The Central Turkey Mission included the larger, western part of Anatolia, predominantly Turkish, but including large numbers of Armenians and Greeks, most of whom used their own languages, and all kept their very separate culture and social life.

The Central Turkey Mission covered the area anciently known as Cilicia, the southern central part of Anatolia. Here, too, the Turks constituted the bulk of the population. The Christian population, Armenians and a few Greeks and a few Syrians, for the most part spoke only Turkish, as they had been forced by the Turks to abandon their native tongue. But under a tyranny which, in earlier days, forced them to accept the language of their conquerors, the Armenians of Cilicia were as intensely Armenian and as ardently Christian as any of the Christian minority groups. This was probably in part due to the fact that Cilicia was, for a long time, the Kingdom of "Lesser Armenia."

The Eastern Turkey Mission included the main part of what once was Armenia, and throughout most of that Mission the Armenian people continued to live in their ancestral homes, retaining unchanged the language and the customs of their ancestors. Here the Turks were in the minority and their hold on this part of the country was precarious; but the majority of the inhabitants of this region were Kurds, most of whom were Moslems, and who therefore, when it came to relations between the races, made common cause with the Turks, though they never abandoned their national language and habits of life. The Kurds also were a very important element in the population of the Central Turkey Mission. It was in the midst of this conglomerate population that these four missions found themselves.

The Turkey Missions were, at that time, eagerly calling for more workers; yet, as compared with other fields, or with other times in Turkey, they were remarkably well manned, with a total of 216 missionaries at work. And the force of workers was not only numerically strong. Among these missionaries there were no less than sixty-five seasoned veterans in active service who had been in the field for twenty-five years or more; among them might be mentioned such names as Andrus, Barnum, Haskell, Herrick, Riggs and Tracy and others—twenty-five in all who had seen service for over *forty* years. But there was also a goodly portion of younger men and women, as the Board steadily sent new recruits,

> so that in 1910 there were forty men and women under permanent appointment who had been five years or less in the field, and were therefore to be counted on for long years of service in the unfolding work of the Missions in Turkey.
>
> In the educational field, the Turkey missions had a complete system of schools to meet the needs of almost every section of their field—schools from Kindergartens to Theological Seminaries. There were five Theological Seminaries, made necessary both by the difficulties of travel and by differences of language in the different areas. ...The number of colleges is less easy to state, partly because it is often difficult to decide to use that name for an institution whose curriculum fits the need of its clientele, but does not easily classify according to American terminology. And partly because the Colleges of Turkey, as they have grown up, have stood more or less on their own feet. The Board's report for 1910 lists seven colleges in the Turkey Missions, those already named at Samokov and at Smyrna, Anatolia College at Marsovan, Central Turkey College in Aintab, Central Turkey Girls' College at Marash, St. Paul's College at Tarsus and Euphrates College in Harpoot. All of these colleges were open to students of all races; but the number of non-Christian students in these colleges was very small indeed...
>
> So far as visible results are concerned, the Turkey missions in 1910 were hardly touching the Moslem races who were the rulers and constituted the majority of the people of Turkey. This fact was not at all in line with the wishes of the missionaries, and it was a subject of constant study and prayer in their meetings. But it was a fact, nevertheless...[6]

Henry Riggs completes the picture of missionary work in Turkey by mentioning the eleven missionary physicians working in nine hospitals scattered through the Turkish Empire, as well as the extensive work of the Publication Department in Constantinople which for decades had been printing Christian literature in the native languages. "No more striking evidence of the creative power of these periodicals could be imagined," writes Henry Riggs, "than a visit to a simple home in a remote village, where a man who never had more than an elementary schooling showed himself a well-educated man, able to converse with intelligence and good judgment about a very wide variety of

6. Henry Riggs, "The Turkey Missions in 1910." Unpublished manuscript, Houghton Library, Harvard University.

subjects concerning all parts of the world, all because for twenty years he had habitually read the *Avedaper* (The Bearer of Good News) from cover to cover every week."

Perhaps this was the same villager somewhere in the Taurus mountains who had been so impressed by the speeches of President Lincoln, reprinted in this paper, that he had long stretches of them committed to memory so that he would be able to teach others the lessons of "malice toward none, and charity to all."

All this publication activity built on the work of former missionaries:

> Besides the complete equipment, already mentioned, of the Scriptures in all languages, the Christian churches in Turkey were equipped with a very substantial literature of commentaries, Bible notes and dictionaries, devotional and didactic books, and apologetic literature. All of this literature, without exception, was the product of the labors of the missionary Fathers, and represented, in the aggregate, hundreds of years of patient and scholarly work by Goodell, Schauffler, Riggs, Herrick and many others, whose work still lives.[7]

Theresa seems to have been far too impatient for the tezkerehs to take in much of the sights of the Queen City. She was also not much given to flowery language. A woman visitor from England provides us with a word picture of the Constantinople of that time: "The glittering cupolas of the mosques, the minarets like tall white tapers around each sanctuary, the brilliant white marble façades of the numerous palaces, the brownish roofs and greyish wooden balconies of the Turkish houses, projecting over the sea, and surrounded by dark cypresses, and the soft green foliage that covers the hills on both sides of the straits; lastly, the sea itself, like a blue satin ribbon with silvery ripples, alive with sails of every hue—all these together make up a picture which it would be difficult to match anywhere else."[8] But while Theresa was waiting for the official travel permits, she did make a voyage out to the Princes Islands in the Sea of Marmara:

> Dear family,
>
> Yesterday was a delightful day. Seventeen people, including ourselves, went on a picnic to one of the Prince's Islands in the sea of

---

7. Henry Riggs, "The Turkey Missions in 1910." Unpublished manuscript, Houghton Library, Harvard University.
8. Mrs. Max Müller, *Letters from Constantinople*. London: Longmans, Green, and Co., p. 11.

Marmora. We took a steamer from Bebek at 6.15, and left Galata Bridge, where we met the others, at 8.15. The sail to Antigone, the island to which we went, takes over two hours. At the wharf we engaged two or three donkeys for the ascent of the high, steep hill. Soon several more little beasts came rattling down the stony road, so that in all we had ten donkeys, which we took turns riding. They don't seem to understand English but will respond to Turkish. It was very shaky business—this riding—because most of the saddles were for men and we rode woman-fashion. On the way up, I tried several times to make my donkey stop but every time the donkey-boy saw me gesticulating and talking to him, he gave a yell and began to ply his stick and hurry things up a little. I found the best thing to do was to run the donkey into a tree. On the way down I cut a great "dash, as my steed went thundering by." I wasn't well mounted and the boy made my donkey trot most of the way. My skirt blew out in the wind and I hung onto the back of the saddle with one hand and to the reins in the other. The stirrups were too long and of no use, so when we swung around a corner, my feet flew up and my legs stuck out straight at one side. Everybody cheered as the grinning donkey-boy and I went bumping by. Some of the others when they couldn't make their donkeys stop called friends to their assistance to hold the donkey by the tail.

The island is almost covered with a growth of small pines. On the southern side it slopes very abruptly to the water. The view over the sea of Marmara is magnificent as, indeed, are the views of the coast range of Asia Minor, and of Constantinople. The temperature of these islands is on an average ten degrees higher than it is along the Bosphorus. This means that we had a wonderfully soft, warm air as well as a clear blue sky. We ate our dinner sitting on the pine needles on the hill-top. After some merry games of puss-in-the-corner and three-deep, and some conversation and naps, we started for home at about 2.30. We reached Bebek at six, just before dark. The Turkish day ends at sunset, that is at 5.15 just now, and no boat starts from the city after that. Accordingly it is compulsory to keep early hours.

Finally, there is good news, and the family in Milton a world away get the last letter from Constantinople:

Bible House
Constantinople
October 26, 1898

Dear Ruth,

This is in no sense a birthday letter, but, after all, I'm not sure whether anything I may send later will reach you before the festive day. Here is a kiss for each of your dear slanting eyes, or rather, eight apiece.

I'll begin with my most important news. We start for Samsoun at four o'clock tonight on a French steamer. Dr. Gates has had the tezkerehs for himself and his family for some time, and the rest of us are going without any. Mr. Strauss sent a letter to the Sultan this morning, giving our names and destinations, and saying that we were to go without our tezkerehs today at four o'clock etc., etc., also, that he, the Sultan would be responsible for our safety and for any extra expense for delay, etc., which our lack of tezkerehs might cause, moreover that he, the Sultan again, thro' his officials, must telegraph ahead at his own expense to our various stopping-places, to insure our passing through without trouble. He also remarked that the relations of the two governments were strained now and that if the tezkerehs were not granted today, or if anything disagreeable happened to us, he would telegraph the situation to the U.S. government and wait their instructions etc. etc. Mr. Strauss put the whole matter most strongly, and is himself taking the thing very seriously. I think we shall get along all right. The worst which could come would be a little delay in some disagreeable place, perhaps. The English government is doing just what Mr. Strauss is.

We have done little at the Green's since Sunday. We went in a kaïk (small boat) to call on the Herricks and Mrs. Browne one day, we made some gingham bags, etc for the journey yesterday, and have studied Armenian a little every day.

Much love, my dear little sister from
Theresa (L. Huntington)

Chapter Four: Khans and Mountain Passes: Constantinople to Harpoot

The leader of Theresa's travelling party from Samsoun on the Black Sea, four hundred miles east of the Bosphorus into the interior of Asiatic Turkey was no newcomer to the land. At this point, Caleb Gates had been living in Turkey for sixteen years. Like Theresa's brother Ellsworth, he went to Beloit College and after graduate work at the Chicago Theological Seminary, headed straight for missionary work in the Ottoman empire. He disembarked at Alexandretta, "a malodorous, malarious place," in 1881, an eager twenty-four-year-old. He and his wife Mary Ellen Moore (Nellie) lived in Turkey for fifty-one years until his retirement from the Presidency of Robert College in Constantinople at seventy-five, and he was President of Euphrates College in Harpoot during most of Theresa's stay there. Caleb Gates was a man of extraordinary intelligence and charm with great administrative abilities. In addition to being a missionary, he was an educator, a teacher and a diplomat who knew many of the ambassadors and statesmen of the day. He had an intimate knowledge of the country and spoke Arabic, Turkish, and Armenian fluently.

When Caleb Gates met Theresa's party in Constantinople in 1898, he had just passed through the most trying time of his life, as the man responsible for the lives of the missionaries of the Harpoot station and the Armenians connected to it during the massacre of 1896. He had seen his home there destroyed by a mob. He had sent his wife and two young sons to safety in Switzerland, and had spent a gruelling two and a half years trying to help thousands of Armenian refugees and orphans. When the family was reunited in Constantinople a week after Theresa's arrival, his children did not recognize him. He had aged, and his hair and beard had turned white. But now, with the situation in the interior looking up and reconstruction started, he was impatient to return to Harpoot and insisted on going even though the missionaries lacked the necessary papers. The American official in Constantinople, Oscar Strauss, said he would back him up and that he would let the Ottoman government—the Sublime Porte—know that they would be held responsible if anything happened to the missionary party. Having made this decision, they took the first Black Sea steamer toward Samsoun.

The interior of Asia Minor that they were headed to was not a happy place. It was an area forgotten by a despotic government, except for the purpose of squeezing taxes out of an impoverished population. The representatives of the government were equated in the minds of many people with oppression and suspicion. The justice system was corrupt, spies abounded, and nothing could be done without extensive bribes. Roads were often no more than tracks, rivers had to be forded, bandits and robbers threatened at every turn. Mail took weeks to get to the interior, and was sometimes held up for even longer by snow during the severe winters.

Theresa was going to get a first-hand taste of some of this very soon. They were finally on their way:

> S.S. Circasse
> Paquet Line
> Black Sea
> October 27, 1898
>
> Dear Papa,
>
> That is a most elaborate heading, but I want you to know just where I am. It is now a little after eight P.M. and I am writing in my stateroom, which I share with Miss Hall and Miss Ellsworth. The latter is lying in her berth reading, while the former is getting ready for bed.
>
> We sailed yesterday at 4.30. By paying between four and five dollars, Dr. Gates put our baggage through the custom-house at Constantinople without its being opened. We had no trouble at all about boarding the steamer. The cavass of the U.S. Embassy, and likewise the English cavass escorted us to the steamer and put us safely on board. I don't know what they said, but their presence brought with it authority, and Dr. Gates' tezkereh was enough. A caváss (pronounced exactly as it looks-hard c) is a man attached to an embassy, legation, or to some educational or church institution. He is licensed to carry fire-arms, and has authority beyond that of a policeman, tho' of a different sort. He wears a striking uniform with a good deal of gold about it, and carries a sword at his side and pistols at his belt. Seven or eight of the American missionaries and teachers came to the boat at different times before we sailed.
>
> There are only two first class passengers on this steamer beside our party. One of them is, I think, a Greek. He wears a fez on deck and talks both Turkish and French. The other is a young English-

man who has just come from Australia and is on his way to Russia, where he is going on a gunning expedition with a friend. Counting in the captain, this makes sixteen people at the two tables in the dining saloon. The Browns, Stapletons and Gates are at one table and all the rest at the other. We had a great deal of fun last night trying to talk French to the captain. The Englishman is a very jolly young fellow.

It is, after all, a bit funny to talk about my sitting at a certain table, for I have only been there at one meal. Miss Hall, Miss Bushnell, and Mrs. Browne had to leave the dinner-table last night, and most of us had been more or less sea-sick—chiefly more. We three didn't leave our stateroom till after noon today, but since three o'clock I have been very much myself again and feel equal to a long voyage. We all have felt much worse than we did on the Atlantic, and that is queer because I have been out in a row-boat on a sea seemingly no rougher than this.

A great many land-birds—beautiful ones of several varieties, have flown about the ship today, and alighted on the rigging and deck in an astonishingly tame fashion. We have been in sight of land about half of the day. The weather has been cloudy and damp, yet it is rather warm, and it has not rained since we left the Bosphorus. This steamer is much more comfortable than I expected to find it. The table is fairly good—French cooking, of course, and the fat stewardess is very kind and obliging and quick to catch ideas from our vague communications. There are deck passengers on board as there were on the vessel Ellsworth took. They sit cross-legged in the midst of their possessions or gather about in a circle and talk and sing their droning, minor tunes. They are a dirty, picturesque lot—tho' I must say I have almost ceased to see the picturesque in these people. We are at the stern end of the ship, entirely separated from these passengers.

We expect to reach Samsoun at about five o'clock tomorrow morning and to leave the steamer not before seven. Dr. Gates is going to leave us early, go ashore and bring back with him the cavass of our consular agent at Samsoun. If we are not delayed there we hope to reach Marsovan before Sunday. Otherwise we shall go by a different route and not pass through Marsovan at all. Four of our party, the Stapletons, Miss Lord, and Miss Bushnell go on to Trebizond, in this ship, reaching there probably Saturday morning early.

I enclose two stamps for Harry which I meant to use on a letter from Constantinople. They are of no use to me now.

I will add something to this if possible tomorrow. After that you will not hear from me again, probably for a week or more.

I long for a letter from home.

Very lovingly, your daughter,
Theresa (L. Huntington)

Samsoun

Fri. 9 A.M. Came thro' custom house etc without the least trouble. We start this morning. Pleasant weather. The U.S. consular agent on board to meet us.

Sivas
Nov. 7, 1898

My dear Mamma,

It is a mystery to me that Ellsworth wrote so much about that journey from Samsoun as he did. I don't see when he found his opportunities to write, or how he remembered what had happened a week after it occurred.

We left the comfortable French steamer upon which we had been so uncomfortable—most of us—at seven A.M. Friday October 29. According to the plan I wrote of, Dr. Gates went ashore first (he had a tezkereh) and brought back, with him, the U.S. consular agent, who, by the way, brought with him an American flag, to display if necessary. Wasn't it sensational? We and our hand luggage, with two or three other passengers were taken to the landing in a small boat. I don't know just what was said and done, but I do know that while Dr. Gates and the agent talked with the officers we were told to slip quietly along ahead, and before I knew what was happening, we had passed through the custom-house where our bags were examined very superficially and nothing disturbed, and were on the street. That morning the tezkerehs for which we had waited nearly four weeks in Constantinople, were obtained in as many hours. A little extra present was necessary, but that is always to be expected in this country. The agent, who is a Greek, was very helpful to Dr. Gates.

We spent the morning at a "hotel," repacking our trunks. Ellsworth has described the streets full of shouting men and donkey-trains and buffalo carts. We started off at about three o'clock. I told you of our arrangement in the arabas. Two of the árabagis are

Turks, and the other a Greek, Geregos. Ours is one of the Turks. We put the mattresses and quilts from our beds upon the flat bottom and pile up shawl-straps, baskets, and what pillows we have behind. It is very comfortable for the first hours, and would be later, if it weren't for the incessant shaking and jolting. The spring-arabas are black, lined with red or some gay color. I feel as if I were climbing into the side of a steam-roller when I get into one. The driver sits cross-legged on the seat, and shouts d-r-r-r-r-r to his horses when he wants them to start or to stop. I wish you could see Darok, our driver, early in the morning, in a big sheepskin coat, and a battered fez with an old colored handkerchief twisted about it, and one corner trailing down his back. He smokes ten or twelve cigarettes a day, lighting them by means of a flint. The horses have beads, blue or red, about their necks, and here and there on the harness.

The first day we passed over the coast-range. We met a great many donkey-trains, a few camels, and many buffalo-carts. These native buffaloes are ugly, black things, with horns lying back close to the head—very dirty and slow. They suggest the hippopotamus to me. The wagons they draw are of a primitive type. Two thick, flat pieces of wood are rounded and shaped a little, and an axle run through them, to which is attached the pole. A rude platform is laid upon this foundation. Sometimes a sort of basket-work fence is built up upon the boards—narrow in front and broad behind. They usually leave the wheels ungreased, because they think the noise helps the buffaloes on. The noise is excruciating. You have no idea what shrieks and whines can be produced by one pair of wheels.

That night we reached our destination, the Jackal Khan at about 9.30. I'll describe the proceedings of an average night. After driving into the courtyard of the khan, we wait for a few moments in the arabas till Dr. Gates makes his bargain with the khangi. Then we carry all our traps up the dirty stairs and dump them down upon the divans in our three rooms. In a khan a divan usually means a raised board platform, built across one end of a room. It is usually covered with something like carpeting. This, with one or two strips of matting constitutes the furniture of the room. On the flagging of the open hall-way or balcony outside, Muggerditch spreads out his utensils and builds his fire in the brazier. When water is hot somebody makes tea or coffee. Meanwhile Dr. Gates sets up the beds, and then we make them up, shaking in a good deal of flea-powder between the sheets. If Muggerditch has time to get us a jar of water somewhere, we get out the basins and wash a layer of dust from our faces. By this time supper is ready, and we sit about a little native table, a foot or so high, upon the floor, or rather upon our pillows. Perhaps we have boiled rice, or semolina and some cold meat and cookies from the last mission station, likewise the native bread. Then we prepare our luncheon for the next day. For this we may have bread and boiled eggs and apples. This is, in fact, the regular luncheon. After supper we have prayers, and then go to bed as quickly as possible. If we get in by sunset, we go to bed between 7 and 8, and you don't know how delicious the bed feels. About three o'clock in the morning, there is a knock at the door, and the mild voice of Muggerditch is heard, saying, "You are up," with that lack of expression or emphasis peculiar to English-speaking Armenians. Poor Mugger! He doesn't sleep more than four hours a night. He always smiles when you speak to him, and if you thank him for anything, invariably murmurs, "That is nothing," with an intonation which paper fails to convey. He wears a rusty cut-away coat, and Turkish trousers—baggy in the seat and close at the knee. He has a peculiar cat-like tread.

We tumble out of bed—cautiously, on account of possible fleas, skirmish about for a little water, and dress just in time for M's breakfast. For this meal we may have a boiled chicken, killed in the courtyard for us the night before, or perhaps we have eggs. Otherwise the meal resembles supper. All this goes on by lamplight, the lamp standing on a little shelf high up on the wall. Then we fold up our bedding and beds while Muggerditch washes our breakfast dishes, things are taken down and stowed away in the arabas, and we start off in the moonlight (at first) or this week, in the starlight. I often fall asleep early in the morning, but sometimes I stay awake and watch the sunrise over the mountains. The children always sleep after we have started. I forgot to say that a crowd of Turks usually assemble when we come to a khan and watch all our operations with the most intense curiosity. As yet they have not ventured to come into our rooms, although they do not hesitate to peer in at the door. Since I have mentioned that enemy of oriental travellers, which it is vulgar to name in America, I will add, lest you be troubled about this matter of fleas, that we have had very little annoyance from them, because of the cool weather and our carefulness at night. This is something to be thankful for, since they are more numerous than flies and mosquitoes are together in America, and the khans are full of them.

The second day of our journey, we arose at 1.40 A.M. because we had a 16-hour journey ahead of us. About three, we rattled out of the court-yard. Early that morning we met an enormously long caravan of camels, carrying grain to Samsoun. There must have been over 700 of the great creatures, tied together in chains of 8 or 10, led by a donkey, with a man astride. 'Tho we have crossed higher mountains since, that was the only day when we found ourselves in the clouds. The day was along, hard one, with a delightful ending. At sunset we began to descend the mountains, which had been unusually varied in their scenery, toward the Marsovan plain. It took 2 1/2 hours or more to cross the plain and pass through the garden outside the city. The Marsovan missionaries, three or four of them, had come out in their wagon to meet us, but turned back on account of the coming darkness, about 20 minutes before they would have met us. Dr. Tracy went back with them and then started out again on foot with a servant. He met us just outside the city.

There hardly could be anywhere a more delightful company of people than that at Marsovan. The Gates family were entertained by the Tracys, Mrs. Browne, Harold, and Miss Hall stayed with the Riggs family, and Miss Ellsworth and I slept in the girls boarding hall, and took breakfast there with Miss Willard and Miss Susie Riggs. The other meals we had at one or the other of the two homes I mentioned. For mere lack of time I must condense. Sunday I went to an Armenian service at the boys college in the morning. Of course I understood nothing, but I knew all the tunes they sang and could use the English words and so join in. In the afternoon I went to the girls' Sunday-school, and said a few words to them at the close, at Miss Willard's request. Miss Ellsworth spoke to them at their morning prayers the next day. In the evening, just after supper, they, the missionaries only, always have a little gathering which they call the children's meeting at one of the missionary houses. They each say a verse, the children choose the hymns etc. We went to the parlors of the teachers at the girls' school for this. Later in the evening Dr. Gates spoke in English at a general meeting. The next day, we visited the orphanages and work-shops, went all over the girls' dormitories, visited the hospital with Dr. Carrington, I repacked my trunks, went for a drive outside the city with Mr. Riggs, Miss Cull, Miss Ellsworth, Harold B., and Marjory Carrington, in the station wagon. Then we had washing and sewing done. I had my dress-skirt shortened temporarily, for comfort in travelling. I found one picture glass broke. Otherwise things were in very good condition.

Monday evening there was a big birthday party at the Tracy's. Dr. Tracy and Mrs. Smith, the step-mother of Ellsworth's Beloit friend and a lovely woman, celebrate their birthdays on the same day. The children—there were six of them—had a table in one room under the supervision of Chester Tracy, an Oberlin student spending a year at his home, and all the other people sat at the long dining-room table. There were, I think, 22 of us. We had a good supper, with a great birthday cake, which had the figures 110 upon it, Do you see why? and in general a happy time. I forgot to say that in the day-time we received any number of calls from teachers etc.

We started off at about eight Tuesday morning. We spent that night at Amasia, the old city of Mithegdates, where there is an old, old castle, and some interesting tombs in the cliffs. We saw these only from a distance. The next night our stopping-place, externally at least, was beautiful. We were in a pass between two mountains, and whenever I woke in the night, I could hear the steady rush of a mountain stream which poured thro' the khan court-yard. Thursday night we spent at Tokat, famous for its connection with Henry Martyn. The city is a large one, and thriving for a Turkish city. We reached Yeni Khan at about 7, Friday night. It is rather a poor khan, standing in a little village on a bit of table-land among the mountains. On Saturday we crossed the highest mountain of the journey—Chamli Bel. The climb up is long and winding, and the views beautiful. I had a long drink of sweet water from a spring. It was exceptionally good, because at the khans we only dare to drink boiled water. The rivers of the plains are sluggish and dirty. In general the hills and plains are very bare and brown, and the roads rocky and dusty. A bit of green grass or a group of trees is a refreshing sight. I appreciate the Bible prophecy about the thorn and the fir tree. I have seen great stretches of plain covered with nothing but dusty, dry thistles. Some of the mountains are beautifully colored red, green, yellow, etc, by mineral deposits in the rocks.

I have no time to write more, but will have to write about the Sivas visit after we reach Harpoot next Tuesday. I was more than glad to receive a letter from Mamma at Marsovan and a whole package here telling about the Gorham visit, the last dated Oct.

11. We have found letters from the Harpoot people all along the way. We have spent Sunday and Monday Nov. 6 and 7 here in Sivas, and expect to reach Harpoot Tues. Nov. 15. My journey letters, Cornelia, will almost hold out to the end. I think the last is dated the 9th or 10th. I have enjoyed them ever so much. A good many which I have read since I reached Samsoun have spoken about my sitting on deck enjoying the sea breezes. Somehow the voyage across the Atlantic seems a mere speck to me out of the whole journey.

Goodnight, dear little mother. Do all please keep well.

Lovingly,
Theresa (L.H.)

Harpoot, Turkey
Nov. 16, 1898

My dear Father,

I left myself, so to speak, just out of Sivas. Two hours from the city Mr. Hubbard, and his son of 12 or 13 met us, on horse-back, and a few minutes later a carriage (such a carriage!) came up, containing three ladies, Swiss and German, who have charge of the orphanage work, and two more Hubbard children. A little way out of the city we passed some of the Armenian orphans lined up by the road-side with their teacher, and listened to a German hymn from them. It was expected at Sivas that a Swiss physician would come with us, hence the coming of the ladies and the orphans. There are only two American families at Sivas—the Hubbards and the Perrys. The Hubbards have three children with them and five in America, the Perrys have no children in Turkey. Miss Hall, Miss Ellsworth and I stayed with the latter family. They all welcomed us very warmly and did a great deal for our comfort. We visited the schools and orphanages, as at Marsovan. Their girls' school is not in as prosperous a state as that at Marsovan, because they feel the need of an American teacher to give her whole time to it. We received a call from Dr. Jewett, the American consul, and his wife, and returned the call on Monday. Their life must be very uninteresting. I found them most agreeable people, but very quiet. You remember that he is Mrs. Blair's friend. We left Sivas early Tuesday morning, much rested, with a store of bread, cookies, meat etc for the next two or three days.

I found the second week of araba-travel more comfortable and more interesting than the first. We crossed more mountains and I walked more. Asia Minor is nothing but mountains with a dusty, barren pain or a little fertile valley here and there. There are villages scattered about on the lower land where water can be found. We passed through two or three of these every day. Most of the houses are built of mud mixed with straw, and are just the color of the earth, of course. The houses are crowded closely together, and man and beast make one family. In the winter the shepherds have to live with the animals, for the sake of the heat from their bodies. We saw more flocks of sheep and goats than we did the week before. I don't see what the creatures feed upon, for most of the mountains, at least, have practically no vegetation upon them, but are masses of earth and rock. Have I told you already of the colors of the mountains? Many of them are a soft greenish gray, others have patches of yellow, olive green, bright red, deep red and brown. The fertility of the land went with the trees.

I won't name the khans at which we stopped, because you would have a sad time with pronunciation. Some of them were in villages, others stood off by themselves among the mountains. They were much alike, on the whole. Sometimes it was easy to get water, sometimes not; one day we had large rooms, another small. We rose generally at three or a little later and started off about five or before. We went to bed somewhere between six and eight o'clock. Every day we met trains of donkeys or pack-horses or, less frequently, camels, with brown, ragged drivers, Kurds, Turks, or Armenians, more often the first, who stared at us, open-mouthed, and pointed at our dress. We met women, wearing full trousers like the men, and carrying great bundles of crooked sticks upon their backs. I also saw women ploughing, with the primitive wooden plough of the country. The shepherds wear a most curious garment. It is the shape of the boards the "sandwich men" wear, who advertise something to cure corns, in the streets of Boston. It is made of sheep or goat skin and has no openings for the arms.

One day our arabagi killed a bird which they called a wood-pigeon. It looked to me more like a partridge than like any pictures of wood pigeons which I have seen. He gave the bird to Dr. Gates. The magpie is very common here. He is a handsome, black and white fellow, but rather tiresome.

At Sivas we received word that Mr. Browne and Miss Bush, who had been off on an eight-week tour, would wait for us at Malatia and spend Sunday with us there. That word is not pronounced

Malasha but every letter is sounded and *t* has its own proper sound. The *a*'s are like *a* in father.

They came out on their horses to meet us, about two hours from the city. We recognized them at a long distance, because of Miss Bush's side-saddle. They came up on a canter and we had a happy meeting. Instead of going to a khan we rented, or rather, Mr. Browne rented for us three rooms in private houses near the pastor's house. They were, of course, unfurnished. Native furniture, anyway, means only rugs and low divans with cushions. We reached Malatia at about two, ate our luncheon, set up our beds etc, and at sunset went to the pastor's where we were invited to dine. We saluted our host and hostess and sat down with them upon cushions arranged about the walls. There was a mangal to keep us warm. Soon one of the daughters of the house brought in a low sort of stool and set upon it a large, round tray (I call it that, for lack of a better name).

Now I'm sorry to stop right here, but it is Wednesday morning, and in five minutes this must go to the mail. I'll tell all the rest next week. To be brief, the whole station came out to meet us, and we had a very joyful time. I rode into the city on Mrs. Gates' white donkey, like the kings of Bible-days. The people, the rooms, everything, in fact, is beautiful. Ellsworth is well, and looks very happy and manly.

Much love to each one,
Your affectionate daughter,
Theresa (L. Huntington)

In a letter written after her arrival in Harpoot, Theresa describes the last part of the long journey:

We started off soon after five o'clock Monday morning, our party increased by Mr. Browne and Miss Bush on their horses, and their man Raspár with his pack mule. He cooks for them, takes care of the horses etc when they go on a tour. That noon we crossed the Euphrates—a slow-moving, muddy river, with sandy shores. Two of the scoop-like ferry-boats which Ellsworth described were in operation, so, tho' we made two loads, we were able to cross comparatively quickly. I cannot imagine a more primitive concern than one of these old scows, carried by the current and guided by a pole. We reached our khan early that night, and found it a very comfortable one, standing all alone in the midst of the mountains. On

> Tuesday we were off before daybreak, as usual, crossing our last high mountain. Most of the morning from 8 o'clock on we spent on the Harpoot plain. Ellsworth, Dr. Ussher and a German gentleman from Mezereh, who had all come out four hours to meet us, hailed us at about twelve o'clock. There was nothing exciting about our meeting. Ellsworth jumped from his horse and spoke to Dr. Gates first, for he was in the araba in front. I hopped out of our araba. We said "Hullo," then I said, "Is that the way you look, Ellsworth?" and he said "Yes, is that the way you do?" The poor German had been thrown from his horse just as they caught sight of us, so he came up a little later. We all rode on together a mile or so to a village where at the khan they had a luncheon waiting for us (in care of the station zaptieh) which Miss Barnum had prepared. We sat down on the floor, as usual, and had a good homelike meal. About two hours out of Harpoot we met Dr. Barnum, Miss Barnum, three Germans from Mezereh, and the Armenian pastor from Mezereh, all on horseback, and in an araba, Mrs. Barnum, Miss Seymour and Miss Daniels. Very soon, the English consul, Mr. Jones, and his cavass came upon beautiful horses. We stopped out in the plain and Ellsworth took a picture of the party, as did Herbert Gates, also. Counting the zaptieh there were fifteen people on horses. The occupants of the arabas changed about a little, and I rode with Miss Daniels for an hour or more. When we reached the foot of the Harpoot mountain a man from the station met us with Mrs. Gates' white donkey and a mule which belongs here. As Mrs. Gates did not care to ride, I took the donkey and Laura the mule, and, as I said before, like the kings of old, I entered the city on a white ass. We had to go through the city only a short distance because our buildings are on the outskirts of the town, but in spite of this boys and men accompanied us in a great crowd, and the roof-tops and windows were filled with people.

Theresa's arrival in Harpoot came thirty-two years after the first rugged missionary party had crossed the same immense plain which constituted the last stretch of the two week araba-journey. Some years later, Dr. Gates' successor Henry Riggs described what Theresa also saw as she approached the Harpoot station that was to be her home for the next seven years:

> The traveller journeying eastward on the great Constantinople-Bagdad highway crosses the Euphrates just above the point where that mighty river takes its wild plunge through the Taurus range of

> mountains. Climbing up the left bank of the river the traveller comes to a point where there opens before him a great plain, and a brown patch on the brow of the upland fifteen miles away is pointed out to him as the city of Harpoot. Hour after hour, as he rides along the monotonous length of the plain, the brown patch keeps in sight, gradually taking shape as he nears it, till by degrees a group of buildings, prominent above the crowded houses of the city, commands his attention. Standing on nearly the highest ground in the city, at the top of a steep slope twelve hundred feet above the plain, the seven buildings of Euphrates College, together with the orphanages and missionary residences of Harpoot station, form the most conspicuous feature of the city of Harpoot, visible for miles from the west, south, and east.[9]

Although Henry Riggs' description of the road may not correspond to our notion of a highway, Theresa's journey to Harpoot had been relatively comfortable by the standards of the day. In Harpoot, she was to get acquainted with some of the early missionaries who had ventured into the interior thirty years earlier, a generation before she did. Some of them were women whose hair-raising travel experiences were similar to this quaint account of how the Ely sisters, who were to spend their entire lives as missionaries, reached nearby Bitlis in 1868:

> The only method of reaching Bitlis then was through horseback travel over the worst possible roads and through dangerous mountain passes. It is a month's journey from Trebizond; and as they started in the Fall of the year, they encountered cold and storm and every kind of discomfort. Now they began to meet the real hardships of missionary life. Some of us shrink from the fatigue of Pullman cars and good hotels. I wonder how we would enjoy a month on the road in constant danger of robbers, with no conveyance but a horse and no decent refreshment by the way! The higher up they went, the colder and more disagreeable it grew and one night their misery was full. The muleteers who were engaged for an early morning start, put in an appearance late in the afternoon. Then a cold, drizzling rain had set in, the wind was blowing fiercely and with night before them, the prospect was dismal enough, but there was nothing to do but to go on. Miss Charlotte was unable to ride

9. ABC 16.9.4., American Board of Commissioners for Foreign Missions Archives, Houghton Library, Harvard University, Cambridge, MA.

horseback so a board was strapped across the horse's back and a kind of basket chair arranged for her to sit, while the opposite end was balanced by some articles of baggage. In some places the way was so narrow that the horse scarcely had a foothold, and as the road wound round the mountain, she was often suspended over some awful chasms where it made her sick and dizzy to look or even think. The rain changed to snow and sleet. Darkness settled upon them and the wind blew open their wraps, so that the moisture trickled down their necks and they were drenched to their skin. To add to their trials, they became separated from the muleteers in charge of their baggage and it was impossible to go on without them as they were liable to get robbed and murdered, if left alone. Their guide began to look around for some kind of a shelter, till morning dawned. Nothing could be found but a native hut, a stable, but they were glad even of this. No warmth but the breath of the animals, no lights but the dim flicker of a single candle, no food, no clothing, not even a place to lie down. That our Lord had not where to lay down His head, has a new meaning to these sisters now.[10]

10. ABC 16.9.3, 92.

Chapter Five: The Rigors of the Early Work; an American College in Anatolia

The ancient town of Harpoot, perched on a steep hill near the upper Euphrates, had been the center of the American Board's "Eastern Turkey Mission" ever since the arrival there in mid-nineteenth century of the first missionary. An important city in the ancient historical land of Armenia, in Ottoman times it became the center of the vilayet or province of an area that included several other large towns and hundreds of villages and hamlets. The majority of these communities—in an area that in the missionary frame of reference was "three times as large as New England"—were Armenian. The name of the city itself attested to this fact: Harpoot is derived from the Armenian Kharpert, from khar (stone), and pert (fortress). The ruins of this ancient stone fortress are still standing, not far from where the missionary compound used to be.

Harpoot was richly blessed by nature. The region with its mountain ranges and plains irrigated by rivers and tributaries of the great Euphrates was fertile and the climate ideal for growing a variety of fruits and grains. Harpoot grapes were famous; mulberry trees supported a substantial silkworm population and silk industry; grove after grove of nut trees thrived on the plains. There was a sizeable cotton industry; sheep and cattle raising supported local tanneries. The peasant population was mostly Armenian and worked hard on the land, and they also dominated the commerce of the towns in the area. "The Armenians," wrote the last President of Euphrates college, Henry Riggs, "are the bankers, merchants, artisans, and farmers of this part of the country, and are inferior in native ability to no nation in the world."

The first missionary who lived in Harpoot was the Rev. Dunmore who with his wife established residence there in 1855 and founded a Protestant school in the town that same year. His wife seems to have been unable to withstand the rigors of the Ottoman interior and returned to the United States after one year. He employed a sixteen-year-old Armenian, M.A. Melcon, as a teacher. Fifty years later, as one of the first Armenian members of the faculty of Euphrates College, Mr. Melcon wrote in the *Missionary Herald*: "No one would have thought then that this school would, in the course of twenty-five years, grow to be a college, including a male and a female department. Then there was only one woman in the place who was able to read, and she was pointed out as a person of extraordinary ability. The first female pupils I had were only two, my sister and another girl of my acquaintance, studying with the boys."[11]

Two years later, Rev. Dunmore was joined by two missionary couples, the Rev. Crosby Wheeler and his wife Susan; and the Rev. Wheeler's sister Caroline Allen with her husband Orson. Mr. Dunmore himself, "having a taste for exploration and pioneer labors," was transferred to the town of Erzroom in 1858; for him, his native country proved more dangerous that the wilds of Turkey: he was killed on a battlefield in the Civil War. "It was the time of the Civil War in his native land," says a contemporary account, "and his public spirit led him to accept an invitation from a regiment of cavalry to be their chaplain. A detachment, with which he was connected, was surprised early in the morning of August 3, 1861, and he fell, shot in the head before he was fairly out of his tent. [...] The Lord forgive the Texan whose bullet cut short a life so valuable."[12]

In 1859 came Dr. Herman Barnum and his wife Mary. These three couples; the Wheelers, the Allens, and the Barnums, all devoted their life's work to the Harpoot station and their names were a legend in missionary circles. The Barnums were still there when Theresa arrived and figure prominently in her letters; they remained there after she left; they died and were buried there after fifty years of service. The Allens spent just short of forty years in Harpoot and left shortly before Theresa arrived—four of their children were buried in the missionary cemetery on a hillside just outside the town. The last of the original couples, the Rev. Crosby Wheeler and his wife Susan, had also left the Harpoot station after four decades there before Theresa arrived. A bronze bust of Dr. Wheeler was prominently displayed in the assembly hall: Dr. Wheeler was the founder of Euphrates college.

This tall and rugged man, born in Maine in 1823, was a graduate of Bangor Theological Seminary. After ten years in the field, the Rev. Wheeler wrote an influential book about his early experiences in Harpoot. An anonymous introduction describes the task of this "earnest, practical" man:

> To evangelize a region of country larger than the State of Massachusetts, covered with hundreds of villages and cities, with a popu-

---

11. *Missionary Herald*, January, 1903.
12. Rufus Anderson, *History of the Missions of the American Board of Commissioners for Foreign Missions to the Oriental Churches*, Boston: Congregational Publishing Society, 1872, vol. 2, p. 56.

lation of from four to five hundred thousand souls,—this was the work undertaken by three married missionaries, assisted a part of the time by one single lady in a female boarding-school. They entered upon it in humble reliance upon Bible truth, the blessing of the Holy Spirit, and the presence of their great Leader. They made Harpoot the base of their operations; selected fit centers for influence amid the surrounding villages, set up schools, and put young men of promise upon special training to become preachers and teachers, gathered believers into churches, ordained pastors over them, and taught the people to support their Christian institutions, and to engage vigorously in the work of home evangelization...[13]

The Rev. Wheeler seems to have taken an instant liking to the Armenians:

They are a very interesting people, naturally intelligent, enterprising, and ingenious, as is shown by the fact that in Turkey the most skillful and successful artisans and the chief merchants and bankers are from among them. But the one thing which raises them I may almost say infinitely above all the other races of the East, as hopeful subjects of missionary labor, is the fact that, amid all their ignorance, superstition, and degradation, which are especially great in the central and eastern portions of the country, and while addicted, like those about them, to most of the sins which are peculiarly oriental in their character, and pre-eminently to lying, still, buried beneath all the gathered rubbish of centuries of oppression and sin, is found a conscience, which the first touch of divine truth is often sufficient to waken to new life and saving energy.

As I have stood in their dark old churches, begrimed with the smoke and soot of centuries, from lamps kept burning even at midday, and seen the white-haired old priest reverently take from its recess a timeworn book all covered with silver crosses, and hold it forth from the altar for young and old to devoutly kiss, as for centuries past their fathers have done, though I knew that the contents were alike unintelligible to him and to them, and that the fixing of these crosses upon the sacred cover, in the hope of thereby saving infants that had died without baptism, was but another token of their own deep spiritual darkness, yet the fact that, by

13. C. H. Wheeler, *Ten Years on the Euphrates*. Boston: American Tract Society, 1868.

> that devout though ignorant act of reverence, the poor people were keeping alive in their hearts the feeling that that book has in it something more than any and all other books, made me grateful to God that the memory of a living though departed ancestral faith in the Bible has thus been perpetuated even by this its dead and petrified ceremonial form.[14]

The Rev. Wheeler set down some very clear guidelines for his missionary work, some of which sound surprisingly modern. Nothing, not even the cheapest religious pamphlet, was to be given away for free, because the gospel is "worth more to those to whom it costs some pecuniary sacrifice." The churches had to be made self-supporting as soon as possible. The people—and this included the women—had to be convinced that they could learn to read. "It was sometimes amusing to witness the wonder and incredulity with which our assertion was received, that an adult man, and even a woman, can learn to do this." The missionaries had to remember that "many things which are highly beneficial and even necessary to us, because we have been educated upon them, and because, as a fruit of our own national culture, they are peculiarly our own, may not only be unsuited to any other people, but, in their peculiar circumstances, positively pernicious in their influence."[15]

Ten years into this work, in a quiet moment in his room, the Rev. Crosby Wheeler penned down his assessment of the work in Harpoot:

> Sometimes, in early spring, the morning light shows the plain of Harpoot covered with a dense fog, the deposit of the past night's darkness and chill, which seems a vast leaden sea, its farther shores the distant mountains. But by and by the sun rises, and, at first agitating the outspread mass, and here and there revealing an outcropping hill, at length lifts and dispels it all, or pours it over the Taurus to be dissipated by more southern heats; and the populous plain, in its vernal bloom and beauty, lies outspread before us.
>
> A deeper, deadlier mist of superstition and sin, the deposit of a longer night of spiritual darkness, has covered its people, and rising higher, buried all the land beneath its chilling weight of death. But already has the Sun of Righteousness arisen, and here and there outspringing forms of spiritual life and beauty, in living Christian churches, tell that He too shall at length dissipate all the deadly

14. C. H. Wheeler, pp. 57- 58.
15. C. H. Wheeler, p. 87.

Theresa Huntington (1896)

Above, Theresa Huntington's graduation picture, Wellesley College, 1896. *Facing top,* Rev. Henry Strong Huntington and family, Milton, Massachusetts. (*Standing, from left,* Ellsworth, Theresa, George. *Seated,* Harry, Cornelia ("Kindie"), Henry, Mary, Ruth.) *Facing bottom,* Theresa Huntington (holding banner) as a member of the women's varsity crew at Wellesley.

LOCH LEAROCH

American Board of Commissioners for Foreign Missions.
CONGREGATIONAL HOUSE, BEACON STREET,
Boston, Sept. 7, 1898.

Miss Theresa L. Huntington,
Milton, Mass.

Dear Miss Huntington:-

It gives me very great pleasure to give to you the official notice of your appointment as a missionary of the American Board by the Prudential Committee at its meeting held yesterday. You were designated to the Eastern Turkey Mission. We congratulate you upon the consummation of this your desire and ours and upon the goodly fellowship of Christian men and women into which you have come. We join our prayers with yours that God's richest blessing may rest upon you at all times and for many years. We shall hold you in warm Christian affection. Will you kindly bear to your father and mother and family my assurances of warm regard, and believe me,

Very sincerely yours,

C. H. Daniels

Above, Theresa Huntington's letter of appointment as a missionary in Eastern Turkey. *Facing,* a page from one of Theresa Huntington's letters home.

still in the office of the Turkish censor in Samsoun.

Last Sunday Miss Hall and I, in acceptance of a very shy and halting invitation given me by one of the orphan girls, visited Pompish Leah's orphanage. It is by far the sunniest and brightest of the six orphanages in the city. Leah herself met us at the door, all smiles, and conducted us from the stone-flagged lower room, -always a dark, illsmelling part of an Armenian house,- to the sunny upper floor. The place would seem plain and bare to you, but to most of these girls it is paradise after their squalid village homes. The youngest of the sixty girls under Leah's care, is four years old and several others are mere babies,- fat, bewitching babies, in their big, white, wool stockings, long, coarse gingham dresses, and

Right, Theresa Huntington Zeigler, 1937. *Below,* The Zeigler family. (*Standing, from left,* Constance, Carol, and Lyman. *Seated,* Charles Zeigler, Theresa Huntington Zeigler, Miriam.

gloom, and pour his own light and life in upon the darkened populations so long buried beneath it.

The labors of the Rev. Wheeler and his wife in Harpoot, however, ended with a more literal "chilling weight of death" in the aftermath of the massacres of 1895. In May 1896, according to the *Missionary Herald*, the Wheelers, "their home and all their household goods having been destroyed at the time of the massacre at Harpoot, in great weakness and suffering they set out from the city in which they had spent so many years in active service for the Master, turning their faces to the homeland. They arrived at Auburndale, Mass., on the twenty-ninth of June, after months of painful travel, and on the eleventh of October Dr. Wheeler's weary, pain-racked body was at rest."[16]

The person who accompanied the Wheelers on the first part of their journey all the way to Constantinople was a young man by the name of Egbert Smyth Ellis. His name, like Mr. Dunmore's, is only a brief flash in the station's history, but even the sketchy details surrounding his work and premature death in the field are compelling. Word had gone out from the station and its overburdened workers that they needed urgent help: "two of the very best men attainable." Ellis, the son of a Maine minister and a graduate of Williams College and Andover Seminary, had "left behind the one whom he expected after a time to return to and claim as his wife" and ventured out in 1894, just a few months before the massacres. He learned Armenian quickly, and started doing "evangelistic work," distributing religious literature among the hundreds of Armenian villages in the Harpoot field. He was the first one to reach the village of Ichmeh after the massacres and witness the devastation first hand. There, he was "taken with a violent chill" and watched over by the "Christian brethren" in the village whose ministrations including "snow from the mountain to cool his head" were all in vain. Mr. Ellis, too, is buried in Harpoot.

In addition to these founding couples, there were two women whose names are intimately connected to the early days of the Harpoot station: Caroline Bush and Harriet Seymour. By the time Theresa arrived, the beloved 'Aunt Caro' of her letters had already been there for eighteen years, and she continued on for another three after Theresa left. Both these remarkable women were sent out by The Woman's Board of Missions, an offshoot of the American Board especially dedicated to evangelistic and educational work among women, whose support and collaboration was seen as crucial for the work to proceed. In the annals of the Woman's Board, whose work we'll return to later, 'Caro' Bush and 'Hattie' Seymour were shining examples of the

16. *Missionary Herald*, 1896.

work to be done among 'native women.' They were in charge of what was quaintly called 'touring work,' which involved visiting the hundreds of villages in the field, holding women's meetings, organizing literacy groups, teaching home and child care. This meant spending months every year in the saddle on steep and perilous bridle paths—in the case of 'Aunt Caro and Hattie' riding side-saddle in a long dress, often sleeping in huts with dirt floors, fording ice-cold rivers, and running the risk of encountering robbers and bandits. An example in 'Aunt Caro's own words from 1878: "From Arabkir we had nine hours ride to reach Vank, during which we lost our way four times, plunging through muddy fields and wandering over barren hills, until I began to wonder for what purpose the Lord let us waste our time, which was so precious to us. I became so discouraged that I wanted to cry, but finally concluded I would laugh instead. Tired, hungry, wet and cold, we esteemed the wee room we reached by six o'clock a welcome haven of rest, and after supper we were ready to go to work to improve every moment for the souls about us. "At Aghun and Vakhshen," she continues, "our next meeting places, the preacher's wives were graduates of our school. With them I was able to visit many of the houses and at both places to hold a meeting with the women. At Vakhshen I had at one time quite a little congregation of Turks and Armenians in the street, where I sat before a shabby door-way and tried to turn their thoughts a little above spinning wheels and cattle-tending.[17]

By 1878, the evangelical and educational work in the outlying areas had gotten firmly under way with a dozen self-supporting native churches headed by Armenian preachers operating in the outlying areas; there were over eighty primary schools in the Harpoot field villages with close to three thousand students in all. In Harpoot proper, resistance to the idea of education had long since been overcome, even for girls: primary and secondary schools for boys and girls—with boarding-schools for the students from the villages—had been in operation since early on. The mission station also taught its students in a variety of trades or 'industrial work.' A Theological Seminary was established; classes were beginning to be taught in English as well as in Armenian. Earlier, there had been an effort to avoid teaching English in order to discourage emigration. Keeping in mind the fact that twenty years before, the Rev. Wheeler and his colleagues had had difficulty persuading the local 'Harpootsis' that they would profit from being literate, it is interesting to take a look at the curriculum of the Theological Seminary of Harpoot in 1870:

17. ABC 16.9.5.

> For the first year, Exegesis, the Synoptic Gospels and Pentateuch, the Turkish and Ancient Armenian languages, Algebra, Physiology, Reading, Writing, and Spelling Armenian.
>
> For the second year, Exegesis, Isaiah, Daniel, and Revelation, Geometry, Natural Philosophy, and Astronomy, Rhetoric in Ancient Armenian, Evidences of Christianity (Turkish.)
>
> For the third year, Exegesis, Acts, Pauline Epistles, except Romans and Hebrews, Mental Philosophy, Moral Philosophy, and Theology.
>
> For the fourth year, Exegesis, Pastoral Epistles, Romans, Hebrews, and Gospel of John, Sermonizing, Pastoral Theology, Church History, and Logic.
>
> Weekly exercises in composition and declamation through the first three years; and lectures on Physical Geography, Geology, History, and Chronology, and lessons in singing, distributed through the course at convenience.[18]

Despite all this, there was an increasing need for an institution of higher education: in spite of the hardships of taxes and conscription on the local population as a result of the Turko-Russian War of 1878, Harpoot wanted its own college. Responding to this need, the Rev. Wheeler set out to do fund raising work, and in 1875 he collected over $140,000 for the establishment of a college while on a furlough in the United States. An additional $40,000 came from local Armenian contributors, and Armenia College in Harpoot was founded in 1878, with local Armenian representation on its Board. The Turkish authorities soon objected to its name and it was changed to Euphrates College in 1888. The Rev. Wheeler remained its President until ill health forced him to resign in 1892. He was succeeded by James Barton, who also became ill after a short period and was forced to return to Boston, where he took up his life's work as Secretary of the American Board. Barton was succeeded by Dr. Barnum, who stayed on in Harpoot and who will appear often in Theresa's letters but who was no longer President when she arrived there. At that time the Presidency had been taken over by Dr. Caleb Gates.

The first men graduated from Euphrates college in 1880, the first women three years later. Many of the faculty were Armenian:

> Among them was Prof. Haroutoun K. Avakian, a graduate of the Marash Theological Seminary, who taught languages and mathematics until 1895 when he migrated to America. Prof. Hachabed

18. Anderson, vol. 2, pp. 445-446.

> Benneian taught at Harpoot for twelve years before going on the United States in 1896, where he was editor of the Armenian newspaper, *Gochnag* (The Church Bell) in Boston after 1907. Prof. Garabed Beshgoturyan taught Armenian language and literature both at Harpoot and at the International College, Smyrna. He relocated in Detroit where he was active as a writer until his death in 1941. Prof. Haroutoun Enfieyjian was a Euphrates college graduate who attended Yale University before returning to teach at his Alma Mater in Harpoot. Prof. Arshak Shemovonian had studied in Switzerland and knew five languages in addition to his native Armenian. He taught at Euphrates College for twenty-five years. Prof. M.A. Melcon, the pioneer Armenian teacher in Harpoot, collaborated with the American Board educators there for eighteen years. He later taught in Iran and immigrated to the United States in 1898. Melkonian was a translator of Goethe, Schiller and Shakespeare into Armenian.[19]

To complete the cast of characters on the scene in Harpoot, we need to mention a few more names. First of all, there were Theresa's travelling companions on the SS Winifreda whom she has already mentioned; Miss Laura Ellsworth and Mrs. Leila Browne. Laura's stay at Harpoot was not destined to be long: maybe it was during their stay en route in Sivas that she first set eyes on her future husband, Mr. Anderson, who worked for the British Consulate there. At any rate, Laura married him two years after her arrival and moved to Sivas.

Mrs. Browne and her spirited son Harold, Theresa's young friend, had left the field for safety during the massacres and were on their way back to Harpoot that had been home to them since 1876. Leila Browne was 'a Mt. Holyoke girl' and the daughter of a Cambridge Deacon, Edward Kendall. Her husband, John Kittredge Browne, a man of 'genial friendliness and buoyancy of spirit, who never doubted clouds would break,' was a Harvard man from Framingham, Mass., and a graduate of theology from Andover. The Brownes spent thirty-seven years in Harpoot and left in 1912 when Dr. Browne was seventy years old.

And then there was Emma Barnum, whose poignant story will emerge gradually through Theresa's letters. Emma was the daughter of Dr. and Mrs. Barnum, born and raised in Turkey, and destined to die there. She and Theresa became great friends.

---

19. Frank Stone, *Academies for Anatolia,* Lanham: University Press of America, 1984, pp. 179-180.

Miss Mary Daniels, too, was there when Theresa arrived. She was by then the head of the Women's Department of Euphrates College, a strict disciplinarian who was prone to jealousy toward her co-workers. She was to cause Theresa no end of trouble, although she rarely lets any of her feelings show in the family letters. She does refer, however, to a romantic interest on Mary Daniels's part for the newly arrived Dr. Clarence Ussher—who was also being very attentive to Laura Ellsworth—proving that not everything was work and prayer at the Harpoot station.

This, then, is the scene onto which Theresa steps in 1898. But before we can get back to her letters, it is necessary to look more closely at the tragic 'events' that we have already referred to: the Hamidian massacres of 1895.

Chapter Six:
Massacre: "This Fearful Storm of Murder"

Seventy-five years after the arrival of the first Protestant missionaries in the Ottoman empire the future of missionary activity in that part of the world seemed bright. By the mid-1890'ies, there were not only American missionary societies in Turkey: there were German, Scottish, Irish, English, Dutch and French ones as well. Some were Presbyterian, others Methodist, but the largest missionary society by far was the American Board, which, as we have seen, was the representative of the Congregational Churches in America.

In 1895, the activities of the American Board in Turkey were centered around eighteen stations, of which Harpoot was one. Forty years after the Rev. Dunmore's arrival in Harpoot, the small elementary school he established there had grown into a mission station of dozens of buildings that was a source of great pride for the American Board. Occupying over four hundred acres on the crest of the hill above the city proper, the station schools were drawing pupils from a wide area of outlying villages.

Yet, there were signs of trouble ahead. Outbreaks of cholera threatened the populations of several towns. On the heels of the cholera came crop failures; in some parts locusts ate everything in their way. Famine was widespread and the government did little to help. The oppression and persecution of Armenians was increasing. In 1894, a massacre of Armenians broke in Samsoun, the town on the Black Sea coast where Theresa's party had started out on their overland journey to Harpoot. News of it spread like wildfire through the missionary community in Turkey: What next? Where next? Generally, the mood was one of faithful stoicism. In Harpoot, the old Dr. Barnum wrote: "We are glad to be here whatever may happen. If the Lord permits us to be cut off in an uprising of fanaticism, it will be because we can bless the country more in that way than in any other. Perhaps something of this kind is necessary. If so, for my part, I am ready."[20]

Dr. Gates had only been President of Euphrates College in Harpoot a few months when the massacres in Sassoun occurred. The origins of this attack are somewhat sketchy, but it appears that an Armenian from Constantinople

---

20. *Missionary Herald*, vol. 92, January 1896, p. 3.

had been agitating among his people in Sassoun, without much success. This was the pretext for an attack by the local Kurds on the Armenian villagers, which the Armenians repulsed. That, in turn, led to an attack by the Sultan's own troops, and up to 8,000 Armenians were killed in the ensuing atrocities.[21]

The massacre at Sassoun caught the attention of the European powers who pressed to institute reforms. The Sultan temporized. The Armenian Hnchag party, one of several Armenian nationalist organizations, organized a protest march in Constantinople. The marchers were attacked and a massacre of Armenians took place in Constantinople. This was the prelude to the storm: between October, 1894, and January, 1896, a wave of massacres swept the country. In the end, an estimated 200,000 Armenians in various Ottoman provinces were killed and thousands more left homeless. As this storm was gathering, the Harpoot missionaries realized that they were about to be put to the test of their lifetime.

At the time of this crisis, 'Aunt Caro' and 'Aunt Hattie' were returning from an extensive 'touring trip' of several weeks to the outlying villages to visit and offer help and encouragement to the small Christian communities in their field. In a letter dated a few days after the massacre, 'Aunt Hattie' wrote the following:

> I was away from home for more than seven weeks—Miss Bush and I were in Arabkir, one of our largest and wealthiest cities, fifty-four miles from Harpoot. The political horizon looked so stormy that we felt we should hasten home. Three times on our journey robber bands of Koords were at the roadside, and if it had not been for our resolute gendarme, we should have been robbed and perhaps murdered. They said to our gendarme, "You stand aside and we will cut them to pieces." They took a fancy to Miss Bush's horse and said, "We will dispose of her and take her horse." God put it into the heart of that Turkish soldier to protect us, when he might easily have joined those who robbed us."
>
> How glad the Harpoot missionaries were to see us. They had been full of anxiety for us—every mile of our journey of fifty-four miles seemed a miracle of mercy. I must not forget to say that we left Arabkir on Tuesday; the day but one afterward, Thursday, that city was plundered and burned. That same day the Turkish governor of Arabkir telegraphed to Turkish officials in Harpoot, "There

21. Robert Melson, *Revolution and Genocide*, Chicago: University of Chicago Press, 1992, p. 45.

is nothing to be seen but burned houses, and nothing to be heard but volleys of musketry."

Friday, the day of our return, the Koords and Turks began to burn the Christian villages on our lower plain: Saturday, we counted from our window eight burning villages. We hardly thought Harpoot would be attacked so soon, but after the morning service on Sunday, Christians, Protestant and non-Protestant, came in crowds to the large door opening into the courtyard belonging to the premises Miss Bush and I occupy. I appointed a doorkeeper and told him to admit every Christian who came seeking shelter. Oh, what a pitiful sight! Strong men with blanched faces brought their families, and there they sat day and night. All day Sunday, Nov. 10th, and Monday morning, Dr. Barnum and Dr. Gates and prominent Christians consulted with city authorities as to the safety of the city. The Christians voluntarily gave up all arms, that the authorities might see that there was no thought of rebellion; and it was a wise move, for those who resisted were cut down without mercy. What solemn promises the officials made! The chief of the troops of the city said, "Dr. Barnum, my body shall be cut into pieces before a Koord shall enter this city." And yet when they did come, not the slightest attempt was made to check them, and the cannon which the military chief said he had brought up from the barracks on the plain for *our* safety, instead of being directed towards the Koords, were turned in the direction of Dr. Barnum's and other Christian houses. Cannon balls and an exploded bomb were found in Dr. Barnum's study.

Monday noon all the missionaries gathered in Mr. Allen's house; the crowd also from my rooms, about 150, and other refugees left their houses to the mercy of the plunderers, which were chiefly Turks. When they broke open the large door of our courtyard, we all left the building. Dr. Wheeler and Mrs. Allen, both invalids, were carried in the arms of strong men and we started to go up the steep hill back of our premises; where, we knew not. But soldiers came running down to meet us and said it was not safe to go farther, for Koords were all about. So we took our way back to the school premises, and the great crowd, weak from terror, sat down on the ground in the girl's school yard in perfect quiet to await further developments. We heard the Koord going through the girl's school building, breaking open doors and cupboards with their axes. When one Koord opened the door leading out into the school yard, and another peered around the corner of the house, we thought it time to move again. We then went to the boys' College building, and the crowd surged in there. What a haven of rest it seemed. In an incredibly short time, all our premises were thoroughly plundered, and then with the exception of Mr. Gates' and Dr. Barnum's houses, were soon in ashes. Dr. Barnum's house was fired several times, but the Lord did not permit it to be burned. Soon after we entered the College building, word was sent that we must leave it, as the Koords were going to burn it; that if we would come out the soldiers would protect us. Dr. Barnum told them that we had no longer any faith in their promises; that they could protect us in the building if they wished; that we had *all* resolved *not* to leave the building, and that if they burned it, we should burn with it. The guard was withdrawn with the chief and we *fully expected* to perish in the flames. But there were no outcries; death by burning seemed desirable rather than falling into the hands of the Turkish soldiery, especially the women and our school-girls. *What* mercy would they have found!

But God sent another officer with soldiers, who set guards about the four buildings that remained of our twelve. The Protestant church was burned that night, and that was connected with the Preparatory school adjoining our refuge, so that if the latter had burned, the College would have been in great danger. But the school fire-engine was brought out and the building was saved.

We stayed about a week with 450 refugees in the College building. The massacres, plundering and burning have been universal. The object at first seemed plunder, but it merged into a religious war, and there is now a great pressure upon Christians to become Mohammedans, to save their lives. *Very many* have joined the noble army of martyrs; among them, right in our vicinity, a white-haired pastor, and two preachers, members of our last theological class. I grieve to say that whole Christian villages have outwardly accepted Islamism by putting on the white turban and repeating the formula, "There is no God but God, and Mohammed is the Prophet of God." Of course we know that they inwardly loathe Islam. But in one village on the Euphrates the alternative was given to die or disown Christ. Ten men were killed and fifty-five fled with their wives and children to the river and drowned themselves.

We are still holding on, though our work has received a terrible blow. There are many Sassouns in Turkey now. Thousands are homeless and hungry, and unless aid, speedy and abundant, be sent, thousands will die of starvation. The Christians have no food, no homes, and many no clothes, and a winter is just before us. Oh, that God would bring out of this terrible desolation and distress a holy, purified people.[22]

Two days after the attack, an exhausted Dr. Gates wrote his account of the devastation to his friend, the Treasurer of the ABCFM in Constantinople, Mr. Peet:

Harpoot College, Nov. 13th, 1895.

Dear Bro. Peet,

We are in the college building with a crowd of refugees. The first attack began on Sunday by a few Koords. These were easily driven off. Monday there was another attack in the morning, also repelled. These attacks amounted to little. The *set time* had not yet come.

Monday the Aghas from the village gathered in the city. The Koords and Turks from the surrounding regions attacked Husenik and slaughtered many. The soldiers went down the road to meet them. Some of the principal Moslems also went down. They had a conference with the Koords. Then the bugle blew and the soldiers led by their commander withdrew to the city dragging their cannon in a very leisurely fashion. After the soldiers had reached the city the Koords and Turks came on yelling and firing. The soldiers made no attempt to stop them. They fired their cannon once harmlessly toward the city, and they fired off their guns over the heads of the enemy. The Turks of the city joined in the plunder and attack. The Armenian school was fired first, then the greater part of the Christian quarter. Christians were shot down everywhere.

I saw all these things with my own eyes, for I watched things with a field glass until it became perfectly plain that the whole thing was definitely planned and arranged. The Christians had given up their arms and cast themselves on the protection of the Government. No Christians fired on the assailants, so far as I know. We took refuge in the girls' school until that was attacked, and Mr. Allen's house burned, and the school set on fire; then we gathered in the yard and prepared to die together. [...] We decided to go into the college building. As we left the school yard a Turk fired upon us from across the yard twice, first at Mr. Allen, then I

22. ABC 16.9.10.

said to him "God chastise you," and he fired at me. He was a very bad marksman or else God withheld him from accomplishing his purpose. There was no panic in our crowd. My family were the last to leave the yard.

At last the Alai Bey (Mehmet Bey), a Circassian, arrived. He was the first and only man who acted as if he meant to do anything for us. The soldiers had left. He called them back. We got out our fire engine and fought the fire, and he helped us. For three days I have fought fire, and cannot write now. We saved our house, Dr. Barnum's house, the Varjaran, the College building, eight of our buildings have been burned. All our houses were plundered before our eyes. The soldiers *made no attempt to stop it.* We are stripped of everything but the clothes we wore, but none of our company were wounded or killed. We owe our safety to *God alone.*

The Turks of the city were very much disappointed that any of our buildings were spared and they were determined that Dr. Barnum should be killed. Tuesday, the Alai Bey told us that he could not protect us here. Dr. Barnum told him we would not leave the building. If it were fired we would die in it. If we had left they would have burned the buildings and forced the refugees to become Moslems or suffer the penalty.

Four hundred souls are gathered here and we are feeding them.

Say to the foreign ambassadors: This work emanates from high quarters and only the strongest means can prevail. Do not let them be hoodwinked.

We may not yet escape with our lives, but if we do there will be great need of relief work.

This whole business has been hellish and the government deliberately abandoned Christians. We put ourselves under the protection of the government again and again, but their protection was a sham.

We shall send a telegram, if we can, to you and Minister Terrel. We cannot trust anyone, but we do not want to be ordered out of the country. If we abandon the Christians they are lost."[23]

As the days wore on and the stricken missionary station of Harpoot along with those of its sister stations all across Asiatic Turkey struggled to get back on their feet, the question of where the blame for the devastation ought to be put arose again and again. Dr. Gates continued to write to Mr. Peet at Bible

23. Gates to Peet, typed copy of letter, ABC 16.9.12, p. 6.

House in Constantinople, foreseeing the ways in which the Sultan was going to deflect the blame for the massacres away from himself:

> Nov. 21st
>
> Dear Brother Peet,
>
> The apologists for the beneficent and genial ruler of this land will doubtless try to make out that all this is the fault of Moslem fanaticism and quite contrary to the wishes of the Sultan. The government itself will represent, it has already begun to represent, that the Armenians provoked these attacks.
>
> As to the Armenians, in most places in this region they had given up their arms and cast themselves wholly on the protection of the government.... To us it is perfectly clear that this thing emanated from the Sultan. For two months the Dersim Koords and Moslem Koords have been declaring that they had orders from the Sultan to kill the Christians. The Turks in the cities also have said the same. Prominent Turkish officials have acknowledged that such an impression was prevalent.[24]

Page after page, Dr. Gates sets down the details of what happened as more information started to trickle in from outlying areas. Slowly, the extent of what had happened was becoming clear to those on the outside as well. The Rev. Judson Smith, attempting to sum up what these events meant for the missionary work, wrote:

The events of the past year in Asiatic Turkey have brought us face to face with the greatest disaster which has ever yet befallen any mission of the Board. Indeed, the occasions are few in the whole history of Christianity, in earlier or later days, in which the powers of evil have dealt the Church more heavy blows. To a casual view it may seem that the results of all our seventy years in Turkey have gone down in the general crash, and that the only thing left for us to do is to withdraw from the field and count all as lost." He continues: "The Armenians... were the only people assailed. In the short space of a few weeks, from being the most prosperous people in the empire, they became the poorest and most wretched. The leading men of the nation in many communities were struck down in cold blood by the ten thousand, their possessions carried off by murderers, and their wives and children, homeless and destitute, thrown upon the charities of the world....This did not happen in one village or city alone, not in one district or province of the empire merely; the six eastern provinces, including the territory occupied by the Eastern Turkey

24. Gates to Peet, typed copy of letter, ABC 16.9.12, p. 6.

Mission and Trebizond, were swept from north to south, from east to west, in cities, in towns in hamlets, with this fearful storm of murder and greed and lust.... In all this vast region business and agriculture and every form of productive industry were silenced; the winter's supply of food, the very implements of labor, were destroyed, and the victims left paralyzed and hopeless.[25]

Dr. Gates and his Harpoot missionaries were not the only ones who concluded that orders for the massacres had emanated directly from the Sultan. There was a similarity in all the reports from missionary stations across the land, attesting to a chilling orderliness in which the slaughter took place: it would begin in the early morning at the sound of a bugle, and the bugle-call would end it at sundown. But when looking for the cause for this nationwide bloodbath, the missionaries tended to look beyond the affairs of man and to discern, somehow, the workings of a Divine purpose behind it all. One day, they told themselves, those terrible days would be seen as the necessary prelude to a time of peace and Christian love.

In terms of politics, however, the Great Power pressure for reforms which would have guaranteed a greater measure of human rights for the Armenians came precisely at the time that, from Sultan Abdul Hamid II's point of view, he suspected the Armenians most. His empire was falling apart. The Armenians lived on both sides of the Russo-Turkish border, a potentially seditious minority. The way to deal with them was to teach them a lesson, "to diminish the number of Armenians—first, by dealing a vital blow at those most capable of taking part in any scheme of reconstruction, and, secondly, by leaving as many as possible to die by starvation, exposure, sickness, and terror, during the rigors of winter."[26]

The massacres and the losses sustained by the American Board in Turkey never sparked a serious debate in missionary circles as to whether the Board should leave its work in Turkey and simply clear out. "Those who look at [the missionaries] merely as American citizens, with no reference to their work and their responsibilities, as it is natural for government officials to do can very easily say, 'Let them flee as people flee from a burning building,'" editorialized the *Missionary Herald*.[27] It went on to make much the same point that many other writers made, and that we find in much of the private correspondence written by missionaries as well: This, if ever, was the time to stand firm. To leave now would spell certain doom for the Christians in Turkey, and ruin for all the work that had been done so far. Was there ever a time when they could do as much good for the people as they could at just that time? A noble future

---

25. Rev. Judson Smith, "The Crisis in Turkey," *Missionary Herald*, 1896, p. 447.
26. *Missionary Herald*, Feb. 1896, p. 56.
27. *Missionary Herald*, Feb. 1896, p. 57.

lay before them if they would stay put, because now, as never before, would the two and a half million Armenians in the Empire be ready to accept "the messengers of the gospel."

This, clearly, was one of the reasons Theresa felt compelled to follow her brother Ellsworth into this recently devastated land to try to alleviate that "great need over the water." We, of course, can appreciate the terrible poignancy of her decision to take part in the work of reconstruction: Whereas Abdul Hamid II's massacre was meant to teach the Armenians a lesson, his successors, the Young Turks who deposed him in 1908 had another purpose in mind: to wipe them off the land for good which, in fact, is precisely what they did in 1915. As we read Theresa's letters a question presents itself: Would she and her colleagues have gone ahead and toiled as ceaselessly if they had known what lay ahead?

Chapter Seven: Theresa Has Her First Christmas and Learns the Armenian for 'Behold the Cow.'

Theresa now turned to the business of unpacking her trunks and settling into the room she was to occupy for the next seven years in Harpoot. After the loss of eight of their twelve buildings in the massacre two years before, the Harpoot station had acquired three new two-story buildings connected to each other by second-floor hall-ways. One of the end buildings housed Dr. Ussher, the other end was occupied by the Browne family. The upstairs of the middle part had two bedrooms, one for 'Aunt Caro' and the other one for 'Aunt Hattie' who shared a sitting-room on the same floor. The ground floor had rooms for Laura Ellsworth, Ada Hall, a young woman from Liverpool who had also just arrived, and Theresa. The people at the station had gone out of their way to make the room welcoming and cozy:

> The people here had made our rooms very attractive and had put into them everything necessary for our comfort, stoves, beds, soap, towels, everything. I don't see where the things came from. I know that someone at the Barnums' had no pillow the first night. In our sitting-room had been put rugs, a hanging lamp, *growing plants*, curtains (from Ellsworth's rooms) and table, couch, chairs, etc. Chairs are still rather scarce. We have here one apiece in our bedrooms, and sometimes I have had to take my only one for use in the dining room. Before I forget it I want to speak of the beautiful pink chrysanthemums which Mrs. Barnum had put in every room.

Laura, Ada, and Theresa started Armenian lessons right away with Prof. Garabed Soghigian from the men's college, and daily conversation lessons with one of the twelve Armenian teachers from the girls' school. Theresa immediately took to the girls in the boarding school and found them "attractive and winning." She also started giving English lessons to the Armenian teachers, going for long walks or horse-back rides for exercise, and, as would be her custom during all her Harpoot years, spending her limited free time writing letters home:

Sunday, Nov. 27, '98
Harpoot

Dear Mamma,

Day before yesterday came your letter telling about your visit to Springfield and a good letter from Harry. I am sorry that you were so disappointed about the pictures. I did not like them especially, but I do not feel as strongly as you do. As for my looking sad, I was feeling very happy when they were taken, and I am as happy as can be in Harpoot. I love the missionaries here and the girls in the school, and I already like my work a hundred times as much as the teaching in Milton. (You had better not repeat that). I'm afraid you were feeling sad about me yourself, dear, and that you put that feeling into the picture. The one hard thing about being a missionary was over when I had left New York. I do sometimes worry a little about you people at home, but I know that is wrong. Otherwise I am more than contented.

As far as material things go I am well off. My room is pleasant. Our sitting-room is uncommonly cheery and sunny. The food at the Browne's is almost as good as home food. The Barnum's table is *just* as good as ours. We have rice and mutton in various forms, more than at home. Of course we have no beef, but to offset that, eggs are cheap, and we have quinces (cooked), honey, and delicious grapes very frequently. We have breakfast at seven, luncheon at 12.05 and dinner at 5.30. Prayers come directly before breakfast in the morning and right after dinner at night. We take turns leading prayers, i.e., choosing the hymn and praying. We are reading Isaiah in the morning and John at night. You remember that the Brownes, Miss Seymour and Miss Bush and E. and I constitute our family.

You may be interested to know (Remember that this is a private letter and you *mustn't* speak of this outside the family, above all not to Miss Wheeler or Dr. U's father) that Dr. Ussher and Miss Ellsworth seem to have taken a great fancy to each other already—I was going to say, have fallen in love. It is truly funny. The whole station looks on with some amusement and some doubt, because it is so sudden.

I have liked horseback riding from the very first. Yesterday Ellsworth and I had a fine ride of an hour over the hills above the city. I rode Miss Bush's horse, a lively little pacer, called Brer Rabbit. Four dogs chased us, and we had a hot run away from them.

I have bought some linen materials (figured) with a good deal of red in it for outside draperies for my bed-room windows, to cover my wood-box, make into a table-cover, etc. The white muslin I brought from home, I shall use for short inside curtains, close to the windows, which open in the middle and swing like doors. There are very broad window-seats. Altho' my room is on the second floor, people can look straight into it from the walk above, because we are on a steep hillside, you know. Ellsworth had a fairly good chest of drawers made for me, and I have had to buy a little sheet-iron stove (costing about two dollars) because our things won't come for a long time. I have had to borrow toilet-soap, table cover, etc, but in general I am pretty well off. I know you want to ask a thousand questions—I know what they are, but you see my time for letter-writing is limited. I must go now to the sitting-room of the "Aunties" for at 6.30 we have the one meeting of the whole circle of the week. It is wholly informal and family-like. We sing a good deal.

I must tell you know about Thanksgiving. In the morning we had school as usual, but in the afternoon a half-holiday was given. At 3.30 "the circle" had a little meeting at which we all gave some reason why we were thankful. Little Moore said, "I'm fankful 'cause I'm at *home*." Then we had a most excellent dinner, all sitting down at one table at the Barnum's, or rather at two tables united into one. Celery and cranberry sauce were missing but the turkey and pies were there. We had likewise mashed potato, delicious pillaf with almonds in it, quince jelly, canned corn and chicken pie. The pies were mince, squash and apple-tart. After dinner we carried out a sort of impromptu program which Miss Barnum got up. Miss Bush had paraphrased a song called "Over the waves," so that it fitted our circumstances. This was to be sung by Miss Bush, Miss Barnum, Ellsworth and Dr. Ussher, but after it was announced impressively by Dr. Gates, they said they were not going to sing it after all. This was because they agreed privately that it fitted Dr. U. and Laura altogether too well. He didn't know why they left it out. Then Ellsworth made gestures from behind (you know how we have done it at home) while I recited Lochinvar and later, "Give me turkey," etc. We all sang The Battle-Hymn of the Republic. Laura recited a bright little poem, Mrs. Gates read a Thanksgiving story by Eugene Field, Dr. Gates read the poem of Mr. Millard's which I enclose, Dr. U. did some sleight of hand tricks, and finally, we sang two verses of America and one of God

Save the Queen. In the course of the evening we had lemonade, nuts and raisins and candy served to us. Isn't this most extravagant for missionaries?

Nov. 29 Sunday was a very full day. I went to the service in the church (really a large school-room) at 7.15. We had breakfast at about 8.30. At 10.45 I visited the two girls' Sunday Schools, at 12 went to a C.E. [Christian Endeavor] meeting for the day pupils. The service, corresponding to our morning service at home, comes at 2.30 here and I went to that, together with all the circle except Mr. Browne and Miss Daniels who have been sick with the grip (Miss Hall had it last week). It was a communion service, and three people were received into the church. Dr. Barnum preached in Turkish and afterward Dr. Gates in Armenian. Of course all the hymns, Bible-reading, etc. was in Armenian, as were all the other meetings I went to. Usually the native pastor preaches. All these gatherings are in school-buildings. The missionaries sit on benches in the front. All the people here take off their shoes at the door and go about the house in thick woolen stockings.

Isn't it queer that Miss Ellsworth has a brother named George Henry Ellsworth? No time for more.

With much, much love,
Theresa L. H.

What good letters you and the others do write. Where are George and Cornelia?

Most loving Christmas and New Year's wishes for you all. I cannot get used to thinking a month ahead. I have some little things to be sent to the feminine portion of the family, when I learn how Cornelia's table cover gets through.

Dec. 4, 1898

Dear Papa,

Ellsworth and I were very glad to receive your letter which arrived last Thursday. It was, by the way, the only letter either of us had. Mr. Browne's letter for some reason did not arrive till Saturday. I haven't much time to write, so I'll just give you an idea of an ordinary day such as I am spending now. I dress by lamp-light as you probably do now. At 6.45 we (those who board with them) have prayers in the Browne's parlor. At 7.00 comes breakfast. After that I study or do "odd things" till 8.30, except on Thursday when we have a teachers' prayer meeting at 7.50. At half-past eight all the schools have prayers. I go often but not always to college-prayers, sometimes to lead, sometimes to listen. These girls understand English if it is spoken simply and slowly. At 8.45 Monday and Tuesday I have the Second Freshmen in English till 9.15, at which hour I have a conversation lesson of half an hour in Armenian with one of the native teachers, the first three days of the week. Her name is Aghavni. I have forgotten her last name. She has a sweet, refined face and a gentle voice, and is (I judge by her clothes) of a family in comfortable circumstances. I should suppose her to be about my age. Like all Armenians she is a little lacking in "snap." After this lesson I have until now studied Armenian, prepared for my English classes etc till the luncheon-hour, 12.05. Beginning tomorrow, however, I am to give Herbert and Harold a "language" lesson (Eng. grammar and composition) for half an hour every day. Laura is to teach them Arithmetic, Ellsworth, Geography, and among us they will be taught two or three hours every day in a room in the Gates house, which Mrs. Gates has fitted up as a school-room. After luncheon I study or take my ride till 1.45 when Br. Garabed Soghigian comes to give an hour's lesson in Armenian to Ada, Laura and me together. He is one of the young teachers in the boys' college. We sit in a row on the sadir (couch), while he sits before us in his long, mouse-colored coat of European cut, and his fez, and very diffidently asks us to translate into Armenian, "Behold the cow," or "The horse eats barley and green grass." Br. Garabed stays until 2.40. On Thursday and Friday I have the Seniors and Juniors in English at 3.00, other days I am free at that time. Monday there is a teachers' business meeting at 3.40, Tuesday the Christian Endeavor meeting is at that hour; Thursday I have a teachers' class in English then. I suspect I have made this all very confusing to you when I might have expressed it very simply by giving you the program which I made for myself.

We have dinner at 5.00, prayers immediately afterward and then we go our own ways.

We have made a slight change in our rooms, at least, some of the others have. Laura has one room now for a sitting-room and bed-room (a large, sunny room) and Ada and I have separate sleeping-rooms and the sitting-room together. You may be interested to know that I pay about twelve cents a week for having all my room-work done, sweeping and all, (and this includes both rooms) and about fifteen cents a week for washing. To balance such cheapness as this, you must remember, it costs as much to get furniture here as it does to buy it in the first place in America. Nothing is so cheap as work in this land.

Miss Daniels has been ill for more than a week. It began with grip, but she is nervously used up and is very slow in recovering. Ada and Mr. Browne are just over the grip. Laura has been a little troubled with malaria. I am almost the only one who is perfectly hale and hearty, for the doctor has been vaccinating everybody, and it has very generally "taken." I believe it hasn't with Ellsworth. Fortunately, I was all through with this unpleasant little performance before I reached here.

Mr. Browne and Miss Bush expect to start off on another tour—of three weeks this time—day after tomorrow. They will probably come back just before Christmas. We do not have vacation in the schools at that time, for Christmas is celebrated here among the Armenians on the twelfth of January, I believe.

Last Saturday, the Juniors called upon Miss Ellsworth and me. The Seniors (five in number) had asked to come to see us about a week before, and that called forth the note, a copy of which I enclose. Of course after that we asked the Juniors to come too. I enjoyed both calls. Most of the older girls are winsome and attractive. They are rather shy and giggle upon very slight provocation. We showed them our photographs, which interested them greatly. It really takes almost all of one missionary's time to receive calls. The women, and men, too, come at all hours and stay indefinitely. We have to do a good deal of smiling and nodding in lieu of talking. I have to leave my guests on account of my lessons, but people like Aunt Hattie and Mrs. Browne, whose time is not so rigidly planned for, give a great deal of that precious article for this purpose, very patiently and cheerfully. Last week the two ladies whom I just spoke of, and the three new-comers returned some calls. We did not go into the first house because the washing was being done, and the women of the household were not ready for company. We made four calls, offered our parevs (salutations), sat down upon the rugs spread upon the floor, and made ourselves agreeable by smiling and saying the few Armenian words we knew. Sometime I will try to remember to tell you more about the calls in detail.

Sunday afternoon I visited three orphanages with Mrs. Barnum, Ada, the doctor and Ellsworth. The children sang for us, some of them recited Bible verses and answered questions about Bible stories. The children seem as happy as can be. You would laugh to see them walking in single file to school. I know when they are passing from the clatter of their flapping shoes on the paving stones. I look down upon the meandering line of fezes, the funny coats, and the switching, striped skirts, such as the men and boys wear here, and I smile frequently.

Yesterday was Dr. Barnum's 72nd birthday and we were invited over to have ice-cream etc at his house in the evening. He is a charming old gentleman. We have had a great many letters of welcome from the missionaries at neighboring stations. They are all most friendly. The weather here has been beautiful for weeks, clear weather such as we sometimes have at the beginning of November.

Every week I think I must stop writing such long letters, but my pen runs away with me. It would be a great comfort to me if you could sometime say We are all happy, or something of that sort.
With much, much love,
Theresa (L. Huntington)

We have had a delightful little prayer meeting tonight at Dr. Gates'—the American teachers, Dr. Ussher, Mrs. Gates and Miss Hall.

Dec. 14, 1898

Dear Harry,

You have been very good about writing to me. Your two bright letters to Ellsworth and to me reached here together last week. I think they were meant to come a week apart.

Just now I am sitting in our parlor by the table. It is about 7.15 P.M. Tonight the Brownes took dinner with the Barnums, and as "Aunt Caro" is away on a tour, that left "Aunt" Hattie, Ellsworth, and me to have our dinner together. Since dinner I have spent some time in covering, rather, preparing to cover a combination wood-box and pew arrangement for my room. Perhaps settee is the best name for it. The cloth is a sort of chintz which a merchant brought here from the market. I have had the frame of a screen made, likewise a wash-stand, which is merely a good box on end with shelves. The sides and front are to be covered with a piece of the chintz, a little ruffled. I may use white cloth, something like muslin, instead. I haven't bought any rugs yet because all which have been brought here are either ugly, too large or too expensive. It isn't easy to find rugs, because they don't make now the kind which foreigners like, and the natives know that the old rugs are in demand in America and elsewhere and charge accordingly. Ada and I have had a sadir or couch made for our sitting-room, and a wood box, too. As to the rest we use chiefly borrowed furniture.

We have hung the pictures, most of which were mine, and they look very well indeed. I am thankful for every picture I brought, framed or unframed. Aunt Caro admires very much the Fra Angelico angels which Cornelia had framed so beautifully.

The other day Mrs. Barnum sent over to us as an early Christmas present several pots of plants,—a rosebush, a tuberose, just starting, a primrose plant, some freesias, some little carnation seedlings, several geraniums etc. These, with what Ellsworth had started, fill up our windows pretty well.

Let me tell you what special things have happened this week. Friday night Ellsworth and I took dinner at the Barnums. We sang for a while in the evening. Miss Daniels, who is slowly getting better, came to dinner that night. She will not teach again this term (which ends in four weeks).

Sunday I did not go to the early service, but went to two Sunday Schools for a short time, to a C.E. meeting, to the afternoon service, to the meeting for the boarding pupils at 5.50, which Aunt Hattie led, and then to our own pleasant little station meeting. It was at the Doctor's this week. He had just furnished his parlor the day before (chiefly with rugs, couches, and pictures) and the room looked very cheery and attractive. We had a delightful, helpful little meeting as we always do. It is very informal and homelike. The children say their verses and choose some of the hymns. The one who leads takes any subject he pleases, and we, the rest, speak or keep silent, "as the spirit moves." Emma led our teachers' meeting on Tuesday. That is the best one of the week. We always have it at eight o'clock (P.M.) at the Gates' house.

You will wonder that I don't say more about the people. As long as I can't talk Armenian, there is a wall between me and them and I cannot really know them and understand them. I don't feel this way about the older school-girls because I see them so much. It is queer how quickly one gets used to their ways. It seems the most natural thing in the world to see people sit on the floor and to do it oneself. Chairs are always provided for the Americans, however, if we want them. I'll own up that I can't sit still on the floor as these people do. My feet go to sleep.

It is hard to tell the ages of the women, for the little girls wear long dresses and aprons, and all the women wear their hair down the back in one or two braids. I have had a funny little woman sewing for me today. She crouched down on my rug and worked silently all day. She brought her own dinner—bread, I suppose—and I pay her three piastres, or 13 1/2 cents a day. She had a shawl twisted round her head and neck and the bows of her spectacles which came over the shawl were tied together behind by a string. I find most of the school-girls very attractive personally but the older women who call are much less so.

Miss Bush went on her tour alone, after all, that is she had with her an Armenian pastor but Mr. Browne didn't go because he has been having a good deal of trouble with his throat. He means to join her this week at Palu. Miss Daniels is living with the Gates family now. Yesterday she made candy, with the three boys, chiefly for the purpose of amusing them and keeping them still, and I helped for a little while.

It has snowed off and on for the last two days. Today, looking down upon the roofs of the city, we could see dozens of men shovelling the snow from the flat roofs into the street. This afternoon Ellsworth and I went to ride. I used the Doctor's horse and saddle. It is the first time I have tried a man's saddle, and I didn't like it very much. I haven't had a genuinely good ride since Miss Bush went. Her horse and saddle spoiled me for anything else. I tried Mr. Browne's horse and Emma's saddle one day, and the Bagir with Ada's saddle at another time, and both saddles were abominations. This afternoon when we were riding over the hill-tops, in the snow, and looking down upon the clouds which were rolling over the plain, the strangeness of it all struck me, that Ellsworth and I should be riding on horseback together on the mountains of Turkey.

Tuesday afternoon, instead of the regular C.E. meeting, we had a missionary service which our committee had planned. I am the chairman, you know. The subject was Turkey. I wish there were more time to tell you about it.

We are going to have our Christmas celebration Monday evening. The Brownes have invited us all to dine there. I said "The Brownes," but Mr. B. and Miss Bush will not be at home then.

Much love to each one,
Affectionately,
Theresa (L.H.)

We enjoyed Mamma's and George's letters last week.

Ellsworth Huntington's notebooks—now in the Ellsworth Huntington collection in the Yale University archives—are full of observations that provide an interesting complement to what Theresa was seeing. Theresa seems much more interested in people; Ellsworth provides us with more details about the physical conditions in the towns and villages. Here, from his Harpoot notebooks, is his description of winter in the town:

> That street is very narrow and has several uses beside that of a way for men and animals. Everything that is not wanted in the houses is thrown into the streets which are not made cleaner in that way. In the middle of the street flows a stream of water, small ordinarily but after a heavy rain increasing with great rapidity until it fills the whole street and no one can cross. If anyone goes to make a call on a rainy night it is wise to keep on his own side of the street for fear that he may not be able to get home. In winter the snow from the roofs is all shoveled off into the street which often makes it easier to walk on the roofs of the houses in order to save going up and down flights of stairs every 40 or 50 feet. The houses are all built adjoining each other and the people dig out the snow in front of the doors. Often the piles of snow in the streets are higher than the roofs so that as our doctor remarked, 'One can sit on the street and hang his feet over the roofs.' I heard of a case last winter where a boy fell off the street onto the roof and broke his arm.[28]

Theresa didn't just write letters to her family. This is one to the high-school class she taught at Milton, where her sister Cornelia had succeeded her:

> Harpoot
> Dec. 21, 1898
>
> My dear Class,
>
> My sister Cornelia and I own a good many things together, and you are one of them. I have received letters from several of you, and you will have answers soon. You don't know how much I think of those letters and how interesting I find them. Please don't forget when you think I am a long time about writing to you, that I was two months in reaching here, and that it takes a letter a whole month to go from Turkey to America.
>
> I must tell you first a little about how I got here, and then what Harpoot is like. I spent ten days on an ocean-steamer, six days in

28. Yale University Archives, Ellsworth Huntington Papers, Notebooks, 1898.

London, one night crossing the British Channel, then five days in crossing Europe, and we were at Constantinople. We waited here over three weeks for pass-ports, and I saw much that was curious and interesting. The streets are narrow and rough, and very dirty, and crowded with men in baggy trousers and fezes, and gaily-colored skirts or robes. There are quantities of dogs lying about the streets, or hunting for food in the piles of rubbish which are collected in the middle of the path. The dogs yelp if you do not turn out for them, and the men shout, and the shop-keepers who sit cross-legged in their little stalls with their goods about them, call to you as you as pass, to come in and buy, so there is plenty of noise. You see very few women in the streets and those who are visible are covered, except the eyes, with a great cloth thrown over the head and shoulders.

We spent two nights and a day on the Black Sea (and I was seasick, together with most of our party) and then landed one Friday morning at Samsoun, a town in Asia Minor, on the Black Sea coast. The same day we began our eighteen-days journey in wagons to Harpoot. These wagons look like the pictures of emigrant wagons which you may have seen. We used to stop over night at khans or inns, reaching there usually between four and seven at night and starting off between four and five in the morning, before it was light. These inns are much like that where the little child Jesus was born. On the first floor, the animals and wagons are kept, and often the drivers sleep with them. The second story is for the guests. The rooms here are generally empty, except for matting on the floor, and the windows frequently have paper instead of glass. We had to carry folding beds with us in the wagons.

I should like to give you a little glimpse of the sights we saw—of the long trains of camels with great packs on their backs; of the lines of patient little donkeys and pack-horses, of the flocks of goats on the mountains; the rude buffalo-carts, drawn by buffaloes, which look very much like the pictures of the hippopotamos; the strangely-dressed people who stood open-mouthed to stare at the foreigners; of the little houses built of mud, and oh, so many more things.

We crossed one mountain after another. One day we had to turn out of the rough, rocky road more than twelve times, and drive over the dry beds of streams, in order to avoid broken bridges. I have never seen such a stony, barren land as this. Only near the rivers in the plains can anything green be seen, except, as they tell me, in spring. The day before we reached Harpoot we crossed the Euphrates River on a ferry-boat, which looked very much like a gigantic sugar-scoop. A man put this craft into motion by means of a long pole.

Now I want to tell you a little about the place where I live. The missionaries' houses are on the edge of the city, and on the side of a mountain. From the window of my parlor, I can look down upon the flat roofs of some houses, and far below them, upon the great plain at the foot of the mountain. I can make out the villages upon this plain by the smoke which rises from them early in the morning. Beyond the plain there is a range of great mountains. Indeed there are beautiful, snow-covered mountains looming up along the horizon wherever I can see it. Sometimes the clouds hang over the mountains and hide them; again we can see the clouds down below us, between us and the plain, and sometimes Harpoot city itself is in the clouds. It is very much like being in a fog.

Every Sunday I go to a Sunday School for Armenian girls about your age. I cannot teach them because I know so little of their language. They meet in a house made of mud, though that is not as bad as it sounds, for the house which I myself live in is plastered with mud on the outside, because wood is scarce and bricks are not made here. When I open the rough, wooden door, and the girls catch sight of me, they all stand, and do not sit till after I do. Many of them make the pretty, native salute, touching the chin and then the forehead with the right hand. Near the door, I see a number of shelves, one above the other, and upon these stand quantities of shoes, arranged neatly in pairs. They are like very heavy, coarse slippers than like our boots. All the people here leave their shoes at the door, and go about the house in heavy white or grayish woolen stockings. The floor of the room is covered with carpeting, not like our carpets however, and upon this the girls sit, each class grouped about its teacher, who sits on a low bench which runs about the sides of the room. These girls all have their hair parted in the middle, and braided in two or more braids. They are, as I said before in their stocking-feet, their dresses of dark, heavy calico or gingham come to their ankles, most of them have a little square shawl of a reddish-brown color, over their shoulders. This they draw over the head when they go out of doors. Some of the girls wear aprons, and some have on woolen jackets which you would call very queer and old-fashioned. But in spite of clothes, most of the faces are bright, and many are pretty, even to American eyes. Pretty or not, some of them are very attractive and loveable. In making the attendance of a class, the teacher always puts down opposite the name of a scholar, the number of verses she has learned. Some girls learn fifteen or more for one Sunday. After the lesson is over one of the teachers asks some questions about the lesson of the whole school, and some of the verses are repeated. I visit the different classes in turn. Some girl offers me a bible and I smile and say "Shenór hagályem" (Thank you) and look on, altho' I can hardly read a word. I can pronounce the words but cannot understand much as yet. You would enjoy hearing the girls sing our dear old tunes with strange words, and you would notice how eager and talkative they are during the lesson. After Sunday School is over one of the girls scampers to get my jacket and holds it for me just as some of you used to.

Now my third sheet is full. I send my love to you all,—Ziblah, Polly, Adelaide, Sarah, Jenny, Emma and Louise, and I hope that each one of you is trying to obey and imitate our dear friend, Jesus Christ,

Very affectionately, your teacher,
Theresa L. Huntington

Harpoot
Dec. 28, 1898.

Dear Mamma,

What a good family you were to send so much mail for us to receive just at Christmas-time. Cornelia especially outdid herself, and what shall I say to Harry's weekly letters? All this beside Papa's and Mamma's epistles! When little Ruth hasn't too much studying on hand, she must write someday to her missionary brother and sister. It sometimes seems impossible that we are really missionaries, because the houses are so comfortable and pretty and we have such pleasant social times together. The touring missionaries do suffer a good many hardships, but they take it all joyfully. I never saw a cheerier, braver, happier woman than Miss Bush. Just look at her face in the report of the Red Cross Society in the relief work in Turkey and see if you don't admire it.

Since I must leave out some things, I'll tell about Christmas first, and then write of other things if there is time. You know that the Armenians celebrate Christmas about the fifteenth of January, and New Year's a few days before that. The school vacation comes at that time. Nevertheless, as the week of prayer comes just before the beginning of vacation, it seemed best for the schools to have their celebration now. Friday afternoon all the school-girls crowded together into the Mangaran (Grammar School) room, and we had a sort of Christmas concert, consisting of recitations and songs in Armenian and English. I said something about giving, which Emma translated. She is normally our interpreter. The children brought gifts for the poor that day,—money, bulghur (barley), bread and various kinds of food. Most of the children are very poor themselves and can only bring a few paras, or a handful of grain. Earlier the same day I went around with Emma and Laura to the different schools, and we gave something to each child. The little kindergarten girls each had a paper doll, cut from a colored fashion-plate; the kindergarten boys each a card and a pencil; all these little ones had some leblebs, too. (Leblebs are dried peas, browned and salted. They correspond in a way to our popcorn, and are very good.) The older girls received more,—an eraser, several pens, a ruler, and a sheet of blotting-paper, in addition to the pencil and card. The college girls had their presents in the evening, when the boarding pupils, of whom there are some thirty, had a sort of party. Dr. and Mrs. Gates and Miss Hall were the only missionaries present beside the three American teachers—Miss Daniels wasn't able to come. We played games, such as "passing the key" or ring, and pinned appendages onto a tailless donkey. Then the girls received their gifts, each having a little bag containing a paper of pins, a pin-ball, a spool of thread, a card and a thimble or a little pocket-book. Four of the younger girls had dolls. They were speechless with pleasure. One child was delighted because I told her that my little sister once had a dress of the material of which her doll's dress was made. It was interesting to see the disposal of the things which I saw packed at home. Since there weren't enough dolls to go around Mary has saved most of them for special prizes. If she hasn't acknowledged the box yet, it is because she hasn't been well enough to do anything. She has been in the school only a week since we came.

On Sunday there were of course no general Christmas services, but in the evening we had a "station" Xmas meeting at the Barnum's. Ellsworth led it. The day was snowy and blustering. It hardly seemed like Xmas. The poor little children came to Sunday-School half-frozen and crowded about the fire, seated on the floor, to warm their poor red hands. The people here don't wear mittens.

The next day, I was wakened at about six o'clock by singing somewhere near me. I thought it was out of doors, but as I was groping about in the darkness for my matches, someone knocked and Aunt Hattie's voice said, "The girls are singing out in the hall." Sure enough, there were some eight or ten of the older girls, singing Xmas songs. I pulled on a few garments hastily and went out. They shouted, "Merry Xmas!" Then Ada appeared and we talked merrily for a few minutes, till they went below to sing for Laura. They had sung at the Barnum's and Gates' before coming to us. Most of the morning I spent in completing and doing up Xmas gifts. At one o'clock I went for a ride with Dr. Gates, Dr. Barnum, Dr. Ussher, Ellsworth, and Emma. It was snowing and the wind blew hard, but the sky and the clouds were wonderful, as always, and it was exciting to have the horses plunge through the drifts. Ellsworth's horse tried to roll with him in the snow and we all looked on and laughed.

At 4.15 before dinner, the little boys recited some poetry and we sang. Dinner came at 4.30,—turkey, mashed potato, rice, quince dolmas, gravy, (of course) currant jelly, and madzun; then chicken salad, and for dessert, ice-cream and cake, pears and oranges, and nuts (walnuts and almonds). They had prayers at the table after dinner was over. Meanwhile E. and I slipped upstairs and I dressed him up in some Santa Claus toggery which had been prepared. Laura had made the bay-window into a remarkably successful fire-place. Before this were hanging three enormous stockings, and several small ones, filled with gifts. The organ and floor were likewise heaped with presents. Santa with a great pack on his back was filling the stockings when the people came in. The children were wild with delight. Little Moore was afraid of him. I had ever so many presents. People were too good. I will enclose a list of what Ellsworth and I gave to the other people, and what I received. I forgot to say that Saturday night all the Browne household hung their stockings, and on Monday morning before prayers had our stocking opening.

Now for the presents from home. How much you did put in! I am more than glad to have the studs because I broke and lost one of my silver link studs at Con'ple and I broke one of the little studs for the front there, too. George's table-cover is a beauty. I haven't a table for it yet, but I think the one which is coming from America may fit it. Cornelia knows how glad I am to have the Northfield pictures, especially that one of Mr. Morgan and Mr. Macgregor.

The Wellesley Songs are a joy. I shall feel very swell, using a seal upon my letters. The Turks will suspect me of being a person of some importance. I spoke of the wax once in a letter. I didn't discover till the other day that that was a part of Christmas and was for both Ellsworth and me. "The children" will please count themselves thanked for the photograph frame. Cornelia will tell them how I valued my other one, and this is just the same in shape and size. I am glad of every ornament for the top of a book-case or desk. I don't know what I was about when I left my china at home, especially the yellow rose-bowl and my vases. I think I have mentioned all the home presents. I hope you had as happy and merry a time at home as we had.

Yesterday was rather a busy day with me. In the morning I straightened my room a little, then had an Armenian lesson, then taught the boy's at the Gates' house, made a little call upon the invalid (Mary), came home, and studied Armenian till luncheon time, after that I studied more, had another Armenian lesson with Br. Soghnigian, slipped out early, and went to a hantess (performance) at the Mangaran. Every school has one at the end of each term. The parents, especially the mothers, love to come and hear their children recite poems, dialogues, etc and sing in English and Armenian. When the affair was over I was talking to some of the women, one of the mairigs, Leah, translating for us. One old woman pointed to my eyes and said something in Armenian. Pompish Leah translated thus, "She says she loves you very much because your eyes are brown like the Turkey's eyes. The Americans have blue eyes." These women are continually telling us that they love us. That mistake of Turkey for Turk—the people of Turkey—is very common. The girls often make it.

By this time it was about four o'clock. Ada and I were longing for fresh air, so we went to the Gates' to look for a man to go with us to walk. We found no one there, but we stopped for a few minutes with Mrs. Gates, and she insisted upon lending me her short walking skirt. Then Ada and I went out onto the water-course above the yard, and walked up and down in sight of the building for half an hour or more. We should have gone to the end, if we had had a man with us. I wish you could stand with me sometime on the height above us, or even at my window and watch the sun set behind the snow-covered mountains, and the mist roll over the plain. In the evening, that is at 5.45 just after dinner, E. and Ada and I went up to the Gates' by informal invitation and had some ice cream. Then we all had a real frolic with the children for an hour or more and afterward prayers. When I came home I wrote till bed-time.

Chapter Eight: Theresa Gallops Through the Snow, and Mr. Browne Steps into an Armenian Dinner

The Harpoot missionaries welcomed the infusion of strength that Theresa and her newly arrived co-workers represented, and although the workload for each person was heavy and the hours long, there was a gradual sense that the political situation was stabilizing and that the government would permit the work to go on and to spread. Dr. Gates, aided by Ellsworth, devoted himself mainly to the college. Dr. and Mrs. Barnum and Mrs. Seymour were in charge of the extensive orphan work with the help of Ada Hall. There were twenty-four orphan homes in different parts of the Harpoot field housing a total of over one thousand children whose parents had been killed in the massacres.

Mr. Browne and Miss Bush did the 'touring work' among the forty out-stations in the vast Harpoot field. The year Theresa arrived, this work kept them in the saddle going from place to place, covering hundreds of miles. It was not unusual for them to stay on the road for a total of twenty-five weeks of the year.

Dr. Ussher, who according to Theresa had "a rather high opinion of himself" got himself entangled in a romantic relationship with Laura Ellsworth soon after he arrived. But as the only American physician in Harpoot, he had plenty of other things to worry about as well. "The halt, the blind, and the ill flocked to him by the hundreds," wrote the *Missionary Herald*.[29] This is how he describes his work as a doctor in Harpoot:

> But in the nineties the churches at home and their mission boards had not yet begun to realize the importance of the physician's work; so this large station of the ABCFM, with its schools and churches in sixty villages and towns, its college and theological seminary, and its orphanages where a thousand children left father-

29. *Missionary Herald*, 1899, p. 73.

> less by the massacres of 1895 were fed and clothed, was without a hospital.
>
> The houses of the missionaries had been destroyed by Turkish soldiers during the massacres, and President Gates of Euphrates College was superintending the construction of three new houses in a solid block to economize space and material. The eastern end was given to me. In this I opened an office, also a dispensary which I stocked with the medicines brought with me from America, and found an Armenian of some experience in this line to act as my apothecary and interpreter. Here I saw patients at all hours, many of them before breakfast; for Orientals, the original daylight-savings people, begin the day early.
>
> Operations had to be performed in the patient's own homes. During my first operation for cataract the woman lay on a mud floor of a small room under a window fourteen inches square from which I had to tear the paper glazing to obtain sufficient light. When I performed my first operation for stone I took a door from its hinges and laid it across two stools, placed the man on it, and knelt beside him...[30]

Theresa, Laura, Emma Barnum all helped Mary Daniels who was frequently ill with the Female Department of the college. As the new year began, Theresa, her health as robust as always, continued to delight in the view from the Harpoot hill, her vigorous riding excursions, and the work in general:

> Harpoot
> Jan. 4, 1899
>
> Dear Ruthie,
>
> Our mail from home instead of reaching here last Thursday or Friday, came yesterday (Tuesday). There had been a storm which delayed its passage over the mountains. It brought me Mamma's letter telling more about the great storm, and your new clothes etc. Likewise it brought a letter from you to Miss Barnum which I was glad to read.
>
> I wish you people could have some of my pleasure in riding. We usually follow the same path in our rides, for we have a limited amount of time, and the choice of riding down the mountain toward Mezereh by a much frequented road, or riding thro' the

---

30. Clarence Ussher and Grace Knapp, *An American Physician in Turkey*, Boston: Houghton Mifflin Co., 1917, pp. 10-11.

city, or on the hills behind our buildings. The horses would have to walk all the way if we took the first route; the second of course is not to be thought of, so we are restricted to the third. This is beautiful, however. It is a path which is, now that the snow has come, only wide enough for one man or horse. For a mile or so it runs along the side of the mountain, twisting and bending according to the ravines and slopes, and then comes up onto the hill-tops. Here there are opportunities for a good canter or run. At this point we can branch off in several directions—to the garden or to the ice-cave etc, but we usually choose a less frequented path than those, and we leave that too, to ride onto the tops of the hills. You understand that Harpoot is on a mountain, but it is such a big mountain that it has upon it lesser hills and many valleys and hollows. One side is steep, the other falls off gradually, by ups and downs till it meets another mountain. As there are practically no trees, we always have a wonderful view before us of the vast plain below and ranges upon ranges of mountains on every side of us. If I wrote many pages, I could never give you a worthy idea of the clouds and the varying sights in the mountains. Today in one direction they were of all shades of blue and in another—just golden in the sunlight. It is a most exhilarating thing to have one's horse flying over the ground with several other horses, on a height like this.

Harpoot
Jan. 23, 1899

Dear George,

I mean to make you the recipient of my home-letter this week and as there is to be only one, will you please send this home when you have read it? My recent epistles have been very hasty and scrappy.

I don't know where the vacation has gone. School begins again tomorrow noon. Term-bills are paid in advance here, and each child when his bill has been paid is given a ticket of admission. Since Miss Daniels isn't able to sell the girls' tickets for the coming half year, Dr. Gates has been taking her place yesterday and today, and Ellsworth has attended to the boys. Two days and a half have to be devoted to this work. It is by no means a pleasant task. Some of the people who can afford to pay for their children tell lies and make themselves out as utterly poverty-stricken. There is weeping and wailing and beseeching, and he who would sell tickets successfully and not be sold himself, must be just and immovable. Yesterday a stream of poor people banged away upon our knocker, in the hope of seeing Miss Seymour—(Miss S'more, they call her) and begging something from her, to get their children into school.

Yesterday Mary Daniels spent here, lying on my bed most of the day. She has been living with the Gates' family, but now they need her room, and she plans to exchange rooms with Laura for a week, and then for a week with me. That is, we go to her room at the girls' school and she comes here, to escape the noise and confusion. She will probably take her meals at the Barnum's again. I have been with her a good deal lately because Mrs. Gates is not well.

I enjoy living at the Browne's very much. Mr. Browne I like immensely. He is jolly, quick at repartee and hearty and wholesome in general. He can be very severe at times, and he is not at all afraid to rebuke a man who deserves reproof. Miss Bush and Miss Seymour are just part and parcel of the Browne family, having lived with them, and taken care of their babies from the beginning. They call Mr. Browne Papa or Parson and he calls Miss S., Aunt Hattie or Auntie, and Miss Bush, Caro. The people, by the way, call her Meester Push, and Mr. Browne, the Badvelli or Meester Bravóne. The Brownes have many ways like our family, and little home-jokes and by-words, just as we have. For instance when the children were little, they used to put on Christmas presents, "Dear Papa from Dear Me." This corresponds to "My loving Ruth."

On Saturday Aunt Caro started off alone, that is without Mr. Browne, for one of the villages of the plain. He had some work to do here, but this he finished yesterday, and this morning he left us to join her. She took the travelling servant, and the pack-horse, laden with two enormous hoorjes or saddle-bags, and he went alone, both plunging down from our sunshine into the chilling fog which has covered the plain like a blanket for days. I wish you could see some of the interesting, cheery letters they write, and I wish you could see them—Mr. Browne big and burly, with a long sweeping beard, Miss Bush sprightly and sunny, and slender and quick-footed as a girl.

Mr. Browne told a story to illustrate the politeness of the Armenians, the other day. Once he had been preaching in a village in the large living room of a well-to-do family. There were some forty or fifty people and the service had been very solemn. At the end he stepped forward to speak to someone and one leg went down almost to the hip in one of the big native ovens which are made in the floor. Not a muscle moved on anyone's face, then a little boy called out "O mother, the Badvelli has walked into our dinner." Mr. Browne could see the muscles tighten on the peoples' faces, but there was not a smile. He heard them roaring with laughter outside afterward, but no one showed amusement in his presence.

Here are some little scraps of news. Laura has bought a horse. He is about four years old and not fully grown. Our boxes have reached Samsoun, and will probably arrive here in March. The little sheet-iron stove which I bought for less than a dollar has kept my sleeping-room very comfortable, and as for the sitting-room, I am sitting there now with the sun streaming in at the windows and no fire at all. We usually have one morning and evening, and all day on cloudy days. Our plants are doing well. Two pansies blossomed, but then the miserable plant-lice appeared and since its soap-suds and kerosene bath, the plant has hardly recovered. Our fresias are beautifully budded, likewise two geraniums, and two violet plants, while our candy-tuft, marigold and yellow oxalis bloom cheerfully in our sunny windows. . . .

This vacation some seventeen girls and four teachers, who have no homes or live far away, remained at the girls' school. Ada and I made a little call upon them Monday evening. We found them, as usual, sitting upon the floor about the stove. Most of them were knitting, or crocheting thread edging. Some girls rushed off, as always, to bring chairs for us, and when we refused these, insisted that we sit upon some cushions that were brought. We attempted more Armenian remarks than ever before, and spoke with greater brilliancy. Ada has a funny way of rolling her eyes, putting her finger upon her lip, and plunging into a long Armenian sentence, using the English order and floundering about desperately in the middle. A droll one-eyed girl from Diarbekir, who sat at one side shook with silent laughter all the time that we were there. I suspect that our accent overcame her.

Yesterday Aunt Hattie, Laura, Ada and I invited these same girls and teachers to spend the evening with us. They came at six and we played games in Aunt Hattie's parlor for an hour or so, and then had tea, native candy and wafers (from Mrs. Browne). We borrowed our dishes from the Barnums and Brownes. The girls play some games which are much like ours. There is one good one which I never saw before. The people all sit in a circle. One who is leader, twirls her hands about one another, while each of the other players make some motion with her hands, no two people making the same motion. The leader keeps changing from her motion to that of someone else and then returning to her twirling again. When the leader takes another player's motion, that person must twirl as the leader does, till the leader ceases to make her movement, when she herself takes it up again. Any one who is caught napping and doesn't imitate the leader when she should, leaves the game or else pays a forfeit. These Armenian girls sing a funny, quick little song, when they play this. Our leader was very dexterous and lively, so the game was a success. At eight o'clock, the girls left, and we went to our little Tuesday evening meeting at the Gates' house.

Much love to you my dear brother. Be a good, true boy.

Lovingly,
Theresa (L. Huntington)

Harpoot
Feb. 9, 1899

Dear Mamma,

I told you that the time would come when I shouldn't write very good letters, and here it is. My life is pretty full with studying and teaching, with the C.E. Society and S.S. (Sunday School). The extras are what will interest you most. Yesterday was a real holiday. Miss Riefgold, one of the German ladies, is engaged to a count back in the Fatherland, and is to start for Germany next Monday with Pastor Ehmann and another Pastor who have been making a tour about Asia Minor this winter, inspecting and building up the missionary work of the Germans.

Accordingly in honor of the guests and Miss Riefgold, we were all invited to take luncheon at Mezereh yesterday. Seven of us went—Mrs. Barnum, Mrs. Browne and Miss Seymour in an araba, and Dr. Barnum, Dr. Gates, Miss Bush and I on horseback. I rode Miss B's horse, using Mrs. Gates' saddle, and she rode Mrs. Browne's. It was the first visit I had paid at Mezereh, though I had met four of the German friends before. They were most hospitable and genial, and I liked them all. Including the two guests, they now number eleven. There are four recent comers, a young man of about twenty-one who teaches the boys carpentering, an older gentleman (for he is surely that) who is to buy land, and train the boys in agricultural methods and two ladies, just arrived, who will soon open another orphanage.

Our conversation would have amused you, for we talked in four languages,—English, German, French and Armenian. For instance, Mrs. Browne had to talk to young Mr. Shutz in Armenian, for they had no other language in common; Mrs. Barnum and the newly-arrived German ladies had no means of communication except through French. When I found anyone who absolutely could not understand English, I boldly attacked German, tho' my vocabulary was very rusty. Because I'm sure that one or two of you would like to know, I'll tell you what the menu was. 1. chicken-soup, with egg in it, and native bread, 2. fried fish and boiled potatoes, with an oddly flavored gravy, 3. roast fowl and fried potatoes, 4. quince-sauce and cake, 5. oranges and pears. We had tea in the parlor afterward. Just before we went, we had prayers. Dr. Barnum prayed in English, and we sang Rock of Ages in German. Pastor Ehmann and his wife have two little orphan boys whom they treat in some ways as they would treat their own children, for instance, having them sleep in their room at night. The house to which we went is good for a native (rented) house but not as comfortable and pleasant as ours. The Germans have their orphans right about them, and live among them. They have also a hospital, and a widows' home where some of the ladies live. The latter place contains some thirty-three women who through age, blindness etc. are unable to care for themselves. Our horses were very frisky when we started for home, and we had a lively canter from Mezereh to the foot of the mountain. We reached home at about 4.20, just in time for me to go to a C.E. committee meeting. We are planning for a missionary meeting on China to be held next week.

Yesterday little Moore reached his fifth birthday, so we were all invited to have ice-"cheem", as Moore says, at his house at half past six. It was very good, as was also the birthday cake. We had a real children's evening. Moore showed us his presents, one of which was a little fez from Muggerditch, the cook. This pleased Moore more than anything else, and he wore it the whole evening. This morning when I saw him, the fez was still on his curly head. To return to yesterday evening, Mr. Browne and Miss Bush at Miss Gates' request told the boys something about their touring life. Then came prayers, Moore choosing the hymn which the boys always choose, America. After this there was a pillow-fight in the next rooms, in which the small boys and younger men participated. The battle was going hot and heavy when a pillow burst, enveloping one side in a white cloud. The carnage ceased abruptly. After the combatants returned to the parlor, Dr. Gates read aloud an amusing chapter from Robin Hood, and at about 8.30, we went home.

The clock has struck for twelve. That means that the mail must go and luncheon is ready. Much, much love,
from Theresa (L.H.)

Harpoot
March 1, 1899

Dear Papa,

I haven't kept a letter-record and so I really don't know to which one of the dear family my letter should be addressed. Last week we received no letter directly from home, although a note from George enclosing a letter from Harry came. I had by the same mail a letter from Hetty and another from Elizabeth Zeigler. [The sister of Theresa's future husband George Ziegler, and a classmate of Theresa's at Wellesley.]

We read in the papers that grip has raged in America. I hope you all have escaped it. I spent a day in bed with something of that sort about two weeks ago—my only sick day since my arrival—but wholly recovered very speedily. This climate seems to agree with me excellently. Our station invalids are fast mending. Mary looks almost like herself again, and Dr. Gates was able to take his ride today.

We have had much snow this last week, especially on Sunday a good deal fell. This means some suffering for the people from cold, and from dampness—poor drainage—when the thaw comes, but it is excellent for the wheat down on the plain, and for the spring growth generally. Water, you know, is very precious in this land. The streets are heaped with snow. That means much in Turkey. The snow from the flat-roofs has to be shovelled into the streets, there being no other place for it, else the water will soak into the dried mud of the roof, and much damage will ensue. The streets you know are very narrow. The day after a storm, the roofs are alive with men, clearing off the snow and for a time, the streets are well-nigh impassable. When a track is made, it goes up, up and down, down, and wanders from one side to the other, till it becomes a weariness to the flesh. There are no houses opposite us, for all were burned, so we are spared this difficulty in progress close by. The last time I made calls the snow came up to the tops of the doors. Yesterday Dr. Ussher was coming home from visiting a patient, and being weary of ascending and descending, he sat down by the wayside upon the roof a two-story house to rest. He told of another house where he had some difficulty in swinging himself down into the house, by catching hold of the top of the door. In passing through the streets after a storm, one has to frequently give a warning call, that he may not be killed and buried by zealous shovellers. These roofs correspond to lawns. After they have been cleared they must be rolled. Then the children come out and play tag and ball till you shut your eyes in the dread that they may fall over the edge.

My work changes a little from week to week. I have three English classes twice a week, one being a class of teachers, and the two boys five times a week. On Friday I conduct a teacher's meeting for the older S.S. teachers. This includes some of the native teachers of the day schools, and some of the older pupils. I found that they were losing a great deal, because of their insufficient knowledge of English, so I have just begun to have one of the older teachers interpret for me. It is much harder to speak in this way. The S.S. Times reaches us just too late to be of any use.

We are well supplied here with papers. The London Mail, the Spectator and the Levant Herald, a miserable little sheet published in Con'ple, bring the weekly news. Then various members of the station receive the Con'list, Outlook, Independent, Advance, McLure's, Review of Reviews, Century, C.E. World, Miss'y Herald, etc., so that one who will wait for his turn, and read fast when he does get a paper, may read any of these which he wishes.

Mr. Browne and Miss Bush returned from a long tour on Monday—long in time only, for they have not been far away. Yesterday evening we all were invited to the Brownes' to hear the story of their tour, according to a good old custom. They say they have never found the field more encouraging, but the trained, *consecrated* and *self-denying* native workers are very few, sadly few. That brings the responsibility back upon the college. It is true, however, that quantities of the best young men have gone to America. They told some droll things—how the women didn't want to learn to read in one place, and the men made them learn their letters etc by beating them, because they said the missionaries had said that the women must learn to read the Bible. In another village, the service was a good deal disturbed one afternoon by a rooster which insisted upon standing in the doorway and crowing. They shut the door, but it had to be reopened on account of ventilation, and every time his opportunity came, the rooster reappeared and blew a blast. They told of still another little village where there are the blackened ruins of 70 houses. I believe it was from this village that 67 men were led out by the Turks into a field and killed one after another in order.

As Tuesday happened to be Mrs. Browne's birthday, we had a little celebration in the way of chocolate cake and candy, and an acid drink, to finish off the evening. We always have prayers together when we meet in this way. While I am speaking of food let me tell you that we are still having fresh pears upon the table. Last Friday, Mrs. Barnum invited our household to dine and spend the evening with them. We had ice-cream for dessert, and passed the evening sewing and cutting out pictures, while the Doctor read aloud to us Dr. Van Dyke's "The Other Wise Man." On Saturday I had a woman to sew, mend my clothes etc. The sewing is cheap, to be sure, but I have to be on hand all the time to direct and explain (chiefly by illustration) and such patching! You would smile to see the woman come in from the snow, shake off her shoes, and then pull off her big trousers and shake out her skirt.

Ellsworth and I had a delightful ride today through the drifting snow, I using Miss Bush's horse. It was bitterly cold. I haven't yet found the right horse.

Kounus goukah, that is "my sleep comes" so good-night dear Papa, Mamma, and all the blessed family,
Theresa (L.H.)

Harpoot
March 2, 1899

Dear Mamma,

I send much, much gratitude to you and the others for all the good things in the box. To mention things as they come on my list, the chairs are very satisfactory, especially the steamer chair is a beautiful one and very comfortable. Ada enjoys that, particularly. My stoves I shall not use till next winter. The chocolate we expect to enjoy very much some day in fudge. Somebody was very thoughtful to put in that candlestick. It was knocked into a little cocked hat in the box, but can easily be straightened out at the market. The bureau scarf is lovely, Cornelia dear, and very much better than a towel, especially a towel ironed as our woman irons. She is being trained for the first time in civilized ways. I was glad of the writing paper. It is good to own a silver thimble again. I have discovered a most dishonest proceeding on my part. I have Miss

Merriam's silver thimble. It must have been in one of my little work-bags. I might send it home by mail, but there is a good deal of risk of entire loss in sending merchandise from here. It is safe enough from Con'ple. It may be best to wait till Ellsworth's return. The bathrobe will be a joy forever. All the people here (feminine) think it a beautiful one. Indeed, I hesitate to use it. Ellsworth has gladly appropriated the seeds. I haven't yet used the lemon tablets, but am waiting for warm weather. Ellsworth is to have half. The small brass lamp makes me think of the kitchen table at home, "and other things". I had a tea kettle made in the market, but it grew dull with mortification and envy when the new one came. I keep the old one upstairs, and the other on our sitting-room stove. I was delighted to find the pillows in the box. We had some made for our couch and stuffed with cotton, but these take away all the glory of the native coverings, which weren't much to begin with. I kiss the fingers that did the embroidering and all the work. The colors, being rather dull, harmonize excellently with our things. If I have not mentioned anything which ought to receive notice, please consider it appreciated.

Now to answer some questions. I really haven't time to look up older letters for more ancient inquiries. Ellsworth has all the rights in our sitting room of which he chooses to avail himself, but as he has two rooms of his own, and all his books etc are there, he only comes here when he wants to talk or read with me. He always knocks at our door, and I do at his.

Yes, I wore the old brown dress (shortened) all the way from Samsoun, except when we were at Marsovan and Sivas, when I wore the blue. "Night arrangements" is very general. At first I wore a cotton night-dress, but as it was pretty cold sometimes, I finally wore my pink wrapper, knowing that it could be washed. We always undressed completely, excepting the first night. No, we didn't buy pillows. Dr. Gates provided three or four for each araba. I think he brought them on from Harpoot, and left them at Samsoun while he came to Con'ple. We banked these up upon our bags. While I was at the Green's I made some gingham bags, in which I carried many of my things from Samsoun, on. Yes, I bought a travelling bed. It is a small iron frame with canvas stretched across it. It folds up into very small compass. Yes, we used white sheets. Dr. G. provided a "doshag", a sort of thin mattress for each person, and we sat upon these in the day-time in the arabas. Then he bro't along some heavy dark blankets and several comforters—big heavy things, such as the natives use. I think he bought these, some of them in Con'ple. I used my steamer-rug at night and one blanket doubled, and often put my cape etc on top. I didn't buy any Turkish towels, because I had no room to carry them, and tho't they could be procured here. They can be to be sure, but they are not nearly so good as those bo't at Marsovan. I haven't bo't any yet, because I wasn't satisfied with those which were bro't. On the whole, I needed more warm clothing on the overland journey, than on the ocean. For one thing, it was later in the season, and then we travelled so early in the morning. I didn't use my fur gloves. They were too good, and I could wrap my hands up in my cape, and keep them as warm as toast. All of Mrs. Brown's furniture has come, some books—the last arriving with my things.

Ellsworth or I or both have written every week since I came. After this, I think we must take turns, he writing one week and I the next.

The mail goes in twenty minutes.

Very much love,
Theresa

Harpoot, Turkey
March 15, 1899

Dear Ruthie,

I haven't been keeping a letter record, and I really don't know whether or not you deserve a letter, but here goes. I feel like writing quarts, but I must confine myself to gills. It is just nine o'clock and Auntie Hattie appeared a few minutes ago, and asked me if I wasn't going to bed, reminding me that she was the mother of us all in this part of the house, but I want anyway to write this letter. [...]

Dear me, there is so much to tell! On Sunday afternoon I went with Ada to Pompish Leah's orphanage near by. It is the pleasantest, sunniest one of the six in the city. She has sixty girls, some of them mere babies of four or five—fat, bewitching babies, surpassing all other Armenian babies I have in that they were clean. If you could only see them, their white Turkish drawers coming down to their ankles, their toes wriggling inside their woolen stockings, their coarse gingham dresses hanging down long and full, and their ridiculously small "tiers" fairly bursting asunder from the plumpness of the wearers. Then their big eyes were bright as stars, their hair hung down in their eyes, and their general solemnity of expression was irresistible. They came up to us, four or five of them, at Leah's summons, gravely and coyly saluting and plumped themselves down upon the floor. Of course the older girls take care of the little ones a great deal. We talked a little with Leah and her mother in her room, and then went out into a bare, sunny room where the children had gathered. One of the teachers and three college girls conducted a simple little meeting. There was a good deal of singing in which even the babies joined, all but little Mariam, who was too much interested in pulling a hole in her stocking. This little one will probably be sent away soon, for we have just learned that she inherited a little land, so her place must be filled by someone who is wholly destitute. Pompish Leah is a cheerful smiling woman, well-fitted for her place. [...]

This evening Ellsworth and I took dinner with the Barnums. In the evening they brought out the scales, and we were weighed, I for the first time since Thanksgiving Day. I have gained, advancing from 131 pounds to 137 1/2. Ellsworth had gained a pound or two, Laura had lost four pounds. She weighs now 148, and Ada about 115.

We are thinking a little anxiously now about the permission to rebuild which was long ago sent in to the government. The work ought to be begun this summer and as yet nothing has been heard from the request.

Just now Ada has on her table, in process of being read a book by Rev. Geo. H. Hepworth, entitled "Thro' Armenia on Horseback." It seems to be very brightly written, and some of his travelling experiences so closely resembled ours that it amused us much. I wish you could get hold of the book.

Well, dear little elephant, I don't believe you go ahead of me in size. Keep all the other precious people merry. I wish I could send home our three red roses.

With my dearest love,
Theresa (L. Huntington)

Chapter Nine:
Spring Awakens Amorous Feelings and Theresa Visits a Village

Before Theresa left home, she promised to send occasional letters to the ladies of the Norfolk and Pilgrim Branch, the auxiliary that supported her work in Turkey. She kept her promise, although she complained to her mother that "these missionary meeting letters are hard to write." While these letters are clearly more formal in their tone than the 'home letters,' they are succinct and impart a great deal of information about the world of the missionaries. They were written to be read aloud at the Branch meetings, and these were the ones that were deposited in the archive at Harvard. This is the first one, addressed to Miss Lord:

> Harpoot, Turkey, March 16, 1899
>
> My dear Miss Lord,
>
> Your letter was most welcome. I will gladly write something to be read at the April meeting, though I feel that for a year or two my letters cannot be very satisfactory. Before one had learned the language, it is as if there were a cloud between her and the people, and until I can talk freely in Armenian, I shall not feel that I really understand or know them.
>
> The girl's school is my first interest and care. As yet my share in the work is necessarily small, being limited chiefly to teaching several English classes. Miss Daniels is at the head of the girls department, and Miss Barnum was her only assistant till Miss Ellsworth and I came last November. Our girls, from Kindergarden to College, number about four hundred and fifty. They meet in five different buildings, four of which are rented houses, and hardly adapted for school purposes. There are sixty girls in the boarding department. They study, recite, hold religious meetings, eat and sleep in three small rooms. During the day, the mattresses upon which they sleep are piled in one end of the room behind a curtain. When mealtime comes, large round pewter trays are brought in and placed each upon a low stool about a foot high. Inasmuch

as chairs would be an uncomfortable luxury to the girls, and they are not afraid of cold air, our whole Senior C.E. Society has been able to meet weekly in one of these rooms, with some degree of comfort, all sitting close together on the floor.

I want you to know something about our society. It is as wide awake and active as the one to which I belonged in America. We have nine committees, most of them doing excellent work. Some of the ways of the Society, for instance, giving several moments to silent prayer at the end of every meeting, and having regular, weekly committee meetings, are worthy of imitation.

We lately had a very good missionary meeting on Turkey, and still more recently, one on China. The girls are supporting a student in Inanda Seminary, South Africa. If any CE Society, for the sake of increasing interest in missionary work, would like to hear more particularly about our work and would like to write to us, I think that our letter-writing committee would gladly write an answer, though it might be in rather curious English.

Recently we have felt that some of the girls who call themselves by Christ's name, were keeping their pledge rather carelessly, and outwardly were differing little from the girls who are not Christians. We have had several meeting for prayer about this matter. Last Tuesday a good many of the girls took the "quiet hour" pledge—not an easy pledge to keep either for the girls in our crowded boarding department or for the day scholars, most of whom come from large families, which live in two or three rooms. We are hoping and praying for the speedy rebuilding of the school. We trust that the indemnity may some time come, but it is also necessary to obtain permission from the government to rebuild, and as yet nothing has been heard from the request, which was sent in long ago. The government is in steady opposition to the missionary work. Two of our orphanages in outlying places have recently been closed by the authorities, and the children scattered.

Yesterday a pet plan of Miss Daniels was carried out. The older girls were asked to bring their mothers to the school for an informal meeting. About thirty came, both Gregorians and Protestants. The girls sang very well, several times. We had a little Bible reading and prayer and then a social get together. Many of the women had dull, worn faces—they grow old very fast here—but when I spoke to them, they could not have smiled or patted me on the shoulder more cordially than they did. My broken Armenian may have been productive of some of the smiles, but most of them should be attributed to good will and friendliness. We hope soon to invite them again.

I thank you for all your kind words. May the missionary meeting be a blessed one.

Sincerely and with love,
Theresa Huntington.[31]

March 28, 1899

Dear Home people,

It's very hard *not* to write to you, in spite of what I said about sending a letter every other week. Last Friday night Mamma's last letter from Galesburg came by the southern mail, although it was plainly marked "via Con'ple". Saturday morning her first letter written after reaching home was brought by the northern mail, and in the afternoon the letter written on the cars came, probably having been overlooked in the morning. That same day letters from Harry and Ruth came, all *very* interesting.

Our spring rains have begun and the snow line on the mountains is gradually creeping up. Sometimes at this season it rains every day for a month, with some sunshine, of course, now and then. Such a droll sight as the children were the other day, on their way to school in a hard shower! (Poor little ones!) Some of the boys had old handkerchiefs tied over their fezes, some bundled up their skirt-like garment about their waists and pattered along with their long, baggy white drawers receiving the spattering. One boy carried a small umbrella of a brilliant pink color. He walked in a dignified manner while other boys ran alongside, poking their heads in under, when they had a chance. The plain is beginning to be beautifully green in squares where the early crops are springing up. Yesterday, Mary, the Doctor, Ellsworth and I had a short ride together, and for the first time we found the snow so far disappeared that we could ride almost wherever we pleased. The horses seemed to enjoy the freedom and played and circled about and performed real spring capers. Bare and rocky as the ground was, little white flowers were thrusting up their heads here and there all about us. I will enclose some. I think they are different from those which I sent last fall.

The Diarbekir travellers expect to start Monday morning, tho' there is still a question as to whether they can cross the mountains

31. ABC 16.9.13.

without difficulty. Ellsworth and I shall take our meals at the Gates' table for the next two months. I shall miss Ada very much. She is a lovely girl and I enjoy sharing the room with her. While she is gone, Laura will use her sleeping-room, opposite mine. On Tuesday the table and the second chair came. I am very glad to have them. Who selected the pretty table? The chair is exactly like my other one, you know. Ellsworth has now one of the large rocking chairs and one of the small ones. I have the other small one in my bedroom. The other four chairs are in our sitting room, together with one of Ada's (she brought very little furniture, because she is here for so short a time) and two borrowed ones which we intend now to return.

In brief, these are the unusual things which have happened since I wrote last. Friday evening we invited the circle to our room. Laura made some fudge, Dr. Gates read a funny story aloud, we read some letters of general interest which had just come from the south, and played a game of twenty questions, where the unknown object was a famous person, instead of an inanimate object. Saturday morning Ellsworth started for the plain (he will tell you about it) and Eleeshpá (Elizabeth) sewed for me, chiefly upon curtains etc for Ellsworth's room. Ada covered a foot stool for him and in the afternoon we went up to his room, and "fixed it up" a little.

Saturday night I took dinner at the girl's school. We had little meat-balls, fried in mutton fat, and so dripping with it that I don't believe that you could be induced to touch them, native bread, which is far better than the sour stuff they sell in Con'ple, and a very good sort of tomato pickle. For dessert we had dates.

Sunday morning I led a children's meeting, and went to four other services, including Sunday School and our informal circle meeting in the evening. In the afternoon I slept for almost two hours. Today we are having a holiday, in which I mean to write, sew and study Armenian.

Harpoot
March 30, 1899

Ruthie dear,

How is everything and everybody? I am insatiable in the matter of letters, and tho' you dear people are very good about sending them, I don't feel as if I knew much about you. I suppose you have the same feeling about me.

Last Tuesday the Diarbekir party left us, and we do miss them. Last week we had beautiful weather, but they waited for more of the snow to go off from the mountains, and they had difficulty too in finding cartejees (or cartegis) that is, men with pack animals. This week opened stormily, and they started off in a pouring rain. I wish you could have seen them, in their long rubber cloaks, riding-skirts and big helmets. Their saddle-bags, shawl-cases etc covered up the horses pretty well. Harold rode on a pack-horse, his legs sticking straight out in front of him, because the animal was well-loaded. They had four cartegi horses beside the ones which Mr. Browne (Mrs. B. used his) and Harold rode. That seems a good many, but you know they must take their beds and bedding, clothing, dishes, and cooking utensils with them, and they will keep house in a fashion, at Diarbekir for two months. I'm afraid their journey has been a hard one, for it rained very hard the first day, and the first night seven inches or more of snow fell here, probably more in the mountains. Then they will have to spend the night in stables two or three times before their arrival.

Almost all of the Diarbekir orphans are supported by English people. That is why Ada goes. There is some trouble in the orphanage there, because the Protestant brethren are unwilling to maintain a school large enough for all the orphans and the other children of the city. We are not allowed by the government to have an independent school for the orphans. Two of the orphanages have been closed by the gov't, one at Palu, and the other at Choonkoosh. The Gregorians have made a good deal of trouble for us, stirring up the Armenian patriarch at Con'ple, who conspires with the Turkish gov't, altho' he denies it, against the miss'y work. The Gregorians would rather have all the children in the streets again, than to have them educated as Protestants. We have just made a concession, rather a necessary one, and now allow the children to go to the Greg. church on feast-days, and to receive instructions in the teaching of that church once a week. Every Sunday the children from one of the six orphanages in the city are to be taken to the Greg. church. Protestant training all the rest of the time ought to over-balance this, and it is only fair that the children should know what their national church is like. We do this, however, to placate the Gregorians who are stirring up a good deal of trouble for us.

The other day when I went to ride, we saw six or more great vultures sailing majestically with the wind over the plain. Hawks are plentiful now, and the magpie, the jay of the land, has been here all winter. There are no sweet little singers such as come in the spring at home. The irises are blooming on the plain, and the almond trees down below are almost out.

What Theresa reveals here about the missionary attitude toward the Gregorians may be closer to the truth than what the *Missionary Herald* professed that same year: "The missionaries have not attempted to make Protestants of them or to prejudice them in any way against the Gregorian church. They have simply attempted to elevate their intellectual and moral life and help them to become sincere, earnest Christians. It is the expectation that many of them will remain in the old church. In fact, it is the hope that this will be the result, but that they will carry into that church a purer Christianity which will make itself felt upon every organization and lead to marked reforms."[32]

April 5, 1899

My darling Mother,

It is much easier to write on people's birthdays than to remember them five weeks ahead. I hope this has been a happy day for you. You are a precious little mother, and I realize more every day what sensible, wise Christian parents I have.

I think my letters would give the impression that I go out to dinner or ride most of the time. That is because I naturally tell of the special events and the recreation, and I don't write much about the routine of work, just as you don't tell me when you bake bread or sweep your room.

I have just been writing to Mrs. Browne. We received a telegram Monday from Diarbekir saying that the travellers were there, safe and happy. We expect to receive the first letters from them tomorrow, eleven days after they started. I enjoy eating with the Gates' very much, but to tell the truth, though it is no important matter, the food is better and more varied at the Browne's. Yesterday morning Moore asked at breakfast if we mightn't say some verses. His father told him he could begin if he wanted to, so he said, "Blessed is de man who does what dey do to him." We smiled and he was so embarrassed that he was obliged to cover his head with his bib.

Last Friday evening we all, that is all who are here, except the Doctor who was spending the night with the Consul at Mezereh,

32. *Missionary Herald,* 1899, p. 71.

dined with the Barnums, and spent a delightful evening there. Emma put a slip of paper with a conundrum upon it at each place at the table, and these called forth a great many other conundrums. After dinner, as it was letter day, a good many letters were read aloud, then Laura played on her guitar, and later while we were eating some candy and drinking root-beer, we told stories, in response to requests made upon slips of paper which Emma handed to us. We were asked, for instance, to tell of some college-scape in which we had part, or the worst accident which ever happened to us, or a good practical joke, etc. I told of Cornelia's losing her bag at Poughkeepsie, and the joke of Ella and her friends at the wedding in Maine. Next Friday I believe Aunt Hattie intends to invite us to her room. She is a dear, saintly soul, and it is a delight to live with her. She sometimes comes down in the evening to send us to bed. Don't think by this that we are often late for we're not. Aunt Hattie herself goes to bed at nine, and gets up at five.

Saturday afternoon Ellsworth, Laura and I went down on to the plain. The other two wanted flowers for their Botany classes. As far as that object went, we were unsuccessful, but I enjoyed the ride. I used Dr. Barnum's horse. It is tiresome to ride up or down hill, but had some good canters on the plain. I really enjoy it more ordinarily to ride on the hills behind the station, for we meet very few people and aren't obliged to wear veils. A veil bewilders me a little, especially on horse-back. On Saturday we turned off from the main roads to Mezereh, at the foot of the mountain and went down a dry water-course. When we passed the large Turkish school on the main road, some boys threw stones at us. I think they meant to frighten our horses, and not to hit us. We rode along the brook-bed till we came to a grove of mulberry trees. They are not yet in leaf. In shape they suggest willow-trees which have been cut down many times, and are not very beautiful. They were planted in double rows, which ran in various directions, and between the lines were irrigating ditches, thro' some of which water was flowing. There were numbers of birds in the trees, which strongly resembled song-sparrows, except that their song was weaker and less cheerful. We passed from the trees along the ridges between the planted fields. The grain had begun to spring up in many places, but I wish you could see the stones which seem nearly to cover the earth, and see, too, how far apart the little green blades are. These fields are laid out very irregularly, and one man's property is separated from another's by a ridge of earth. We saw farmers working with very primitive implements, the woman wearing full trousers and a black handkerchief bound overall the head except the eyes, working with the men. We came home by a different road and passed through the village of Husenik. Some forty boys ran along after us for a little way. We are foreigners and conspicuous wherever we go. Of course these boys knew who we were. Indeed, I think they belonged to our orphanage. Close to the village we passed a Turkish grave-yard, where I saw for the first time the common sight of a tent pitched near a newly made grave. After the burial, the friends of the dead live close to the grave for three days to keep off the evil spirits. All their food is brought to them! We climbed the mountain again by so steep a path that we had to lead our horses for some distance. It was easier for them and for us.

Speaking of horses, I have tried Ellsworth's twice, and like him, so far as I can see. It is very probable that we shall own him together. During the week we can rarely ride at the same time, and on Saturday someone is always willing to lend a horse. In the summer it is much of the time too hot to ride for mere exercise and recreation. Aunt Caro has just sold her horse. She offered him to me for four liras, about eighteen dollars, and I thought very seriously of buying him, for he is a gentle, playful, pretty little fellow. Dr. Gates, however, advised me not to, because the horse is old—ten or eleven years—and he sometimes stumbles, tho' that depends much upon the rider. One reason for my owning the horse with Ellsworth is that he will go home in two or three years and will probably be obliged then to sell the horse for much less than its value.

Sunday wasn't exactly like Easter at home. Mary asked me to put some Easter-cards at the Gates' table at breakfast, so on my way to the early morning service at half-past six, I stopped to leave them in the dining-room. I went out by way of the kitchen and tried an outside door (the one which Ellsworth commonly uses) which was locked. When I attempted to go back into the kitchen, I found that the spring latch had caught and I was a prisoner in a small hall way, with six locked doors about me and four useless keys in my pocket. I rapped in vain, and then resigned myself to an hour's waiting. It wasn't so bad as it seems, for the place was lighted by a transom, there was a step to sit upon, I had my winter jacket, and my Bible and hymn-book to read.

Mrs. Browne has started a little Junior Endeavor society which has for members Herbert and Harold. Moore is a regular attendant, but not a member. While she is gone I take her place with the two boys. She left two mite-boxes for them, which were duly presented and used on Sunday. Then Moore said meditatively, "Whall sall we do wid dis money? We must give it to de poor and needy. Herbert can give his to de poor, and I'll give mine to de needy." He is a remarkably sweet and sunny child.

In the morning I went to Sunday School, and listened, as usual. Before the afternoon service (which I shouldn't have gone to, if I hadn't missed the one in the morning) I helped Mary give medicine to twelve or thirteen girls who were sick in bed. In the evening I led the meeting for the boarding pupils.

With Emma's kind help, the Senior class of four, has invited the American teachers and Aunt Hattie who used to teach in the school, to spend this evening with them in the Barnum's parlor. Yesterday we had the last of our mother's meetings, for a time! Very few came because it was stormy. That afternoon Laura, Herbert and I rode for less than an hour, with Maderos, the man who cares for the horses as guard, because it wouldn't be safe to go alone. It was snowing a little when we started but on the hills we were caught in a sharp little hail storm and well pelted and drenched. It has rained or snowed every day for a long time.

I suspect you're tired of quotations from compositions, but I'm going to give you one more. This is from a composition about St. Bernard dogs. They "find him" (the lost man) "with their sharp smell. Then everyone begins to bow loudly, until the monks will hear."

I think it will amuse you to know that our front door can be opened by pulling a rope at the head of the stairs. It is so hard for the women to go up and down stairs constantly to open the door, that this native device was adopted. We keep all our outside doors locked all the time, because beggars and all sorts of people would otherwise come straight in.

I enclose some violets from a little bunch which one of the girls gave me. They are of a beautiful, rich color. Ellsworth won't write this week. He is well but very busy. You do write such good letters.
With love for each dear one,
Theresa (L. Huntington)

Harpoot
April 13, 1899

Dear Papa,

I haven't time to write a good letter this week. I have sent a long one to George and asked him to forward it later to you.

The calendars are lovely, and by no means too late to be useful. Mine were all small, except a W.B.M. calendar which, tho' valuable is hardly beautiful. I am surprised that it cost so little to send them here.

Your letter and Mamma's, mailed Mar. 8 and 16 were received gladly last week. Yesterday and today have been beautiful, with clear blue skies and a fresh breeze. The green patches on the plain daily grow greener, and the snow line on the mountains slowly creeps up. The hillsides about us are at last perfectly dry.

The other day when we were riding, we approached a flock of sheep and goats, cared for by two or three shepherd boys. When they saw us coming, one child threw his arm about the neck of a little white goat, and dragged it out in front of Dr. Barnum and laid it before him. He expected ten paras (a cent or more). This is a common custom. The idea is that the lamb or kid is offered to you as a gift. You refuse it, and give a little present in return for the compliment. If you really took the creature, you would be expected to pay its full value. There is a similar custom at harvest-time, when a handful of grain is offered to each passer-by.

Have any of you had the grip this winter? It seems to have been very prevalent in America. We are both very well. I can't answer your questions today. They are hard ones, Papa, which have to be looked up.

Love to each dear person,
Theresa (L. Huntington)

April 18, 1899

Dear Kindie,

Your nice letter, with all its enclosures came last week. Dear child, its just as hard to be good, not to care for clothes, and comfort and "the world" out here as it ever was at home, if not harder. I really believe that if the people were more degraded and our comforts fewer, our temptations would not be as great. Then it is a good deal of a test for one to be surrounded by people who consider him and treat him as their superior. We are treated in two ways. The Protestant Armenians look up to us. The Turks have no words to express their contempt for us. The Gregorian Armenians vary. When Mary went to the other side of the city last Wednesday, a little Gregorian boy called out, "Leper, leper." This is not uncommon. The Armenian word for Protestant is Prod; for leper, prot, so it is easy to see how the epithet is suggested. On the other hand, the attitude of the Gregorians in our schools, and those who know us is much the same as that of the Protestants.

Vacation begins next week, Wednesday, and lasts for two weeks. People from several villages have invited the varzhoohees (teachers) to visit them then, and we, Mary, Laura, and I, have finally decided to go to Houlakégh, a good-sized village down on the plain and stay for two days. We shall go on Saturday, and come home the next Tuesday. The woman who invited us is a graduate of the college. I don't know anything more about her except that Mary isn't very fond of her. The Armenian Easter comes on the thirtieth of this month. They have a salutation on that day which I know you will like, "Christ is risen from the dead." The answer is, "Blessed be the resurrection of Christ."

The days are warm and clear now, the thermometer ranging between 60° and 72° and still higher in the sun. Today when we took our hour's ride, we went past our garden, leaving Laura there to get some specimens for her Botany class, while the Doctor, Mary and I rode on a little farther. Spring is lovely anywhere. The almond trees, mish-mish (apricot) and other fruit trees are coming into blossom. The almond blossom is about the size of the apple, but whiter. It comes out before the leaves and crowds close to the stem as the peach-blossom does. There is an almond which has an intensely pink blossom. The fragrance is sweet and rather faint. When we stopped for Laura, we made a little pause at the garden and bro't away some of the sweet violets which were growing near the "gurl" and in moist places around. A "gurl" is a pool or cistern in the ground, fed by running water. It is a necessity to every garden house. I usually ride at one o'clock, because I have work in the latter part of the afternoon, and Ellsworth takes his exercise later because his work lasts from one to half-past three.

This week I am leading prayers every morning in the college. The teachers take turns doing this. Prayers last from 8.00 to 8.15. Dr. Gates left early this morning for Arabekir, where he expects to stay nearly a week. It is a two days journey. There is some trouble about the industrial work (weaving) there which he must settle.

Where are the books for Baron Muggerditch? Did Brother Greely send them to you? Tell me about him. Does he ever call? Has he fallen in love with any new girl? How is his business? I ask this from pure curiosity, for I don't care for him any more than I ever did. You funny child, you thought I'd fall in love with the doctor, didn't you? Well if you should see much of him you would understand why I never could. He is one of the handsomest men I ever knew, he is generous, courteous, an excellent physician, but oh, he is conceited. It is the one conspicuous thing lacking, and is very noticeable all the time. I feel rather ashamed of writing this, but I feel pity for him rather than a spirit of criticism. His attentions to Mary, who is some seven years older than he, are very pronounced and I do think she is pretty fond of him. He doesn't act, however, like a man in love. The whole business does make Ellsworth fume, so whenever we speak of it together, that I have to laugh. He thinks the Doctor doesn't mean anything serious, and is valiant in Mary's corner. Well, this is all silly gossip.

Let me tell you a droll thing which is very characteristic of oriental customs. On Monday a pastor from a native village, who has a nephew in America, came to see Mary on business. The nephew had written that he wanted a wife and would be satisfied with anyone whom his uncle should choose. The pastor said to Mary that he had thought of Aghavni Toporzián or Anna Avakian, and asked her opinion of them. He also asked if he might visit their classes the next day to form an opinion himself. They are both nice girls, particularly the latter, whom Mary wishes to be a teacher. Accordingly she will discourage any alliance for Anna.

Long ago I said I would send some bastegh and some manna. Laura ate up the best of the bastegh, not knowing that I wanted to send it away. What is left is as dry as a chip, so perhaps you'd better wait till next fall for it. The manna has melted and run together, but I may send some. I'm quite ashamed that I said I would do something which I haven't done. It is hardly safe to send valuable things out of the country by mail for they are often appropriated before they leave Turkey. With very much love for my dear sister and all,

Theresa (L. Huntington)

Harpoot
April 27, 1899

Dear Mamma,

I enclose some edging, which I think perhaps you can use, or if you don't want it, the girls can. One of our girls wanted to earn some money for missions, and I found that she could make edging. This is not especially beautiful or unusual, but as I have enough now, I send it on to you. I cut it into pieces half as long again as my dress collar, and put it in as I would rushing, slightly ruffled. It really looks very pretty, and can be washed again and again.

By dint of perseverance on the part of missionary teachers, most of the school-girls have been taught to wear something white in the neck, and sometimes the sleeves of their dresses. You have no idea what an improvement it effects. We must practice what we preach, and now, tho' at first Mary asked me to do it, I feel only partly dressed, without a collar or ruching.

I have begun to put my clothes away from the moths in big white bags which all the people (Americans) here have made for that purpose. Will you please, mother dear, (and don't forget it) send me by the next shipment a good sized roll of stiffening for collars and the bottom of skirts. My dress collars are beginning to look broken and decrepit. Did I tell you before that if you please, I would very much like to have you send me one of the duck hats by post. I really need it now. I am wearing now on horseback a cap, light brown, of the regulation boys' shape, which Dr. G. got for E. in Con'ple. He bought one like it for himself, and Mrs. G. has appropriated that.

Since Dr. G. has been gone at A., the boys, Herbert and Moore, have had an especially good time with E. They are very fond of him, and he tells them stories, romps with them, and sometimes scolds them roundly, too.

Day before yesterday we had a good missionary m't'g for Senior and Junior Endeavorers together. Our subject was a very broad one for we took up in general, the miss'y work done by all Protestants in all lands. I was very much interested to know what England, Germany etc. are doing, and what other denominations are accomplishing. We made large charts, copied from books, which showed the progress in various ways, and the relative strength of the different non-Christian religions etc.

If I have time to make it, I will enclose a rough plan of the house and the pag (yard).

Love and a kiss for each dear person,
from,
Theresa (L. Huntington)

Spring vacation presented Theresa with her first chance to catch a glimpse of Armenian village life. Her description of the trip comes in a letter to Miss Lord of the ladies' missionary circle at home:

> My dear Miss Lord,
>
> It seems like ancient history to write what happened in our spring vacation, but I had my first village experience then, and I want to tell you about it. The Armenian Easter came this year upon the thirtieth of April, and Miss Daniels and I spent that day with its accompanying Saturday and Monday at the village of Hoolakegh. It was a genuine visit in response to an invitation from the preacher's wife, Lucintag, who was an old scholar of Miss Daniels. Lucintag's sister, Pailadzoo, a pupil of ours, and her cousin Eunice, the teacher of our boy's kindergarten, were spending their vacation with the preacher's family, and no two girls could have devoted themselves more diligently to our entertainment and comfort than they.
>
> Miss Daniels and I set off on a Saturday morning, taking a faithful servant and one baggage horse to carry our beds and a little clothing. After a ride of almost two and a half hours over bare hills we reached the plain and the flat-roofed mud houses of our village. I have hardly seen enough villages yet to draw comparisons, but this one impressed me rather favorably in point of cleanliness, though in New England it would be considered too filthy for habitation.
>
> The preacher's house has glass instead of oiled paper in the windows and is far more attractive and clean than the other village houses. Such a house and family give one new enthusiasm for the work of our schools. Lucintag and her husband Avedis are honestly trying to train their three little ones in truthfulness and obedience, though they go to extremes of over-petting and over-severity. I was glad to see that Baron (Mr.) Avedis sometimes helped in the care of the children and Monday, when we were taking a long walk he carries one of them instead of letting his wife do so. I don't believe another man in the village would have done this. Baron Avedis is a graduate from our Theological Seminary. He told me that he studies now five hours or more every day. The trouble with many of our preachers is that after leaving school or college, they stop studying. He has a little library of some fifty volumes—mostly English books. Among them I noticed Torry's "How to Lead Men to Christ" and some of Girkie's books. He is a genial, kindly young

man, but his heart doesn't seem to be wholly in his work. It is the same restlessness which we see everywhere. He wants to go to America, for safety and for the sake of educating his children. He has been refused a passport to leave the country, however, by the government.

Sunday we went to a morning service at about six o'clock, and two hours later we held a meeting for the women. The church building is most bare, and yet very comfortable for an Armenian village. The pulpit and a chair or two, and some dirty cushions on the floor comprise the furnishings. A railing running across thc middle of the room separates the men, who sit in front, from the women. The oiled paper has been taken off from the high, little windows for the summer, and the birds dart fearlessly in and out, and find resting-places on the rafters. Some of the women offered prayer. Though I was a newcomer, they didn't leave me out of the meeting. Many of them merely saluted me silently, touching chin and then brow with their right hand; others crowded up close and stared in a friendly way. One woman grasped both my hands in the impulsive oriental fashion and drew me about after her for a few minutes.

After a luncheon of cheese and bread we started for Bizmoshen, a village about two miles away. Miss Daniels rode her horse, but I had sent mine back to Harpoot, so I walked with Eunice and Pailadzoo. Makar, the leading Protestant of the village also went with us. Just as Miss Daniels dismounted from her horse at Bizmoshen, a woman came up carrying a baby, and insisted upon shaking hands with Miss Daniels. In a few moments we discovered that the child was suffering from smallpox. We had heard before that the disease was in the village.

The young preacher and his wife had been expecting us, but as it was afternoon, one women's service had already been held. However, a bell was rung, and the news seemed to go about for the women began to gather. They were more untidy than the Hoolakegh women and brought more children, even the smallest babies, with them. There were fewer who could read. (We have no school in Bizmoshen.) The women listened attentively. One can't speak too simply for them. It is more important to love much than to know much. Afterward they greeted us warmly, though you would say rather rudely. Poor, dull souls! They are slow to understand, and not over-eager to learn. They work all day in the fields, each taking with her on her back the smallest of her children. In this village, they told me, the men stay at home to weave, except for two months at harvest time. One woman in each household stays at home to cook the food.

After the meeting at Bizmoshen we waited for an hour or more while Makar tried to settle a difficulty between the preacher and his people as to his salary, which they declared they were unable to pay in full. Meanwhile Miss Daniels and I talked with the women who had come in. I was unable to say much, but one can show friendliness without words. I feel more every day the darkness in which these people are and how without Christ, they are without hope in the world, and without joy, too.

I see that the hands of my little clock are fast creeping toward post-time, so I cannot tell you of the rest of our visit.

With kindest greetings to all the ladies of our Branch who are interested in my work.

Faithfully yours,
Theresa Huntington.

Ellsworth, too, had ventured into the Armenian villages and made some observations in his notebook:

In villages inhabited only by Christians the women walk about the streets with their faces uncovered, they talk with men in public and their opinions are respected. Where Turks and Armenians live together, the Armenian women lead a harder life: they are always closely veiled and are treated harshly and without respect by their husbands.

From Hoolakegh I went to two other villages, in both of which I stayed in a stable. For the sake of warmth the people live in the stables. The human quarters are in one corner of the square room and are raised three or four feet above floor on which the animals stand. They are enclosed within a railing a foot or two high. While we were in one stable, a drunken priest came in. He took me for an Armenian and began to berate me roundly for not treating him with enough honor.

Omriin—village in the mountains. Paradisical place where fruit is so plentiful it is considered a shame to sell it. 400 houses of which 20 are Christian. We are at the house of the richest men in the place, three brothers, Krikor, Bedros, and Boghos Aghas Boyajian. They are merchants and the most influential men of the place among Turks as well as Christians. They are old style Armenians,

> large competent looking men, sharp at trade but kindly & with a good deal of common sense. They send their children to Malatia to be educated. They talk about the oppression of the Turks but as far as they are concerned it amounts to nothing. They walk the streets with their heads up and make all the Turks step around. Even the government would hesitate to oppose them.
>
> The place of meeting would not make a decent cow stable in America. It is a room about 22 feet by 16, and by actual count there are in that space ten pillars to support the roof. Of course the walls, roof and floor are made of mud. The latter is covered by cheap straw matting. Light is admitted by a circular hole in the roof about a foot in diameter and the room is so dark that from where I sat it was impossible to see about a quarter of the congregation. The people listened very attentively.
>
> In one place I tried to photograph the interior of a very poor house. It consisted of one room with an earthen floor, walls, and roof, light enters only by a hole in the roof about six inches by eight, everything was damp and it was much like an unfinished cellar in appearance, feeling, and furniture. The last consisted chiefly of two or three earthen jugs and a few pieces of old matting. The room was about fifteen feet square and five or six people live in it. A little boy sat on the floor while the picture was taken. He had on almost no clothes and was so weak from lack of food that during the exposure of three minutes necessitated by the darkness of the room he scarcely moved a muscle.[33]

And, in a letter to his brother Harry, Ellsworth made another observation—this time about his sister Theresa: "I just want to say that Theresa improves all the time. She is very bright and merry, and her character has gained a great deal of strength."

33. Yale University Archives, Ellsworth Huntington Papers. Notebooks, 1897.

Chapter Ten: The School Year Comes to an End, and Life in the Garden Begins

By the end of the school year, Theresa had managed to learn the Armenian alphabet well enough to manage her first letter in Armenian. This she used to write an invitation to some of the Armenian women teachers to visit the summer house of the missionaries, the so-called Garden, which lay a good hour's walk away from Harpoot. The Garden was a modest place, but it was surrounded by fruit trees of all kinds, it was quiet, the air was fresh and the views of the mountain scenery splendid. It was also equipped with two fine tennis courts that saw a lot of use. One day during the summer, Dr. Herman Barnum celebrated the fortieth anniversary of his coming to Harpoot. It was an occasion for much story-telling on his part, and of some stock-taking on the part of other missionaries as well. All agreed that the shadow of the massacres, "the event" in Theresa's letters, still lay heavy on the people. Many of the best young men, the ones trained by the missionaries to be teachers and preachers, sought to emigrate to America, and "the moral and spiritual condition of the people" did not appear to be the best. No one was about to lose hope, however, for improvements in the future. It was thought just to be a matter of time, and of hard work, for the Christian spirit to spread.

In strictest confidence, Theresa tells her family that Dr. Ussher might be transferred from the Harpoot station to Van, also within the Eastern Turkey Mission. His presence had become increasingly troublesome: he was being exceedingly "attentive" to Mary Daniels without, it seemed, having serious intentions. But there were reinforcements on the horizon: the missionaries were preparing to welcome a new family, the Knapps, due to arrive before the winter.

Harpoot
May 10, 1899

Dear Mamma,

I said I would tell about my visit at Houlakegh, but as I have been writing an account of it to send to the Woman's Board, I believe I'll send you a copy of that, as soon as I finish it.

This vacation has been a very pleasant, restful one, but I am just ready now to begin to sew and write letters, and plan some school work. Last Friday Mrs. Gates, Emma and I worked on riding-skirts together. I cut mine and basted it partly, but have gone no farther. On Saturday, Mary, Laura and I spent the day at the village of Husenik at the foot of the mountain with the pastor's family. It is he and his wife, Mr. and Mrs. Antreasian, who have visited the Ruggles family. One of his daughters, Esther, a really fine woman, is a teacher in the Girls' College. She is a widow with one daughter. Twelve or more orphan girls live in the pastor's family. This Mrs. Antreasian is the woman who wrote the account of Anna which I sent you. She taught in Smyrna with Miss Lord, and afterward, I think—no, it was before, she studied at Marsovan. She is an interesting, kindly woman, who talks a good deal about herself. We took luncheon with them, a native meal, with a few European modifications. The afternoon we spent in calling upon a few of our school-girls who live in Husenik, and some old pupils of Mary's. They were very glad to see us—Mary hasn't been in the village for five years—and the welcome in some of the houses just warms one's heart. At first we drank whatever they brought us, but later we had to entreat them not to prepare anything for us. I can stand Turkish coffee, for it is hot and the cups are very small, but sherbet is almost too much for me. It is water, faintly flavored and *very* sweet. It is served in goblets.

We saw a stork's nest with the mother stork upon it, upon the chimney of one house. It is the only stork's nest in that village. The people who live in the house, the Vartabedians, are comparatively well off. At the time of the event some Turkish friends of theirs saved their house and property for them, but took the liberty of reserving some things for themselves, as a sort of commission I suppose. They kept some dishes, a sewing machine, etc. Accordingly when the Vartabedians wish to use their sewing machine, they send to their Turkish neighbors and borrow it, and afterward return it. Similar cases are common. The missionaries bought back a great many of their things. One day Mrs. Browne saw a little child's rocking-chair of wicker at the Gates's. "Why," she said, "That is the little rocker which all my children used." It had been brought to the Gates's from the market, and they had bought it, not knowing where it came from originally. We called at eight houses on Saturday.

Sunday was much like other Sundays. The early morning service began at 5.35, it begins an hour after sunrise, but I like to go to that better than to the afternoon service. I don't usually attend both. Much of the morning I spent with the boys, because Mrs. Gates wasn't well, and the servants come on Sunday only to get breakfast, and dinner at four o'clock. Ellsworth led our evening meeting.

On Monday we took a real holiday. The six young people (from 22 to 35 years old) took a long ride, being gone from eight till one or later. We went to the most beautiful place I have seen in Turkey. I just wish you could see the mountains, the great rocks, the clear brook rushing down in falls and cascades and the fresh springs gushing out from under and between the lime stone boulders. Grass grew along the sides of the stream and though the place was lonely, villages had planted trees in some places. We found a great many beautiful wild flowers. I always feel like apologizing for writing so much about our recreation, and so little about work.

Harpoot
June 21, 1899

Dear Mamma,

No letter from home again last week, but I suppose that will mean two home letters tomorrow. This has happened several times recently. I wonder if all our letters reach you. I have written every week since I left home, except twice, when I had something like the grip for a day or two, and when I had the measles. Both times I think Ellsworth told you that I would not write. I'm afraid that several of our letters have been lost.

We are almost in the last week of school. The college graduation comes on Thurs. June 29. This week and next there are oral examinations in the lower schools. This really means little more than the ordinary recitations, but the missionaries turn out in full force, and of course ask the children questions and give suggestions. When I have finished this letter I expect to go to the Girls' Gertaran (Grammar School) for an hour or two. Part of the Gertaran girls are in the building with the Varjaran (H.S.) girls. The two lower classes are in a private house which we rent. Tomorrow the Kindergarten girls receive their certificates, the next day, the Kind'n boys and so on through the schools until Wednesday. We are civilized and western enough to have a baccalaureate sermon, which will be preached next Sunday, the service beginning at 5.30

A.M. Really when one keeps good hours in the evening, it is much pleasanter to go to church in summer in the early morning than in the afternoon. The Protest. pastor from Mezereh is to preach the sermon. There are four girls and four young men to graduate from the college.

Last Sunday afternoon, Ellsworth, Ada, and I went to the church at the other side of the city. The audience was not as large as that in the church on this side, but we have here a great many orphans, and all the boarding pupils. A young pastor from a village near by preached. They are without a pastor just now. They have a small organ which certainly does improve the singing. Ellsworth had to sit on the men's side, while Ada and I sat on a funny, high upholstered set on the women's side (The few chairs made here are always very high). I wish you could have had a glimpse of us, for I know you would have laughed to see up beside us an old woman sitting cross-legged on the broad seat. The church, alas, was rather dirty.

When the service was over, we went to a boys' orphanage which is near. The others had been there before, but it was my first visit. The rooms are large and clean. First we went to the room of the hairig and mairig (father and mother), Ada and I taking a peep at their baby, as we passed an open door. The baby was in a hammock, and had a cloth thrown over its face, in native fashion. We talked for a little while with the father and mother, and the preacher and teacher who had come in with us. Then we went to another room where the boys were gathered—sixty or more of them, sitting in orderly rows on the floor. If they had been American boys, there would have been rows, (to give a new pronunciation) but these little chaps sit close together by the hour, in school and elsewhere without pinching or punching. The boys chose a hymn and we all sang together. Then each one repeated a verse which he had learned that day. One little fellow forgot his verse or was afraid to say it, and it pleased me to see how the mairig gave him a loving little rub and pat on his head and cheek, like a real mother, instead of reproving him.

Well, I want to say more about the orphanage, but there are other things too. I think I said once that the Barnum family have already moved to the garden, though they come to the city every day for their work. They invited us all to come out Monday evening "for strawberries." Accordingly we had dinner at both houses early and started off at about half past five. Horses and people were shuffled about so that almost everybody rode, that is, excepting the gentlemen. I walked part way. It isn't really a long or hard walk. We sat on a little platform on the shady side of the house or on the steps and talked, and ate our strawberries and cake. Later we had prayers. A little before eight while it was still light we started for home. We all had a most delightful time.

The new part of the garden house is almost finished, indeed it will be ready for use in two weeks. I will tell you more about it when we go out. Ada and I are to have a room together. You would laugh to see how crooked it is. One of Laura's windows is four inches wider than the other and our floor has a decided slant, but it goes ahead of native garden-houses. . . .

Most lovingly,
Theresa (L. Huntington)

Harpoot
July 5, 1899

My very dear People,

I have quite made up my mind that there is too much to write about, for me to ever tell all, and that I must be satisfied to tell a small part. Last week was very interesting. The various schools had their exhibitions and graduations, one after another, on different days till Wednesday, when there was a brief lull. That afternoon the college boys had their Prize Declamations—to me the most interesting affair of the week. Three Freshmen learned the same Armenian declamation, three Sophomores the same Turkish one and three Juniors one in English. They threw themselves into it heart and soul, and some of them did *very* well. I am really beginning to admire an enterie (pronounce, ontery) when it is clean and well-worn. It is a cotton garment, sometimes white, more often of some dark striped material. It comes within 10 or 12 inches from the floor, is scant, and opens all the way up the front and part way up the back. It is fastened by buttons from the throat to the waist and often by a girdle in addition. I also like to see a big broad-shouldered young man, whose feet have never been squeezed by tight shoes, standing before an audience in coarse, white wool stockings, and no shoes at all. It is a great improvement upon the peculiar French shoe which many of the educated men wear.

I was one of the judges in the English contest. Five young men sang in turn a song and a prize of half a lira was awarded to the best. No prize exceeds half a lira. The professors and teachers offer the prizes.

I am going to omit any account of Commencement Day proper because I want to write a whole letter about that.

On Saturday, all but the Gates family moved to the Garden house. I come into the city every other day for an Armenian lesson. Just now at 11.45 A.M. Ada and I are sitting in our dismantled parlor in the city. We come in some eight of us at about eight o'clock and work in here, bringing our luncheon with us. I usually walk from choice, tho' most of the ladies ride. Our horse has been very sick, but now he is much better.

I wish there were time to describe the garden house. E. took a picture of it once before the new part was finished. He will send it, if he has not already done so. From Mrs. Browne's end we can see the Anti-Taurus mountains which still bear streaks and patches of snow in the valleys. All about us are hills and mountains. Ada and I have a room together, with two windows at the East end and two windows and a door at the west. The door opens upon an aivan,—that is a sort of broad piazza, or to be more accurate, a long narrow room, with one side entirely open to the sun and air.

On Sunday I came into the city, straightened out four Sunday Schools of 60-100 scholars apiece. This is, I saw that they were in working order, helped form the classes etc. The teachers I had planned for before. You see, when school closes, our boarders go home, and we lose 20 or more teachers. Of course most of the little children live in the city and continue to come to Sunday School. Then I went with Aunt Hattie to one of the orphanages to see a little sick girl. This is a strange case and a beautiful one. The child has eaten nothing for over a week. The doctor expected that she would die long ago. She whispers incessantly, "Heesoos, kezeé gookám."—"Jesus, I come to thee." It is part of a hymn. She says Heesoos hundreds and hundreds of times a day. Often she prays for the mairig and the other children by name. She keeps her eyes closed all the time, but smiles frequently and seems perfectly happy and contented. I believe she has seen the Lord. She talks about him and to him all the time. This was true last week. Since Sunday she hasn't talked.

I wanted to tell about the Fourth, how we spent the evening on our ivan and ate ice cream and talked and sang, but the others have come in to eat luncheon with us, so with my best love,
Theresa

Harpoot
July 11, 1899

My precious Cornelia,

It is just now about two o'clock, and I am sitting in our ivan, off at one end to get away from the sun. Yesterday morning Ellsworth started on a trip to a village nine hours away, taking with him the Turkish zaptieh, (touring servant) Shabán. We expect to see him again tonight. He went on Ada's horse because ours is sick.

Sometimes I feel really impatient because I can't make you see this place. I don't mean that you are stupid, but that pen and ink are unsatisfactory. Let me tell you what we see and do when we come to the garden. Supposing we have been in the city all day, studying etc. At about half-past four we water the plants, make a bundle of clean clothes or whatever we want to take out with us, lock up the house and go down to the street. We go near to the stable-door and call "Mardirós." In a minute he runs out saying, "Hramé," which means "What" or something a little politer,—"at your service" perhaps. We say, "badrasd yenk,"—we are ready, and he scuttles off. It is a long time before he returns. A little company of small boys, beggars, and passers-by watch us mount, and we start off at a walk, because it is too warm to canter and our bags or bundles prevent.

If no gentleman appears to go out when we do, we take an Armenian servant who walks along beside us. He is needed too, to take the horses back to the stable. We turn to the right just after we pass the girls' school and then follow the level path which runs in and out along the hillside for perhaps three quarters of a mile. On our right the hill rises steeply. On the left it slopes quite abruptly in long valleys and ridges to the plain. The sky is cloudless, as it is all summer, excepting a few days here and there when it is cooler and groups of white clouds gather in the sky. Dear me, I must continue that exception and say that there are often a few clouds in the west at sunset, just enough to make the sunset glorious. The air is wonderfully clear and the Taurus mountains are in sight until the path curves very decidedly to the right and we go up a little hill. When we reach the top, there are the Anti-Taurus mountains spread out before us. They are grander than the others. Range after range rises, one behind the other. Once Ellsworth and I counted five distinct ranges rising from the plain, one after another. On the highest the snow still lingers. We are standing with mountains as high as the White Mountains on one side, and much higher ones on the other.

On the way we pass two fountains where men and boys loaf as they do on the street corners at home. A fountain is usually sheltered by a three-walled enclosure made of stone and mud, and roofed over with similar material, the grass or weeds growing on the top. The water pours out from the hill-side into a shallow stone trough. The men gather out of the sun, inside the enclosure. Sometimes we see little boys taking a bath in the trough.

As we ride along, sometimes a very strong wind rises and blows the dust along in clouds. We meet a prosperous old Turk now and then riding upon a donkey. His feet swing back and forth,—they seem barely to escape the ground, his mouse-colored dressing-gown flaps gently; and he holds a white umbrella majestically over his fez and turban. Then we meet a picturesque Koord in dirty white garments. He prods along two or three forlorn little donkeys, bearing loads of sticks. Perhaps we meet two or three Turkish women of the lower class, wrapped from head to feet in garments of black, barred with orange. They stop and stare at us curiously, tho' we can see nothing of them but their eyes and feet.

From the top of the hill of which I spoke we can see the roof of our garden house, which is about a quarter of a mile off. If we take the lower path to the house, we shall find the way stonier, but we may find a little shade, as we pass the garden of our nearest neighbor,—a Turk. You know the land is very, very bare. Each garden is by itself—a little clump of green, nestling in a valley. It looks to me as if a giant had pushed plums into a pudding with his thumb, for each dark plum is in a little dent of its own.

Our house looks toward the south west. It is a little hard to know which side is the front, after all. On that side, at least, there are two stories, while on the other there is but one, the house being upon the hill side. Most of the trees about us are mulberries, and almonds. There are a few English walnut trees, apricots, pears, etc. We have one fine tall clump of poplars. Underfoot it isn't very beautiful, the ground being stony and weedy or wholly bare, except where vegetables have been planted. There are always some dirty little Turks about, the children of our gardener.

I suppose you wonder what we do at the garden. Much the same that we do at the city. Indeed if we want to work very hard, we go to the city. Today I have been lazy. This morning I slept for nearly two hours, and much as I love you, my dear sister, it is a "regular pull" for me to write this letter now. After our 5.30 dinner nobody works. We play tennis on two very good courts, or walk on the hills near by. The air is as dry by night as by day, but of course, much cooler. This is a wonderful climate–almost ideal. South of us in Mardin it is very hot, and Sivas and Marsovan are much lower than Harpoot. Mr. Browne was saying yesterday that he believed there was no place in Turkey where there was so much fruit in variety and quantity. Since the first week or two of "toots" (mulberries) I can't bear to taste one, they are so sickeningly sweet. Everybody else likes them. Perhaps I shall some day again. I have eaten a great many mish-mish (apricots) today. They are large and delicious. But the nectarines are better still. The sweet cherries have gone, but the sour cherry or fishna is still in the market. Most of the plums which I have had as yet have been rather sour, but the best ones haven't come. This is a wonderful land for fruit. I am continually wishing that you all could have the good things which come to me, especially the views, the climate and the fruit. However I shouldn't want you to share all the characteristic features of the country.

The other day the Doctor found a big tarantula in his room and Ellsworth's. There are more attractive biological specimens. Last night after dinner, Laura and I went on a hunt for ant-lions. It is easy enough to find the holes, but harder to capture the proprietors. The other day I saw a praying mantis (How about the spelling?) for the first time.

The little girl about whom I wrote last week is getting well. She doesn't remember anything of what she said when she was sick. She seems likely to recover soon unless they kill her by letting her eat what she wants. When she first began to eat again, they gave her a cucumber.

The Doctor found it out and protested. "But," said they, "she wants it. She cries." This is very characteristic of the people in their treatment of the sick.

...

You dear people at home, have you forgotten my request? Ellsworth hasn't more than three decent neck-ties. Won't you please send him a little package by mail? One of the three is a black satin tie for evenings, one is a dark blue four-in-hand which Mrs.

Barnum brought here and one is a cotton wash-tie. He needs two or three rather dark string ties for common wear.

Dear sister, do please write a little wee, short letter to us some day.

Most lovingly,
Theresa

Harpoot
July 26, 1899

Dear old Harry,

Please don't feel insulted by my form of address, and please excuse this ponderous sheet of paper. I can't find any other in this deserted room without wasting a great deal of time. I am in my city bedroom just now.

I thoroughly enjoyed the "Dial." It struck me as very sensible and unpretentious. School papers are apt to have a great many unsuccessful attempts at wit, and you were wise enough not to attempt much of that. I recognized a story of yours which you wrote when I was at home. The cutting-down improved it. Didn't I see L.L.'s hand there? I am glad of the bits of news which the paper brought. May I make a small criticism? Is there any reason for putting the initials after the name—e.g. Brown, F.E. '92. It is confusing to me. We shall be glad of future numbers, if you have them. I suppose that next year you and Ruth must leave the editorial board.

Yesterday was the fortieth anniversary of Dr. Barnum's arrival in Harpoot. Accordingly we were all invited to spend the evening together with the Barnums. As on Fourth of July some rugs were spread on the broad aivan, chairs were brought (There are always a good many there. Mary says it reminds her of the deck of a steamer), the little organ was brought, too, and a low table on which were flowers, and some candies which Emma had made. For drinks we had lemonade and root-beer, not the genuine thing, of course, but the sort made from tablets, etc, which is nevertheless excellent. When we sang we had some common lanterns and a great Japanese lantern for lights. Afterward when the moon rose we put out the lesser fires. I wish you could see us when we meet in this way. It is just as comfortable and pretty as any lawn-party at home. Then the little boys are always scampering about, and they make life enough, for their fathers and uncles, especially Dr. Gates, the Doctor, and E, are continually spanking them or tossing them

> up into the air. This makes them tough little mortals. I wish you could see little Moore standing erect and fearless on his father's shoulders, just grasping the tips of his fingers. Then he takes his father's hands, tightly, stiffens his little body, falls forward and with the aid of his father's strong arms, turns a complete somersault in the air and comes down on his feet. I will come back to Moore again when I have finished up with Tuesday evening. Dr. Barnum told us a good deal about his coming and the early work here and then we fell into a general discussion of the work at present and the Christian leaven among the Mohammedans. It was a dclightful evening. Dr. Barnum spoke of the changes in the homes here within forty years. His own has furnished a most beautiful example for the people. Dr. Barnum has the power of a remarkably, clear and sensible judgment. Dr. Wheeler who was the aggressive factor here, used to say that he often presented ideas and plans without thinking them out carefully, because he knew that if they weren't wise Dr. Barnum would condemn them.

Aunt Hattie' Seymour's account of that evening was later published in *Life and Light*:

> I must tell you about a pleasant gathering to celebrate the fortieth anniversary of Dr. Barnum's first arrival in Harpoot. A new Estey baby organ, sent by Miss Emily Wheeler for the college, had arrived the day before, and was used to help us in our song of praise. In his reminiscences Dr. Barnum spoke of his experiences in his early days, when persecution met them in every place they tried to enter; yet officials dared not refuse to protect them, as they were men who wore hats, and English prestige was in the ascendant because of the Crimean War. One cannot but marvel at the great changes wrought since then. The hardest work to start was among women. They would not come to Protestant meetings because there was no latticed gallery where they could sit apart and be unseen by men. When the missionary ladies accompanied their husbands to the villages, they used sometimes to take with them native sisters who had become Protestants, that their example might persuade the village women to be present at the meetings. When Mrs. Williams had her first meeting in a village where there is now one of our largest and most intelligent congregations of men and women, Dr. Wheeler had to flourish his cane among the women to insure sufficient quiet, that Mrs. Williams' voice might

be heard. It gave us new courage when we remembered what the gospel had done for women in these forty years; not only for Protestants, but in Gregorian homes.[34]

Harpoot
Aug. 1, 1899

Dear Little Mother,

You would smile to see me dressed for church. I usually wear a shirt-waist and skirt, my small white sailor, trimmed with a blue scarf (part of the over-long sash of my silk dress), some silk gloves, and a little black crocheted shawl which Aunt Hattie gave me. For custom's sake it is necessary here to have some sort of outside wrap, and this is the thinnest thing I have. Several of the other missionaries wear similar shawls.

Yesterday I sent my first Armenian letter, asking the teachers of the summer S.S. to come to a teacher's meeting. Last Sunday I said something to the scholars in Armenian for the first time. Of course I have spoken to individual girls before in their native tongue. I don't tell you very much about the work, do I? I believe I ought to. Tomorrow the pastors and preachers of our field have a meeting in Mr. Barnum's room for prayer and discussion of work, I suppose. They had a similar meeting last week. Mr. Browne is a good deal discouraged about the work just now. It seems to be going backward to him. It isn't that he can't hold revival services in the villages and here with apparent success, but the standard of Christian life is so low. There is constant quarreling among church members. We educate and train young men and half or all their way thro' the college and then they fail us as teachers and preachers and go off to America where they feel safe and can make money. There seems to be so much self-seeking and so little self-sacrifice among the pastors. The Armenian character is one that doesn't hold out well. Don't think that I am discouraged for I'm not at all, only we have to look at these things and think of them. You see the Missionary Herald prints only the bright half of the missionaries' letters. People don't want to hear the other.

I am sitting in Ellsworth's new garden room just now. It opens from the Gates' dining room, has an earth floor and the sort of ceiling that scorpions and centipedes tumble down from. We killed a small specimen of the former creature on the wall over

34. *Life and Light*, 1899, vol. 29.

Ada's bed the other night. I wish you could have some of the white grapes and great delicious melons which we have daily.

Do you remember that I wrote you about a sick little orphan girl? She died last Saturday and according to the universal and necessary custom in this land was buried on the same day. She thought she would die on a Sunday and wanted to. She was a gentle patient little creature. The Doctor told me the other day that only four orphans had died since he came last August, those brought their weak constitutions if not their sickness, with them from their native villages. That is not a bad record for 600 children. A great many of the orphans have the measles just now. That disease seems to be more serious in its nature here than at home. The people say that after small-pox, there is danger of weak eyes, but after measles, danger of death. They don't distinguish between scarlet-fever and measles. One cause of the fatality of these two latter diseases in this country is the injudicious, insufficient care which the patient receives. He is given whatever he asks for and allowed to eat and do about what he pleases. Little Lucia who just died, would have lived, the Doctor says, if she had been cared for properly. The Doctor told me that she would die if they continued to treat her as they were treating her then. But the Mairig and her helpers said, "What shall we do? She cries if we don't let her eat like this. She doesn't like the medicine."

With love to each blessed one of the family,
Theresa (L.H.)

"Infant mortality in Turkey," wrote Dr. Ussher about this period, "was something frightful, about sixty percent of all the babies dying before completing their second year."[35] There are no statistics on the babies of the missionaries in Turkey, but the little missionary cemetery in Harpoot received many of them. In the first few years of the Harpoot station, the three families lost two babies each to the hardships of missionary life.

Harpoot
Aug. 22, 1899

Dearest Mamma,

Ellsworth and I are sitting in his garden-room, very cosily writing. He is sitting by himself and I am in a rocking chair with my feet conveniently propped up on his clothes-box. Most of the

35. Ussher, p. 13.

things in his room suggest activity. Beside me in the corner are two tennis rackets, his and mine. Near by is a large glove which he used this morning in his Geography lesson with the boys. In the next corner is a stout walking-stick with a spike at the end, and likewise a surveyor's compass on a tripod. He used it today on the roof in getting the noon mark. Not having a noon-whistle, we depend on Dr. Barnum's or E.'s noon-mark and have a lively time correcting our watches every few days. Just now, Dr. Gates is living (with his whole family) about 15 minutes ahead of the rest of us. He thinks he has the right time. In the city we all have to keep together.

Last Thursday we were all invited to a little celebration of Herbert's birthday which had taken place some time last July. We had ice-cream and cake on the ivan, where some Chinese lanterns danced about gaily in the wind and we had to put on shawls to keep warm. Then Ellsworth and the Doctor, with a little help from Mr. Jones, told us about their last trip. That evening was a sort of double celebration, for a telegram came about four o'clock saying that Mr. Knapp and his family would be at Con'ple Oct. 22 en route for Harpoot. I wrote you, did I not? that the station had invited him to come and help in orphan work. The family will live in the house which the Doctor has now. I don't know where he will go, poor man. He may rent a new house which has just been built opposite the Brownes. The older people are ordering the Knapps' winter supplies now, putting up fruit, making pickles for them etc. Nobody here knows just how many children the Knapps have, but the prevailing notion is that they have four under seven years of age.

Let me tell you something funny. An Armenian or Turk never, if he can avoid it, speaks of his wife by name or in any other way. The other day Manoog, a man who helps Aunt Hattie in orphan work was looking for the Doctor and encountered Emma in his search. "Who is sick?" she said. He stammered and mumbled and at last said, "Our bride." (The man must have been married 16 or 18 years.) "Oh," said Emma, "I didn't know you had a boy old enough to be married." This embarrassed him more than ever. At last he got out his answer, "Oh no, it's the mother of my children."

Harpoot,
August 29, 1899

Cornelia dear,

What I am about to write, you, i.e. the family mustn't speak of to anybody, Dr. Barton, Miss Wheeler, or anyone else, unless we write that it is settled. Dr. Ussher may go to Van. (I suppose you think that isn't very wonderful news after all) His relationship to Mary is at the bottom of it. He seemed to think a great deal of her, but really didn't mean anything by his attentions. It has interfered with his work and somewhat with hers, and snarled things up generally. Being strongly advised by our three older missionaries here, he has written to Van where they need a young missionary very much. They may not wish him to come there. This is rather gossipy and strictly private. I know I can trust you people not to mention it outside the home.

Harpoot
Sept. 5, 1899

Dearest Mamma,

Last week we were rich in mail, receiving your fine long letter, Papa's very interesting one and Cornelia's forwarded from Christmas. Of course I read them all to myself first, and Ellsworth and I read them together Sunday evening. He came home Saturday night but that is his story.

While I think of it, I want to tell you how much he enjoys his opera glass. He takes it with him on all his trips. Last night he and Dr. Gates and Ada were studying the stars through it. Papa would find congenial spirits here in the matter of interest in Astronomy. Dr. and Mrs. Gates and Emma especially study the stars together very often and know a great many constellations.

Last Friday Emma invited the girl teachers who live in the city to take luncheon here at the garden. They were invited to stay from nine till two. Five of the six came, one on a mule, the others on foot, except that two of them took turns in riding Mary's horse. The distance is really very little over a mile, but the sun is pitiless here, and there is no shade. When they went home, three rode. I wonder how these teachers would look to you. Three of them, I think you would say, had very sweet faces and all look bright. Their dresses would look a little queer to you, altho' they think them quite European. You would like their hair, simply parted and braided in two plaits. We spent the morning in talking, showing them about the house a little, taking them to call upon Mrs. Browne and Aunt Hattie, and in walking about the garden, eating the grapes and almonds which grow there. We had a very good luncheon. Shall I give you the menu? 1. kuftehs, (a sort of croquette); 2. pillaff (rice boiled with a little tomato juice and butter); 3. egg-plant and meat (I forget the Turkish name of this. The meat is chopped fine and arranged in layers with egg-plant. Don't laugh at that word arranged. Then tomato juice is poured over this and it is baked. It is delicious.) 4. sliced cucumbers. 5. black olives 6. native bread. For dessert we had white grapes, water-melon and musk-melon, cookies and cakes. After luncheon we sang together, had a little prayer meeting, and they started for home.

Last Sunday evening we, i.e. the missionary circle alone, except for Mr. Jones' presence, had the communion service together. We held a little preparatory meeting Saturday evening which Dr. Gates led. Dr. Barnum led the Sunday evening service. It was beautiful. He is remarkably direct and simple in what he says always. Monday morning at 7.30 the circle met to talk about the work and pray about it. This week every evening at 7 o'clock we pray together about the work of the coming year and our preparation for it. The work is in rather a discouraging condition just now, not so far as increase in numbers goes, but in the moral and spiritual condition of the people. Since the massacre when the Armenians lost all and were in such utter destitution for a time, they seem to have lost their sense of honor, their moral sense. They live much as their Gregorian neighbors do, and the Gregorian priests say that their people have degenerated. There is much religious insincerity, or to speak more particularly, a lack of harmony between the professions of the Protestant and their lives. There are many church quarrels, always over money matters, and much criticism of the missionaries and their methods. However all isn't black and Mr. Browne who often takes a pretty dark view of things has great hope. This state of things is not peculiar to Harpoot. It extends all over the Eastern Turkey Mission.

Last Sunday I went with Aunt Caro to Yegheki, a village about an hour and a half away, down on the plain. She had to tell them that the teacher for their boys' school whom they expected had stayed in another village. Now they must give up the boys' school for the year. We went first to the pastor's house where we were welcomed very cordially. Two of his six daughters are in our school.

The oldest who is about seventeen is going to teach this year. We sat down in a room where some of "the brethren" were sitting with the pastor. After some twenty minutes we went to the chapel close by for the regular morning service. After this Aunt Caro had a meeting with the women. After she had spoken I said a few words which she translated. They are a simple, demonstrative, friendly people. One of them patted my cheek. They often do that. The chapel was bright and neat—very. You would smile to see in an American church what I saw there,—two very large cards exactly alike bearing in illuminated letters, in Armenian of course, the words "God bless our home." They were hung one on each side of the pulpit. On our way to the village we rode by vineyards and near gardens, and I saw "a lodge in a garden of cucumbers" indeed, a good many of them. In this particular place the cucumbers happened to be melons, but the custom is the same for either fruit. A little booth is built of boughs or if they are unobtainable, possibly the booth is covered with cloth. The people stay in the gardens and in the vineyards days and night to watch the fruit to save it from thieves. We rode by several cotton fields, also.

It is not decided yet whether Dr. Ussher will go to Van, but it seems very probable. Mr. Browne and Aunt Caro expect to start in a week or two for the northern part of our field. They both dread the journey, I think. It will be cold and as the road is wild and unfrequented there are no khans and they must spend the nights in filthy Koordish villages. There is no little danger too, in crossing the mountains by such paths as exist.

I expect to return to the city to live next Monday. Of course I could stay if I chose, but I can work more easily in the city and really rest better there, and the weather is steadily growing cooler. Lots and lots of love to all. We are very well.
Theresa (L. Huntington)

Chapter Eleven: The Doctor Leaves under a Cloud and the End of the World is Thought Near

The Garden summer was over; as the opening of school in mid-September approached, Theresa, Emma, and Ellsworth were still sleeping at the garden but spending more and more time in Harpoot preparing for their classes. Ellsworth had his birthday and Theresa informs her family that "the Doctor gave him a new pair of reins; Mary, a pretty picture and some note-books etc; I, a clothes brush and some money to use on his journey home." Dr. Ussher was preparing to leave for Van near the Russian border; Theresa guardedly says she isn't sorry to see him go, "tho' he has some very loveable qualities." She worries, however, that his absence will mean a great deal more work for the Barnums and Aunt Hattie in their work with the 650 orphans.

In one of her letters, Theresa mentions "the Germans." These are the German missionaries in Mezereh, with whom the Harpoot group had occasional dealings. The relations between the two groups were not always smooth, and the friction between them was particularly over how to divide up the area in terms of missionary work.

This also seems to have been a time when the local population was fearful of a new outbreak of terror. In some villages, the touring missionaries reported that no one dared venture out to greet them or meet with them. In one of the villages of the Harpoot field, Palu, several Armenians had been thrown in jail on trumped-up charges. But the work was proceeding: To give an idea of the extent of the American Board's work in Turkey at that time, the summary of the Eastern Turkey Mission states that the field contained "5 stations; 87 outstations; 10 ordained missionaries, two of whom are physicians; 1 unordained physician; 23 female assistant missionaries; 18 pastors; 23 preachers; 179 teachers; 9 other native helpers; total native helpers, 253; 48 churches; 2,515 communicants; 225 received confession during the year; average attendance, 11,185; 1 theological school; 13 boarding and high schools; 742 pupils; 101 common schools; 6,830 pupils; total under instruction, 7,577."[36]

---

36. *Missionary Herald*, 1899, p. 70.

Harpoot
Oct. 18, 1899

My very dear Father,

It is raining hard outside tonight. Ellsworth stayed in my room after dinner and we read aloud till seven from a book called "The Conversion of Armenia to the Christian Faith" by W. St. Clair-Tisdall, an English missionary in Persia. It is an interesting book. Today we have been reading the chapter on Armenian Mythology. In some respects the Armenian race is a wonderful one. I want to copy a few words by a Russian writer quoted in this book.

"From the point of view of the struggle for existence, the permanence and continued duration of that small nation causes us to wonder, since for centuries it has remained like a wedge driven in between other great peoples. Mighty Assyria and Babylon, the dread despotism of the Persian empire, the sway of the Parthians, the Macedonians, the Romans, the Arabs, have come to an end. Very great nations have perished and vanished from the face of the earth; but the Armenian nation has not only continued to exist, but moreover, full of hoe and of vitality, is now burning with a thirst for knowledge and a love for exertion… A nation which has been able to preserve its individuality from the days of Nimrod and Semiramis up to our own times, and also in some measure to maintain its own distinctive type, its customs, its language and its religion—and that too not withstanding the fact that no nation, not even excepting the Hebrew, has been called upon to endure such sufferings—must never be forgotten in history."

There is another book which I think you may be interested to read aloud at home, "Through Armenia on Horseback" by Rev. Geo. H. Hepworth. It is very brightly written, and describes capitally the khans, the people and just the things that we see every day. The book is published by Isbister and Co. London. Perhaps you can get hold of it in the Boston Public Library.

Just now Ada and I are sitting in my bedroom, each writing to her father, but her father is in India and mine in America. My big lamp gives an excellent light, and some heat, so it is very bright and cosy here. On the floor there is a very pretty rug which I have just bought from the Doctor for about $4.50. It is about 6 ft. long and 4 ft. wide. It is one which Ellsworth is to take home when he goes. Though it is nearly the middle of October we haven't yet had a frost. For the last two weeks we have had almost daily thundershowers. The clouds rolling about among the mountains, some of them below us, are wonderful. The clouds double the beauty of mountain scenery for me.

Last night there was a great din down below our house all night. It didn't disturb me, but the people on the other side of the house heard it, and thought it must be a wedding. This morning we learned that last summer (Aug.) when there was a mad dog in our quarter, a woman had been bitten, and afterward died, not from hydrophobia, I suppose. Her nephew was bitten at the same time and last night was the fortieth night since the accident. The belief among the people—at least, among many of them—is that unless the person bitten is kept awake all during the fortieth night he will become mad or die from some other cause soon after. Hence all the noise. Don't you feel sorry for the poor little boy?

I want to tell you of something which is by no means new to us, but still is strange to our civilized minds. Last spring or in the early summer, a company of women and children came down from Geghi, and the surrounding villages—a three or four days' journey from us—and took up their abode in this city. They left their homes, because they had nothing to live upon. A few had land, but the Turks took it away for taxes, and now most of the women have absolutely nothing. Their neighbors can barely live, themselves, so begging is hardly profitable in that region, and they have come here where people have more. They live in companies of five or ten here and there in this city, in cellars, or other miserable holes, where they can find shelter. The owners of these places, as a work of merit, allow these people to live in them. The women and children who number respectively about 20 and 40–60 in all, get their bread and keep some rags upon themselves by begging, except that Aunt Hattie has given them a little work from her work-room—as much as she could, and the women for a time had a piaster (4 1/2 cents) apiece every week from the collections of our Protestant church. Now the deacon says the church can't give any more, or rather feels that it is useless to give in this way, and Aunt Hattie is trying to induce them to go back to their villages, but they say, "We shall starve there anyway. Perhaps we shall live if we stay here." I suppose this case has many parallels in this country. The husbands of most of these women were killed in the massacres.

Much love to each dear one,
Theresa (L. Huntington).

Harpoot
Oct. 22, 1899

My dear Sister,

It is Sunday afternoon—about half-past five. We have just finished our early dinner, and I have sat down to write instead of going to the girls' meeting at the school.

After I wrote that line I sat still and thought a minute and decided to go to the meeting, after all, so it is twenty minutes of seven now. I can hear them singing up in the Gates' parlor now. The circle meets there for the usual Sunday evening meeting, but you see I didn't go. I rarely stay away from that meeting.

Today has been a very rainy day. The water has streamed from the skies and the roofs ad libitum. I used to think it would be interesting to be in a cloud, and here I have my wish very often in stormy seasons. The clouds rolled across us many times today. It is beautiful to watch them come and go, but when they stay over us for a long time we forget the poetry of the clouds, and say, "What a thick fog this is." This is a queer climate. The temperature at night varies very little from that of the day, and somehow we don't feel the cold as in New England. For instance, yesterday at about two o'clock some snow fell, melting as soon as it touched the earth, and the thermometer stood at 36°, but our stoves haven't been put up yet and I sat in my room and studied with the windows open. I was amazed when E. told me the temperature. I shall enjoy a fire again.

In the summer I laughed at Ada because on a very hot day, she said, "Won't you be glad when we can have our stoves and sit down on the floor in front of them again?" You see, Ada lives across the hall from me, and in the winter after we have undressed, we often slip on our wrappers, and then we sit down in front of Ada's fire, (She makes one at night and I in the morning) and poke in the wood until it is cozy and cheerful, and when the water is hot we make a cup of cocoa—grateful and comforting, like Epp's—and sip and talk, like two old crones gossiping over their tea. You see the cocoa that somebody put into my boxes isn't all gone yet. Some of the chocolate still remains, tho' I used half a cake on Wednesday in making the Doctor some fudge, at Mary's suggestion. The sugar was hers and the other things Mrs. Browne let me have. I made it on her (Mrs. B's) kitchen stove. Ada made him some "toffy" on my oil-stove the same day. It's a sort of custom here, when anyone starts off on a journey to give him or her some nuts and candy.

The Doctor has really gone. He went at about half-past ten on Friday. We all had prayers together just before he started—another station custom. Do you remember how the brethren went with Paul to the seashore, once upon a time? Well, that is thoroughly oriental and just what the brethren (and sisters) do here. I decided to go out part way with him, when I thought that only one or two of the Americans were going, and so let one of the teachers give some written work to my classes, but when we came to start, thcrc were fourteen people, on horse-, mule-, or donkey-back in the company. They were Dr. Barnum, Aunt Hattie (riding her mule as if she were twenty instead of seventy something) the Doctor, Ellsworth, Herbert, Harold and I; Mr. Jones and his cavass; the apothecary, the head-carpenter and one of the hairigs of our orphanages, the whole company preceded by two zabtiehs. We went down onto the plain and turned after an hour and a quarter's ride.

Well, I'm glad enough that the Doctor has gone, though it will be hard to have no missionary physician for the orphans and boarding pupils. The Dr. seems to expect to return in the spring, but when Mrs. Browne asked Dr. Barnum about it, he said that the Dr. wouldn't be wanted at Harpoot again till he was married. Dear me, you don't know what a snarl things are in. I never would have believed that missionaries could act so. The persons involved are the Dr., Mary and Laura, but the rest of us are made miserable sometimes by them. You see the Dr. is nice to everybody—can't seem to help it. He begins by being nice to Laura and then, because L. isn't always just as loveable as she might be, he is nicer yet to Mary. Result: Mary falls in love, Laura is jealous, without exactly knowing it, and relations are strained between L. and M.—a most pitiable state of affairs for Christian missionaries. These things might pass almost unnoticed to outsiders in America, but, alas, the people here are low and degraded and gossipy, so they notice that the Dr. walks home with Mary in the evening and that he rides with her, etc, and they start their miserable, vulgar talk. Result 2: The missionaries advise the Dr. who doesn't seem to be in love with anybody to go to the relief of Van and he goes. Mary is forlorn. M. and L. aren't yet in harmony. Speaking confidentially to my best girl friend, my dear sister, both of them are rather hard to live with for different reasons, but L. is the hardest. I do love them both, but not as I love the other members of the station, all of whom I admire and some of whom I really reverence.

Now these things have been happening gradually for months and there really isn't any use in telling them except that I am so tired of the whole business that I just felt like telling it and freeing my mind for a while, and then you don't really know much about me unless you know what things I am thinking about. If you want to read this to the others you may, but I trust you all not to let it go outside the family. I should feel very badly to have anyone who knows anyone in Harpoot know about it. . . .

Today will be like many other days, I imagine. At nine I shall have my Bible class. There are only four girls in it. Then comes my Armenian lesson, and following it two English classes in close succession. This afternoon, our Senior C.E. society meets, and afterward I have a com. meeting. I am chairman of the com. which has charge of the Junior C.E. Society. Usually I have one more class than today.

With much love to my dear Cornelia,
Theresa (L Huntington)

Harpoot
Oct. 24, '99

My very dear Papa,

You were very good to spend time in looking up and sending books for me. When the books came and up to the present, we have been studying Joel, and as Sanders' and Kents' book deals only with the earlier prophets, I haven't used the book for my class yet. I think it will be very helpful. I like it thoroughly, so far as I have looked at it. After a few weeks I can give more definite reasons for the opinion that is in me. Although Prof. Smith's book wouldn't have been too learned, still it is just as well that you didn't send it because Dr. Gates has lent me his copy from a beautiful set of the Expositor's Bible which he owns. He also lent me Farrer's book, the "Minor Prophets" but that doesn't go down so far to the bottom of things as Prof. Smith's, and sometimes avoids difficulties.

The "History of the Hebrew People" I am very glad to own, because I have no books at all on that subject. It seems to be ably written as a history. I like a book on the history of the Jews which is written not merely as a story. I don't know whether you thought I asked for such a book or whether it is a gift from you. I hope a

letter will come soon, telling about it. At all events, it is an excellent book to have, and I am grateful for it whichever of us pays for it. Did you know Prof. Sanders, who wrote the other book, in college, or is he a young man?
My best love to you, my dear, kind father.
Theresa (L. Huntington)

Harpoot
Nov. 1, 1899

My precious Mother,

Last week, as always, we had a good letter from you, which, by the way I want to read again if I can get it from Ellsworth to whom it was addressed, and one of Papa's which are always interesting. You both send letters to us very faithfully and you don't know how welcome they are.

Just now I am sitting by a table at the school while the Seniors are taking an examination in English. There are only four girls in the class, and one is absent today. Two of the three are sitting on the floor as they write, and the third is sitting on a low broad seat, about 16 inches high, which runs across one end of the room under the windows. This building is only a native house which we rent. The room is bright and sunny, there are pretty pictures on the wall. Pieces of Koordish carpeting are spread on the floor. There are two chairs for the teachers' use in school-time. Along three sides of the room are 13 little chests in which the boarding girls bring and keep their belongings. Some of the chests are painted a brilliant green, except on the front, where there are gorgeous and wonderful figures in red, purple, blue, orange etc. In the next room, which is much like this, are more of these chests. At one end of the room there appears to be an extensive cupboard or wardrobe, built against the wall, and closed in front by a curtain. You find this in every native house. It is the place in which the beds are rolled up and stowed away during the daytime, for you remember that these rooms are dining- and sleeping-rooms as well as recitation-rooms. The one thing pertaining to them which you would like to have, is the view, which I don't believe is excelled by any which Papa sees at the White Mountains.

In these days there are various arrivals and departures to write about. Monday a brief telegram came from the Doctor announcing that he had reached Bitlis. The next day came one from Mr. Heizer, the treasurer and Factotum of the Turkish Mission saying that the Knapps reached Samsoun on the 26th. Last Friday Mrs. Browne invited us all to her house, "the Browne Konak (mansion) for a brown dessert." Just before the time for the guests, who should turn up but Mr. Browne and Miss Bush from Erzroom. We hadn't expected them for three days. They reached here after dark, contrary to their principles, having been twelve hours in the saddle on Friday. Nevertheless, after eating a little something they came in their old clothes and spent the evening with the others. They lead a most difficult and wearing life. As it happened, some of the others had on rather old clothes because Mrs. Browne had asked us to dress in brown if we could. I wore my brown suit of course. As far as possible everything carried the brown idea. Our napkins were brown paper. Mrs. B. made some little changes in the furniture and ornamentation for the room to introduce the desired color. The refreshments were hot chocolate, chocolate and sponge cake and some candy. When we meet together in the evening in this way we don't have dessert or prayers until we have them together. If it seems to you rather giddy to have an evening affair with refreshments almost every week, don't forget that we don't have any other dessert, and this is almost all the social life we have, unless you include our rides.

I have eaten my luncheon since I began this letter and now Ada and I are sitting in our parlor, both of us writing. I can look straight at my organ. It is a nice little one and a tremendous temptation to me. We have larger, handsomer organs in the station, but they cost twice as much, and don't sound any sweeter than mine. Emma's is larger, that is, the case is, but it has no more stops. The injuries it received are slight, with the exception of a split at one end which was mended before it reached me by the cabinet-maker at Sivas. I haven't written to Auntie since it came, but mean to.

I have begun to wear the brown jacket and the green skirt now. The jacket-lining is very nice and sensible. All my jackets need to have the buttons changed a little. I'm bigger all over than I used to be. However, not much. The one criticism I have to make on the skirt is that it is too large on the hips. I think I can remedy that by changing the darts.

Ada's stove has been mended and put up in our parlor. It is an odd thing—very English—an open stove with pretty brown tiles. But alas, although they told her that it was adapted for either coal or wood, it smokes abominably, and we've got to do something about it. Our parlor is a very warm sunshiny room and just now we get along without any fire at all. Ellsworth has my smaller stove, and the other is waiting to see if Ada's proves to be a failure. I keep my little native stove in my bed-room. It is better than anything else for my purpose, because it warms the room in eight or ten minutes, heats water in less than no time, and goes out as quickly, unless you feed it pretty well.

There is one other thing in this room which I want to speak of—a lovely chrysanthemum plant with three big pink blossoms and many buds. Mrs. Browne gave it to us. Wasn't she good? She often sends her love to you, but I forget to give it. She is so hungry for news about her girls and boys and Mr. Browne is too. It is possible that Mr. Browne may spend the winter in the Erzroom field. I know he dreads going, but they need an experienced man there to straighten things out, and have asked him to come. He hasn't decided yet what his duty is, but is waiting for further communications from Erzroom. I know that Mrs. Browne is feeling badly at the thought of his going, for she left her children on purpose to be with him, and now may be separated from him for four or five months. Mr. B. has been sick with malaria yesterday and today.

Has Ellsworth written you about the fire? I think it happened last Thursday night. At about two o'clock in the night a zaptieh came to Dr. Gates' house to ask for the use of the little pump for a fire which was raging a ten or fifteen minutes walk from here. Mrs. G. called E. and he and Dr. G. started off with the hand-cart and our fire-apparatus. They worked until seven o'clock in the morning and, the people say, helped a great deal in putting out the fire. All the water had to be brought in digs (goat skins) so the odds were against them, and the fire had been burning two hours or more when they sent here. These mud houses have their peculiar dangers in time of fire. The fire gets into the wooden framework within the dried mud, and smoulders for a long time, bursting out in unexpected places. The great danger is from falling walls and roofs. Two children and a man were buried in this way at the beginning of the fire. The man and his family had been drinking new räky wine until they didn't know what they were doing and threw the dregs of the wine into a pan of smouldering coals. Dr. G. and E. were pretty thoroughly soaked and tired out. Dr. G. could hardly see for a day from the effects of the smoke and E. caught a cold from standing in water, and "knocked up his hand a bit" (as Ada says)! They are all right now. Two houses were burned.

There is another danger peculiar to these houses. After a long rain, the walls of an old house become water-soaked and the whole thing caves in. It is as dreadful as a fire because it comes suddenly. A week or two ago, a little boy was killed by the collapsing of a house a little below us.

The Germans are becoming a little disheartened about their work, and are becoming more willing than at first to ask advice of the missionaries who have been here a long time. Mr. Ehmann suggested that the Germans and Americans have a prayer-meeting together, and we had a most pleasant one last Monday. For a time at least we shall continue them. Usually they, the Germans, will come up here, though next Monday some of us will go to Mezereh. Mr. Jacobs, their missionary at Palu, a most excellent Christian, but an injudicious one has gotten into trouble with the government, through the relief-funds which he has been distributing, etc, and at last has become so sick that he had to be brought to his friends at Mezereh in a litter. He is better now. Partly as a result of Mr. Jacobs' foolish acts, and for other reasons such as the government is always able to hatch up, a hundred Armenians or more have been thrown into prison at Palu. When Mr. Browne and Miss Bush were at Palu six weeks or more ago, the people didn't dare to come and call upon them. It was the same at Diarbekir, when they were there last spring. The Armenians were in a state of terror and were afraid to call upon the missionaries, hardly daring to walk in the streets.

For almost two days, now, a drum and fife have been played in our neighborhood practically without intermission. It is part of a Turkish wedding, which I hope will be completed in a day or two.

Well, I have more to say, but no room or time to say it in. Next week I don't believe I can write so much.

If you don't receive a letter from me every week, please let me know.

Much love to you. I thank God for my dear family.

Lovingly,
Theresa (L.H.)

Harpoot
Nov. 22, 1899

Dear Ruthie,

I don't know whose turn it is for a letter and am too lazy to go up stairs and find out. It must be just about Xmas time as you read this, George is at home, I suspect, and you are all feeling rather festive, and being a little extravagant (I hope) and going to oratorios "and things."

You want to know about the Knapps, don't you? Last Wednesday came a telegram, saying that they would reach Harpoot on Thursday. With Thursday came a pouring rain, so that several people who had expected to go out to meet them had to give up their plan, and the welcoming party was reduced to Dr. Gates, Ellsworth, Herbert and Harold. The last named rode on Ada's horse. All wore mackintoshes etc. but were cold enough after their five hours ride in the rain. Touring must be hard work. Well, the clouds hung around and below us all the morning so that we couldn't see the plain but between two and three they rolled away a little, and Mrs. Browne got out her opera-glasses. About three o'clock she spied them way down on the plain, on the Malatia road. They were still an hour and a quarter away from us, but we could make out very plainly two arabas and four people on horseback. So the fires in the Knapp's house were started up, and after a while we all went to their house or to the gate to meet them. The boys Harold and Herbert came on ahead, because arabas travel slowly and all they had to say was "There's a boy." (We had tho't there were three girls) and "They're way behind." At last they arrived and the children were handed out from the araba and carried up the long flight of steps to the house, and finally all were in the house getting dry. In the evening the whole circle had prayers together.

This week the new family are eating at our house, but soon they will get a kitchen-stove, a servant etc, and start out for themselves. Mrs. Knapp is a sweet, gentle woman of about 34, I should say, a little deaf, but having a very bright smile to make up for it. She graduated from Mt. Holyoke in '86. Mr. Knapp is "a Harvard '87". I haven't made up my mind about him yet. He is young, and of course suffers a little in comparison with our three mature missionaries.

Winifred Knapp is seven. She has pretty, fair curls, and is on the whole a nice little American girl. The two older Browne boys who had privately said that they didn't intend to play with a girl are quite captivated by her, and they have royal times together. Addison is five–a nice, sturdy, little boy, with a strong will, when he wants to be naughty. The baby, Margaret is three. She has short dark hair and round blue eyes. Just now she is very bashful, and not quite well after the long journey.

Has Ellsworth written that a week or so ago when astronomers and other people were looking for a shower of meteors, the people here and in Mardin etc, (many Armenians and pretty nearly all the Turks) expected the end of the world. They tho't a comet was going to strike it. They had especial services here in the mosques. One day the public baths were closed and business in the market was almost at a standstill.

I send by this post (I really do this time) two little packages of native sweets. In the larger box, the candy which looks like our gumdrops, is called "Turkish delight" or rahátlakoom. The "stuff" with almonds in it which looks like oiled silk is mulberry bastegh. The mulberries are boiled and I think a little flour added. The concoction is spread when soft upon a large sheet to dry. The combination of grape bastegh and walnuts has a special name which I forget. This was made especially for Mrs. Browne and we often have it for luncheon. You would hardly think from the color that the grapes were white ones.

In the small box I have put some grape bastegh which was rather dry to start with and something else which is more or less solid now, but will, I fear, be only dust or else a sticky paste when it reaches you. It is made from dried mulberries, ground fine, spices, etc. I am afraid that all the stuff will be rather dry and leathery when you eat it, and I don't believe you will like anything very much, unless it be the rahátlakoom.

I hope you all had or will have a lovely, happy Christmas. I anticipate the home vacations happily, for it sometimes means a letter from one of my brothers or sisters. Last week Ellsworth had a letter from Mamma.

I thought of you on your birthday, little sister, and prayed for you

Most lovingly,
Theresa (L. Huntington)

The Rev. George Knapp was another one of those missionaries whose whole life was inextricably bound up with Turkey and the Armenians. His parents were missionaries in Bitlis, a town in a mountainous and remote area of eastern Turkey where, the *Missionary Herald* informs us, "the marauding Kurds have made life a terror to the Armenians and the rule of the Turk has been harsh and bigoted." When he was of college age, he was sent to the United States and graduated from Harvard College in 1887. He went on to Hartford Theological Seminary and was ordained in 1890. That same year, he married Anna Hunt from Barre, Mass., and was appointed missionary by the American Board. He spent the next six years—which included the Hamidian massacres—in Bitlis, and in 1896 he became involved in an incident which made headlines in the missionary papers of the day: "In 1896, in his first term of missionary service, he was suddenly arrested on the absurd charge of inciting sedition, and was about to be bundled out of the country, with "expelled" stamped upon his passport, when his resolute demand for a trial at Constantinople brought a stay to the proceedings."[37]

George Knapp was a welcome addition to the missionary group at Harpoot and the Knapp family remained part of the Harpoot group for as long as Theresa was there. He took on the work of station treasurer from Dr. Gates, started a number of agricultural projects and taught vocational skills to the hundreds of orphans who continued to be a heavy responsibility for the station. Partly as a result of Mr. Knapp's initiative, the missionaries introduced potatoes to the Harpoot region at this time, they taught the farmers how to use winnowing machines to separate the chaff from the wheat, and they brought in windmills for power.

Harpoot
Nov. 29, 1899

My very dear Cornelia,

Sometimes I almost feel as if I didn't have any sisters, I know so little about them. My precious sister, if I stay here eight or ten years before coming home, we shall be almost like strangers to each other, unless we write about what we think and feel sometimes, at least about what we do. I think I do write to you once in four or five weeks, but you hardly write to me once in four or five months. I think your last letter reached me sometime in July or early in August, and there haven't been more than two others this year. Confess, haven't you written much oftener to Gertrude than to me? I don't feel at all jealous, but I think you wait till you can send a long fine letter, and don't send me the little scribbled half sheet which I am so hungry for, once in three or four weeks, telling that so and so took tea, that you didn't give a lesson because it rained, that Priscilla is good, or naughty, that you have had a new blue jacket, that Jeny finds the work hard etc. Mamma says she doesn't like to send a letter about trivial things so far, but don't you see that

37. *Missionary Herald*, Nov. 1915, p. 511.

when we are in a foreign land, we don't want to hear any wonderful things, but only the little things that will make your life real to us and bring a picture of home before our eyes. I should just love to have Ruth for instance tell me what things of Aunt Martha's were brought home and where they have been put in the house; and what clothes she is wearing to church just now and whether Bessie Young seems any nearer to Christ than a year ago. I am not complaining a bit about the lovely letters you have sent, but about the lovely little ones which you have not. I guess you are longing for a change of subject. Here is a kiss under your left ear, asking forgiveness for two pages and a half of this.

Tomorrow we expect to have Thanksgiving dinner at Mrs. Browne's. It will be a great squeeze for the twenty of us to be given places at the table although the storeroom which opens by folding doors into the dining-room will be used and, I believe, the ironing table. She has three turkeys. They don't cost here what they do at home, but still are not easy to obtain. All fowls are bought at the market alive and killed by the cook. These gobblers have lived in the stable for a month, getting fat on English walnuts. They, the missionaries' cooks, always have to keep and fatten turkeys here before killing them. Mr. Browne and Miss Bush are at Arabkir and won't return to Harpoot for two or three weeks.

Each week I speak a little more Armenian than before and find it easier to pray in Armenian at a meeting, for example, but I still have to think out beforehand what I want to say and ask if certain phrases are right. This morning I led one teachers' prayer-meeting. My "remarks" were in English, all the rest, giving out of hymns, prayer, etc, in Armenian. I find it pretty hard to understand others. It is almost, for me, impossible to understand villagers, they use so many Turkish words, make mistakes in grammar, and almost every village has its own peculiarity in pronunciation.

The Knapps are still taking their meals with the Brownes but today their new cook came and they will leave us tomorrow. I am glad to see that Mr. Knapp is firm with his children and not afraid to punish them when they need it. Addison has had to stay alone in their house during two meals and eat only bread, because he was naughty! One day he cut his hair and the baby's.

I suppose Ellsworth sent his pictures by this mail. I did want to comment upon some of them, but I can't remember all. Dear Aunt Hattie looks old-fashioned enough in her picture, but you must look at her kind face and her dimples. She usually wears smaller sleeves than that. Mary isn't a bit pretty anyway, but in her picture she looks much less attractive than she really is. Ellsworth's picture is pretty good. I look tremendously fat in mine. I must hold my chin up more. I wonder if some day it won't be a double one like Aunt Theresa's. My complexion is clear almost always now and my cheeks always have some color. I think that warm water, lack of worry, and enough sleep do this. Yesterday Ellsworth and I had a beautiful walk on the water-course. The sun was setting and shining on the grand, snow-covered mountains north of us, so that their eastern slopes were in shadow and their peaks and western slopes glowed like coals. All the west was cloudy and rosy. We ran most of the way home in the bracing November air. We haven't had any snow yet.

I wanted to tell about the bath and about the fear in which the Armenians are, all the time, but it must wait.

With any quantity of love,
Theresa (L. Huntington)
No home letter last week. Probably two, this.

Chapter Twelve: A Severe Winter, and a Baby Dies

As 1899 drew to a close, Dr. Gates redoubled his efforts to secure the indemnity from the Turkish government for the mission property that had been destroyed in the massacres and to get a permit to rebuild. His attempts to do this sheds light on what passed for town-gown relations in those days between the Turkish authorities and the missionary colleges. It would stretch well into the year and would have tried the patience of a saint, as this excerpt from the Report of the Euphrates College makes clear:[38]

> The event that especially marks the year are the protracted negotiations regarding the permit to reconstruct the destroyed college buildings. Over two years ago carefully prepared plans were sent to Constantinople accompanied by a petition for permission to proceed with construction in accordance therewith. About Dec. 15, 1899, Minister Strauss, about to start for the United States telegraphed President Gates "Permission has been given to rebuild your school." Dr. Gates at once put himself into communication with the head governor or Vali, but could get no satisfaction whatever. Telegrams and letters passed back and forth between Dr. Gates and the Seceretary of the Legation at Constantinople, Mr. Griscom, until on the first of May a telegram came from Mr. Griscom to Dr. Gates, "Am officially informed of the issuance of an Irade for reconstruction of your college buildings." This was also followed up at Harpoot, but the local officials seemed to block everything. By May 20 the Governor at Harpoot had what purported to be the permission in his possession and on May 30 Dr. Gates was permitted to see it. This, however, was permission to build a few teacher's rooms on the old site, which was interpreted by the officials as meaning one or two rooms and at the most, five.
>
> Again, telegrams and letters in large numbers passed between Dr. Gates and the Legation, while the local officials were given lit-

38. Annual Report of Euphrates College, 1900. ABC 16.9.9.

> tle rest. Things reached such a strained condition at Harpoot that a plot among the officials was revealed to Dr. Gates to get him outside of the city under the pretense of making a decision about the college water course, and there have him set upon by a band of roughs there for the purpose. The plan did not succeed.
>
> Dr. Gates confessed that during these times he frequently used the punching bag that he had hung for winter exercise in one of the corridors to relieve himself of the stress that these negotiations produced.[39]

In early December, the whole Harpoot station along with Dr. and Mrs. Gates rejoiced in the birth of their "long-desired daughter" who makes her first appearance in Theresa's December letter to her brother George:

> Dec. 12, 1899
>
> My dear old Brother,
>
> I began a letter to you a week or two ago and then found that E. was writing to you, too, so I sent a letter to Milton instead. What do you do and think? Please tell me now and then. You don't know how much I want to see you. Tell me how you look. Ellsworth and I are always talking about you and the rest of the family. All the circle think you must be very delightful people, but you are, so that's all right. Yesterday at the table we happened to speak of making fires, taking care of a church building etc, and E. said, "I've been most everything in a church except minister," and then as I thought of it I said, "Why, all of our boys have been members of the congregation, janitor, librarian, sung in the choir, and more or less regularly have been Sunday School teachers. "You do know the business, don't you."
>
> Have I ever told you about the Turkish bath? We have our own for the use of the boarding and orphan girls. It used to be at one end of the girls' school and when the school was burned the bath was only partly injured. It is a funny little place. There is an outside room—very small—where we undress and dress. There are some hooks on the walls and one hanging down in the middle for the lantern if you go in the evening. The inner room is wholly of stone—floor and walls. The walls are dome shaped and at the top is a hole where the steam escapes. The floor slopes a little so that the water can run off. At three places in the wall there are faucets,

39. Annual Report of Euphrates College, 1900, ABC 16.9.9.

i.e. three faucets in all, one for cold and 2 for hot water. Beneath each is a small stationary basin. There are little wooden stools, and you sit on one of these before a basin. There are a good many large pails in which to draw the water and little pans in which you dip it up and pour it over yourself. Nothing but clean water is ever put in basins, pails, or pans. You make yourself clean by pouring water upon yourself and rubbing. There are little "cubby holes" in the wall for soap etc. The room is very hot and steamy and your face becomes dripping wet before you put any water upon it. Now I'll go back and tell what you have to take to the bath. Into a bogcha (a big square of cloth in which things are wrapped) you put a big, thin towel, to tie around your waist in the bath (they make large square ones for this purpose) a Turkish bath-towel, with which to dry yourself in the other room, a piece of carpet on which to stand in the outer room, while dressing, a pair of bath-shoes, and soap, bath-mitten, comb, clean clothes etc as you wish. I use E's bath-shoes. They consist of a flat piece of wood the size of the foot, two blocks of wood which raise the foot above the wet floor, and a leather strap to go over the instep and keep the shoe on. The beauty of the bath is that you can spatter all you please, can use plenty of hot water, the pores are thoroughly opened, and of course the cold water which you pour over yourself at the end is delicious. I go to the bath once in two weeks or even less often and pay a piastre ($.045) a time. Usually Laura and Ada go at the same time. Eight or ten girls have to go at one time. Even the poorest people think they must go to the bath. It seems rather luxurious, having a private bath, but we save a great deal of money by having this for the school-girls and orphans. Otherwise they would have to be sent to the city baths. The boys are now, and Mr. Barnum has a scheme for making a bake-house (very small) for the bread used in the orphanages etc and utilizing the heat also for a bath for the boys. If we ever get permission to build, this will save us several hundred dollars a year.

Ada has just gone over for the Knapp children to bring them here to play for the afternoon so that their mother can sleep. She stayed with the Gates baby last night because Dr. G. had lost so much sleep the night before. Of course she slept a little, but that baby, good as she is, does her sleeping in the day-time. We hope that Mr. Browne and Miss Bush will come home from Arabkir next week. If they don't they will have neither Thanksgiving nor Xmas at home. Aunt Caro wrote a very droll letter about one freezing, wild, stormy night at Arabkir when her window blew in and she tried to fill up the opening with cushions from a divan.

We feel sorry for Dr. Ussher just now. He is probably on his way from Erzroom to Van, conducting Miss Barrows and two English ladies from there to their new home. A tremendous amount of snow has fallen north of us. For almost three days the snow came constantly. Many roofs were crushed in by the weight upon them. In Mardin, on the other hand, they are having a real water-famine, and Armenians have to go in the night to fountains if they hope to get any water at all. . . .

Please send this letter home, because I shan't send any other there this week.

I pray very often about your work for next year. How I should love to be at your Commencement.

With much love,
Theresa (L. Huntington)

Harpoot
Jan. 2, 1900

My dear Miss Loud,

I thank you for yr. last letter and yr. kind words about my father. I always enjoy your cheery letters. I did want to write last week, but we seem to grow more and more busy as vacation approaches. Our vacation you know comes at the time of Arm. N.Y. and Xmas in the middle of Jan.

About three weeks ago I went with Mr. Knapp and my brother to the village of Ichmeh to spend Sunday. The village cannot be more than 18 miles away, but it took us some six hours on Sat. to reach there, going on horseback as we did. Indeed there is no other way of reaching the place unless one wishes to ride a donkey or go on foot. We took with us one animal loaded with our bedding. Before we reached Ichmeh he had taken occasion to roll himself and his rider in a pond where he was allowed to drink. Fortunately our things were not much wet, but the poor man had a cold ride afterward.

Ichmeh is at the foot of a steep mountain. The green fields about it and the fruit trees made it even on a chilly Dec. day look more homelike than any place I have seen for a long time. But the rough stones in the streets and the deep, sticky mud were thoroughly Turkish. My brother left us before we reached the village, and crossed the Euphrates spending Sat. and half of Sunday at a village where no missionary has been since the massacre. You know there are over 500 villages in our field. He found the few Protestants rather disheartened.

Mr. Knapp and I were met by the Prot. minister (preacher) about half an hour from Ichmeh. The people had been expecting us and had been holding meetings that wk. preparatory to communion. They had brought their cushions, pieces of carpet and wood for the fire and with these made ready for us a room in the preacher's house. It was very comfortable. In the middle of the room was a little sheet-iron stove. The windows were covered with oiled papers instead of glass.

The preacher has four sweet children. The oldest one, a little girl of about eleven is in our boarding-school at Harpoot. It's her first stay away from home and when I told her that I was going to see her father and mother, it made the child cry. They seem to be a loving household. I heard the father and mother joking together—a most unusual proceeding for Armenian husbands and wives. The smallest girl said to me, "Why do you say Degen Takoohi to my mother?" "What must I say?" said I. "Why, Mairig," (that is, Mamma) she answered. These three were baptized on Sunday by Mr. Knapp. They had been told by their parents what baptism meant, tho' of course the younger two couldn't really comprehend it. It was sweet to see with what seriousness and interest they stood up to be baptized on Sunday. In all 15 children were baptized. One encouraging thg. about this service was that people had finally yielded to the missionaries and consented to give up general baptism, a hard thg. for those who have come out of the Gregorian Church. Only the children of church members were baptized.

Sunday morning the board on top of the preacher's roof was pounded at sunrise to call the people to the chapel. I have described our chapels to you before—bare and empty except for some flat cushions on the floor. The woman's part is usually only one half as large as the men's. Later in the morning I led a women's meeting where about a hundred were present. Then came a church member's meeting and finally communion service where two men and two women were received into the church. One of the latter, a poor young village woman, didn't know how to read, but her neighbors all said that she was ready to come to the Lord's table. The other must have been 50 yrs. old. The people all stand to receive the bread and wine and there is somethg. in the services in these poor villages wh. goes to my heart more than the services in our comfortable Americ. churches. In the evening many men and women came to talk abt. their church and school and their own selves.

In the morning we started for home accompanied for some distance by a large company of friends—men and boys. The preacher's little wife, like any Amer. mother, didn't forget the daught. away at sch. but sent her some raisins tied up in a colored handkerchief while the tiny brother brought me a shrivelled apple for his sister.

Yesterday was a most pleasant day to us all here. A notice was given out in church that the missionaries wld. be at home and glad to see all the people on New Year's Day. School and all other work were given up and from half-past nine to 4.30 four miss'y households rec'd guests. All sorts of people came, the professors of the boys' school, the orphanage fathers and mothers, the Syrian Bishop, little schoolgirls, our new U.S. consul, Dr. Norton, our washerwomen, the Armen. doctor, the preacher, women with their babies, a poor ragged water-carrier with bare, dirty feet and many others. Abt. 140 people came to the house where I helped to rec. To one house 200 came.

I send my cordial greetings to all the ladies of the Branch.

Lovingly yours,
Theresa L. Huntington

Harpoot
Feb. 8, 1900

Dear Papa,

I have been wanting to write you a letter for a long time, and now have time for only a little note. I wrote once about the books but wanted to say more. I have only just begun Dr. Clarke's book, but I mean to make it one of those books that I have "on hand" in process of reading (according to advice given often of old) even if I am a long time about it. I am glad that you sent me a "solid" sort of book. It is what I need to read. Since the book came I have seen in the papers notices of other books of Dr. Clarke's. "Comfort" I know will be a comfort. Thank you for both, Papa, dear.

I often feel thankful to you and Mamma in these days for things which as a child I disliked very much. I am so glad that you made me obey, that you taught me to be respectful, to pick up my room, open my bed and my window carefully, use my knife and fork in the right way, eat good things which I didn't like, and that

you gave me a taste for good books and a correct ear in music and I am thankful for ever so many more things which I can't name. E. and I talk so much about you all that the circle here, particularly our household feel that they know you all. Now I have no room left for news. Mary is at her work again. Two of our teachers are sick, so it makes more work for us all. I have more lessons this term, anyway. Today is Moore's birthday (He is six) and we are all invited to spend the evening there. The baby is well, but very tiny and white. After a winter of almost incessant cloud and fog, we have a clear day at last.
Love to each dear one,
Theresa L. H.

Mamma dear,

I began a letter about clothes last week, which I can't find now. In brief, I don't want any more summer clothes till a year from next summer. I have enough and I want to wear them out. There is no belt for my blue and white gingham and some insertion is needed like that on the rest of the dress. I enclose a bit. Probably you can't match it exactly. Please send enough to go around the belt twice. Also I need no winter clothes, so save the brown cloth a year longer. I have enough for next winter and I want to wear these things out. One thing I need. I bought some silk for the front of my plum-colored dress, you remember, which isn't at all pretty. I bought it by electric light and it is too purple. Sometime I shall find a use for it. But I want some other silk for the front. Don't try to find anything changeable. Just get surah silk between wine-color and plum. Real wine-color wouldn't be bad, I think, like that I had on the dress Mrs. Wadsworth gave me in college days. I enclose a piece of the dress. Please send these things by registered mail. The Sept. shipment reached us day before yesterday. The things are very nicely made and pretty. The baskets are lovely. The coat will be used immediately. The cape is of less use, but there will be a place for it. The two pretty silk bags I shall keep to give to missionaries. No thimble, buckle, or ribbon from Mrs. Young appeared! Were they sent or not? As you see, any clothes for winter use must be sent in July.
With much love,
Theresa L. H.

Feb. 10, 1900
My dear Cornelia,

Sun. Morn.

While I wait for Mariam to finish the work in my room I can write a little. Ellsworth and I printed only one sheet of his chart last night because he couldn't find the cloth. After that I went in to see the baby for a few minutes. Her father was holding her and feeding her, as he usually does when he has any spare time. I hope God will let them keep that little girl, for they are just wrapped up in her. Her food has had to come by mail from Con'ple lately, for the Sept. shipment was so very late in coming. It costs almost as much again to have the food come by mail as it cost in the first place. When the Sept. shipment and the things added to it at Con'ple at last arrived a week ago, they found that Mellin's food had been sent instead of Nestlé's. They can't use it because good cow's milk must go with it and that we can't get here, so the baby will have to be fed by mail a while longer.

Mon. Afternoon.

I don't know when this letter will be finished. Mamma asked once about Ada. You have her picture now, so you know how her face looks. She is thirty-two or thirty-three—I'm not quite sure which. Her hair is a little gray already, but her face and manners are rather girlish. Perhaps it would be truer to say only her manners. She is about my height, but much slighter than I. She always has good fresh English color in her cheeks, which are rather thin, and of course she has a decidedly English accent. Her father is not in the army but is a merchant in the wholesale cotton business. He has just gone back to England. Ada's mother died six or seven years ago. She is the oldest of the family. She has a sister Katie, a few years younger, then a brother Fred in South Africa, a sister Bella, about twenty-two years old, who lives at home, and a brother of George's age, Archie, who is still studying, making a specialty of Chemistry. Now you know all about her.

Wed. Noon

Two days ago some news came to us which we at Harpoot had confidently expected and joked about a good deal, tho' we hadn't thought it would come till a month or two later. The Doctor is engaged to Miss Barrows. They had known each other about six

weeks when the happy event occurred. I supposed the Doctor would succumb immediately, but I did think Miss Barrows would hold out a little longer. I think whoever the girl had been the Doctor would have fallen in love. Perhaps I'm a little hard on them, after all. Such a journey as they took together must have made them feel that they knew each other very well.
With much love to my dear sister and all the family.
Theresa (L. Huntington)

Harpoot
Feb. 28, 1900

Dear People,

I have been gadding about a good deal today—at least since 3.30. At that time we, that is, all the teachers native and American were invited to Aghavni Varzhoohi's house. She is the teacher who has given me Armenian lessons ever since I came. She is the very choicest and sweetest of our teachers. Tomorrow she is to be married to a man who has lived in America ten or twelve years. Probably they will both go there in the summer. Meanwhile she will live in one of the worst villages on our plain. We really know very little about his man. (She knows almost nothing of him herself) and we Americans have been praying that the marriage would never take place, for we don't wholly like what we have seen of him, and Aghavni is very sad and unhappy over the matter. You want to know why she marries him then. This is the Orient, you must remember. Aghavni is twenty-four and has refused to marry all the men who have wanted her before. Now her parents insist and make her life miserable.

Well, there were sixteen or seventeen of us. Of course we all sat on the floor in the little room or on the low divan. At first they brought us tea—very sweet, and strongly flavored with cinnamon. Later a tray was brought in with dishes of dates, figs, apples, almonds, and candies upon it.

Theresa also comments on this event in a letter to the Norfolk and Pilgrim Branch, hinting that the Christian education of Aghavni may have made it very difficult to continue living among her own people:

Aghavni (dove), our most winsome and refined teacher is just leaving us to be married and to go immediately after to America. We feel sad about this, for she has really been forced into the marriage by her parents and friends. It is a disgrace for a girl to remain long unmarried. Various men have asked for Aghavni and her parents have always yielded to her refusal to accept any of them, but at last they insist upon having their way, and have made her life a burden over the matter. She said to me the other day, "I should not care so much if I knew whether he was a real 'Christian'. You remember that marriages here are arranged by the parents. The girl is often only fourteen or fifteen years old when she is married,—though there has been a great improvement in the matter of such child-marriages, since the missionaries came—and she hardly sees or speaks to the man chosen for her before the wedding. Aghavni said, "I do not see how other girls can feel happy when they are going to be married. It is better in our country for girls to be given when they are very young. Then they cannot feel sad about it." The touching thing to me is to see that her education, her reading, and above all, her Christian character have given her ideals which she cannot realize among her own people. Yesterday all the older girls met together for a little farewell meeting with her, planned by the native teachers. It was very hard for Aghavni, because she is not only marrying against her wishes, and about to leave her home and country, but the school is very dear to her. She gave a beautiful talk to the girls whom she had taught.

March 21, 1900

Dear Mamma,

We are constantly hearing new, pitiful reports of the cruelty of the tax-gatherers. They are even beating the women in some of the villages, because a son or husband is dead or unable to give anything. A poor käturgi (the owner of a pack-animal, which he rents to travellers) told Aunt H. that he had no money to give the tax-collector and that they would take his animals. They take the beds and the rags of clothing of the very poor. Today four or five men came here from a village about a week's journey distant, hoping for shelter or help of a little work here, but there is nothing here for them. Some of their neighbors, women from the same district, Geghi, have been here all the winter, and the men expected to find a place to sleep with them, but they are afraid that the house will fall down on their heads, and do not dare to stay there. Auntie gave each man some money to get across the river, and tomorrow they will begin the journey back. They told Aunt Hattie that in their village, the tax-gatherer was never out of their sight. I suppose they meant that every day he came about. Some people who have paid their own taxes have had part of their few possessions taken away to pay the taxes of their relatives in America.

Speaking of houses, reminds me that Mrs. Browne's washer-woman said this morning that their house fell in last night—only a part of it, I suppose. At this season several houses always collapse. There is so much rain and snow that the mud walls and roofs are thoroughly soaked and often cave in.

Harpoot
March 28, 1900

Dear People,

It is after nine in the evening and Ada and I are writing in my bed-room. I'm afraid you won't have a very long letter this time. Nothing very uncommon has happened. I have gone about my regular work, teaching, leading meetings now and then, making a few calls, riding, etc. The last two Saturdays the Gates' have invited Ellsworth and me to come up at half past six in the evening and eat ice-cream with them. That article of food in winter-time isn't an expensive one here. The labor is nothing and the snow and ice all about us are used for the freezing. One of those two nights they invited the Barnums who couldn't come, so we took their place.

The Barnums have been inviting all the teachers (and their wives if they have any) in groups to dine with them or take luncheon. It was a difficult task to arrange them not getting any unmarried young men and women together, for that would be highly improper. Indeed some of the younger girl teachers refused the invitation, according to their parents' wishes, because some of the young men, already safely married, were invited, too. The Barnums have invited the various members of the circle to come in at different times after dinner to help in entertaining the guests. E. and I have been twice.

Today Mr. Browne and Aunt Caro are here again for a brief rest before they go to Malatia. They are a constant wonder to me. They had been for a few days just before coming home at the village of Houiloo on our plain. The night before he left just as Mr. B. was about to go to bed in the house of Br. Hagop where he was staying, they heard a pounding at the door. It proved to be three Turkish zabtiehs who demanded food for themselves and their horses.

"Why should you come to this house?" said Br. Hagop, but he was too frightened to refuse their demands. So he had to bring barley to their horses, make a fire and cook food for them. Then they went on to Mezereh, of course not even leaving a Thank you behind them. This is only an example of the treatment which the Armenians receive. They do not dare to wear good clothes or have a good house, even if they can afford to. We hear that 400 or 500 Armenian families will leave this summer for America if they can obtain teskerehs, which is hardly probable in the case of all. From six to ten Turkish pounds is necessary, judiciously presented to get a pass-port from the government, that is for an Armenian. We can get one for about a dollar. We have heard too that one or two hundred Turks want to go to America, but I hardly believe that the number is so large.

Another one of our girl teachers is engaged, this time the young man is a teacher in the boys' school, and the match is very suitable. The young man, Br. Hovhannes is rather advanced in his ideas, beyond his people. He wanted to see Vartiter and hear from her own lips whether she was willing to marry him. So it was finally arranged that they should meet in Mary's room. The young man came, and then Vartiter was called, though she didn't know why. She wouldn't have come if she had known. She was dreadfully embarrassed and hid most of her face except her eyes in her shawl. Another teacher, an older woman, was present, who had been a sort of go-between, such as always is necessary in such an affair. After some general conversation in which Vartiter took no part, Mary sat down at her desk and tried not to hear what they said. After a great deal of difficulty in persuading Vartiter to sit down in his presence he said, "Zees gesirrés?" which means, "Do you love me?" or perhaps "Do you like me?" for like the French the Armenian has only one word for like and love. Now considering the fact that they had never spoken together, that he had hardly seen her face at all, and she had seen him only at church etc, one would hardly expect her affection to be very strong. What do you suppose she answered? "Haires yev maires keedén," that is, "My father and mother know." That was all he could get out of her. He asked Mary afterward what she thought of her answer, whether she would consider it satisfactory. She answered that Vartiter was a very modest girl, and under the circumstances she should think it was. He wasn't fully satisfied even then, however. Tonight their engagement ceremony takes place.

The storks have come back to the plain. They come at exactly the same time every year, that is, the same day. Irises and crocuses are open on the hills and violets on the plain, but please give me green grass first.

Very lovingly,
Theresa (L. H.)

Harpoot
April 3, 1900

Dear Papa, Mamma and All of you,

Our dear little missionary baby went back to the Good Shepherd last Saturday, so we have all felt sad for the last few days. She had a cold last Friday night and they sent for the Armenian doctor. He left some medicine and directions about her care. The next morning she seemed better and was laughing and crowing in her usual way. About noon she woke from a long nap, choking. Fortunately Dr. and Mrs. Gates were both at home. They worked over her for some time with the doctor who was hastily summoned, but it was of no use. The step between life and death for such a delicate little spirit and body seems nothing. Word came to us just after luncheon that she had gone. Ellsworth had but a few minutes before started on a long walk with the school-boys. In this land it is necessary if possible, to bury the dead on the day of death, so it was decided to have the funeral between five and six o'clock. The little box had to be made and the missionary ladies covered it with soft white cloth. I helped a little.

After we had gathered for the service Ellsworth came in hot and tired. It was a pitiful surprise to him, for like the rest of us he supposed that the baby had gotten over her cold. We would have sent for Ellsworth (Dr. Gates especially wanted him) but we didn't know exactly where he was and it would have been almost impossible to find him. It was a very touching little service. Several of the Armenian teachers and servants were present and all the missionaries. We sang and Mr. Browne offered a short prayer. Then Dr. Barnum in his gentle, tender way said a few words. Six little children of the Barnums, most of them when still babies, died in this land. He referred to that, and mentioned a little incident which I want to tell you. Once he and Mrs. Barnum were travelling to the coast, and they saw a shepherd carrying a lamb while the mother sheep walked behind keeping her eyes anxiously on her little one and on the shepherd. "That is like us," said Mrs. Barnum. "Christ took our lambs so that we would follow him more closely." After this Dr. Barnum prayed and we sang again. Then we walked together to the place on the hillside where the other babies lie. Meggerditch, the Gates' faithful servant carried the little casket. Mr. Knapp prayed here. Then we came back. It seemed strange to think that only a few hours before the baby had seemed bright and well. She was always a delicate child but not a sickly one.

Mr. and Mrs. Gates are wonderfully brave and cheerful. Elizabeth was their one little daughter whom they had prayed for, for years, and they were both wrapped up in her. Sunday evening we had expected, that is, the circle, to have a communion service at the Gates house, when the baby was to be baptized by Dr. Barnum. We had the service, without the baby, and it could not have been a sweeter, more tender service. Tonight Ada and I went up after dinner, to see Mr. and Mrs. Gates. Ellsworth had been in several times because he lives so near. She sent her love to you, Mamma.

In a letter written a few days later to James Barton, Dr. Gates said: "Last Saturday our little girl was taken to her heavenly home in a very sudden manner. She had a cold and bronchial trouble, which the doctor called slight. She woke from sleep gasping for breath and in a few moments her spirit had taken its flight. She was a beautiful child, the light and joy of our home, but the Lord knows best and He will take such care of her as we could not."

Chapter Thirteen: Turks Watch in Amazement as New Buildings Go Up

The death of the Gates' baby daughter saddened the whole Harpoot station for a time. This was the second child Dr. and Mrs. Gates buried in Turkey; they had lost their first-born son at Dr. Gates' first station in Arabic-speaking Mardin to the south of Harpoot. In fact, the death-toll among missionary children continued to be very high. Caleb Gates might have found some consolation in the fact that others had been even worse hit: one missionary family in Van lost three of their children within three weeks during an epidemic of scarlet fever; they had already buried two older children there.[40]

Laura Ellsworth was packing and seeing visitors before she was to leave the Harpoot station to take up her new work as principal of the girls' school at Sivas—and, eventually, to become the British Mr. Anderson's bride. The Barnums—after eleven years of continuous work—had already left for their furlough in Switzerland, where they were met by two of their boys and Mrs. Barnum's sister from the United States. The school year came to an end and teaching gave way to other tasks and more excursions, and "the Garden" became home once again.

During the spring, Theresa and her friends frequently spent their free time visiting their Armenian friends in outlying villages or exploring the countryside with budding geologist Ellsworth:

> Dear Family,
>
> Last Thursday Mary and Ada planned to go to Mezereh to buy some things and make some calls. Just as they were about to start, they asked me if I didn't want to leave my work and come. And I did. The girls were thankful enough for a holiday, and I was too. We took a servant, Avedis, and rode down on to the plain. "Let's do what we want to all day, and not try to get home at any particular time," said somebody. So we were gay and foolish and rode on through the fields (very rocky fields) for an hour or so, just because the sky was blue and the sun was bright and we felt like staying out

40. Caleb Gates, *Not To Me Only*, Princeton: Princeton University Press, 1940, p. 87.

of door. After a while we came near the village of Keserik. "This is where Aghavni (she was my teacher) lives," said Mary. "Let's go to see her," said I. We all wanted to, and rode on toward the village. Just outside we came to a broad stream. Ada said rather fearfully, "My horse always likes to lie down in the water." But we said, "Hold his head up high and whip him if he tries to lie down." So in she rode and in the middle of the stream the old beast prepared to roll. Ada tried to whip him and Avedis joined the fray on his mule and lashed the horse with his stick. He, the horse, went round and round like a top and finally rushed for the shore. Ada's breath and courage were gone. Inasmuch as this stream winds through the main thoroughfare into the village on the side from which we entered, it was necessary to cross it five or six times. Ada didn't dare to cross again on her horse, so Avedis took him and he did have a time of it. The horse backed, and twisted and reared in the water while Avedis beat him with his stick or clasped his neck affectionately as need required. Finally after some funny and trying experiences we reached Aghavni's house. It was far more comfortable than we expected and she looked very sweet and ladylike and seemed delighted to see us. We stayed there over an hour. She and her sister-in-law brought us tea to drink, and later brought in a tray upon which were plates of apples, figs, dates, peanuts, barstegh, and candy. It was after one and we were hungry so we ate a good deal and she insisted upon our carrying away in our pockets, a quantity of the last three dainties mentioned. Then we made a little visit at the girls' school and Mary planned for a meeting with the women a few Sundays hence. Afterward we called upon another school-girl recently married. Here they brought us tahn to drink. I sort of gathered up my grit and gulped it down. It is like buttermilk, only worse. You would have liked to see the storks' nests which we saw, one on the roof of a house, another in a poplar tree. The stork is a dignified bird and seems to command respect wherever he lives, whether in Germany or Turkey.

From Keserik we rode through the fields, and past the soldiers' barracks—horrible places they are, I imagine—to Mezereh. We left our riding-skirts there and went to the market under Avedis's wing. It was the first time I had been in a shop since I left Constantinople, and I must say I haven't missed a great deal. Of course we went to Armenian shops and Avedis went ahead to clear the shop where we were going, of all other customers. Isn't it ridiculous? In Harpoot women never enter the shops, in Mezereh only a few foreign women do. We went to only two shops. At one I bought a few little notions for birthday gifts to the children etc. At the other we bought some cloth. How we were stared at in the market-place! I become very tired of always being strange and foreign and always being stared at.

After making our purchases we went back to the [German] orphanage and found Mrs. Ehrmann at home. After a pleasant call with her and a cup of coffee, we went to the Protestant pastor's house to see his oldest daughter, Mariam, who has been one of our teachers, but left us a month or more ago because she was sick. She really was very ill, and though we were cheerful and hopeful, we couldn't seem to brighten her up. To complete our drinks for the day, they brought us more Turkish coffee. We reached home about six o'clock after a happy restful day. I really think that our calls did good, too.

Harpoot
April 11, 1900

Dear Harry,

I can't find my letter-record just now, but it must be very nearly your turn for a letter.

The spring comes earlier here than at home. We have some branches of almond blossoms in the room and some little daisies.

Last Saturday Ellsworth wanted to take a geological ride, so Laura and I went with him. First we had to pass through the Koordish quarters of the city where we rarely go. It is horribly dirty there, but that is true of the whole city. You ride through narrow streets where your feet almost hit the walls and you on your horse tower up above the tops of the low door-ways. As always we were the objects of much curiosity, and Ellsworth who understands a little Turkish caught fragments of the usual conversation as to whether we were men or women. Laura was the puzzle this time, she is so tall and rides astride. We both wore caps like men (to their eyes) and our hair was out of sight. Then men wear skirts here, you know. They were in difficulty because we seemed to be of three kinds.

We rode to the beautiful rocky valley which I have written of twice before. It is about an hour and a half from here. It is so wild and high that it reminds me of the descriptions of the haunt of the Doones in Lorna Doone. Here we began to eat our luncheon by the brook, finishing it on our horses about two hours later. We followed this brook by the path near it for nearly two hours, down its steep, winding valley, hoping to reach the river Euphrates, but we had to turn just before reaching the river because our time gave out. At one place we had to ride back and forth through the brook, then a broad stream, for some distance. At another we exclaimed over the fragrance of violets and I held E's horse while he dismounted and picked some. They were like our green-house violets, that is like those called Russian violets; a deep reddish purple and very fragrant. In other places it was very barren and desolate. We went near to a village and a little lamb which had strayed from its owner followed us for some distance. The point at which we turned was about 1000 feet lower than the highest point we reached, so we found almond trees which had hardly thought of opening in Harpoot, in full blossom and we found many other flowers in bloom. In the high rocky places the blue grape hyacinth was growing in great quantities. The little wild Ladies' delight was open, too.

Tonight the teachers of the girls (Armenians) invited the Barnum family, Aunt Hattie, Mary, Laura, Ada and me to take dinner with them at the school, a dinner which they planned, cooked and paid for. It was delicious. They roast meat beautifully here. The great difficulty with the native way of eating out of one common dish is (for me, at least) that I never can tell how much I have eaten, so I always eat too much. After dinner we played "tea-kettle" and some other games. The girls are sometimes like children in their noise and hilarity, but they are very quick at understanding our games and enjoy them immensely. We played the games sometimes in English, sometimes in Armenian. After that we sang some hymns, and Dr. Barnum told something about the condition of women 40 years ago in this country, when he first came. Then Emma read the Bible and he prayed.

Harpoot
May 19, 1900

Dear Ruthie,

Is it your turn or not? I find in these days that I have to begin my letters before Sunday or I have nothing ready to send for the Tuesday night mail. Last Thursday a wonderfully long letter from Cornelia came, which was a regular feast. When she does write a letter she quite outdoes herself. Also there was a lovely birthday letter from Papa and one from him for Ellsworth too, enclosing Dr. Lehrmann's letter.

What are you going to do next fall, my big little sister? I am very anxious to know. And will Harry go to Yale in the autumn? We were delighted to hear that Yale had been decided upon. None of you ever commented upon Ada's picture? Were you disappointed in it? I wish you would say what you thought of it. I don't know many girls of her kind. She didn't go to school very long, only till she was fifteen, but yet she is very intelligent and refined. She hasn't the all-around information which most Amcrican girls get. I think the horizon of the middle-class English girl is narrower than that of our girls. Ada has travelled in Switzerland and Scotland and spent a year in New Foundland. I use middle class, referring to money.

Ada hasn't returned from Diarbekir yet. We got her room all ready four days ago, but last Thursday a little note came, saying that she was sick but would try to start Friday (yesterday) and spend Sunday on the road somewhere, i.e. at a khan—a delightful resort for things that bite. It is much warmer at Diarbekir than here. They say that in summer the lead waterpipes on the houses melt. You can believe or not, as you please.

This week we have spent two evenings in discussing the location of next year's teachers, their salaries, the amount of aid to be given to certain scholars. It was a discussion in which the touring missionaries, representing the outside schools, and all the American teachers were concerned. We have lost four teachers from our school this year. Two were married. One is going to her husband in America. The fourth is sick. The official papers authorizing us to build are still not forthcoming. They will come through our local government. Dr. Gates has men at work on the foundations, but no wall can be begun. Our schools are still closed on account of scarlet fever, though there seem to be few cases, at least, the disease is not spreading.

I think that Mr. Browne and Aunt Caro will give up their tour to Kurdistan. At least, put it off till fall. You know our work there is among Armenians who speak Kurdish. We have no work among the real Kurds. Their religion is a form of Mohammedanism. . . .

I wish you could see our plants. We have two big ivy geraniums. One has six or seven large clusters of double pink flowers and quantities of buds. Then there are two or three other geraniums in blossom. Our carnations are full of buds. Two cactus buds will open soon. There are three blossoming petunias—one white, one a sort of pinkish lavender, the other purple. We have two big ivy plants, some mignonette, a wall-flower, a great many little chrysanthemums etc. I gave them a washing this morning as I usually do on Saturday. It doesn't take a great deal of time now that I can put them out of doors. I carry them from the parlor to the front door. There my little Vartuhi takes them and sets them on the ground. Then I sprinkle them with my watering pot.. I just soak them and they love it. It helps to keep off plant lice. If there are many of those on a plant, Ada and I mix up some soap suds and pour it over the plant. Then after an hour or two we sprinkle it thoroughly with clean water. Last winter we didn't wash our plants and they didn't do half so well. Some plant-lice may live through this process, but they're not happy after it. It takes away their courage.

Harpoot
July 9, 1900

Dear Cornelia,

I almost began this letter to Papa but I remembered in time that he would probably be away on his vacation when this reaches America, and I want this letter to be read in Milton first. Perhaps you are away yourself. I surely hope you will be sometime in the summer.

My life has been rather uneventful and stupid for the last few days. I have been into the city almost every day. Mary and I, with the help of three girls have been going over all the books of the Loan Library, numbering them and labelling them again, sorting out those which the girls can mend, those to be rebound, to be thrown away etc. They are rather a dirty lot of books and as there are quantities of them, the task has been long and tiresome. I usually walk into the city and ride out at night. I pay a boy 20 paras (about 2 1/4 cents) to come out and take my horse back for me. E. and I usually walk in together and eat our luncheon together. Otherwise we work apart. I wish you could see us working in the girls' kindergarten—a most bare and dismal looking room, but cool in summer. I sit on a foot-stool surrounded by piles of books and wielding a fountain-pen. Mary sits by the table. Near by are two girls Yéva and Rakel squatting on the floor, as only Orientals can, and dipping their fingers recklessly into a big pan of paste. They don't work as daintily and nicely as American girls would, but they keep at it steadily, whispering together in low tones. They are both pretty girls, even from our American standpoint, and Rakel is a straight, vivacious little person whom you can't help liking. We expect to finish this work tomorrow. Then we have to plan for next year, make out the program and prepare for own special lessons. Tomorrow afternoon I expect to go with Aunt Caro to call on some Turkish women.

A few days ago some Turkish women called here on Aunt Caro. (She, Emma and Mrs. Barnum are the only ladies who speak Turkish in our circle). They wanted to see the "teachers", so Ada and I went in. I can only say about three sentences in Turkish, "Thank you," "I don't understand Turkish," and "Give me some hot water," so I make up for the deficiency by smiling profusely. Turkish women usually have shrill, high voices and rather sharp, inquisitive dissatisfied faces. Two of these women who lived in gardens near us were rather attractive. Two others, strangers—one from Beirut and one from Egypt—were more like the type I have described. They tried to dress like Europeans, which usually results in an ugly costume. Turkish women usually cut their hair in front so that it hangs down in front of and over their ears in locks five or six inches long. These women asked the usual questions—whether we were married, why we weren't married, etc.

The other day E. and I had a pleasant little experience. We started for the city on our horses intending to go by a roundabout way for the sake of the ride. We went down into a valley where there was no path and after riding along the edges of fields and vineyards and under trees and bushes where my thoughts constantly turned to Absalom, we came out into the dry rocky bed of a stream. Then we tried to climb the other side of the valley, but it was very steep—in fact almost impossible and I finally jumped off my horse and began to lead him. Just at this point a man began to shout to us from the other side of the valley and wave wildly. He prudently was trying to show us another path. He gradually crossed over and came to us,. E. talked with him a little, for he knows some Turkish, and then said, "Let's go with this man. He wants to help us." He took my horse's rein—an unusual courtesy for a Turk to show a woman—and following his lead we went back to the garden we had come through on the other side. This man had been working there in the field and had seen us. He insisted on tying our horses under some trees and leading us to a tiny pond, such as is found in every garden. Then he ran off and soon reappeared with a big "doshag", or mattress for us to sit on. Then he brought a box of tobacco and some papers for us to make cigarettes and smoke. Most Turkish women smoke as well as the men. Of course we refused pleasantly and then he hurried off and brought us green apples and plums, ever so many and ever so green. After that he mentioned coffee and tea inquiringly, but we shook our heads. Then he suggested water and hating to refuse so much, we accepted and away he went to be gone some minutes. He finally returned carrying a tray, which he put before us, spreading a big towel over our laps and saying "A la Franc" with much satisfaction. On the tray were bread, cheese and a bowl of tahn (the sourest of sour milk). So we had to eat, tho' it was about as poor food as I have tasted in Turkey. He ran to the garden and brought us parsley and young onions which he washed in the pond. At the end, he poured water over our hands very politely and saw us on our way. He accepted a little "token of gratitude" from E. tho' I don't think he offered us his hospitality for that purpose. He was evidently rather a poor man.

I suppose Dr. Barton has told you of the consul on his way to Harpoot. From his record in science, in travel etc he seems to be rather a remarkable man and he seems to be genuinely interested in missions too. We hope for a great deal from him. This constant haggling of the gov't is wearying Dr. Gates very much. Mr. Browne hasn't yet returned from Sivas. This morning at about 5.30 Ellsworth started off for a ten day's trip among the Taurus Mts. He took one man with him. Possibly one of our preachers will join him. He took very little baggage, expecting to eat and sleep among the Koords.

Last night just at dusk, i.e. about eight o'clock E. and I heard a great deal of bubbling laughter and squealing from the Gates' house. The boys were just going to bed, and when they were all undressed, they skipped out onto their own little private back porch and Mr. and Mrs. G. each took a watering-pot and thoroughly watered the boys.

An owl is calling away as he does every night from the poplars close to the house and that is a sign of bed-time. The people here say that the owl says "Eésahäk" or Isaac and it does sound like that.
With limitless love to you all,
Theresa (L. Huntington)
I do think my duck dress and the woolen shirt-waist are lovely.

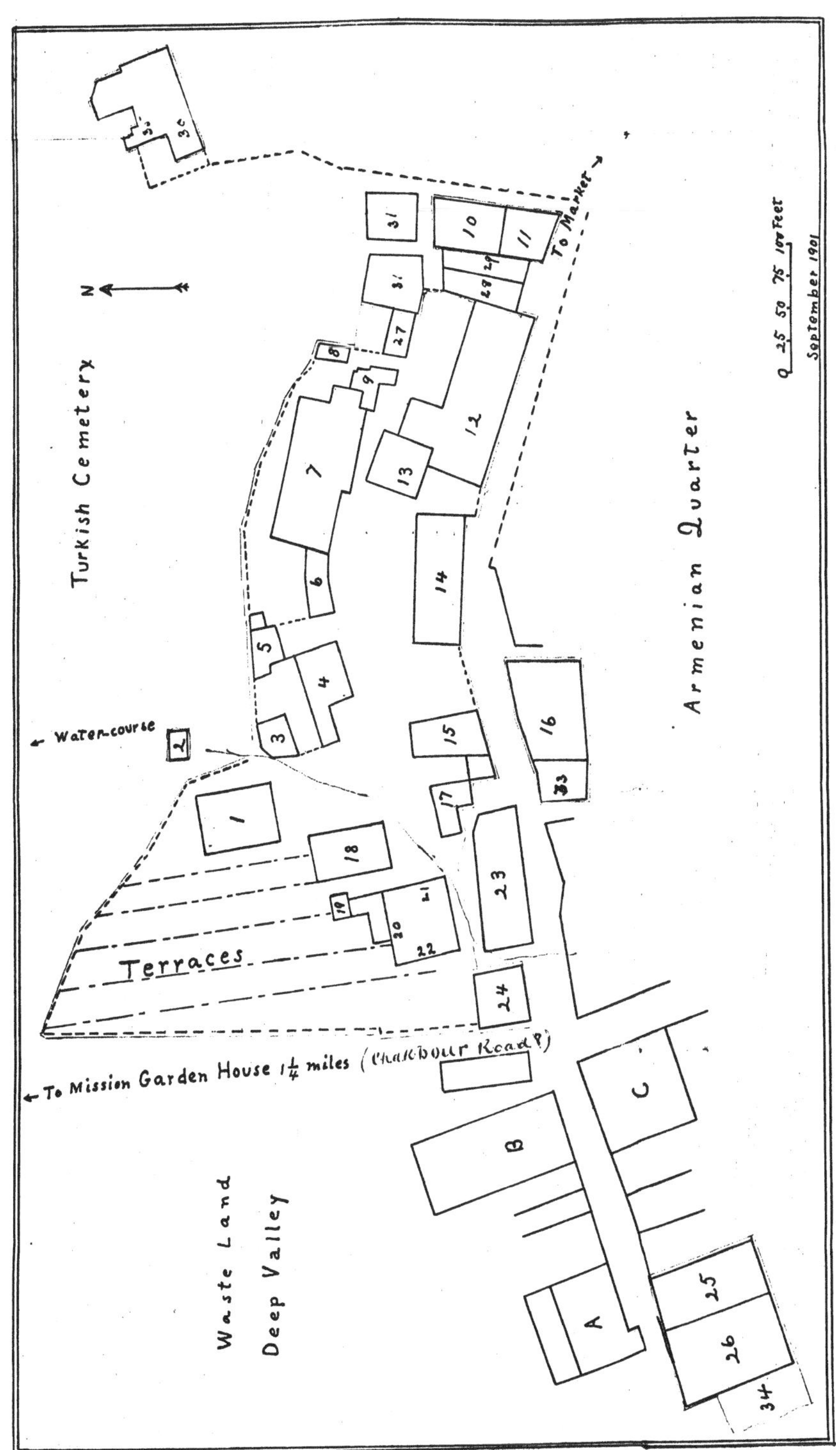
Turkish Cemetery
N
To Market
0 25 50 75 100 Feet
September 1901
Armenian Quarter
Water-course
Terraces
To Mission Garden House 1¼ miles (Charbour Road?)
Waste Land
Deep Valley

EXHIBIT OF PROPERTY OF A.B.C.F.M. AND EUPHRATES COLLEGE

at Harpoot, Turkey, to accompany Chart.

No.			Valuation
No 1.	Euphrates College,	Male Dept. 50'x 60'. Title C.H.Wheeler, Lot 225' square, Bldg. 3 stories. 1887. Value Land 50 Bldg. 1200.	£1250.
2	"	Reservoir included in above title	25.
3.	"	Wood shed " " " "	10.
4.	"	President's House 45'x 60', 2 stories & Basement, Title C.H.Wheeler, Built on land in No32. Estimated.	500
5.	"	Reservoir & Laundry included in No 4.	50
6.	"	Old Girls' High School, 75'x 25', 1 story. Land in Title Deed No 32. Bldg. School.	225.
7.	"	Girls' College & High school, 100'x 50' 3 stories Basement & Attic. Title to site in No.32	1500
8.	"	Gate Keeper's Lodge, 25'x15' 2 stories. Title to site in No.32	40.
9.	"	Bath for Girls. Title to site in No.32.	50.
10.	"	Boys' Orphanage, 50'x 45'. Title Miss Huntington 3 stories. The house & 2 lots were bought for.	280.
11.	"	Bakery & Bath for Boys 45'x 40'. Title Miss Huntington. Bakery & Bath cost	250.
12.	"	Girls" Grammar & Primary Schools, 100'x 50' Ell 50'x 50' Built on tract No.32, 2 stories	900.
13.	"	Teacher's Rooms, 25'x 25', 2 stories & Basement. Built on tract No 32, ~~2 stories~~. Bldg School.	200.
14.	A.B.C.F.M.	Residence Browne, Ladies, Knapp. 100'x 45'. 2 stories Basement & Attic. Built on Tract No.32. Houses in name of Dr-Ussher, Mr.Browne, Miss Bush	1000.
15	"	Residence H.N.Barnum, 60'x 30'. 2 stories. Deed for this and adjoining Rooms (No 17) H.N.Barnum. Present value.	150.
16.	"	Stable, 90'x 50'. On land formerly occupied by Dr.Wheeler's house & Theol.Sem'y. Deeds in names of Dr.Wheeler and Mr.Browne, cost unknown, buildings burned. Plan to build College assembly Hall on roof. Stable.	500.
			£ 6930

Previous page, "Property of A.B.C.F.M. and Euphrates College at Harpoot, Turkey," September 1901. *Above and following two pages,* "Exhibit of property of A.B.C.F.M. and Euphrates College at Harpoot, Turkey, to accompany Chart."

2

			Valuation
		Brought forward	£ 6930
17.	College	Rooms for students, one occupied by guard 45' x 15' Included in deed 15. Present worth	40
18.	"	Boys' High School, 60'x30'. 2 stories. Cost unknown. Built on tract No. 32. Worth	500
19.	"	W.C. " " " " "	
20.	"	Former Dormitory, burned	
21	"	" Chapel	
22.	"	" Kindergarten, pulled down to make way for New Dormitory. New Dormitory is built on site of these three* 60'x 60'. Built on No 32.3 stories & Basement. Cost will be about	800
23.	Protestant Community house, occupied 1896 - 1901 by Girls : now by Orphanage		—
24.	College	Schmavonian House. Transfer not complete.	75
25.	"	One lot Mr Shushanian 50'x90' Quit claim to C.F.Gates Aug 1 1316. Title Deed no.25 enclosed	50
26.	A.B.C.F.M.	One lot Prof. Melcon 60'x 100' Temporary Deed No 26. C.F.Gates - enclosed -	10 cost
27.	College	House & lot, Title Miss Emma Barnum. To be pulled down. Deed 27 enclosed (Present worth 80 £)	180 cost
28 & 29	Two houses the purchase of which is desirable.		—
30 & 35	Orphanage.	Reverts to College. Deed Artin Adanli Oglou. Quit Claim to Miss Seymour and Miss Ellsworth. Aug 9th 1315. June 21, 1315	380 "
		Title to 35 in name of Stepan Harpootlian's wife. Quit Claim to Kevork Habibian & C.F. Gates. July 26 1316	45 "
31 & 31	Two houses the purchase of which is desirable		—
32	A.B.C.F.M.	The whole tract on which the Mission is for the most part built, Cost unknown. Area about 4 14/100 Acres. Bought about 40 years ago. Boundaries, North, House 27 & Street (south	
			£ 9010

3.

		Valuation
	Brought forward	£9010
	south, street, West, Chakhpoor Street: East, private way. Present deed is a copy of one given about 20 yrs ago, and is in the name of Dr. Barnum. Estimated value	500 -
33. A.B.C.F.M.	Lot & Ruined House, purchased of Arakel Demirjian. Quit claim to C.F.Gates July 26, 1316. 30'x 50'	44 -
College	Two houses have been built upon it. One is rented, one is occupied by hostler & shop.	200.
34. "	A lot of irregular shape purchased to get rid of a troublesome neighbor. Quit claim to C.F.Gates. Dec.14.1316 (AH)	3. -
35 "	Part of orphanage. See No.30	— -
A.B.C.F.M.	2 Gardens & trees. Deeds in names of Dr. Barton & Dr. Barnum. 16 22/100 Acres.	102.50 -
"	3 Houses built on the same. 115'x 35'	350
	1 Garden across the road from the above. Quit claim. July 3, 1315. A.H.	37.
	Water Garden. 2 lots. 2 Quit Claim Deeds Mch 19, 1900. Oct. 2, 1891. Area 20 37/100 Acres.	75.
		£t10,321.50

HARPOOT
Aug. 31, 1901

C.F.Gates.

Top, Euphrates College buildings at Harpoot. *Left,* The Rev. Orson Allen. *Right,* The Rev. and Mrs. Crosby Wheeler.

Top, Dr. Herman Barnum and Mrs. Barnum. *Below, left,* Emma Barnum Riggs. *Right,* Emily Wheeler.

Harpoot
July 12, 1900

Dear Mamma,

I have been spending rather a lazy day at the garden today. Now dinner is over and I feel as if I mustn't let the day pass without accomplishing something, so I begin this letter. This new paper I have just bought from Mrs. Browne because I was very short of stationery. I don't like the lines on it. Mary and I are sitting on the ivan—the broad semi-piazza of which I have written. It is a pretty place. The ledge running the length of it and serving as a railing is covered with plants. There are various chairs standing about, a jar of drinking water, a watering-pot, and two hammocks make things look comfortable and luxurious. I can just imagine how Papa would delight in the view, of rolling hills and mountains. The sparrows are just flying in to perch for the night on the beams overhead and Herbert's white doves come and alight near by. It has been a very hot day. The hard thing to me about the climate here especially in summer is the monotony, the inevitableness of it. When it grows hot, it stays hot and dry, day after day and week after week. It is perfect weather, but one longs for some that is imperfect. We do have fresh breezes almost every evening, but the temperature at night varies very little from that by day.

Today I have put up some curtains in E.'s room, cut down our plants mercilessly, helped Mrs. Browne get luncheon chiefly by toasting bread, read some to her some old letters from home, sewed a little, studied a little Armenian, read in the Levant Heralds (Con'ple) about China, and played house with the children for an hour or more, being Harold's wife. Tuesday I called upon some Turkish women with Aunt Caro (Did I write that before?) and yesterday made two other Turkish calls with her. Tuesday we didn't find the people whom we wished to see at home, and as we stood in the street a moment, debating what to do, some Turkish women called to us from a window to come and see them. As Pompish Elmas, an Armenian woman who was with us, knew them we went in. We found two rather elderly women, the wives of the same man. They seemed to have very kindly relations with each other and we heard afterward that they live in unusual peace and love, considering the circumstances. They served us with sherbet (a sort of fruit drink-very sweet) and coffee in immediate succession. Aunt Caro read to them from the Bible. Probably it was the first time they had ever heard it. They listened politely and attentively. Their husband is of the better upper class. I forgot to say that they offered us cigarettes first, as they always do at a Turkish house. Our first call the next day was upon a young unmarried woman who keeps house for her father. They live in a large house but such a house! So wild and untidy! The father is at the head of a Turkish school. Of course we didn't see him. The daughter talked very fast and in a high tone, but it was interesting to watch her, she was so vivacious, her eyes so expressive and her gestures made with such abandon. She was barefooted, tho' she slipped on her shoes at the door when she stepped outside the living-rooms. Her dress was dirty and not half fastened together. The bare feet and unbuttoned dress are characteristic of the Turkish women, even of the highest class.

We made our third call upon the wife of one of the high city officials and her mother. The former was sick once at Arabkir and her husband begged Dr. Hubbard of the Red Cross to come and see her, Aunt Caro went too, visited the woman several times and won her strong affection. Our zabtieh accompanied us on this call. We were taken to the women's part of the house. Here we found some eight or nine women sitting. Most of them didn't show us the courtesy which Armenian women would, not even rising, but the mistress of the house and her mother both kissed Aunt Caro on the cheek and were very cordial. The women were of all sorts. There was an old toothless woman in coarse village clothing and with a voice as deep as a man's. She smoked her cigarette with the rest. Her husband has three other wives. She was a pitiful object to me. Then there was a very pretty young girl with teeth and hands and eyes too, that any American beauty might envy. She was playing with a doll of a baby. I found that she was the mother of the child, and was eighteen years old. She looked younger. We were offered cigarettes and later sherbet and coffee. The Turkish lady herself honored us by waiting upon us. She was the most refined-looking Turkish woman I have seen. Her trailing silk dress was a broad white and purple stripe and her delicate little shawl was of silk. She wore a dark handkerchief upon her head and many rings on her hands, and bracelets—four or five—on each wrist. The mother was barefooted and wore a common cotton dress. She or the mother asked Aunt Caro to read the Bible. They had heard her read it before. Then the Turkish lady came up close so that Aunt C. might "read over her." She felt as if there were a sort of charm in the reading. She showed us a beautiful copy of the Koran, but I hardly believe she has ever read a word of it, if she is able to read at all. The other women looked on with a mixture of indifference and curiosity.

Later a tray was brought in upon which were apricots, cherries, apples and cucumbers. The latter the people eat like a fruit, rubbing a little salt upon them. When cold they are delicious so. When we went, after a long visit, the old mother kissed me too.

I shall probably not go to Egin and Arabkir after all. Ellworth I look for tomorrow. One of our pastors went with him. Mr. Browne came home last Saturday, tired out. He had had a hard attack of malaria. It was so very hot that he travelled chiefly at night. The day he reached home he set out at one a.m. and reached Harpoot just twelve hours later. We have had letters this week about the Doctor's wedding. Very soon after it the bride became so sick that they feared she might not live, but she is better now.

Love to each dear one,

Theresa (L. Huntington)

I am enjoying my blue gingham with the white yoke. All the missionaries like it and say so.

July 23, 1900

Dear Harry,

The city government is very much against us just now—all because Dr. Gates wouldn't give the $500 they asked for their new government building. He was willing to give less, but they would take all or nothing. The kayimakam is hostile, but there is another official who is quite rabid. He declares that he will make us pay the money, that he will hinder us all he can and close our schools if possible. He threatens to send a crier through the streets to announce that any man who works on any building for us will be fined and imprisoned. This is only a threat, however. Last Wednesday the city gov't put a stop to some repairs which were being made on the inside of an orphanage and stopped the work on our water-course. As a pretext for the latter interference they said that we were drawing off some of the water from the city water-course, which was absurd. Yesterday, tho' it was Sunday, the kayimakam and another official came to call upon Dr. Gates. I believe it was intended to be rather a conciliatory visit. They saw the hammocks and the kayimakam asked Dr. Gates to give him one. This is not the first time that the government has been hostile to the mission-

> aries. More than once the latter have expected that the schools would be closed. Last Thursday one of our teachers, Mariam Khachadoorian, died, after a sickness of five or six months. She was the daughter of the Protestant pastor in Mezereh. Mariam was a sweet girl and a great help to me in my C.E. committee work. The funeral was long-drawn out and hardly in good taste according to our ideas, but funerals and weddings here always are in bad taste.

Here is Theresa's description of one wedding she attended. She is writing to Miss Loud, the Corresponding Secretary of the Woman's Board of Missionas in Boston:

> Harpoot, August 6, 1900
>
> Dear Miss Loud,
>
> Yesterday I went to the wedding of one of the teachers of the boy's school. They sent no messenger for us as they often do to announce that the wedding-feast was prepared, so we started out for the Protestant chapel with no escort. At the door we met the groom accompanied by his men friends. They had just come from the bride's house, whence they had brought her. There is something pathetically amusing to me in an Armenian wedding. This one had more European features than usual. The chapel had been decorated with greens and a few apples and flowers for color. The guests all sat on the floor, the men separated from the women by a railing. During the ceremony there was a constant commotion in the rear of the church; children were running in and out, babes were crying at intervals and one was evidently being chastized outside the door.
>
> The groom entered first with the godfather and then came the young bride supported by the god-mother and another woman. She was entirely enveloped in a crimson silk sheet, and over her face was a thick, black veil. The two sat down in the front on the Armenian pastor. A hymn was sung, prayers offered, then another hymn was sung, the last part of the last chapter of Proverbs read, and then followed a long discourse on "a virtuous woman." Finally the minister asked the pair to rise and joined their right hands—a strange sensation to them, for they were utter strangers to one another, their parents having made the match, as usual. Then the ceremony was concluded and we walked in a troop to the bridegroom's house, the men ahead and the women following.

At the door the father and mother of the groom met us, the mother in a work-a-day dress and apron, for it was not her part to go to church but to prepare for the guests at home. The old parents joined hands, and the son and his bride passed in turn underneath. This was to show their obedience to the heads of the household. The wedding guests then came trooping in, the men passing into one room and the women into another. The poor, warm, damp bride was unwrapped from the folds of silk, her head covered with a light veil, and she stood by the wall, with downcast eyes, speaking only in a whisper, as is the wont of modest Armenian brides. Later she came and kissed our hands, and we begged the godmother to let her sit. After this we were offered a fruit drink and four or five kinds of fruit. Then the bride's dresses were exhibited. This wedding had so many European features that it could hardly be called a native wedding. There is little that is solemn and sacred about an Armenian wedding. The people are changing rapidly in externals. Indeed they are only too willing to adopt our dress and the outer things of western lands, but the spirit changes more slowly. They are no more ready to hear and receive the truth that is in Christ than are Americans.

We expect the new consul, Prof. Norton in September or the first of October. How our hearts will leap to see an American flag floating! Of course we put out little ones on Fourth of July, but they are nothing compared with one on the top of a consulate. You hear the news from China a good many days before we do. For example last week our mail came on Aug. 2. Our last copy of the Mail from London was dated July 18. Our latest news in the Herald from Con'ple was dated July 23 or 24. This paper is not a very satisfactory one, but I do enjoy the English newspapers which we have—the tri-weekly Mail and the weekly Spectator. They are up to date, not at all sensational and look at the world as a whole in a broad, interesting way.

In early August that summer, Dr. Gates received a telegram from Secretary Griscom which promised to end his long fight for the permission to rebuild. The annual report states:

For a week, [Dr. Gates] went back and forth to Mezereh trying to find where the "instructions" had lodged, but in vain. All denied having received any. But on August 15 he was informed that he

> had permission "to rebuild all of the American school that was burned down on the old site without enlargement."[41]

On Saturday, August 18, there was put into Dr. Gates's hands properly signed and sealed a document which he himself dictated, giving him permission to build all that he had asked for, except one building which was not destroyed, but which he had asked permission to reconstruct. This was a full and complete authorization to erect five new buildings of ample dimensions and also to raise the Theological Seminary buildings to a height of three stories where it was not expected they would grant for more than one.

Thus from December 15, 1899, when Mr. Strauss wired that permission had been given, until August 15, when it was actually received—just eight months—the college administration was in one continuous state of negotiation, uncertainty and anxious waiting. Dr. Gates showed wonderful skill and patience by the way he treated with the officials at Harpoot and kept himself in touch with the Legation at Constantinople. Had he been willing to pay a bribe he might have closed negotiations with the governor earlier, but he declared to them that the question was one of pure right and not of favor.

> He received the permit to build on Saturday the 18th of August, 1900, and on Monday, the 20th, the work began in force. With the money appropriated by the Board a year ago, stone had been collected, doors, windows and floors prepared so that everything was ready for rapid work. The Turks watched the construction in utter amazement, affirming most openly that never did a building go up with such rapidity and precision, and declaring that it was not the work of man, but of Allah. In just ten weeks from the laying of the foundation, the main college building of the female department, two stories high on one side and four upon the other, was all roofed in. Another building of such size hardly exists in that part of the country, and under ordinary circumstances it would require from one to two years to erect, if done by the Turks.[42]

There remained the question of the indemnity, which Dr. Gates had no intention of letting the government forget. He had support in high places; President McKinley's Secretary of State John Hay declared that "the United States Government will insist upon the payment of this indemnity as a protection for American citizens in Turkey and as a just debt."[43] But for the mo-

---

41. Annual Report of Euphrates College, 1900. ABC 16.9.9.
42. ABC 16.9.15.
43. *Missionary Herald*, 1900, p. 64.

ment he was pleased: instead of the eight buildings destroyed, they now had ten new ones. Much later, reflecting on those years, Dr. Gates wrote:

> Looking back upon those years of strenuous labor, with the great expenditure of money for feeding the people, reconstructing their homes and their industries, and rebuilding the College, it may seem like labor lost. The World War and the deportations [of the Armenians] destroyed what had been achieved at such cost. But we could not foresee the future. Hundreds of thousands of men, women, and children were left helpless in imminent danger of perishing from starvation... Some day, perhaps, the sufferings of refugees driven from their homes will teach the nations that a world dominated by selfishness is a bad world. The cry of the Old Testament prophet seems to ring in our ears today—Lord, how long?[44]

44. Gates, pp.152-153.

Chapter Fourteen: Theresa Swims in a Pink Ruffled Nightdress, and Receives a Marriage Proposal

In mid-August, Ellsworth invited Theresa, Ada, and Mary to accompany him on an excursion to Lake Gyüljük at the foot of Hazar Baba, the highest mountain in the Taurus range. The excursion was in part prompted by Ellsworth's wish to map the area. It resulted in delightful letters from Theresa to her Milton family. They were written by the light of a swaying lantern in a tent buffeted by high winds on the slopes of the Hazar Baba, the region's highest mountain. Theresa tells her family about the astonishment of the local people at her great rowing skills. How could they have known that this missionary lady was a former member of the Wellesley crew?

Theresa's younger brother George makes an appearance in these letters. George, three years Theresa's junior, had just graduated from Williams College and was on his way to visit Theresa and Ellsworth in Harpoot. George was to spend a major part of his life in Turkey: after a short stay in Harpoot he took a job as tutor at Robert College in Constantinople, the first American institution of higher learning in a foreign country. The college had opened in 1863, three years earlier than the American University of Beirut, and was founded with a missionary impetus but was independent of the American Board. George remained at Robert College until 1904. A year before Theresa herself returned to Milton, George left Turkey for graduate school at Hartford Theological Seminary and was ordained a Congregational minister in 1907.

Harpoot
Aug. 6, 1900

Dear Mamma,

What do you think we are going to do tomorrow? Mary, Ada, Ellsworth and I are going camping for a week to Lake Güljük. As long as we stay here we do more or less work, and the children do make a great deal of noise, so we are going to run away from it all for a while. I can tell you about it better when we have been than beforehand. We three girls will sleep in a tent and Ellsworth and the men outside. You know there is no dew in the summer. I am going to wear my very oldest clothes, and so are the others. We shall be rather a tough-looking crowd. We are not to do any work except write letters. Ada and I have quietly slipped in an Armenian Bible to read when we are tired of recreation. It seems rather luxurious to take a zabtieh, a cook and a guide, but we are obliged to take the first and we don't pay any of them much. They receive as much as they are really worth.

Lake Gyüljük
Aug. 10, 1900

Dear Cornelia,

Here we are camping out as we planned. We have decided to stay two days longer than we expected to when we came, that is, ten days in all, including the two days of travelling. That means that we must send our letters for the American mail to Harpoot early tomorrow morning by Shaban the zabtieh instead of taking them ourselves three days later as we had expected. That is very confused to you, I am sure, but it is an attempt at an explanation of my short letter this week and a promise of a long one next week telling in detail of what we have done.

It is now about eight o'clock in the evening and a high wind is blowing. We three girls are sitting in the tent, two of us on the floor and all writing by the light of a lantern which stands on a folding stool in the middle. Ellsworth is outside, pounding in tent-pins and tightening the ropes. The two zabtiehs and Boghos the cook are sitting under the shelter of a large rock not far off, laughing and talking. The horses are tied to their stakes close by the men.

I must tell our doings in mere outline. We came three days ago, i.e. we have been here three days. The lake is beautiful, a great blue sheet of water in the middle of the mountains. We are up on a hillside a little distance above the lake. There were pleasanter spots down on the shore under the trees, but we didn't want to run any risks of taking malaria by living there.

The first day we straightened out our possessions, rested, read and went in bathing. The second day we rowed across the lake in a great clumsy boat. The owners of the boat did a large part of the rowing, but E. and I took our turn. It was a delight to get hold of an oar again, tho' it was such a primitive affair. Of course we bathed. The temperature of the water is just right. It is excellent water for washing clothes, because it contains a great deal of borax. That makes it unfit for drinking.

Today E. and I took Shaban, the zabtieh, and climbed the highest mountain in this region—Hazar Baba. They gave us a delicious luncheon in a Kurdish tent. But more anon.

It is blowing a regular hurricane as it does every night and the sand is flung up constantly into my face. That with the flickering light makes it hard to write. I am astonishingly brown and red—mostly the latter.

E. sleeps out of doors here. I slept under the stars too, one night, but the wind was a little too much for me.

Always most lovingly,
Theresa (L. Huntington)

Lake Gyüljük
August 15, 1900

My precious family,

I promised last week to tell about our vacation here at the lake. It was Ellsworth who proposed it, and I didn't know how delightful and restful a change of place would be till I tried it. This is Mary's first outing for six years. We decided at first to take the Barnum's cook, Boghos, who is of course temporarily out of work; Bedros, a sort of guide, and the nuisance of a zabtieh. When our mission zabtieh went to Mezereh to notify the government of our intended departure to another village they said we must have another zabtieh because of the depredations of a certain Turkish chief somewhere or other, so we unwillingly took two zabtiehs and gave up Bedros. He was very much occupied anyway just at the time we wanted him to go in trying to recover some sheep and goats which this same Turkish chief had stolen. Of course we have to feed all these men as well as pay for their services. It is fortunate that we don't have to pay American prices.

I wish Ellsworth had taken a picture of our procession. Unfortunately for picturesqueness we never could keep together, because the zabtiehs rush ahead always and the cätergis (men with the pack-horses) dawdle behind. There were four of us and "we girls" wore big pieces of white cheese cloth over our hats and hanging down upon our shoulders to keep off the sun. All sorts of people when they travel here in summer throw a big cloth over the head as a shelter from the heat. I carried a parasol of Ada's all the way, too. That sounds funny, but it is a very common sight to see a rich old

Turk in a sort of gray dressing-gown and white turban riding out to his garden on a little ambling donkey, and holding a big umbrella over his head. Our cook rode in just this way on a tiny donkey. When progress was too slow to suit him, he would shut up his umbrella and give the animal a poke with it, and then sail along grandly for some moments. The man who drove the two pack animals had a hard time of it for one of them frisked like a kitten and playfully kicked up behind at most unnecessary times, while the other marched up a steep bank and did other stupid things. We started at about 9.30 A.M. and after a long, hot ride across the dry plain, we reached the foot of the mountain in the middle the afternoon. Here we met Ellsworth who had left us in order to see a man at a village on the plain. Then we ate our luncheon—chiefly fruit brought by villagers. After the climb up the mountain by a narrow, winding path, it began to be cool and breezy and we saw the beautiful blue lake before us.

It took some time to decide on a camping place so we didn't begin to put up the tent till after sunset and we ate by moonlight as we have several times since. I have told you about our sleeping arrangements. As for eating we brought with us cake and cookies, jelly, pickles, cracked wheat, semolina etc. and we buy milk, eggs, fruit, fish and sometimes meat and vegetables from the Koords near by or from the village across the lake. We buy bread there, too. They put up their prices for us fearfully, so we have to deny ourselves some necessary things. Such milk as they brought last night! It was fully one fourth water. When confronted with this by the indignant buyers, the man said that his wife washed out the bucket so that we might have the milk in something clean, and that she must have left a little too much water in the bottom. So even the Koords have something of the old Adam in them. "The woman tempted me," you know.

The first day by the lake we spent in reading and resting. We sat on or rather near a little beach and under some willow trees. There were white gulls flying about or floating on the water. Opposite us on the farther shore of the lake, 2 1/2 miles away is the village of Gyüljeik, snuggled in between the lake and the mountains. On the slopes near it are vineyards and cultivated fields. The people are poor and ignorant, but full of questions for the few strangers who come their way. We have not been into the village at all. That first day, they saw our tent and half a dozen or more men came over in a boat toward evening to see if we wanted to hire their boat. It belongs to six Armenians who earn their living by fishing and working in their fields. They had a passenger, a handsome, straight young Koord who strode about like a lord, in a brilliant yellow costume, with a gun slung on his shoulder. The Armenians are afraid of the Koords, tho' there is no special cause just now. The government really gives them much more trouble. We took a little row that night and engaged the boat for the next day. The oars and the boat itself are very rude and clumsy, and the men row abominably, helter-skelter each for himself. They insist that there must be four men at least to row so with us four, there is a boat-load tho' the boat could easily hold half a dozen more. The four men who have been with us several times interest me very much. It is not their custom to talk to women, but they pry Ellsworth with questions constantly—about America, what he has done, where he has been, what languages he knows etc.

I have said before that this lake is in many ways like the Sea of Galilee. I often think of it and imagine Christ among these villagers. I call one of our fishermen James the Less and another Andrew. Those two might easily have been just like these men before Christ called them. One of our rowers is blind and a look at his face marked deeply with small-pox shows the cause of his blindness. He is the most intelligent of all. I think the man who was cured of his blindness and put out of the synagogue for his consequent loyalty to Christ may have been like this poor fellow. One day as he was pulling away, he asked E. if he could sing. E. answered, "A little, but I'm very sure that you can." That delighted the simple-hearted man, and afterward E. asked him to sing. He said he didn't know any song but he could sing a chant. So he sang an old Gregorian chant, in a minor key, full of quavers and long drawn-out notes. You should have seen his smile when Ada told him that his singing was sweet.

Ellsworth and I sometimes row and steer. The men were much astonished at my rowing. We pay at the rate of four cents each for three hours use of the boat. On this particular Thursday we went to see the ruins of the old vank or monastery which has been almost submerged by this slowly rising lake. There is not much to see but a wall and stones here and there with rude crosses upon them.

That afternoon we sent Shaban around the end of the lake to the village of Gyüljük with Ellsworth's and my horses. His own happened to be there. The next morning we all got up before five, had breakfast and Ellsworth and I crossed the lake by boat. By the way the night before, we reached the tent at perhaps four o'clock and the men when they found that we wanted the boat again early the next morning said "We won't go back tonight. We have our bread with us." So they slept on the ground, by their boat. We met Shaban on the shore and started on our climb up Hazar Baba. It is 7,300 feet high, 3,300 feet above the lake, the highest of the Taurus range near the lake. The path we took was new to Ellsworth who has climbed the mountain before and was rather a bad one. Most of the scant vegetation on the mountain side is dry now, but sometimes a few trees or bushes marked a mountain spring, which poured its cold water in a rushing stream down the slope. Sometimes I thought my horse would be pulled over backward by the saddle and my weight. Sometimes I had to jump off and lead him, or one of the other two led him for me. It took about two hours I think to climb the mountain. At the last we led the horses some distance and finally left them with Shaban and scrambled up the rocks to the summit. It is useless to try to tell about the view. The lake was spread out before us, the Harpoot plain, over a range of mountains beyond. To the south was a jumble of mountains and beyond them the Diarbekir plain, which is the beginning of the long regular slope to the Persian gulf. Ellsworth took some pictures, but they can give no idea of the distances. Indeed only the near mountains can appear in them.

The particular peak which we climbed is a holy place to Turks, Kurds and Armenians alike. They all sacrifice there. We could see the blood on the stones. We asked "Andrew" some particulars about the sacrificing later. He said it was for sickness and that a lamb was usually killed. We asked him if he had ever sacrificed a lamb there and he said he had. The rocks are piled up strangely. Each pilgrim to the spot puts up a "stone of remembrance". We saw some piled up so as to form a cross. Tho' it was a hot day below, there was a strong cold wind on the mountain top. We found flowers there which had ceased to bloom and dried up long before on the plain. On the way down we stopped at some Koordish tents out of curiosity. Ellsworth found some Koords there whom he had visited last year. The tents are a dark brown, woven from goat's hair. They are like those which Paul probably made. Under the open sides stones and brambles are piled to form a wall on three sides of the tent. They brought us rugs to sit on and were very courteous in their fashion. They insisted upon bringing us food, tahn (whey) for Ellsworth and goats' milk for me. It was the best milk I have had in Turkey. Then our old white-bearded host, Ali (Ahlee) brought us butter or rather madzun in a lordly dish and most delicious bread and cheese. It was a royal feast. I don't know whether the sweetness came from the food itself or the long climb. A woman tried to talk to me, but my side of the conversation was limited to Yah or Huh, with varying inflections. She took me to see all the other tents. The descent was by a new and more travelled path and was easier. We came home by the shore of the lake, about ten miles from the foot of the mountain. We saw quantities of storks wading in the marshes, as well as wild ducks and gulls. I was rather tired the next day and just scorched as to my face. We bathed and read and loafed near the tent. On Sunday our program was similar, without the bathing, and we sat where we are sitting at this very moment near the shore under the shadow of some mulberry and willow trees. We go to bed comparatively early here and get up at about six. One can't read much by the light of a lantern, especially in a high wind. I forgot to say that Saturday we sent Shaban to the city for the mail. He brought the papers, and for E. and me two letters from home, one from Mamma—a fine long one, and one from Harry written in Gorham. Thank you both. Shaban started at 2 A.M. He didn't need to go quite so early. Sunday evening we climbed part way up the mountain behind the tent and watched the moon rise from behind the mountains and sang. The moon has been full since we came here. Yesterday we spent the day in rowing, going to the upper end of the lake, where E. took some geological photographs. It was very hot and the water too calm for the greatest pleasure. Our baths at night time are delicious. The borax in the water gives it a most pleasant, smooth feeling.

Today Ellsworth, Ada and I climbed the mountain behind the tent—rather a hard, hot climb. We reached home again by noon. We stopped a good many times to get breath and pull the thorns and "prickers" out of our stockings. I had to tie one of my shoes on with a string. From being in a state of partial collapse it has become a complete wreck since my climb up Hazar Baba. In fact we rival each other as to shoes and hoses. Tomorrow we hope to row again and on the next day return to Harpoot. It has been a delightful rest and work waits for us.

Mamma, do you want to know what I wore in bathing? A pink ruffled nightdress and flannel drawers of Ada's with a brown belt and some old stockings of Agnes Browne's. It is bewitching but it

doesn't rival Mary's costume and then, nobody sees us. I am reading Richard Carvel and Mackay of Uganda. We are reading aloud "Chinese Characteristics" by Arthur Smith.
With unending love,
Theresa (L. Huntington)

Harpoot
Aug. 28, 1900

Dear Papa,

I almost always stay at the garden on Tuesdays to write letters for Wednesday's post, so here I am in my garden-room as usual. We are having deliciously cool weather just now—thermometer 65 or "thar abouts" in the early morning.

And so dear old George is tossing on the Atlantic now or perhaps is on the Continent seeing wonderful new sights. I can't get over the strangeness of his coming to Turkey, too. Often the Armenians ask me whether my father is coming to Harpoot or why he doesn't come. Very few of the people really understand why we come here. That is, they think we come because we get good salaries or because we can have positions of honor here. Their way of living is so poor that even our simple homes seem very beautiful to them. They think we come to Turkey for the same reasons that they go to America. They are constantly telling us that we are rich and if we would, we could help in such and such cases of destitution. It is a great problem how to live cheaply and plainly without degenerating. I wear my everyday clothes to church almost always and even then I sometimes feel too well dressed when I look at the rest of the congregation. For Mama's comfort I will say that I do wear my best clothes, but I do so at our little missionary gatherings and rarely among the Armenians. Our difficulty which comes from the difference in dress is that the people try to copy us. Poor young men, who ought to use any money they may have for their mothers are continually blossoming out, dressed á la Franc, and the girls and women, naturally fond of dress, seeing our clothes, put ruffles and lace on their dresses too. They want to borrow our clothes as patterns. I have lent a jacket for that purpose and Ada a silk-waist. The people with very few exceptions have no pride about asking for money, clothing—anything they need. One of our greatest difficulties is to find work or make work for the poor to do. They are unskilled and careless—wholly untrained. With constant attention and teaching, our washer-women don't wash and iron our clothes well. They don't see any difference worth fussing over between a well-ironed and a poorly-ironed article. It's of no use to change the women. We should simply find others of the same kind. We have tried it.

The scarlet fever still rages in the city, and all over our field. I was told the other day that 600 children had died from the disease in Harpoot since Easter. A few days ago two children died in one night in one of our Protestant families in Mezereh. In another household there three children have just died. Our watchman Avedis has just lost a little son, brother of the Mariam who used to work for me. While the child was sick I went to the door to ask about him, and explained that I could not come in because I might carry the sickness to the children at our garden. Just after he died, I went to the door again, and they said, "He is dead. You can come in now, can't you? He isn't red any longer." We may not be able to open our schools at the usual time. The people have more fear of scarlet fever than small-pox.

Mr. Jones has just come from Diarbekir where he spent the winter and will pitch his tent in our garden for a month or more. We dread having him come, for he is a tremendous talker and quite breaks up the restfulness of the gentlemen's evenings. Last year they used to take turns with him. Our new consul is still in Constantinople waiting for his exequatur (diplomatic permit to open a consulate). The Doctor in his last letter from Van wrote that the English consul there was attacked by Koords, some distance from the city and all his tents and other possessions were taken. There was a real fight in which the consul killed three Koords. They are utterly lawless in the Van and Bitlis region.

I have spent my time this last week in the ordinary vacation way—making calls, doing school work, writing and reading a little. Last Saturday Ellsworth took the three older children for a Geography expedition, and Aunt Caro, Mrs. Knapp, Ada and I tho' not properly in the class were benefitted by the excursion. We started at noon, took our luncheon and a zabtieh and reached home soon after seven. We rode an hour and a half to a beautiful valley about which I have written before. There is little verdure there, but there is a beautiful clear stream fed by springs and it is a wild rocky place. We went into a large cave where the birds gather and nest. The walls were smoky in one part, where the shepherds had built fires.

I just heard Moore call out, "Auntie Knapp, may Winifred go on a expedition with me?" That means probably that they will go on the hill to hunt for lizards, or else catch grasshoppers to feed the praying mantises already in captivity. The children are wild this summer over bugs and small reptiles. Moore and Addison had such a quarrel one morning over the ownership of a certain turtle which they had lost, that both had to be put to bed for the day.

The work on the school goes on rapidly with 30 or 40 workmen, five or six orphan boys are helping. Yesterday Ellsworth and I bought three rugs. One was an old Persian rug, which we got for Aunt Theresa. It is chiefly dull rose color and black with some white in the border. It is rather large. I hope she will like it. We have bought eight rugs now partly for her and part for home. The orphan girls at Egin have been taught rug-making and do very good work. Mr. Knapp, when he came back from Egin about two weeks ago brought two rugs with him to sell. Ellsworth and I expected to take one of them for two pounds, but he was offered five for it in Mezereh so of course we lost it. The man who bought it was just starting for America, so that rug will cost there something between thirty and forty dollars probably.

You asked once about railways in Asiatic Turkey. You will find just what you want in the Con'list for July 26. You must have read it already.

My heart has ached for you over George's going. He will find the new life very interesting.
Theresa (L. Huntington)

Harpoot
Sept. 4, 1900

My dear George,

I suppose you are now somewhere on the continent. I wish I knew exactly where. Mamma wrote a letter about your plans which we received last week. I wish you were to have some companion, but no company is better than poor company and you have doubtless made some pleasant friends on the way.

I am spending the morning at the garden, but this afternoon I shall go to the city for the wedding of one of the teachers in the boys' school. These teachers are marrying off at a fearful rate. There is only one left now in single blessedness—Aram who teaches me Armenian. It is only the hope of going to America, I am sure, which keeps him from "entering the house of bondage" as Dr. Barnum says.

We had some astonishing news from Sivas last week. Laura is engaged to the English consul there, Cap't Anderson. She had known him barely two months. They will be married in two months more, probably the end of October and will go to Constantinople for the ceremony so you will see them there, I suppose. Please call on Laura, if you possibly can. Mrs. Green took a great fancy to her when we were staying at Bebek, and they may possibly visit there. I take that back. I hardly think they would on their wedding trip. Cap't A. is an army officer. He belongs to the Church of England, is very fond of hunting, is tall and ruddy and suitable in age for Laura. He isn't a widower. He may join his regiment, which is now in S. Africa, after a year or two.

The scarlet fever doesn't seem to decrease and we have put off the opening of school for two weeks. We shall make up the time by shortening winter vacations and lengthening the summer term next year. Did I tell you that I heard the other day that 600 children had died of scarlet fever in this city since Easter. It seems to me an exaggeration, but there is no doubt that the number is large. The government sends around an apothecary to the houses where the disease has been and he is supposed to disinfect things by squirting about some carbolic acid; but I don't suppose the acid touches a small part of the infected things. Miss Bush, or possibly it was one of the missionaries was telling me about being caught in a quarantine on a steamer, when there was an epidemic of smallpox. An official came around with his little squirter to disinfect. They, Miss B. and her friend, didn't propose to have their clothes wet with carbolic acid, so when their turn came, they put up their parasols and from their safe shelter, heard the gentle rain of carbolic acid fall above them.

I have had a little malaria again, but it passed away as before with only one chill and that not a very hard one. Mr. Browne and Aunt Hattie haven't gotten off so well. Yesterday I was told that there wasn't a house in the city where there was not someone who had malaria. It isn't our perfect climate that causes it, but the lack of drainage of an oriental city. By the way I wrote a letter to one of you a short time ago in which I inadvertantly wrote occident for orient. I realized it afterwards and in another letter, wishing to speak of the consul's exequatur.

Two, no three days ago the 20th anniversary of the Sultan's accession was celebrated and we had to light up our houses in the city for the occasion. Mr. Jones who is tenting in our garden honored His Majesty with some fire-works.

In speaking of scarlet fever I forgot one interesting thing. Many of the people think that a frog tied to the foot during sleep will prevent the disease from attacking one, so in the night very often companies of men with lanterns can be seen in the places where frogs are found, searching for the creatures and catching them.

The new building is going up rapidly. Will you please send this letter home, because I don't want to write the same thing again.
Most lovingly, your sister,
Theresa (L. Huntington)

Harpoot
Sept. 10, 1900

My beloved Mother,

How different our household is now from the household I left. You think of George now as near to us, but in matter of time he is nearer to America, and it is time which counts. I have a great hunger to see the dear boy. I do wish some of you would have your pictures taken. We're not a great family for pictures. I long to cover my bureau and walls with pictures of my precious people.

I'll begin with the thing which happens to be on my mind, though it isn't a matter of great importance. Still I wish you would *never* speak of it to anyone except our own family. I had an offer of marriage today from an Armenian. This isn't a new experience to missionaries in this country. Of course the proposal was not made to me, but by the young man's father to Mr. Browne. I feel inclined to resent it, and yet from the standpoint of the Armenian family there is nothing strange in it. On the contrary it is an honor. The young man graduated from our college and then studied medicine at Beirut. He is doing well as a physician in Mezereh. I have seen him once or twice from a distance. He is a handsome young fellow. The parents think no Armenian girl from these parts is fit for him. Does it make you indignant? Well, there's no use in feeling insulted. You see it is our pride which is insulted really, because they should consider themselves our equals, and yet we always try to treat the Armenians as equals. The idea of marriage for love's sake is utterly foreign to these people. The fact that I have hardly seen the young man is rather a desirable thing in their eyes.

You can't imagine, though, what it would be like in an Armenian home. The rule of the mother-in-law would be the smallest burden. Well, there's nothing to do but to forget such an unfortunate little occurrence. There's really nothing disagreeable in it for me, because I only have to speak to Mr. Browne about the matter.

It has been definitely settled that school will be opened Sept. 26, two weeks later than the regular date.

Chapter Fifteen: Thanksgiving and Christmas; Aunt Caro's Touring Work, and the New Consul

The fall semester of 1900 opened on an optimistic note: after a near-frantic construction period over the summer, some of the new buildings were ready to be occupied, and a record number of students were clamoring to be accepted. The new College for Women building was, in the words of U.S. Consul Norton, "the largest and most conspicuous building in the city," and Theresa was delighted with its roominess. Norton described it as "a spacious edifice of stone, surmounted by a roof of American steel. It is 5 stories in height, measures 100 x 50 feet, contains 33 rooms, and has been completed in the space of 10 months. This is unparallelled rapidity in this region for stone construction."[45]

It would be a while, however, before Consul Norton was to see this building. Ever since the massacres of 1895, the Americans had been pressing for consular representation in the interior, but had run into considerable resistance from the Ottoman authorities. "How our hearts will leap to see an American flag floating!" Theresa writes. "Of course we put out little ones on Fourth of July, but they are nothing compared with one on the top of a consulate." Finally, matters had proceeded to a point where Thomas H. Norton, a young diplomat with a Doctorate from the University at Heidelberg, arrived in Constantinople to await his permit or *exequatur* which would enable him to officially open the consulate in Harpoot.

In one of his dispatches from Constantinople, Norton warns that everybody's "patience will be tried somewhat before the deep seated dislike of the Sultan of the establishment of any more inland consulates of our government is sufficiently overcome." He proved to be right: it would be several months before he set out for Harpoot—without the exequatur.

The Barnums were expected to return after their furlough in Switzerland; Emma Barnum was still not well enough to work but another female missionary was expected soon: Miriam Platt, who was to become a close friend of

---

45. National Archives; Consular Records; Harpoot 1895-1906.

Theresa's—so close, in fact, that years later, Theresa named her youngest daugher after her.

Mr. Browne and Aunt Caro continued their touring work, spending weeks on end in the saddle. A great deal of their energies seemed to go towards mediating quarrells in the local Armenian churches.

Harpoot
Sept. 26, 1900

Dear Mamma,

This is rather pretty paper, isn't it? Mary gave it to me. I have just written to George and Ruth and haven't time left for the dear three who make the center of the family.

School opened today at noon. I have been giving examinations, and giving out books etc most of the day. Now after correcting the last exam, I am sitting down with Ada to write. Mary is spending the night in the city. She won't come out here much more. Ellsworth has gone to live with the school boys, at least he will sleep in the house with them and eat breakfast and luncheon there. He will keep his rooms at the Gates's and will continue to eat dinner with the Brownes. Mr. Browne says he ought to have a Victoria Cross for going there. It isn't as bad as that sounds but it isn't a very delightful homey place. That is just why Ellsworth went, to make things nicer for the boys and help them in morals and manners. There isn't a woman in the house, and in America we think that a necessity in a household of boys from ten to twenty years old. We just can't find a suitable Armenian woman. I feel a widow indeed without E. Still I shall see him as much as before, except for the two meals. He told me that today they had bread, cheese and watermelon for luncheon. He will have real native food. It is excellent for the teeth, anyway, especially the coarse bread.

The Brownes will probably move to the city in two or three days and I shall go then. Mr. B. and Aunt Caro haven't been able to find a touring servant yet and so are still here. Mr. and Mrs. Gates have just been in at the end of the evening to chat a bit before going to bed and have used up my writing time. They often come in in this way. Dr. G. loves to joke. As he went out he said, "Well, you're a lot of giddy girls." That meant Ada, Mrs. G. and me.

Please, please do forward us some of Harry's and Ruth's and George's letters. No matter if they do say, "I will take the 6.42 train," or "My blue jacket needs to be dyed." We grow hungry for letters from them. Last week came a letter to George from Constantinople, a letter from Papa for both, and your fine long conference letter. There are some very helpful thoughts in it. Thank you, dear little mother, for writing such a beautiful long letter. It makes me feel badly to think of you spending so much time on it.

If you ever want to make me a present in the next few years, I will give you a suggestion of two, but you needn't feel obliged to send the things at all. I should like a warm cloth hood for riding in winter—dark blue, I think, close-fitting and like a child's with a little point at the top, i.e. cut square and if you have some of that brown fur which we used to have on a blue cloak, that would be pretty on the edge. Then my belt-wear is all worn out and if I had something in the way of a belt to wear with everyday *blue* clothes, I should be glad. I have a cheap brown leather belt. These are only delicate hints, you know. I shan't feel badly if you don't send anything.

Lovingly,
Theresa
Cloth like lady's cloth or broad cloth is best, if you have any.

Harpoot
Oct. 16, 1900

Dear Kindie,

I mean to write to Harry this week, so this epistle can't be long. No word from George yet. It is queer that he should forget us. He has been in Constantinople over a month now. Won't you send us the letters he sends home, that is all of them that you can send? We will return them to you. We know the name of the steamer he sailed on, and that he wanted to go to Paris and Oberammergau (you must correct the spelling). Otherwise we know nothing and are not likely to except through Milton. Mamma wrote last week that you had received two letters from him. I have six or seven letters to Constantinople, and I must confess that I feel hurt, which isn't saying that I don't love the lad as dearly as ever, I know it is only thoughtlessness. It's rather foolish to write this to you. I had no notion of doing so when I began. Don't repeat this to George.

We have had two or three lovely letters from you lately. You have alluded mysteriously to some German lessons and written fragments in that language. Won't you let us into the secret of who your teacher is, and how and when you happened to take lessons?

I must tell you of our doings in brief. Last Saturday Ada came in from the garden to stay; today the Gates family came and tomorrow the Knapps will migrate. We are having as usual, in October, a long succession of beautiful sunny days. The roof is being put onto the new school. The rapid progress of the building is in striking contrast to the progress of the new city government building. They had their money in hand and began to build before we did. They have barely gotten above the foundations, and now most of the money has been "eaten up" by officials and cold weather will soon come on.

Last Friday Mary and I ate dinner with the girls. The house is brimming over with them. There are a great many little ones. We played Jacob and Rachel and how they did enjoy it when Mary swept her long arms about trying to catch nimble me! Afterward we had evening prayers with them.

You have no idea what constant appeals for money are made to us. Our washerwoman dogged my footsteps begging me to help her put her girls into school. Next it was a dress-lining. I gave her some money for that yesterday. Last year a school-girl named Sara served for us. This year she is teaching at Diarbekir. About three weeks ago her mother besought us (Ada and me) for a mejidieh (about $1) to help them pay their rent. We gave it. Today she comes weeping and in dirty ragged clothes asking us to lend them two and a half pounds for them to buy their winter supplies. Sara promises to repay it, but—! We haven't decided what to do. They are certainly miserably poor. I hardly dare speak to a poor person, because of the shower of appeals which will fall upon my head.

Harpoot
Dec. 1, 1900

Dear Papa,

I am sitting alone just now by our open fire, expecting every minute to hear Ellsworth open the front door, and then to put aside writing for a while. Saturday night the school-boys have a prayer-meeting at about 5.30 and as we at the Brownes eat at 5.00 he cannot have dinner with us. The Gates family always dine after the meeting on Dr. Gates' account, so Ellsworth always takes dinner with them on Saturday.

I began to write a letter to the Plymouth Cadres, thanking them for the box which they sent to the school, but I was too stupid to say what I wanted to, so had to give it up and write to someone who doesn't mind stupidity. This state of mind doesn't come from overwork, but from a warm room, a comfortable chair and the fact of its being evening. I had "a good bit" (as Ada says) of exercise this afternoon. Ellsworth and I went to ride for almost an hour and a half over the hills toward the ice-cave. I wonder whether you imagine a bare and stony enough scene when you think of Harpoot, and I wonder too whether you realize the openness and extent of the view and the great number of mountains on every side. The near view, after the novelty wears off, does not compare in beauty with a New England landscape but the grandeur of the distant view can hardly be surpassed.

Our horses had not been out, except to be watered, for a week, so we cantered "nolens volens" most of the way except where the path forbade. The great stretches of un-fenced, uncultivated land over which we ride make horseback riding double the pleasure which it must be where one is confined to roads. My horse or rather our horse, cuts up much more than he did two years ago. If he had shied and danced and seesawed then as he does now, I should never have dared to ride him. Now I am used to him and enjoy his capers. The trouble with him is that he isn't used enough. We walk more and ride less. Miriam doesn't take to riding, Ada's horse "cuts up shines" now and she is a little afraid of him, Dr. Barnum has sold his horse and prefers to walk, Mary has sold hers, Emma is not here and we haven't the Doctor to plan rides at definite hours and drive us all out, so we do much less riding than last year. Ellsworth and I rode to a high hill-top (you would call it a mountain. It is really one small elevation in our range of Harpoot mountains). Being high to begin with we didn't have to climb up much to reach it. From this point we could see the Euphrates River. We had another good ride last week, Ada, Ellsworth, Herbert and I. E. wanted to take some observations from a high rock near the ice cave, so we went with him.

I enjoyed Thanksgiving Day, though it was not like the real home day. I don't have here what Cornelia and I used to call the "Thanksgiving feeling" and the "Christmas feeling". I suppose one reason is that there is nothing outside of ourselves to suggest the holiday. There is no special home-coming, no unusual guests and then I am not really in a home anyway, and see no Thanksgiving cooking going on. In the morning I did my regular school-work, teaching etc. In the afternoon I dropped two of my three lessons. We had our service at 3.30, at the Knapps of course. I donned my silk dress and a pair of new boots and walked along the balcony to the next house. We each, children and all, gave some reason why we were thankful. Of course there was singing and prayer. Dr. Barnum led.

We had dinner at 4.30. The children, with the exception of Margaret, sat at one table, and Ada, Ellsworth and I sat with them to amuse them and keep them in order, to say nothing of carving turkey, serving vegetables, putting on bibs, cutting up fowl and oranges and wiping up what was tipped over onto the table-cloth. Of course the two tables were very near to each other. We sang the doxology before sitting down. Would you like to know what we ate?

Tomato soup. New rolls.

Turkey. Mashed potato. Dumplings. Gravy.

Onions. Canned corn. Cranberries (tiny ones from England. Poor stuff.)

Currant Jelly. Cucumber Pickles. Tomato pickles.

Mince pie, Squash pie, Apple pie, Lemon pie.

Oranges. Pears. Grapes.

It was delicious, but too luxurious for missionaries living in the midst of hundreds of the "miserably poor." In the evening we had Turkish coffee and would have eaten cornballs and taffy if Mrs. Knapp hadn't forgotten them. She sent some over to *us* the next morning. Right after dinner the older people settled down cosily upstairs and the children and the younger middle-aged people went to Mr. Knapp's study and played games—Tin-tin, French Blindman's buff, Rooster and Dumb Crambo. The children never have too much of the latter. We kept missionary hours and went home at 8.45. Ellsworth and Ada however came to my room, and we made some lemonade and talked for nearly an hour. I wish that dear George could have had as pleasant and homey a Thanksgiving. Miriam received a telegram from Poughkeepsie Saturday morning bringing Thanksgiving greetings from her family. It was pleasant to receive it but I would rather have the money put into something else.

Mr. Browne and Aunt Caro did not come home after all I wrote you, I think, about the quarrel in the Diarbekir church. Mr. B. and Aunt C. really didn't want to go there and dreaded it very much, but God seemed to lead them there. Through them a great many reconciliations have taken place. They felt that they could not leave the church at such a critical point and are staying on indefinitely till their work shall appear to be finished. They hope to be here Christmas.

Harpoot
Dec. 26, 1900

My dear People,

A great many things have happened since my last letter—at least, a great deal for Harpoot. Friday morning the post came bringing good letters—some from Papa, Harry and Ruth sent via George, three wee notes from Mamma, and three dear Christmas letters from Papa, Mamma and Cornelia. We sat down in Mr. Browne's study and read them Xmas morning. They were all so loving and cheery! Thank you. There were some enclosures and bundles which I will speak of later.

Friday evening we had station-meeting—this time at the Knapps. It is sort of ridiculous to stop here but I forgot to tell about what I did before that. Thursday morning I was working away in our room with Ada when Miriam came running in saying, "Mary and I are going shopping." (Fancy it!) "to Mezereh and you and Ada must come, too." I didn't think I could at first because I would have to change so many plans and break so many engagements—not lessons alone, but they all insisted. It was then about 10.30. We sat down on the floor in Mary's room. She brought in some oranges and pears, and rang over to the Barnums for some doughnuts and biscuits. I forgot to say that Miriam felt triumphant because she promised the family (in Milton) to make me do something rash, now and then. Ada rode her own horse, who tho' he has a reputation for sobriety has grown so frisky as to make Ada's life quite miserable, tho' she won't own it. I rode Emma's pretty horse, Dòst, so that the man could use ours, Miriam used Mrs. Gates' white donkey and Mary Mrs. Barnum's mule. We were a funny procession. Dost and the Bey were mincing and prancing all the way, pretending to be afraid of arabas. We went to a khan with the horses and as usual, dismounted before a gaping crowd of nearly a hundred men. One gets used here to being viewed with a "cricket's eye." Then we walked to a shop where cloth is sold. Of course it belonged to an Armenian. All the other customers were requested to leave before we entered. Turkish and Armenian women don't go shopping. We walked where we pleased and looked at or took down what we pleased. It was too à la Franc a place for curios, so I contented myself with buying a pillow-covering at Mrs. Browne's request, and four figured handkerchiefs such as the women here wear on their heads. Then we went to a little shop where there were a great many tawdry nick-nacks from Constantinople. I bought there a little balance, which E. gave to Mrs. Browne in her stocking and a key-ring (price 2 cts).

Then we went to a little candy-shop where Miriam had a commission for Mrs. Gates. There I invested in two candy sheep, at two cents apiece. The shop was hardly big enough to turn around in. I wonder how a big, beautiful store will look to me, when I see one again. By this time we were tired enough to trail back to the khan. Avedis (the man) borrowed some saddlebags to bring home the things. We reached home at about four.

The next day we arranged and labelled the gifts for the schoolgirls. We had sorted them before. I gave my lessons, but all the rest of the time I devoted to this work.

Do you remember that last year we had no Christmas treat for the girls, but that they gave it all up for India? Of course the things which had come from America we kept and now this year we give them. The Armenian Christmas is still two weeks off, you remember.

So at last all the things from Milton were used. Some we had given before. Each College and High School girl had a thimble—or rather, will have. Some of the bags are to be given to teachers and some to girls. I kept a few to give away on my own account. Yesterday I sent one of them to my little orphan-girl, the one who used to do my room-work.

Now I come to the station-meeting again. We talked a good deal about the possibilities of Dr. Norton's coming, and even while we talked there was a knock on the door below. It was a telegram from Dr. Norton from Malatia, saying, "Will reach Harpoot tomorrow afternoon." I neglected to say that Emma's letter from Marsovan said that Dr. Norton and his dragoman had come and gone, and there was another from the Consul himself, written at Sivas. The question in our minds had been, when he would arrive. He really made remarkable time, considering the snow. Once they travelled all night. Another time, they couldn't get into a khan and so slept in the araba. It had been decided that Dr. N. was to be the Gates's guest, but it was a question what to do with the dragoman. Ellsworth offered his two rooms in the ell of the Gates house, and Mrs. Browne offered to E. the use of Mr. Browne's study and tho' he has been sleeping at the school, he (Ellsworth) accepted the use of Aunt Caro's bed-room for a few days, so till today he has been living and eating with us. All this meant that E's rooms which were full of stones, and papers and all manner of things, must have an over-hauling. So Saturday morning, after giving a music-lesson, and doing some little tasks, I went up to E's room at about 11.00 o'clock. The woman who usually does his room-work was there to help, and together we worked in the two rooms till nearly four o'clock. Ada helped too, for about two and a half hours. The rooms had a thorough cleaning, such as I ought to have seen to before. We put up a bed of Mrs. Browne's, borrowed a chamber-set and lamp of the Gates' and finally made it look very attractive. The consul who uses the study, too, was quite delighted with the room.

Saturday evening I labelled our Xmas presents for the circle, and took a bath in Miriam's fine rubber tub. I don't go often to the Turkish bath. I don't believe it is good for me. I feel so tired for a day after it. Only four or five of the missionary ladies go.

I think I must be sleepy, for I can't tell my story straight. At about one o'clock Saturday Drs. Gates, and Barnum, Mr. Knapp, Ellsworth and Herbert and a zabtieh set out to meet the consul. The "Government" sent out two or three officials and three soldiers. They went on and on in vain. The Government partly turned back. Then Dr. Barnum and Herbert turned back. The others kept on in the darkness. Finally they gave up and turned homeward. On the road home they met some men going toward Malatia and told them if they met an American to say that a party had come out to meet them and gone back. They went on at a brisk pace. A little later they heard a gun fired several times. The zabtieh was sure that someone wanted them, so they turned about once more and soon met one of Dr Norton's zabtiehs, who had quite exhausted his horse, trying to catch up with them. They had to ride on some distance before meeting the consul. He had been hindered nearly two hours at the crossing of the Euphrates. They all reached the city a little before eight—on a very dark night, too. I didn't see the new-comers till Sunday evening.

(Norton himself described the delay in one of his dispatches as follows: "I was unfortunately delayed in crossing the Euphrates, by the colossal inability, for four hours, of the ferryman on the opposite shore to overcome the laws of inertia.")

Theresa continues:

Sunday was much like other Sundays, except that I took a very long nap, and in the evening we had a Christmas service, Dr. Gates leading.

I like Dr. Norton better now than I did at first sight. He is rather below medium in height. His hair has hardly begun to turn grey. He has a loud rather nasal voice and talks a great deal, especially about what he has seen and done, but as he has lived seventeen years or more in various foreign lands and has tramped through them hundreds of miles, he has much that is interesting to tell and I really enjoy listening to him. If he only wouldn't make so many puns and so many flattering remarks! He is a nephew of Prof. Horseford of Harvard and seems to have many famous or well-known people for friends. He has a wife and a little son of five or six who are with his father and mother somewhere near Buffalo.

Dr. Norton has engaged a house in Mezereh, so we shall not see very much of him after all.

The dragoman is a young Greek of perhaps twenty-eight. He is a graduate of Robert College, where he was later a tutor. He also worked in Mr. Peet's office at the Bible House. He speaks English very well, but with a slight drawl. He wears glasses and is tremendously tall. He speaks French and German well, and knows some Turkish. He was born in Bebék. By the way, his name is Mr. Stephanides (What a hodge-podge this is!) Margaret calls him "the Consul's dragon" and I'm afraid he will be "the Dragon" to the end of the chapter. Margaret said to her mother, "He has a nice face, but he looks just like a dragon." He seems a little conceited and hasn't the level-headedness of an American, but it may be just his foreignness. There are no other Greeks in this city—at least no more than one or two. I have described these new-comers thus at length, because they will be a part of our social life.

Monday was just a regular school-day.

Now it is after ten, and my conscience tells me to go to bed. I'll just outline Christmas Day and fill it in later if I can.

About 5.30 A.M. The school-girls came to all the Missionaries houses in turn and sang Christmas songs, with the accompaniment of bells. It was very sweet, in the darkness.

About 6.25-still dark. Twelve orphan boys, each carrying a lighted candle made the round of the houses and sang an Armenian Christmas song.

About 6.35. Prayers.

6.45 Opening of stockings, which we had hung the night before about the Browne's table. Great enthusiasm all around. We opened the home-books then.

About 7.30. Breakfast.

Morning. Received calls—Eight young men teachers came at once. Rather an ordeal. Many came to give Xmas greetings.

Played Puss-in-the-Corner with the children out-of doors.

Did up some belated Xmas presents.

Read Xmas letters with Ellsworth.

Looked at his map to learn the Geography of the region better.

Noon. No luncheon. Had a cold bite of bread, but didn't need it.

Aftern. More calls—six or more people. Went to ride.

4 o'clock—Dinner at the Gates—the whole circle.

About 5.30. Christmas tree. Grand Chorus—"Mamma, this is for *me*!" "*Look* at this!" Happy squeals and the strains of the harmonicum are heard in the land. Margaret calls it a thermometer, and begs leave to play it all night. We go home by 8.30 and Ada, Miriam, E. and I talk till ten.

Tomorrow I shall try to write a note about your gifts and give a list of my Xmas presents. I enclose a copy of a note which Ada received yesterday.

Always lovingly,
Theresa

Just before Christmas, Mr. Browne and Aunt Caro had returned from one of their long touring trips. "One of the brightest things is the home coming from your tours," writes Aunt Caro, "to the white tablecloth, the good clean china, and nice food, the roomy, clean bed, the books and newspapers, a rocking chair, and the love and cheer of an American home in the wilds of Turkey." Her feelings are easy to understand in the light of the following passage:

> You seek the shelter of a khan—a lonely wayside inn. Your horses and mules and donkeys abide with you there. The odor, as you eat your food, and as you lie down to sleep, is unspeakable. The noises of the night drive away sleep, and in the passing years teach your sleep a coyness which it is almost impossible to conquer.
>
> You think that one flea engaged in an endless circuit of your neck would drive you distracted, but what would you say to twenty who propose to keep possession of your whole body! You cannot like centipedes, tarantulas, and scorpions as roommates,

> ready at any moment to drop down upon your bed from the rafters above!
>
> You are weary with your horseback ride of eight or ten hours; how can you get the courage to open your camp bedstead and make it up, and to prepare lunches for tomorrow? Or, you have arrived at the place where you are to work for days, and the brethren and sisters come in to sit and talk through the evening. Tomorrow you must be at the sunrise prayer meeting, you must write a letter home in ten minutes, you must go from house to house all day long, keeping your spirit intent and strong in the serious work for souls; perchance must lead a meeting at noon, and attend the general one at sunset, then after dinner be cheery and bright to meet people socially, or seriously, again.
>
> The food is rich for your delicate stomach, the time of eating so different from your own, you long for dainties when you are not well, but the bread and cheese are dry at the end of a tour. You long for privacy, but perhaps when a sudden attack of lumbago seizes you, after a torturing ride of four hours, and several of work with poor, discouraged souls, you must sleep in a room with five men, the only woman![46]

At the time of this writing, Aunt Caro was in her early seventies.

The new missionary, Miriam Platt and Theresa became fast friends very quickly. Miriam was born in Poughkeepsie, NY., in 1875 and attended the Lucy Wheelock Kindergarten School in Boston. In Harpoot, one of Miriam's duties was to supervise the lace industry for hundreds of village women who earned their livelihood this way, along with Mrs. Carey. Soon after her arrival, "Aunt" Hattie wrote: "We all like her very much. She is unassuming, and yet independent in her opinion, and always cheerful. We are quite sure she is one who will wear well." President Gates agreed: "Miss Platt seems one well fitted for her work. She is quiet, has a healthy look, and she takes the discomforts of the journey and the country with an ease that speaks of power held in reserve. I like her and think she will do."

---

46. *Life and Light*, 1904, vol. 34.

Chapter Sixteen:
"For the Love of God, I Will Not Eat." The World of Boys and Girls

The orphanages run by the American Board and other missionary societies after the 1894-96 massacres soon established "industries" and "trades" for their young charges, numbering in the thousands, who had to be taught a skill in order to be able to earn their own living as soon as possible. There was tradition to draw from: the Armenians had always been the artisans of that part of the world. The person in charge of these activities was Mr. Knapp, and he proved to be both creative and energetic. He established a tailoring business that was so successful that a branch was opened in Mezereh. A bakery was providing employment for a few of the boys, and supporting four or five other orphans. The girls were weaving rugs that were gaining recognition. "The profit on a number sent to America was $60," reported Mr. Knapp proudly. Cloth and gingham weaving was also proving to be a profit-making activity.

Theresa's letters to her missionary society ladies over the years provide us with a series of vivid, and sometimes heartrending, vignettes from the daily lives of these orphan children, as well as of the ones who attended boarding school in Harpoot:

> Last Saturday I visited the nearest of our three boys' orphanages. The boys who are at trades were in the market, but most of the schoolboys were at home, seated cross-legged on the floor, sewing. I had happened upon their mending-time. Some were patching their white, woolen stockings with cotton cloth—very neatly, too; others were mending torn clothes. All stood, smiling in a friendly way, and made the salaam. They had to be coaxed a little to go on with their sewing, feeling somewhat embarrassed over their occupation. The House-Mother proudly showed me some of their neatest work, while the servers blushed from pleasure & shyness.
>
> There were tidy piles of beds in one end of the room, and Koordish rugs on the floor. The room being devoted to the needle, all the appliances of such work were to be found there. On the wall hung a row of piece-bags. On the other side was a big bag of thim-

bles, wooden eggs for darning stockings, etc. Indeed every room has its rows of bags, all neatly numbered. The House-Mother is justly proud of her system and order.

I sat down with the boys and began to inquire into all their doings from morning till night, while they bubbled over with laughter at my questions. They rise at five in the morning. "The hour is supposed to be 4:30," the Mother said apologetically, "but they are so sleepy." In Turkey five o'clock is really rather late. The sixty-three boys sleep in five different rooms on mattresses spread out on the floor. After dressing, they wash out in the little court. Then for an hour they all study, supervised only by the older boys. After this comes prayers, led by the House-Father, a manly capable Christian.

At this time the monitors read the names of the offenders of the previous day, those who have been disorderly on the play-ground, at meals, at bed-time, in study-hour etc. The punishments are fixed and the monitors see that they are carried out, unless a whipping must be given for some very serious offense, like lying or stealing. However the Father & Mother don't believe in whipping often. As far as possible the punishment fits the crime. The boy who is late for a meal must stand for five minutes without eating. The boy who doesn't play fair must stay in the house. There is one punishment which is used for many offenses—bringing jars of water from the fountain. The Mother used to be in great distress because so many needles were lost or broken, and she decided that for one needle lost a boy must bring water five times, for a needle broken he brings two and a half jars full. At first the boys objected, saying that by carrying water once to a city home they could earn enough money to buy five needles, but the Mother said, "You may earn money if you can that way, but you must pay for my needles in my way." So much water is brought from the fountain and poured about the house that it is as sweet and clean as could be desired from top to bottom. But lest the house should be entirely washed away by these floods of water, the naughty boys are sometimes set to mending the clothes of the trades-boys who have little time for sewing. Of course the boys are often naughty and careless, but on the whole they are a happy, obedient house-hold, and the older boys are becoming competent and mature from their responsibility.

Breakfast is at seven, after which the boys do the morning house-work, shake the rugs, sweep the floors, and mend any bad tears which cannot wait till Saturday. Then they are free to play till they go to school at 8:30. The boys who are learning trades go much earlier to the work-shops. School is much like school in America, only the school-buildings and appliances are not as good and the little boys always sit on the floor. Luncheon is at twelve and the boys eat bread with raisins, cheese, grapes, or milk and then go to school again till 4:30. From that time till dinner they play, usually on the high hilltop back of the orphanage, only the kitchen boys helping in the house. All the boys take turns at this work. Study hour comes after dinner and the boys are thankful enough to go to bed at 8:30, the little ones "turning in" before.

On Saturdays the washing is done in the morning and with two stout women to help, and the boys to carry the water, hang out the clothes, sort them etc, it is quickly finished. In the afternoon they mend and play, and in the evening tramp to the market to the city-bath. If there is extra time the Father translates an English book aloud for them, or they sing, play games and perform their favorite tricks. For my benefit one of the most accomplished performers acted the blind beggar before me and the frog and cotton machine were invited to do their part, while the boys laughing and giggling watched to see the effect of the show on me.

The Mother invited me after that to go over to the house with her. We went first to the great closet where the boys' everyday clothes were hung, everything carefully numbered & in its place. Each boy has three sets of under-clothing, two pairs of shoes, two fezes, two jackets, six handkerchiefs (merely pieces of colored gingham) etc. There are special closets for Sunday clothes. In one room we found the orphanage baby asleep on the floor; in another there were two stocking-machines, with which the boys make stockings at the rate of eight paras a day. It takes a woman four days, usually, to knit one pair by hand, if she gives all her time to it. In the summer the children go barefoot. In still another room and out on the flat roof I saw boxes of flowers & other plants which suffer more from over-watering than neglect. Downstairs in the lower hall hung the boys' rows of towels. In the store-room in great jars were grain, rice, salted grape-leaves, butter, etc. which the boys had prepared in the summer under the direction of the Mother and the cook. Their working-sleeves and aprons hung here in the same long rows.

In the kitchen we found the cook, Sarah, a jolly village woman, preparing the evening meal with the help of two or three boys. A tub full of big, steaming rice-balls flavored with onion stood on the floor. The six low round tables had already been set in the dining-room and the pieces of bread laid upon them. Along the wall were rows of gingham bibs, for even the biggest boys use bibs, not associating them as we do with babies. One little fellow being uncommonly hungry had already put on his bib and was sitting patiently by a table all alone. Soon the boys came flocking in, quietly and politely. I inquired why I had heard no bell, and found that when the boys went up to the hill the day before to wash their feet, as they must before dinner, the bell had been taken to gather them together and had been lost.

Now Sarah and one of the boys brought in the tub and the "kuftes" were distributed, three upon each boy's piece of bread. The boys are not limited to three however, and the older ones can sometimes attain to five or six. One of the boys stood and asked the blessing and then all "pitched in." Only one boy, the monitor, did not eat, but brought bread for the others when necessary and looked after the order.

I was pleased with the system and the loving care of the Father and Mother and with the gentleness and manliness of the boys.

It has been asked what the boys are learning to make with their hands. Of the school-boys in this orphanage one has of his own accord made several large maps of cloth—very good ones—which are hung on the orphanage walls. Two or three others are teaching themselves to cover boxes with colored straws in patterns. Others obtain permission to use the home tools and have made little arabas (native wagons) and other toys, and have mended breakages in the house. The boys have drawing lessons in school and the smallest kindergarten and primary scholars use the kindergarten occupations.

The older boys, however, have no regular scientific manual training, for there is no teacher and no funds for the necessary appliances.

In all, forty-nine of our orphan boys are learning trades. There are tailors, shoemakers, carpenters, machinists, barbers, raisers of silk-worms, gardeners and bakers. These boys work from seven a.m. to five p.m. Many boys have already gone out from the orphanages and are supporting themselves.

I wish you could see what real boys our are, how they shout and play like American boys. Each season has its games, as in America. At one time they all make kites, at another they play a game with sticks, knocking one up in the air and trying to hit it again with another before it comes down again etc. Their favorite game resembles marbles, only it is played with small round bones. These children have not as much law and order in their games as American children. It is a characteristic of their race not to yield readily to a leader from their own race and to have confusion and lack of system in trying to carry out their plans.

If the boys saw you watching them at play, they would run up in front of you one at a time, make a hasty salaam and then rush off again, in order not to lose a moment from play before the school-bell rang. As they come up the stairs several of the older boys stand by as monitors, to see that they do not crowd or dawdle, and that each boy takes off his shoes at the proper place. Once inside, they sit down in rows on the floor, each with his books and fez in front of him. Those who want cushions to sit on are allowed to bring them. Unlike American boys these boys seem to be able to sit very close to each other for hours at a time, without temptation to pinch or push or prick. Perhaps it is because they have been crowded all their lives. Their naughtiness takes other forms. Most of them have bright, attractive faces. When I visit their homes, I sometimes wonder that they are as clean and obedient and intelligent as they are. Obedience is the hardest lesson we have to teach the younger children. Most of them are not used to it at home. When Miss Platt's little kindergarten children first came to her this year, they were like forty kittens let loose. She determined that they should learn to obey this year, if nothing else. She is sometimes discouraged, but judicious and varied forms of punishment & encouragement & most of all patience are beginning to tell. I never realized before as I do now, what an educated Christian home does for a child before he reaches the age of four or five.

I want to tell you some pleasant, hopeful things which have happened in our girls' school. A good many of the older girls are newly awake to their responsibility for others and meet daily in little prayer circles to pray for others in the school. They work as well as pray. Miss Daniels has prepared a pledge similar to the Student Volunteer pledge, only they promise to work anywhere and in any way that God wishes for their people. Several of the teachers and girls have signed it. I hope that means that many girls will be ready to go out next year to little villages to teach. They dread to do that, because young girls in this country are criticized and talked about for going away alone in that way. These girls are naturally very dependent. The parents object for various reasons, one being that a girl's chances of marriage are lessened if she has been talked about in that way, or if she waits till she has taught several years.

My little Junior Endeavor girls recently gave their monthly pledges for money for missions. I was amused and touched at what they wrote. Most of them promised five paras (half a cent) a month. No one could give more than two cents a month. Ten or twelve orphan girls wanted to go without food to earn money. A meal in the orphanage is valued at half a cent, and Mr. Knapp lets them have the money if they want to go without food for any such cause as this. Some of them give up one meal a week, some two. Kohar (Jewel) gave me a list of several girls in her orphanage. Underneath she had written, "These girls consecrate their noon meal to Christ." One little girl Vosgeeg (Golden) wrote simply, "For the love of God I will not eat." No little American would put it so quaintly.

You would be amused to see our girls coming back to school from the villages. They usually ride upon mules or donkeys. The girls' bed, which is simply a mattress stuffed with cotton, wool or rags, is tied upon one side of the animal and the box of clothing upon the other. The box is almost invariably green with red and yellow figures and flowers painted upon it. The girls' other possessions, possibly a jar for drinking-water or a handkerchief full of fruit, are hung on somewhere and over the broad top of the load a piece of carpeting or a cushion is spread. The girl sits upon this, with very little bend in her knees, and having no reins to hold onto, very often rolls off, if the mule is suddenly surprised or goes up a steep place. I often wonder that the girls are not injured more from tumbling off so abruptly as they often do. They do not suffer from the sun, either, as much as we would, often coming long distances, with nothing over their heads but a bit of white cheesecloth, tied over the ears and under the chin. Around the school door, the crowd of donkeys, the bright boxes and gaily-covered beds, piled up, are a great contrast to the respectable heap of trunks at an American boarding-school.

I wish you could have laughed with me today. It has been a holiday and my brother took his Geology class of girls on an expedition to a cañon and a cave five miles from here. Some rode on horses and some on donkeys. Because of the Turks or poverty, several had never been so far from the city before, and the sight of a lizard or a frog was wonderful and delightful to them. They could not get enough of picking flowers. The funny part was to see the girls tumble off their donkeys. The little beasts bumped into each other indiscriminately and trotted at most unexpected and inconvenient moments. Sometimes the girls fell off singly, and sometimes in pairs. One tumbled off five times. But they all came up laughing and ready to try again.

I am often asked how many teachers and scholars we have in our girls' schools in Harpoot,—what they learn and what they do.

To begin at the top, there are three American teachers now,—Miss Daniels, who is at the head of the school, Miss Platt, our newly-arrived kindergartner, and I. All the girls' schools and the boys' primary school are under our care. The schools for the older boys are closely connected with ours in situation and in administration, but the buildings are separate and so is the work of boys and girls, except for a weekly lecture which they attend together and an occasional union Christian Endeavor meeting. At such times the boys sit on one side of the room, and the girls on the other with averted heads and their shawls pulled closely about their faces. All this Oriental propriety, however, does not prevent them from being interested in each other. But this is a digression.

Our girls, from College to Primary School, number 466. They meet in six different buildings. Two of these, only, are real school-houses; three are dwelling-houses which we rent; and one is a large room used by our Gregorian neighbors for their religious services, since their church was destroyed five years ago.

The college girls study and recite in the same rooms in which the boarders eat, sleep and live out of school-hours. There is no denying that our quarters are very narrow, but we all can feel contented when we look up the hill and see our beautiful new school-building.

We have, in all, twelve Armenian teachers, with eight or nine assistants. These assistants are most of them girls who have not completed their course, and are taking some lessons and teaching at the same time, to help pay for their expenses. Beside these, some of the teachers of the young men give certain lessons to the college girls, such as Turkish, and most of the sciences which are taught.

Let us go to the room where the smallest girls are at school. They are seated in rows on the floor—not very straight rows, I regret to say. Each child scrambles to her feet and salutes us by touching her chin and forehead with her right hand. Our rules about cleanliness and whole clothing are very strict, but there are no immaculate little white aprons here. Most of the children wear dull, dark gingham dresses reaching to their ankles. There are no pretty curls either, but the dark hair is drawn back straight or parted and braided. Many girls, both large and small, have been sent home in times past to comb their hair. Now they have begun to understand that it is not worth while to be untidy. The faces which look up at us here, are almost as bright and mischievous as those of as many little Americans would be. In this room Yeranooshee reigns supreme. Pretty Eleeza is her assistant. Eleeza is not very happy just now because her family refuses to give her to the young student who wants to marry her, their reason being that there are two older sisters not yet married, and their chance is gone if Eleeza is given. It reminds me of the old story of Jacob. "And Laban said, 'It must not be so done in our country, to give the younger before the first-born.'"

To return to the children, they learn here the rudiments of Arithmetic, Reading, etc, learn many Bible stories and have some Kindergarten gifts and games. Next year we shall have a genuine Kindergarten in a new building.

Anna's is the next school that we come to. Her girls are from ten to fourteen years old. Her discipline is almost perfect. Even with no teacher in the room, the girls sit and study quietly. This room is rather dark and cold. There is not time for us to go to all the schools. Our teachers are of all kinds, from young, inexperienced girls like Eleeza, to old and tried teachers like our good, crippled Deroshee, who works for her children's souls as faithfully and earnestly as for their minds.

And while I speak of this I want to tell you of the blessing which came to us during the Week of Prayer and afterward. School work went on then almost as usual, but we held several special meetings and many of the teachers and older girls gave much time to prayer for the other girls and talking with them about the Christian life. Many girls began the new life in Christ. It is beautiful to see the change in some. The same Anna who last year refused to obey me and lay on the floor, crying and beating her head against the wall is so tractable, and so smiling and happy in these days, that I look at her in wonder. Miss Daniels has a weekly Bible class with these new young Christians. About sixty girls come to this. Probably there are some in this number who are mistaken about themselves or will fall away, but I believe that a great many of them, though weak, have entered the Kingdom of Heaven. The

Armenian character is impressionable, but not steadfast and persevering, and they need much leading and encouraging. They find it easier to serve God at school than in their homes.

Since I have spoken of the studies of the little girls, I ought to speak more particularly of the College-girls. Our College is higher in grade than a High School, but not up to an American college. We are working up toward our name, however. The girls study the Bible, Ancient Armenian, Turkish, English, History, Armenian Composition, Chemistry, Physics, Astronomy and many more subjects which it would tire you to have me name over. The extras are Singing, Gymnastics, Cooking, a weekly talk on Current Events, a series of talks on Domestic Economy and Hygiene by the missionary ladies, and another series of lectures by Armenian teachers on general and practical subjects. The girls when they come to school must sit on the floor in a small and crowded room, but they do so contentedly, thinking of next year.

Lucene (that is, Moon) is a smiling little orphan, who lives in one of the Harpoot orphanages. The house is on the very edge of the city. Far below it stretches the wide Harpoot plain and beyond are the ranges of the Taurus Mts. Lucene does not know how beautiful the view is, for she has always seen it.

Lucene has sixty-one sisters and a good and kind House-Father and House-Mother. The Mother especially is a very sensible, cheerful woman, interested in each girl individually, knowing the faults and good qualities of each and reproving or commending like a real mother. She often jokes with them and pets them, too, as a mother might.

Lucene is a typical Armenian, with heavy black hair and beautiful dark eyes. Her features are rather coarse, but her rosy, healthy color atones for much. She is short and plump and equal to a good deal of hard work. She may be thirteen or fourteen years old, but "it was not written" and she does not know. No birthdays are celebrated in this land. Her dress is of black and yellow striped gingham and she wears her black woolen jacket indoors and out alike. On Sundays she puts on her best blue gingham dress and her red hair-ribbon instead of a piece of black braid.

It is a Wednesday morning and at five o'clock when the bell is rung, Lucene and the fifteen other girls in her room are ready enough to get up, for they were in bed at nine o'clock the night before and all their people are early risers. If it had been summer, they would have waked up on the roof just as the stars were disappearing, and would have been down the ladder before there was light enough for their neighbors on the next roof to look over and see what they were doing. As it is March, the room is dark and cold, but it is so in every house. There is no room to be very lively in dressing, for the whole floor is covered with mattresses. No one puts on her shoes till she reaches the door where she walks into them without stopping, and then goes down to the dark stone-flagged kitchen to wash. Six or seven big tins of water stand here. The girls do not put their hands into the water, for that would be a very dirty way of washing, in their opinion, but they pour the water over each other's hands and throw it onto their faces. This mutual service continues when it comes to combing their hair for as there are no mirrors they sit down on the floor two by two with their yellow wood combs and braid each other's hair.

Soon the beds are rolled up and stowed away, and an older girl in each of the four rooms conducts prayers, after which each girl reads her Bible and prays alone for a time. Then the bell calls them all together to the big room where the Father conducts family prayers.

Meanwhile the lentil soup has been cooking, which with plenty of the flat coarse bread of the country will make a very good breakfast. This week Anna's circle does the cooking and kitchen work. They spread the seven big squares of blue cotton on the floor and set on each a round wooden table about a foot high, scrubbed last Saturday down at the fountain as white as sand and willing elbows could make it. The bread nicely cut up in pieces is laid around the edge of the table, and in the middle is the big dish of hot soup. The girls sit down on the floor around the tables, draw the blue table-cloth up over their knees, and one of the older girls stands and asks the blessing. Then each one, armed with a big tan spoon does her part valiantly in the general dish.

After breakfast the girls who will spend the day in the work-rooms go to the school-room in another orphanage to study for an hour, while the regular school-girls do the housework. There is no need of the Mother to direct them, for each knows her work. Tooma and Mariam sweep the paved court where the marigold boxes stand in summer-time; Kohar helps to shake out the pieces of Koordish carpeting which are spread on the floors; while Lucene and others fill up the jars with the water which the old water-carrier has just brought in his goat-skin bag, and even little Sateneeg who goes to Miss Platt's kindergarten helps to wipe the sixty and more spoons.

After this till school-time those who have mending to do for themselves or the little ones or for the working-girls who have less time, spread a big, blue cloth on the floor and sit around it with their sewing. A fire has been lighted in the tiny sheet-iron stove, and the room is cheery with the warmth and the happy chatter of the girls. Some are knitting stockings. Yester is sewing her number onto a bit of cloth for each girl has a number with which all her clothes are marked and is very proud of her number, too. The smaller the girl, the larger her number seems to be and the more conspicuous on her stockings. Lucene is mending No. 39's apron, while the merry little owner plays with the family cat. Sometimes someone starts a song which they have learned at school, and all join in.

At 7.45 the bell on the boys' school rings, and each school-girl goes to her own shelf for her books, shawl and shoe-bag, exchanges her house-shoes for her old out-of-door shoes, and joins the procession in the court. The orphans always walk in single file to school or anywhere, and form a very droll, old-fashioned procession, with the long skirts which custom decrees, their flapping, clattering shoes and their white knit shawls drawn tightly over their heads and held demurely under their chins. It is raining, but they paddle along cheerfully, for no other young girl carries an umbrella, and why should they?

School is very much like school in America, only the girls never study with the boys, and the little ones always sit on the floor. This school is under the direct supervision of the missionaries. Lucene is in the Grammar School. She studies Bible, Reading, Geography, Arithmetic, Armenian Grammar, English and Writing, beside having Singing and Sewing lessons. At the end of the morning her Junior C.E. Society has its meeting, and Lucene very happily brings her offering of twenty paras (two cents) which she earned by going without a meal twice in the week. The orphan girls are many of them, real servants of the Lord Jesus and are the most active earnest members of the Society.

Meanwhile the girls who have gone to the work-rooms have passed a busy morning. Sarra sits by a high, old-fashioned wooden loom, and weaves cotton for the orphans' underclothing. She is learning, too, to make gingham for their dresses. The shuttle flies fast and she is proud of her skill. Here is an empty loom because the girl who sat there is to be married soon. In the rug-room there are twenty-three girls at work upon four rugs. It is quieter here and the results of the work are really beautiful. Downstairs in the sewing-room are twenty-one girls cutting out and making underclothing for the boy-orphans. They have two sewing-machines here. All of these working-girls go to school for three hours or more during the day.

At noon there is the same marshalling of clans outside the doors for the walks home. The noon meal is bread and black Malatia raisins today. It is soon over, and the older girls go to school again from one to four-twenty, the little ones till three. After school comes playtime in the court or on the roof if it is pleasant, in the house if it storms. The favorite games are bouncing the ball and jack-stones, with real stones. The heartiest meal of the day is eaten at five. Beside bread this evening they have rice cooked with butter and a sauce made of dried apricots. After dinner-time the girls can play, talk and do what they please, till seven when they have their evening prayers and hymns together. From this time till half past eight they study in four different rooms. In each room there is a leader from among the older girls, and the younger ones submit willingly to her authority. The older girls are in this way having an excellent training in leadership and the protecting relations of older to younger is very sweet. There is a room-pride which makes each girl want to have the family in her room the most orderly and diligent. When the little ones grow sleepy the "little mothers", that is, the leaders, put them to bed. Before undressing each girl has time for her own evening prayer to God. By nine o'clock the great court yard gate is locked and barred, all are in bed and the house is still.[47]

---

47. ABC 16.9.13.

Chapter Seventeen: Theresa Lectures in Armenian, and Attends a Memorable Performance of King Lear

Ever since the massacres of 1895, the town of Mezereh—present-day Elazig—on the Harpoot plain at the foot of the mountain had grown in importance relative to Harpoot. Harpoot, one thousand feet above the plain, was difficult to access; Mezereh two miles away on the plain lay on the caravan route from Baghdad to the Black Sea and was the capital of the province of Harpoot, one of the three provinces within the Vilayet of Mamuret el Aziz. Most commercial and official activity was centered in Mezereh by the time Consul Norton got there, and he soon decided that this, rather than Harpoot, was to be the place for the new consulate. Soon after his arrival, he rented a centrally located building and got himself and his splendidly liveried dragoman Stephanides established. Initially, Norton was delighted with Mezereh: "The Alpine vista from my office windows of the grand Taurus range,—snow-capped during most of the year—is fairly intoxicating. The immediate surrounding, Harpoot perched on her crags, Mezereh with her wide streets and many gardens, the village-dotted plain, are also most attractive. The climate, the food, the essentials of physical comfort, are all that one could wish."[48]

Norton was cordially received by all of local Turkish officialdom. The dragoman of the Vilayet, Husni Bey, was "a gentleman of much culture, trained in Switzerland and Germany." Nevertheless, Norton was clearly worried about a possible repetition of the events of 1895. His dispatches confirm that there existed a good deal of fear among the missionaries at this time, anxieties that Theresa does not allow herself to express in her letters to her family. Norton made sure that he would be able to observe what went on in the missionary compound on the mountain from his office and reported that his windows commanded an unobstructed view of the missionary buildings and that a system of signals would be instituted that would allow the missionaries to communicate any trouble to him immediately. He also made strong requests that they be armed, and that the arms be kept in full evidence as a deterrent

48. National Archives; Consular Records; Harpoot 1895-1906.

and pointed out that just a few rifles would have made all the difference in defending the station in 1895. This suggestion, however, was not taken up by the missionaries, who had learned from hard experience, especially watching the Armenians, how provocative the possession of weapons was to the Turks.

Early in the new year, Theresa and Ellsworth took off from Harpoot on a reckless ride down the mountain to call on the new Consul. Their brother Harry at Yale received this report:

> Harpoot, Jan. 16
>
> Dear Harry-Boy,
>
> Last Thursday, the first real day of vacation, we had a snowstorm—not a very heavy one. I wrote letters till the mail went at one o'clock. Later in the afternoon Ellsworth and I rode to Mezereh in the snow. The horses hadn't been out for nearly a week and were wild to go, so they sidled and pranced down the mountain by the steep path, and when we got to the bottom, we just had to let them go. They pretended to canter but the path was full of rocks and snow. We flew along humpity-bump. The snow in my face blinded me so that I had to shut one eye entirely and keep the other open only a crack. We cantered most of the way to Mezereh and when we reached there my hair had slipped over almost onto one ear, taking my cap with it, which cap, being of fur, looked like a drowned kitten. My veil was a little wet rag which stuck to my face. We were plastered with snow on the outside, tho' underneath we were warm and dry as toast. In this fascinating condition of deshabillé I made my first call upon our new consul. In the courtyard, the cavass swept off the bulk of the snow from "the Hänum" (Madam) but left the water. Ellsworth had business with Dr. Norton, so I was left to the tender mercies of the dragoman, Mr. Stephanides. He speaks English very well, tho' he says *aw* a great deal. He showed me all over the "Consulate". It is a fairly good native house with a pretty garden behind it. The rooms looked dreary and untidy to me, but Ellsworth says they are an improvement upon Mr. Jones' quarters. Mr. Jones never had more than one chair in his reception room and had to send out for another when an American caller came. There are other places where native guests can sit. They love to climb up onto a high settee and tuck their legs under them. We wouldn't let Dr. Norton order any tea or coffee for us because it was so late, and hurrying home at the same rate at which we came, we were barely in time for dinner.

That evening the Gateses (instead of Ellsworth) invited all the boarding boys who hadn't gone home for vacation to spend two or three hours at their house. Ellsworth, Ada, Harold and I helped entertain them. For refreshments they had candy, cookies, and a sort of sour drink—an imitation of lemonade. The boys varied in age from ten or twelve to thirty. They all wore their fezes (except one of the teachers) and began by sitting down in a frozen, solemn circle around the edge of the room. They were thawed out by seeing Moore's bucking donkey and his driver (a toy) perform on the floor and after playing several games such as American boys would, they were chattering and laughing heartily. We played the laughing game where a cap is thrown up into the air—You know the game, I think—and they just screamed in helpless amusement to hear the awful guffaws which Ellsworth managed to extract from himself. That stirred Dr. Gates to similar effort and his remarks and behavior were so irresistibly ridiculous for a little while that the boys could only roll over with laughter and point at him weakly.

After this and some other games, the boys played and sang. One played the organ, two had brought their violins and one his mandolin. They played many queer Turkish tunes, and Armenian tunes which are very similar. They care little for harmony, but much for turns and quavers and trills in the melody. They played Yankee Doodle and Upidee over and over, the boys like them so much. Then three of the boys from Koordistan sang a Koordish song or chant about the Last Judgement. I don't know how they remember these tunes. There is nothing in them which I can catch hold of and remember. After this we had prayers and the boys went home, I am sure they had a good time. Friday the teachers did not have a hantess after all, but the Christmas tree was used for the fifth time for the older orphan boys—all who were not included at the Kindergarten boys' party. I had no special connection with this affair so I didn't go.

Saturday all the missionary gentlemen spent in calling. I haven't made a call this vacation. How are the mighty fallen! For the last three days I have been the victim of a most vulgar and inglorious complaint. I have had a boil under my chin and like Brer Fox, I have been "laying low." I slumbered and slept and ate and drank meanwhile and didn't do much else. Mrs. Browne and especially Ada made poultices for me most patiently and waited on me and Ellsworth too deserves honorable mention. Now I am again among the mighty, tho' my head is still somewhat tied up. I feel quite like myself again.

Very lovingly, my dear brother,

Theresa

Will you please send this home. I haven't time to write the same thing again.

Harpoot

Jan. 27, 1901

Dear Mamma,

Once more the mail has come bringing no letter directly from home. That makes two weeks without a letter from you. By this last post came Papa's letter, via George, telling of Dr. Teeks's anniversary and referring to Christmas and to a long letter written about it by Mamma. We hope that letter may come by the next post. We had only half a mail this week, anyway. No one received his usual supply of letters.

Ellsworth and I both referred last week to my not being well and I am afraid you may be troubled about it. I was rather tired and then this boil came. I suppose it was the very best thing for me, because I just stopped and went to bed for a day or two. Then I loafed about the house for three or four days more. They wouldn't let me go to school the first three days of the term, tho' I really could have gone. So my vacation was a week and half long and I feel and look a great deal better than I did two weeks ago before I had the boil. I am at my regular work again now, and feel tremendously energetic. I have been taking China (the medicine) and sulphur (in molasses!)

Mr. Browne and Aunt Caro are still in Diarbekir and can't seem to get away tho' they feel that Palu, Arabkir, Malatia and a great many other places are needing them. Every week we look for a telegram from them which never comes. Mrs. Browne wishes she could have known and gone with them, but it would be very hard to cross the mountains now. Several times they have suggested the possibility of staying till Easter.

There seems to be little to tell. Dr. Norton comes up every Sunday evening to our meeting and Mr. Stephanides has come once or twice. He isn't used to riding and is afraid to be on a horse after dark. They seem to be very busy somehow, even if Dr. Norton isn't a recognized consul. I saw his cavass yesterday in uniform for the first time. He is gorgeous in a long blue cloak with red velvet lapels and cuffs and silver braid, and a big string of cartridges. I'm not sure whether he carries a sword. His cap is of black astrakhan, the shape of a fez. This sort of show tells in this country. The Turks love it.

My day was full yesterday—chiefly with preparations and plans for school-work. In the morning I went shopping to Mr. Knapp's study. He orders from a London tailoring firm their remnants which they sell at very moderate prices. These our orphan tailor boys make up and sell to customers here in the city. Ellsworth is fast becoming disreputable as far as clothes are concerned and finally is compelled to get a light suit. The tailor who teaches the boys will make it for him and tho' the plaid is a little more pronounced than he might choose in America, and the Harpoot cut may not please the fastidious, still I think he will have a fairly good suit of clothes. I bought some pretty material too, for a dress. It is a rather indistinct brown check. I may not make the dress for a year or two and the thought of dress-making appalls me even now, but it is a saving of money and I think I can manage it. The cloth isn't here now, but I will try to send you samples.

Yesterday afternoon Ellsworth and I took a short ride over the hills. We saw a great many partridge-, rabbit- and possibly fox-tracks. These creatures grow bold in winter. We walk in these days much more than we ride.

I haven't spoken of the new school for a long time. The outside is very nearly finished, though not painted. The floors cannot be properly, or rather, safely laid till late in the spring on account of the danger of shrinkage and warping, I suppose, and though we may be able to enter the new building, as far as the place itself is concerned, two months or so before school closes, I doubt whether we shall think it convenient or wise to do so then. Dr. Gates hopes this summer to build all the other necessary buildings—a Primary and Kindergarten School for the girls, a dormitory for the boys, an assembly hall over the stable (!) and perhaps something else. That is something of a task for a summer vacation. He, that is, Dr. Gates is becoming very tired. He speaks as if he would probably return to America a year from next spring, to stay, I don't know how long. Mary uses herself up fast, and I think that she, too, wishes and needs to go at about the same time, but she may wait for a year longer. Dr. Gates seems to find difficulty in securing someone to fill Ellsworth's place. He wanted Mr. Chas. Tracy of Marsovan to come, but Mr. Tracy is not strong and as soon as he is well enough wants to return to America to carry on his theological studies.

Mr. Knapp and the other orphan workers are trying to send out the boys and girls from the orphanages whenever an opportunity comes, because less and less money comes in for them. The older girls are married wherever there is a chance (Think of it! Being given away to a stranger! But it is no worse for the girls than if their parents were living) and the boys are starting out in trades for themselves or becoming apprentices, while a few of the older ones have been sent out to teach. An orphan girl—a nice girl of sixteen or seventeen, was sent to the home of a wealthy, worldly Protestant in Mezereh to be a sort of companion for his only daughter and a helper in the housework. She has been there only two or three weeks and Mr. Knapp heard at Mezereh the other day that she had been the means of leading the head of the house to go to church more regularly than he has for years, and of instituting family prayers in the house.

Did I tell you that Gertrude sent me a lovely gold hat-pin which came safely and Ida F. sent me a very pretty lace collar?

This winter we have had colder weather than at any other time since I came, the thermometer falling to 5° above zero. Perhaps it was 3°. In Mezereh it went below zero, during a foggy "spell" when we were up in the sunshine.

Very much love, my precious people,
Theresa

Dear Mamma,

Last Friday we looked for Mr. Browne and Aunt Caro and expected them to arrive at about four o'clock, but they came in at about ten, in the morning, weary but happy. The post came that day and in the evening we read letters together, that is, the Browne household. The next morning Mr. Browne became suddenly ill and they sent at once for the doctor. He has been in bed since then and suffered a good deal, but he seems much better now and hopes to get up tomorrow. He and Aunt Caro did a wonderful work in Diarbekir. I wish I had copied some of their letters to Harpoot. They are so modest and humble that they won't talk about it. The Sunday before they left Diarbekir they had a communion service at which sixty were received into the church, about twenty-eight being men, young and old, the rest women and girls. They used no revival methods, except prayer, and worked more for the estranged, quarreling church members than for those outside the church. I would copy part of a letter of Aunt Caro's about the service if I did not think that it might be printed in the Herald, and if I had time.

We have had very warm weather for four or five days, the thermometer going up to sixty and above. We sit with open windows in the day-time and without a fire even in the evening. The white crocuses are out on the hills. It is too early for such weather and I'm afraid it will hurt the trees.

Next Saturday is Paree Gentan, the Armenian feast or carnival which comes just before Lent. In this city the people don't make much of it, except that they visit and feast, but the villagers dress up in their best, have new clothes, eat and drink and dance in circles on the roofs, the men and women at different times.

Aunt Hattie told an amusing incident the other day. She went to see some Armenians and the wife of their Turkish landlord invited her to come into her house, so Aunt Hattie sat down with them for a little visit. Suddenly the woman's husband came by and quickly the woman snatched up a towel which was lying on the floor and threw it over Aunt Hattie's head. Considering that Aunt Hattie is seventy years old this extreme care and modesty is very amusing. The Turks in general have been more annoying and troublesome to us lately. They stoned two of our orphanages, they have followed and annoyed, not to say insulted, our school-girls in the street in mid-day close to our premises, and yesterday, they picked a quarrel with the school-boys at noon, which resulted in the throwing of a great many stones on both sides and high feeling. I do so pity the poor Armenians because if they dare to resist a Turk they only get themselves into trouble. Dr. Barnum has complained to the city government and the zabtieh, Shaban, has been very active with his whip; today, driving Turks from our water-course etc. I hope things will improve as a result.

Last night another of our orphan girls was formally engaged to a young villager. By the time that two or three hundred of our girls are engaged or married, we shall be heartily sick of such things. In the school we have quite a love affair. A pretty, bright girl of about seventeen teaches the smallest tots. She goes to call them in at recess etc and as the school-boys go by that door, and she probably doesn't try to hide, they have had a chance to see her. One of the boys has fallen so much in love, writing her letters etc, that her friends are quite disturbed, not wanting her to be engaged so they are going to take her to Housenik or else she will teach in another school with us. She has no father and mother, but three older sisters and a brother in the Yale Medical School. The boy is quite determined, so he won't be the one to go away. I don't imagine that Eleeza herself wants to, either. It is a queer thing that the boys and girls of our schools, in general don't get along well together. To be sure they see very little of each other, but they are always criticizing and complaining as American boys and girls of from fifteen to twenty-two don't.

Dr. Gates still continues planning for the new buildings and the foundations are being dug, but if the indemnity is not paid, we shall probably not have them.

With much love to all,
Theresa

Feb. 26, 1901

My dear Harry,

I have delivered a lecture on hygiene, "Causes of Sickness"—sickness as produced or induced by bad air, improper food, etc. This wonderful achievement is my second of comparative length, in Armenian. I talked for nearly forty minutes in that tongue, being boosted once in a while by a teacher, when I appealed to her for a word. I think the girls were very glad when the clock pointed to half-past four and they could escape. I gave a talk on games two weeks ago, and as Mary absolved me from teaching the girls how to make soup (!) I hope my trials (and the girls') in the lecture line are over for a time. Every other Wednesday one of the missionary ladies gives a talk on some Domestic Economy or Hygiene subject, and on the alternate Wednesdays they have a cooking-lesson. Every Friday afternoon they go to a lecture in the boys' college on some literary or practical subject. The boys' teachers give these. The college boys, by the way, indulged in a little rebellion two weeks ago, and the thing hasn't been settled yet. They stared too much at the girls during the lectures, so their seats were turned partly around and they had to sit with a side toward the speaker. This was too much for their dignity and they stayed away from the next lecture in a body. I don't know what their punishment will be, but I suppose it will be inflicted next Friday.

After my lecture, to relieve my feelings and for the sake of fresh air, Ellsworth and I went to walk for three-quarters of an hour over the hills behind the college. We started out on the water-course, but we began to meet so many Turks out walking, that we took the regular high-way higher up, and met very few people except shepherd boys with their sheep and goats coming back to the city for the night. When we came back the school-boys had finished dinner and were out playing, with their skirts tucked up into their girdles, showing their full white drawers. Their favorite amusement is throwing stones. They throw heavy ones, too, and there is a great deal of rivalry.

After dinner tonight I tried some songs with one of the American teachers, for her scholars to learn, and then Ellsworth read aloud from the Outlook for three-quarters of an hour. By that time Mary and Miriam were ready to have a teachers' meeting which lasted till nine. We rarely have one in the evening.

Last Friday afternoon the older college boys gave a part of King Lear, which they had translated into Armenian. I said part but it was more than would ever be presented upon the stage as far as length goes. The affair lasted from 1.30 to 5.30. The boys with the help of one of the Armenian professors got it up. They dressed in costumes which you would have shouted with laughter to see, but there was very little acting and practically no change of scenery. Some of the older missionaries didn't approve of having it, but Dr. Gates thought it best to allow it. I wish you could have seen the three daughters of Lear. Of course the boys had all the parts. These three lovely creatures were dressed much alike. Each wore a long, rattling yellow robe which completely enveloped her, and they stood in a straight yellow row most of the time. They wore large squares of cheese-cloth over their heads, bound on with a sort of fillet and I hear that after I left, in the neighborhood of four o'clock they put on hats over these. Some things they did very well. Only the older scholars and teachers were invited to this performance.

As that day was Washington's Birthday, Ada, Miriam and I invited the station and the members of the diplomatic circle to spend the evening with us. Dr. Norton couldn't come, as he had already invited some big Turk to dine with him, but the "Dragon" appeared, dressed very nicely in frock-coat etc. We three were quite giddy (Miriam's influence) powdering our hair, wearing two or three little black patches and putting on our best gowns, pulled up so as to be short-waisted. Our dress seemed to be a matter of astonishment to all the older members of the circle, tho' they all liked it, but the Dragon was floored and finally I explained to him (for he had come late) why we looked so queer. We hung flags about the rooms and put up pictures of Gen. and Lady Washington. We hung up a hatchet (which was really an axe), too. We three called ourselves fine names, Miriam who is plump and wore a white dress and red cherries, being Miss Nellie Custis. The children didn't take it all in, and called her Miss Custard. For refreshments we had two kinds of Washington pie, orangeade and candy. Then we had a guessing affair, called "The Congress of Nations" which we found in a recent long list, and Ada sang several songs. Afterward we all sang Yankee Doodle and other patriotic songs.

I didn't tell you what the invitation was. We cut out a big hatchet from paper and on the head wrote this modification of a Wellesley song,

"There was a famous washing day,
It's action near the Hub;
A Nation's raiment in the suds,
A hero at the tub.
Then come, ye loyal patriots
And rightful homage pay!
We'll honor good George Birthington
On this his washing day"
At home, etc.

On the handle we wrote in large letters, "Who was George Washington?" This hatchet traveled around to the various houses.

Sunday evening Mr. Browne and Aunt Caro told us about the Koordistan work. He is much better now. They plan to start for Malatia next week.

This is Paree Gentan, the beginning of Lent, and last night a bonfire was built on the roof of every Armenian house where there was a bridegroom of less than one year's standing. The children and young men jump thro' these fires and the people everywhere are gossiping and shouting on the roofs. We could see the fires twinkling in many villages down on the plain.

Saturday evening we younger people were invited to spend at an Armenian house. We had a pleasant time, but I haven't time to write of it. Will you please send this letter home when you have read it?

Very lovingly, your sister,
Theresa

Harpoot
March 6, 1901

Dear Mammy,

I have so many half-sheets of paper of various sizes that I am going to use up some on you, please.

Work goes on as usual. Last week we had examinations, and the kindergarten girls gave a hantess. This week, in fact, this afternoon, the kindergarten boys have one. The fathers and mothers come and beam and congratulate each other, if Sarkis, or Sennacherib or Melchizedek has said a piece, while the missionaries sit in the row of honor in front and act as if they had never been to a hantess before, and this were all new and charming. Next week the Varjaran (High School) girls have a hantess, and so on till each school has entertained the public.

The building is going on fast, but with no money. I wonder that Dr. Gates has the faith to keep on so. There must be at least sixty workmen. They are laying the foundations of the Kindergarten and Mangaran (Primary School) now and are beginning the foundation of the teachers' house. I would rather live here than up there with Mary and Miriam, but God won't let us do anything which isn't the very best for us. Mary is always thinking about work and often gets forlorn and blue, but Miriam is just the opposite—always laughing. I am thankful for her. I am half way between the two. Probably Miriam and I will have a sitting-room together in the new house and Mary one alone. I hate to leave Ada, for I love her best of the three, but Miriam is a nice little lady to live with and she has some very pretty things in her room.

Last Saturday, Mary, Miriam and I went over the new school building. I had not been into it for three months. There is a wonderful view from the southern windows. It seems to me to be well-planned tho' the kitchen and dining-room impressed me as small. There are ten or twelve recitation rooms, four teachers' rooms, an assembly room for the College girls and another for the High School girls. The living rooms for the boarders and teachers are all on one floor, separate from the school-rooms etc. The sitting-rooms for the boarders are large, sunny rooms, with bay-windows and a chance for plants.

I've been running about between the sentences of this letter, so that I've quite lost the train of thought.

Last Thursday was Mrs. Browne's birthday, so Aunt Hattie and Aunt Caro invited the circle to spend the evening with them in Mrs. Browne's honor. Of course our American neighbor and his attaché were invited. We had hot chocolate to drink and a fine chocolate birthday cake. Mrs. Gates read one of the "Sonny" stories aloud and the children under Ada's and my direction acted some characters. We often have these impromptu charades. There is nothing which the children like better and the older people love to see the little chickens dressed up, pretending to make calls, teach school etc. Our only preparations are thinking up some words in a few stray minutes and getting an armful of old clothes from several closets.

Harpoot
March 18, 1901

My very dear Father,

It is a Monday night in the middle of March as the heading of my letter indicates. When spring comes I feel more than at other times that we are farther south than you. It is four or five days since we have had a fire in this room, either morning or evening. The number of swallows outside our windows increases daily. The one spring-like thing which is lacking is rain. We have had little snow and rain this winter and unless some comes soon we shall have a water-famine and the crops will be a failure. I never knew the value of water till I came here. When a person is praising up his village, he always tells about the water, and when the people ask me about my "village" in America, they want to know whether we have much water and whether it is sweet.

You people have no idea how much you figure in my conversations with Armenians. One of their first questions is "Have you a father and mother?" Then comes, "Have you any brothers and sisters? Are they married? How could your father and mother let you go away from them? Will they come here? Why not?" etc. They always want to know which is older, Ellsworth or I, and always are surprised at the answer. This pleases E.

Last Saturday Aunt Caro and I took up our beds and a few other trifles and went to Hoolakegh to spend Sunday. You will wonder why I always go to that same village. It has just happened so. The touring servant went with us, using Ada's Bey for a pack animal. It is a ride of about two hours and the weather was perfect—a little too warm for winter clothes. We saw thousands of crocuses and irises by the road-side. This iris grows anywhere and everywhere with no apparent regard to water. It has a faint sweet fragrance. In color it varies from bluish white, spotted with purple and yellow, to a real lavender.

The preacher who was at Hoolakegh when I went there before has gone to America with his family. From his letters it doesn't seem that he is very successful or contented there. I like the new preacher better. He is a young married man from Bitlis who came here to enter the Theological class. When it was decided not to have one, he determined to wait a year and then perhaps to go to Marsovan or Marash. Meanwhile he is working in Hoolakegh.

We had a little room in the preacher's house. It was not very clean, I regret to say, but we were very comfortable there. Saturday night few people came in and we went to bed soon after eight. In the middle of the night we heard shouting and calling and I thought it must be morning. These villagers bellow at their buffaloes, donkeys and cows like the animals themselves. A woman was pounding on a door and crying, "Get up, get up." Aunt Caro said, "Something has happened." We could see the light of a fire reflected on a wall outside our window. We couldn't tell how near it was, so we partly dressed and ran to the other side of the house. It was not dangerously near and before long, we saw that it was dying down. No serious harm was done, because the people woke up in time. It is a mystery to me how these dirty houses with so little wood in them can burn at all.

The next morning we went to the early service at about seven. Then after breakfast Aunt Caro went to Bizmishen, a village half an hour away, to hold a women's meeting, while I led one at Houlakegh. Ten or twelve women came home with me from the meeting and stayed for about an hour and a half. Then they went away to a prayer-meeting and I stayed at home, presumably to rest, but a young woman (a visitor at the preacher's) who had to stay at home on account of her baby wanted to talk, and I wasn't alone till the people came home from meeting, when I went to our little room, put up my camp-bed and lay down for two hours and a half! I really wasn't very tired, but Aunt Caro said she took me away for a vacation and she made me do this. Meanwhile she had come home and then gone to the last service of the day—just before sunset—a church member's meeting. In the evening, eight or ten of "the brethren" came in and as many women. Aunt Caro wanted to talk to them about their wine-drinking, and she did so with a vengeance. She and Mr. Browne reprove, blame and praise the people as they would their children. Wine drinking has increased in this village, as in many others, till almost every church member, both men and women drink. They agree that it is a sin to be drunk but think there is no harm in moderate drinking. Aunt C. went on purpose to speak about this. I don't know how much good it did, but I'm sure it did some.

Do you ever wonder what we eat when we go touring? Saturday evening, we had oyster stew. That was a great luxury in my honor. Aunt C. had a can of oysters and we bought milk in the village. With this we ate some crackers which we brought from here and some native bread—a very nice kind. We each had an apple for dessert, and Pompish Azniv, the preacher's wife brought as a present some squash cooked with dried apricots. For breakfast we had fried eggs and bread; for luncheon, if we wanted any, bread for dinner, pilaf, bread and a cup of cocoa; for breakfast, hot milk and bread. We came home early Monday morning.

Tomorrow is to be a holiday. Ellsworth plans to take his Geology class to a miniature canyon about five miles from here. I think that Ada, Miriam and I will go too. The girls will go on donkeys and make a real picnic of it. Now I must write a letter to Miss Loud. I don't love to write letters of that kind.

Your loving daughter,
Theresa

Chapter Eighteen: The Tax Squeeze, Emigration, and a Splendid Graduation

April was tax collection month in Ottoman Turkey, too, a time that put fear into the hearts of the Armenians. They could count on no mercy from the tax collectors; if there was nothing else to take, Theresa tells us, the collectors sometimes took their household utensils, furniture, animals, or even part of their land. She reports instances where local Armenians, having paid their own taxes, were forced to pay the taxes of their relatives in the United States. At this time of year, Armenians were not given travel permits and many of them, Theresa tells us, were "afraid to go to the market on account of their taxes." In an article published in the *Life and Light*, she told the story of one of the students of Euphrates College, whose father had died two years earlier and who had been put in prison several times since he was unable to pay his father's debts and taxes.[49] Dr. Ussher elaborated on this state of affairs:

> One method of robbing Armenians was to fail to collect some special tax for several years and then suddenly demand cash payment of all arrears. Peasants, whatever their wealth in cattle or land, seldom had much ready money. The tax-gatherer would go to a village with a band of zabtiehs and a number of wealthy Turks from a neighboring village and demand receipts for certain taxes for a period of five, ten or twenty years. For some of those years there would be no receipts to show, because the taxes had not been collected; the receipts for the remaining years would very often have been destroyed in some massacre. But the tax-gatherer took no account of these things: if the receipts were not instantly forthcoming the villagers were beaten and compelled to pay, or to have their fields, cattle, or standing crops sold at auction for one tenth of their value to the wealthy Turks."[50]

---

49. *Life and Light*, 1901, vol. 31.
50. Ussher, pp. 158-159.

Another missionary in Van, Mr. Raynolds, elaborated:

> Of late years, in this vilayet at least, the oppression of the government has been specially manifested in the collection of taxes. As a natural result of what has been narrated above, the receipts from this source have dwindled to a fraction of what they used to be, but the government, instead of changing its policy, and granting the protection which would insure the prosperity and the ability to pay taxes, seems determined to make up the deficiency by squeezing to the dying point the goose which laid the golden egg.... The Turk claims that the amount of taxes demanded is not excessive, as compared with what other governments require... It is a constantly patent fact that the live stock of the farm are so depleted as to make it impossible for the former to cultivate the fields, that the sheep or cow which the poor widow may have kept to provide food for her children, the bedding under which the family sleeps at night, the few copper vessels in which the food is cooked, sometimes the necessary clothing from the person, the fields with the nearly matured crops upon them, which in short time might meet the demand, the timbers, which form the roof which cover them, all are wrenched from the people to satisfy the insatiable tax-gatherer.[51]

At the mission station, however, the mood was one of waiting. Many of the station members were gone, on touring trips, on sick-leave, and were now expected back. Theresa spent her spring break on a tour to the villages of Ichmeh and Palu to visit schools and churches and Ellsworth and Dr. Norton explored a stretch of the Euphrates on a raft of inflated goat-skins—a kelek—which landed the budding geologist on the pages of the *National Geographic*. Theresa and Ellsworth continued to wait for their brother George to come for a visit from Constantinople. Dr. Norton, the Consul, was expecting his wife and son to arrive. And everybody was anxiously waiting for the good Dr. Frank Shepard to arrive from Aintab for Mrs. Barnum who was severely ill.

Dr. Frank Shepard was a legend in these parts. By this time, he had already spent twenty years in Turkey—two of them, by his own reckoning, in the saddle—treating everyone who asked for help. He found there was a great need for him at Harpoot and Theresa reports that "Dr. Shepard gave medical advice to nine of our circle." Mrs. Barnum turned out to have a tumor; the Barnums would have to leave for Marsovan where Dr. Carrington would perform

---

51. ABC 16.7.17.

an operation. Dr. Shepard's visit also resulted in the loss of the leader of the Harpoot station: it did not take the doctor long to see that Caleb Gates—after his unceasing struggles through the massacres and the reconstruction of the buildings—was dangerously close to collapse, and he ordered him to leave for the United States as soon as possible. That however, according to Dr. Gates, did not turn out to be until the following October.

Theresa continues faithfully to write to her family. In May, her sister Cornelia was the recipient of two letters:

> Dearest Kindie,
>
> Ellsworth is sending a nice long letter and it is just ten o'clock, so my letter on clothes will represent me this week. We grow more and more busy as we approach the whirlpool of June. Our new building will be dedicated at Commencement time. Tomorrow the College girls have a hantess, and as I play for all the songs and have trained nearly half the girls for recitations I don't anticipate the affair with delight. This afternoon I had my yearly Junior C.E. social and the girls had a happy time, I'm sure. First they had a grand march, while I played John Browne's Body and the dust flew. Then we had some tricks such as two blind-folded girls feeding each other etc. Then we played chumps and rooster. After that, we had refreshments—candy, leblebs, and raisins and finally we sang a hymn, a teacher read from the Bible, Mary prayed and we went home. Each girl had a little rosette of colored worsted as a badge, the five committees having each a certain color.
>
> The Barnums will start on Monday. News came last week of the coming of Dr. Atkinson and his wife next fall and a new young married missionary to take E's place. This is doubtless old news to you.

> Dear Kindie,
>
> Last Thursday the post brought "Elizabeth and Her German Garden." Thank you ever so much, dear sister. It is a beautiful edition. There is another copy in the station, but I hadn't read it except for bits here and there which Ada read aloud—very little. Ellsworth hasn't read it at all, so there is a treat for both of us pretty soon. It is a book that stimulates one to be sort of clever and vivacious for a while. Do you remember that we used to say that "One Summer" made us feel that way.

For the last few months I have written all my home letters in the evening when I feel sort of stupid and not funny at all. I feel as if I ought to apologize for it.

Last Friday, Mary, Ada, and Mrs. Knapp went off to Ichmeh for a little visit, by invitation. That seems to be the popular resort just now. It is just the rose season now and the gardens are their loveliest. They came home Monday noon. Ada told about a company of Pilgrims returning from Mecca, whom they met. They were dressed very strangely, with tall pointed white felt half caps, large green turbans etc. They were returning to Erzingan and Erzroom. The people (Turks) who met them would kiss the hand and foot of one of the pilgrims. They rode good horses and part of the time went at headlong speed. One rode a fine white horse, half of whose tail was dyed a bright red.

Mr. Knapp, of course, stayed at home and took care of the children. He invited Miriam, Ellsworth and me to take dinner with them Saturday and Sunday nights. They certainly have much the best cook in the station. The Browne's cook Caspar hasn't the Con'ple training which the Knapp's cook had.

We have had several station or school business meetings lately to talk about teachers for next year, salaries etc and to make plans for the last days of school. I'll write down some of the things which come off before school is over.

May 27-31—Written exams.
" 30 Juniors invite Seniors and teachers to a picnic at a garden.
Boys have field-day.
June 1 Boarders picnic at our garden.
" 5 C.E. Social
" 7 Seniors spend evening with teachers.
" 10 Junior C.E. missionary m't'g
" 12 Organ pupils concert for scholars
" 17, 18, 19, 20, 24, 25 Oral exams in different schools.
" 18 C.E. business meeting
" 21 Open house and Dedication of new girls' school
Exhib. of handiwork
" 23 Baccal.
" 25 Hantess—graduat. of lower schools
" 27 Commencement
In afternoon reunion of alumnae.

Beside all this there are the boys' affairs to which we are invited and go. These mean always a great deal of training in singing etc. I don't know that all of this pays yet it isn't easy to know what it is best to omit, they enjoy it all so much. The boys and girls practice together in my room now twice a week. They are going to sing "Praise Ye the Father" together at Commencement.

Tonight Miriam and I went over the new school. I don't see how it's going to be finished in a month. It is a fine large building. Do you realize how much building is going on here now? Two large school-houses—enough to accommodate all the girls, together with the kindergarten boys, are in process of building; a house between there for the American teachers; a dormitory for the boys; a bake-house; and several rooms on the stable-edifice to be used as a Theological Seminary (!) This is a great deal but everything is necessary. I don't know where the money is coming from to finish these. Dr. Gates is in some ways a wonderful man.

Moore is better and everybody is much relieved. Mr. Browne and Aunt Caro start off day after tomorrow on a three or four weeks tour to Temran etc. up toward Erzroom. Dr. and Mrs. Ussher have a baby boy—Neville Thompson Ussher.

Let me tell you what a funny thing I just heard. Yevnege who teaches the older girls Physiology plans to take her class to a garden where they will dissect a sheep after which they will roast and eat him. It is a sort of dreadful plan, isn't it? I don't believe they will do it. Ellsworth may not write this week. He's well and busy.

Very lovingly,
Theresa

Harpoot
May 21, 1901

My precious Father,

This is my birthday, and it has been a very pleasant one. I'll have to do what I used to when I wrote letters as a child—give a list of my presents, which I found waiting for me at the breakfast table.

Ellsworth—set of photographs (of his last trip)
Ada—wood-box–native hand'k
Mary—book– "The All-Sufficient Saviour" by MacGregor.
plant
pencils–envelopes
Miriam—two silver rings for belt.

Mr. Browne—scissors
Mrs. " stocking-bag
Harold—pretty box
Knapp children—roses (Mr. Knapp got up before five o'clock this morning and went to Harsenik for them)
Aunt Hattie—rainbow shawl
Aunt Caro—neck-tie
Emma—little box for dressing-table
Winifred—a sort of wall-pocket which she made herself.

You may notice that the Gates family are left out. They are always loving and friendly, but rarely give presents at such times.

This morning Harold brought his lamb to me, with a note tied to his neck. When I opened it, this was what I read.

Dear Aunt Theresa,

This morning when my master, Harold came down to the stable he told me it was your birthday. So I send you as a congratulation a little cut of my wool. Also many happy returns.
I remain your nephew
Frisk.

A little bunch of the lamb's wool was in the envelope. Isn't that a cunning letter?

This evening I am going to eat dinner with the school-girls. Ada, Miriam, Mary and several other missionaries are invited, too. Mr. Browne and Aunt Caro are talking of starting on another tour soon, this time going to Geghi, a place four days to the north of us in the mountains. It belongs to our field, but is really nearer to Erzroom. Mr. B. is very much better. Moore is still sick and seems to grow thinner and weaker, tho' he is always a merry, cheerful little fellow. We are hoping that Dr. Marden of Aintab will spend the summer with us, but are not yet sure. He wrote accepting Dr. Gates' invitation, but that was before he knew that Dr. Atkinson is to come here in the fall.

May 22, 1901

After writing the above letter we went to the school to dinner. Mary had told the girls that it was my birthday, so when we entered the door, there were all the girls lined up, singing a song of welcome. We had a very nice dinner, sitting with them on the floor by native tables, of course. Do you want to know what we had to eat? Greens (spinach) with salt but no vinegar; bread, of course; little meat balls, like tiny croquettes; rice pillaf; tahn (buttermilk) and for dessert, a poor sort of fried thing similar to doughnuts, and a sort of cornstarch pudding which looked exactly like the boiled starch used for washing.

We talked with the girls and sang and they all came up to me in turn to kiss my hand. We came home at about seven, and lo, Aunt Hattie and Aunt C. had invited all the circle to spend the evening with them in my honor. It was a very pleasant evening. We had chocolate to drink, with ginger-snaps and lemon candy for more solid fare. We were given certain subjects to illustrate by drawings on a black-board, while the others guessed the subject. For example I had to illustrate, "Mr. Browne's favorite joke." Mr. Knapp's subject was "Harpoot time"; Aunt Caro's "Twenty-six years ago today" etc.

Herbert brought to me that evening a very pretty basket from the Gates family and some flowers, with a blotter which he had made himself. Now I am really ashamed that I have written so much about my birthday.

The station has invited Alice Browne to come here as a teacher a year hence. I do not feel at all sure that she will come. We had a telegram two days ago saying that the Barnums had reached Sivas safely.

Ellsworth has doubtless written of his Geology trip. The boys evidently had a splendid time in spite of rain, although some of them were very much frightened in the boat on the lake. It was a rare treat to most of them.

We are already practising music for Commencement time. The boys and girls are learning two things to sing together. One of them is "Praise Ye the Father." I wish Cornelia would send us some more pretty, simple anthems, which she has tried.

The walls of the teachers' house are fast going up. We expect to have the dedicatory service of the school in less than a month. Last night a girl said to me in English. "A man (Armenian) came back to our village from America and he spoke very populously." She meant that he used bad English—the vulgar tongue.

I must go to bed now. Goodnight, my dear, dear father. I grow more grateful every year for all the teaching and the love you have given me ever since the beginning of my life.

Always lovingly,
Theresa

The Garden
June 12, 1901

Dear Mamma,

I am waiting here in the Browne's house for a thunder shower to pass away before I can go back to the city. Mrs. B. and Harold moved out here yesterday. E. still continues to eat with the boys and Mary's woman will prepare all but dinner for M. and me. Ellsworth and I will walk out in the evening to the garden for dinner. We came out for the first time today and it began to rain almost as soon as we sat down for dinner.

Mrs. B. is in the room and reading, "Wild Animals I Have Known" aloud to Harold.

Ada has been having a great deal of tooth-ache lately and last week after being awake and suffering for half a night, she decided that she must go to Con'ple to have her teeth filled. E. who had expected to go as far as Marsovan for George will go to Samsoun with her as soon as school closes. She will go by araba. I may go with them for the sake of seeing E. and G. longer and for the change, but I hate to go so far and spend the money with no more important object. In a year or two I may need to go to Con'ple for my own teeth. They seem to be all right now. There is only one place so far as I can see that needs filling and that can wait sometime yet, I think. There is another place, too, but it is very small. I will tell you definitely next week whether I shall go.

Dr. Norton will start in three or four weeks for Mrs. Norton and Mr. Stephanides' sixteen-year-old sister who is now at the Girls' college at Scutari, will come on with them to take care of her brother, as he said. He frankly confesses that he is very lonely, in spite of the zoo at the Consulate. He says she is taller than he, and he is very tall. "Oh," said he, "she is an awfully grown girl." He sometimes uses very droll English.

I forgot to tell you all about Ada. When she reaches Con'ple she will be only four days from home by the quickest way and we have almost persuaded her to go, so she will probably spend a month or more in England. I don't know when she will come back. Of course, in that case, she will have her dentistry done at home. It is very expensive in Con'ple without being really first-class.

School closes two weeks from tomorrow, the 27th. We are having examinations and all sorts of things just now. Today the girls who have been learning to play the organ gave a concert, for the scholars and teachers only. There was some singing with it, too. At the first some of them had stage-fright which seemed to be contagious and their playing was really dreadful. One girl had begun the same piece four times before she got under way and when she got up, tipped over the organ-stool. I wanted to run away and hide, but finally everybody, myself included was in such a state of laughter that we couldn't hold in. After that however, things grew better and better and some of the girls played very well indeed.

I am writing now in the city. We did enjoy the walk in. Everything was fresh and clean after the rain. The sun was setting. In some directions it was raining heavily, but parts of the sky were clear. The tops of the near hills were in the sunlight, but against the black, dark mountains across the plain there was the end of a rainbow which shone like fire. I have never seen one so brilliant and large before. It seemed to stand up straight at one end of Hazar Baba, like a pillar of fire and its double stood guard at the other end.

It is now nine o'clock A.M. and we just heard a pounding on the stable-door below, on the other side of the street. E. called out of the window and found it was Shaban with the mail, as we supposed. He was going to take it to the garden, but now he is bringing it here for us to take out ours first. Only Aunt Hattie, Mary, E. and I are left here in the city.

Dr. Marden expects to leave Aintab the 25th of this month and will reach here within a week. Little Moore doesn't seem to grow any better. He doesn't walk at all. His father and mother look tired and troubled. He is their ewe lamb and it doesn't seem as if God could take him.

Did I write that a telegram came last week saying that Mrs. Barnum's operation had been successful?

We are still hoping to have the dedication of the new school a week from Friday, but it cannot be wholly finished by that time. Nor do I see how the teachers' house will be ready before September, or October, so that we cannot move our things out in the summer.

You asked me once whether Dr. Ussher ever paid any special attention to me and I have always forgotten to answer. No indeed. I never gave him any chance nor did he ever want to. He is not the sort of man I admire. We were good friends, however. Mr. Knapp was told by Miss Wheeler in America that Laura and I were both in love with the Doctor and that was the cause of his going away etc. Note: I was completely outside of the whole affair and I do hate to be gossiped about that way at "the Rooms," but don't you ever say a word there upon the subject, please. It is much better let alone and they will forget. It is all ancient history now.

The post brings a letter from George but none from home. He says he received none from home the week of his writing.

We are sending away two teachers whose influence in the school has not been good and it makes the school atmosphere a little muggy. They both have some good and attractive qualities but I shall be glad when they go.

Time gone—
Lovingly,
Theresa

Harpoot
June 18, 1901

Dear, dear Papa,

I had been "counting on" writing you a long birthday letter tonight, and an appalling thought has just struck me. If I am to get a letter to Miss Loud in time for the July Branch Meeting, it has got to go tomorrow (I know you will object to all those gots).

I send you a big, loving kiss for your birthday. How I should love to be there to put some more on the top of your head and under your ears and in all the nice little corners adapted to such things. I hope it will be a beautiful day for you. We shall think of it here. Ellsworth and George will probably be travelling that day and I shall be alone so far as the family is concerned.

I often think, dear Papa, of all you did for me when I was a child, and all you do now, too. Ellsworth and I speak of these things many times. I feel so grateful now that you used to come up to my room at breakfast time and have me open my bed properly and my window, too, and to see that my clothes were hung up. I am thankful that you taught me to enjoy a brisk walk, to look at the stars and the trees. Then I am thankful for the way you taught us to enjoy good books and the many you read aloud to us. Oh, there a great many things which I feel grateful to you for. I can't name them all possibly. One more is that you taught me not to toy with my fingers, while talking. The list of what we owe to you and Mamma is endless, and how can we help loving you both dearly—more so all the time.

Only Mary, Ellsworth and I are left in the city now. We walk out to the garden for dinner and back again in the cool of the evening. They bring in our luncheon to us and we all eat together—i.e. Mr. Browne, Aunt Hattie, Aunt Caro, Miriam and I. E. still eats luncheon with the boys. Tomorrow he and I begin to eat breakfast together and expect to keep on with this plan for a week (8 days) longer, when he will start with Ada. Tomorrow morning we shall have bread and milk, boiled eggs, cherries and apricots and perhaps cookies. I paid 10 paras for the bread, 30 for the milk (1 1/2 pints), the fruit cost about 20. That is, the value of our breakfast is about seven cents. That doesn't include the cost of fire for the eggs and the cookies which were given to us.

I have decided not to go with Ellsworth to meet George. I am sure the discomforts of the summer journey, the hasty preparation I should have to make (leaving here on Commencement Day), the work left undone here for a month, together with various other reasons, overbalance the pleasure of being with the boys.

Last Monday Mr. Browne and Aunt Caro unexpectedly returned and have been devoting themselves since to visit the schools and hearing oral examinations. I am much occupied with preparations for the final exhibitions and with the examinations which are going on now. Yesterday we had a C.E. business meeting. The Senior and Junior Societies have this year given between thirty and thirty-five dollars for missions etc. This includes the money which the American teachers give.

Yesterday the January and March shipments from America reached us. I wish you could have seen the train of camels bringing them in and the strange, dark-skinned camel-drivers. All the boxes have not been opened yet, so I have not received all my things. I will try to write to Mamma in detail about them next week. Meanwhile I thank her very much.

We send two photographs of Harpoot by this mail. One is for you from E. and me and the other for Aunt Theresa.

With much love, my precious father,
Theresa

Harpoot
June 20, 1901

Dear Mamma,

I am sitting like Watts, and watching something boil, or rather, waiting for it to boil. You know we always heat milk before drinking it and with the help of Miriam's chafing-dish, I am preparing Ellsworth's and my breakfast for tomorrow morning. Last night Ellsworth went to bed later than I did, and not knowing the habits of the cats who live with the vicinity of our house, he left several doors open. Consequently half our milk was gone this morning and thinking the cat might have walked through the other half, I took it down for the breakfast of our two washer women. They were delighted. I told them we had gotten it for our breakfast and that so much was left. I intended to tell them about the cat, but E. said, "No, they'll think you a great goose not to have drunk it yourself." So I gave them some sugar to make it sweet as all Armenians like it.

I think I wrote to you that E. is sleeping in Ada's room and we two are alone in this big house, and have our breakfast together, walking to the garden for dinner. I told Manoog, a servant, to buy ten eggs for me this morning. He forgot and so tonight appeared bringing forty-two eggs in a sort of bag. I had to laugh to see the heap and think of eating them up in two meals. I finally took 12 paying one piastre (4 1/2 cents).

As I sit here at 9 o'clock in the evening I can hear someone in the street below whistling. "There'll be a hot time" etc. He is probably an Armenian who has been to America.

This has been a busy week. Friday morning there were examinations. In the afternoon the new building was open for inspection from 1 to 3. We began by sending about the people who came, in groups under the guidance of a teacher, but soon they came thick and fast so that it was very hard to manage them. Most of them were women and I really had to push and hold them besides talking to make them go in the right direction. Many of them are only half or three-quarters civilized and have no idea of order and propriety. It is almost impossible to make them keep still at a hantess, though Aunt Hattie says that this "isn't a circumstance to the old days" when they were comparatively speaking, a howling mob.

At 3 o'clock came the dedication of the new school. The windows are not in yet and the walls and wood-work are not finished off, but still things were presentable. All the rooms were empty except the Varjaran (High School) where the service was held. Rugs and carpets were spread on the floor, there were some chairs for the dignitaries and the organ with some plants upon it, and a little table on the platform completed the furnishings. The room holds between 800 and 900 people seated on the floor, with a few in chairs.

The program was something like this. I don't remember it exactly.

1. Hymn—All
2. Reading of the Bible—Mezereh Pastor
3. Prayer " "
4. Address: Progress of the Education of Women in this Country. Prof. Nahigian
5. Paper: The Beginnings of this School. Written by Miss Seymour. Read by one of the girls' teachers.
6. Hymn By College Girls
7. Brief Talk on the Purpose of the School. Miss Daniels
8.The Parents' Relation to the School. Choonkoosh Pastor
9.Remarks by Dr. Norton
10. Dedication Prayer. Dr. Gates
11. Hymn. College Girls (written by one of the boys' teachers)
12. Doxology

There isn't time to tell what they said even if you wanted to know. Only one thing: Prof. Nahigian said that 37 years ago there were only two women in Harpoot who knew how to read, one in Husenik and none in Mezereh. It was considered a shame for a woman to know how to read. Now almost every Armenian girl, except the miserably poor, goes to school for a longer or shorter time. Aunt Hattie's paper was very interesting, but she was unwilling to read it herself. She told how the first school in Harpoot for girls was opened in a stable, just the sort of place where the Lord Jesus began his life. The Armenian teacher who read this paper spoke a few words on her own account, expressing the gratitude of scholars and teachers to Dr. Gates for all his efforts, recalling former teachers etc. She spoke with great dignity and self-possession.

The pastor who spoke of the parents' relation to the school has three daughters in the boarding department. We did not expect to have him speak, but he came unexpectedly from a distance and we couldn't leave him out.

Sunday morning at 7 o'clock came the Baccalaureate sermon. That is an hour later than the usual Sunday morning service at this season. Mr. Knapp preached a good sermon on "Is not the life more than meat" etc. Unfortunately there was a great crowd and before the service a good deal of noise. The graduates, five boys

> and seven girls, sat up in front looking very magnificent in their new graduating clothes. The boys all have suits alike with red (!) neck-ties. The girls all have white cotton dresses—a very pretty material. Next year there will be four girls and sixteen boys in the Senior class.

The 22nd Commencement of Euphrates College on June 27th 1901 was a splendid affair. It was attended by several of the local Turkish dignitaries and close to one thousand people; the ceremonies were held in Armenian, Turkish, and English and started off by the college band playing the Hamidieh March; the graduates—both male and female—read essays on various high-minded topics (Love of Reading Among Women; The Moral Force of a Girl; Progress in the 19th Century; Modern Agriculture) and the male and female choruses alternated between hymns and Mozart. Consul Norton distributed the diplomas. It was a day of hope and optimism, but underneath it all there was a great deal of unease. Consul Norton was well aware that close to two hundred entire Armenian families in the area had applied for passports to emigrate to America earlier in the year. That meant more than one thousand men, women, and children who represented the more enterprising and resourceful element of the population. There was a general feeling of profound discouragement among those elements of the Armenian population who could reflect on their situation; often these were the leaders of the community. For the Protestants, this meant that they were losing the pastors and the teachers faster than they could educate new ones. And those staying behind without their leaders felt even more discouraged. "They lose heart," writes Norton, "in the face of continued oppression and persecution."

Generally, it was easier for entire families to secure passports than it was for individuals, but even for families, the road to the promised land was hard. At every turn, there were new fees to pay, new forms to fill, and new individuals ready to fleece them. The prospective emigrants had to sign a written promise not to return to their native land. This had dire consequences for the marriage market, since so many young men had returned to the towns of their birth in order to seek a bride. More and more, this had to be done long distance, with the help of photographs.

Those who managed to leave, usually went by way of either Samsoun on the Black Sea or Alexandretta on the Mediterranean via French steamer to Marseilles and then on to America, their final destination being New England or California. This was where most of them went. Other countries were beginning to attract Armenian immigrants as well: France, Egypt, the Sudan and many South American countries among them.

From her vantage point, Theresa did not look kindly on those who left. One can assume that her views were fairly typical of the missionaries: they were in the business of educating young men and women to be of service to their own country and people. The massacres of 1895, however, had tempered the missionary reluctance to have the Armenians leave; the continued tensions made it easy to understand their unease, and the initial ban on teaching English that they had imposed in their early mission work in order to make it harder for the population to leave had been lifted long ago. It is safe to say, however, that at the time of the hopeful 1901 Commencement, no one—missionary, teacher, graduate, family member—could in their wildest nightmares have imagined what was coming only thirteen years from then: the First World War, and under its cloak, the genocide of the Armenian people of the Ottoman empire.

Chapter Nineteen: Big-power Politics and New Arrivals

After the Gates family left Harpoot for a long overdue vacation and then on to Robert College in Constantinople, Dr. Herman Barnum took over as acting President of Euphrates College. It was clear that his tenure could not be long; Dr. Barnum was seventy-five years old and getting feeble and forgetful. He and his wife Mary were part of the original group of missionaries at Harpoot and greatly beloved by the locals. Dr. Barnum had never intended to spend all those years in Turkey. He had graduated from Andover Theological Seminary in 1855 and, travelling in Europe after graduation, decided to go on to Constantinople. There, he met the Rev. William Goodell who with Elias Riggs and William Schauffler was one of the missionary pioneers in that city. He also met Goodell's daughter, Mary, who no doubt was an important reason for his decision to stay on. After he and Mary were married in 1860, they headed straight for Harpoot and were there, as we have seen, when Theresa arrived. The Barnums and the Harpoot station were synonymous, and Dr. Barnum, who spoke fluent Turkish and Armenian, was widely respected by all. By all accounts, he was a very capable man and it was said that if he had chosen to, he could have become Ambassador to Turkey. But this unassuming and scholarly man preferred the more simple—and in many ways, more demanding—life of a missionary and the Barnums stayed on in Harpoot.

Dr. Barnum's diplomatic skills were often utilized locally. James L. Barton who spent nine years in Harpoot, from 1885 to 1894, and who later became the Foreign Secretary of the American Board wrote:

> All who knew Dr. Barnum, Turk, Armenian, missionary, and European, learned to put great value upon his judgment relating to all classes of questions. For more than twenty years his counsel has been constantly sought on subjects religious, personal, national, and diplomatic, and every one who sought received the best he had to give, and that was always in high order. He has constantly been in close correspondence with the representatives of the United States government at the Porte regarding political conditions in

> Turkey, while at the same time the local civil governors and officials of high rank have openly declared that Dr. Barnum understood the conditions in the country better than any Moslem. It has been the custom of the country frequently to change the heads of the vilayets, and it was not an uncommon experience for the incoming governor to seek upon his arrival a prolonged interview with the frail, white-locked, modest missionary, whose grasp of the local situation was regarded of too great value not to be utilized.[52]

The Barnums daughter Emma, much admired and loved by Theresa and described by Ellsworth as "not pretty, but the most unselfish person I have ever known," now took over some of the administrative duties from her father. "Emma goes everywhere with her father, to the teacher's meetings, to oversee the dormitory and is eyes and ears and especially memory to him," writes Theresa. Meanwhile, the search continued for someone to fill the Presidency of Euphrates College on a permanent basis.

That this person was required to be a diplomat in addition to an educator was clear from the example of both Dr. Barnum and Dr. Gates. Sometimes, this diplomacy reached far outside the boundaries of the Ottoman empire. The missionaries had clout, and they knew it. From the far-flung corners of the world, they had what we today would call "access"—means by which they could make their problems heard by the Secretary of State and the President of the United States. In November of 1900, Dr. Gates wrote to the American Board offices in Boston:

> Now that the election of Mr. McKinley is assured for another term of service, would it not be a good time to represent to him that permission has been given for the rebuilding (of the missionary compound buildings destroyed in the massacre of 1895) but the indemnity is still lacking and that if we cannot secure the funds with which to build there is danger that our permission will be imperilled. It may be that he would make renewed efforts to obtain it.[53]

Dr. Gates' plea for the President's help did not bear any result, however. But Gates was nothing if not persistent: he loaned the station $5,000 of his own money in order to start the reconstruction. And then, in September of 1901, in the aftermath of the Spanish-American War, President McKinley was assassinated in Buffalo. The news travelled sufficiently fast to Harpoot to

52. *Missionary Herald*, 1910, p. 311.
53. ABC 16.9.15.

enable Theresa to comment on the tragedy in a letter to Miss Lord, but the general news from Harpoot had top priority:

> Harpoot, Sept. 18, 1901
>
> My dear Miss Loud,
>
> I have just received a letter from my mother saying that your meeting may be held Oct. 13, in which case this letter may not be on time. I have waited to write, wanting to tell you about the opening of the school.
>
> Both our new buildings could not possibly be completed before school opened, so Dr. Gates had the work-men give all their strength and time to the building for the older girls and boarders, and the smaller girls and kindergarten children have had to go back to their old quarters for only a month or two we hope.
>
> Our new school is not beautiful architecturally, but it is convenient and large and comfortable and we do love it. Cheap curtains and pretty pictures, with native carpets in some rooms make it all look habitable and homey and I think our school rooms would not disgrace an American town. Simple as it all is, I am sometimes afraid it is too good for the girls, it is so different from their homes. The new girls, and the old ones, too, seemed dazed and lost for a day or two. Most of them are used to living in their houses of two, three, or four small rooms. I hope this "goodly heritage" may make them only more ready to share their benefits and blessings with others. The bed for our sunny little sick-room has come and we renew our thanks to the kind friends who sent the money for it. It is a single iron bedstead made in Constantinople. That, with a table and some pictures comprise our sick-room furniture. I am glad to say that there are no occupants yet.
>
> One feature of the new building of which we are glad is that in the large dormitory there are forty tiny rooms,—rather closets—where the girls can pray and think alone. The girls certainly appreciate this privacy, which we at home think so necessary. As we have nearly eighty boarders, sometimes two girls have to use a room together and the smaller children can have no place of their own.
>
> There is the same desire this year as before among the people about us to have their children go to school. This motive is not always the highest, but everywhere the mothers and fathers want to have their children educated and the children are eager to come. We receive no children free. In every case money must be given or its equivalent in work, or else we or some other friends pay the bill.

A part of the church collections on this side of the city is given by the church to put poor children in school. Our Christian Endeavor girls give a part of their money for the same purpose.

Poor mothers & children beset us on every side just before school opens, beseeching us to pay for their children or themselves or to buy stockings or lace which they have made to earn money for this purpose. Many times, of course, they are unworthy and we are not sorry to say that we cannot help, but often it is hard to say, as we must, "My sister, there is nothing. We cannot give." One dear child who has been to school before and whom I know well came to me to ask for help in paying to enter school. I knew they were very poor, but I asked, "What are you going to do yourself?" She said, "My sister and I worked for a month and a half this vacation from morning till night in a place where they keep silk-worms to prepare the cocoons." "How much did you earn?" I asked. "One medjid together," she said, her eyes filling with tears. A medjid is about ninety cents. That means that she earned a cent a day by working all day for six weeks, in order to be able to go to school in the fall, and then she had to beg for the rest. Perhaps you wonder why we do not receive the poorest children free. I can only say that it has been tried and has not proved to be the best policy in this country. People value only what they pay for here.

We have several new girls from a distance. One comes from Sivas. Two others come from the missionary schools at Hadjin and Aintab to the south of us, where only Turkish is spoken. They have come here to learn their mother tongue and will go back to teach it in the schools from which they came.

Today we have had the great pleasure of welcoming Dr. and Mrs. Barnum and their daughter back from Marsovan, where they went last spring to have a surgical operation performed upon Mrs. Barnum. It was wonderfully successful. Dr. & Mrs. Barnum are the oldest missionaries here and are dearly loved by the people. A great many sent out to meet them on horse-back or on foot. A company of our pastors went out about a two hours ride. Later a troop of orphan boys on foot, then a group of women and after them a large company of school boys with their teachers. It was a real respect and love which brought them out. As they came into the city and up to the gate of the mission yard, the streets were full of men, women, and children all eager to welcome them. It was a touching sight to us younger missionaries to see what a place the older ones have in the people's hearts.

> Our consul has invited the Americans and all the European colony and Turkish officials to a memorial service for our beloved President, to be held tomorrow. Our hearts are full of pain and grief for him as yours are in the home-country.
> I wish I had time for a personal note for you, but this can only be general. Lovingly, your friend,
> Theresa L. Huntington.

Ever since Theresa got to Harpoot, there was one thing which she had been secretly dreading: the day Ellworth would leave. He had already extended his stay by one year; in the summer of 1901, the matter came up again and in Dr. Gates' papers, we find the following:

> ...it is not best for Mr. Huntington to remain and not right for us to ask him to do so. He has already served one year beyond the time for which he came here and he is desirous of continuing his studies. He has received the offer of a scholarship in Harvard which will enable him to do this; moreover, he has the prospect of another opportunity to travel, which would be of great benefit to him. It does not seem to me right for us to ask him to sacrifice these prospects, which may never be renewed to him and continue on in this work. He is willing to do so if it seems the right thing, but he is so unselfish that he really needs a guardian to look after his own interests.[54]

Ellsworth thus becomes another recipient of Theresa's letters. Soon after he left, he received one from her which touches on the big-power politics in the wake of the McKinley assassination. Theodore Roosevelt was now in the White House, and the missionaries thought of him as a friend who would play rough with Turkey, if necessary, to protect their interests. Dr. James Barton who Theresa refers to here, had served a stint of nine years at the Harpoot station before she arrived, and later became the Foreign Secretary of the American Board.

> My dear Ellsworth,
> The Barnum letter-packet had just come to us, and there is a part of Dr. Barton's letter which may interest you. I suppose there can be nothing private in it which it would be wrong to quote, because he says, "You will probably see in the papers something

54. ABC 16.9.15.

> more at length in regard to this visit." The part I wanted you to hear was this:
>
> "I wish to tell you of the visit which had just been made to Washington in the interests of work in Turkey. The delegation, composed of twenty-four men, called yesterday on the Secretry of State & the President, petitioning our Government to demand from Turkey the same rights and privileges that have been grated already to similar institutions in other countries. It is most inspiring to come thus in contact with a President & Secretary of State who are so much in sympathy with the work we are doing. Pres. Roosevelt spoke in highest terms of his appreciation of it and the character of the missionaries who are doing the work, and assured us that our government would secure from Turkey the same rights for our institutions that have been granted other countries, altho' he said he could not promise just how it would secure them: but he added this, "If we undertake the matter, as we shall, we shall carry it through to its only conclusion, that is, the securing that for which we ask, and we shall do this even if it means war with Turkey." And when he made that statement he showed not less than a dozen teeth and the gesture with which he accompanied it was with a closed hand. He added, however, "We shall do everything to avoid a clash with Turkey or any other country, but there are things worse than war." He instructed Sec'y Hay in the presence of the deputation to take the matter up at once.[55]

Theresa did not often concern herself with big-power politics. She felt lonely after Ellsworth's departure for home and graduate school. George, too, had come to Harpoot for a brief visit and returned home to go to college. Theresa continued writing her missives to the Milton home, expressing worries about her Aunt Theresa Gaytes in Galesburg and acutely feeling the distance to her home:

> Harpoot
> October 27, 1901
>
> My dear little Mamma,
>
> I have been thinking of you a great deal since your last letter came, saying that Aunt Theresa was worse and that you were going to her. And I have prayed often for dear Auntie and for you,

55. Yale University Archives, Ellsworth Huntington Papers, Theresa Huntington Ziegler file.

mother dear, not knowing what she might be suffering or what sorrow you might be bearing. I can only hope and wait and keep on praying for you both and for Herbert, and loving you dearly. How I long, little Mamma, to take you in my arms and kiss you, and to help you and comfort you in some way!

This is the end of a very ordinary Sunday, which might have been extraordinary if I had done all in my power to do. I went to the early morning service which begins at about 6.30 now. Then we had prayers at the Brownes and our regular beans and brown-bread Sunday morning breakfast. I went to see Mary, played the organ a little while and did various other little things till it was time to go to the various Sunday Schools which I superintend. Then Miriam, Mary and I ate our luncheon together in Miriam's room—Sunday noon, we don't sit down at the table, except in summer. I didn't go to church in the afternoon, but read and prepared to lead prayers four days this week. In the evening I went to the girls' meeting, which Emma led, and later to our own meeting at the Knapps. I feel that it has been rather a selfish day. I would go to villages some of these pleasant Sundays if only Mr. Knapp could go, but he is kept here by his S.S. class which was Dr. Gates' before, and I rather dread going off with only an Armenian. Not that it isn't perfectly safe, only so many people come to see one at a village and I have had so little experience. Then one is so conspicuous. However, those are poor excuses.

Your little picture I forgot to acknowledge last week. I should know it was you and for that reason I love it, but do you and the others really think it a good picture? It brings your real image more vividly to my mind, but I'm glad that you truly don't look just like that. It is just as well that my face isn't clearer in the pictures we sent you, because I never look well in a picture and you would only be disappointed.

You said in one letter that you didn't think I appreciated the piqué dress. Indeed I do, and I am sure I have written of it. George spoke especially of liking it and Mary said one day that she liked to see me wear that better than anything else. I can't wear it as much as I would like because we have so much sand and dust at the garden and the aivan and dining-room both have dirt floors.

Probably you will not be at home when this letter reaches America, so I will write the rest to Papa.

I kiss your hands, as the children say in this country, and your sweet mouth, too.

Always your loving daughter,
Theresa

Harpoot
October 27, 1901

Dearest Papa,

Although the book you sent did not come last week, it probably will next Wednesday and I must give you my best thanks for it now before I have seen it, and a kiss of gratitude on your dear forehead or anywhere where you would like to have it put. I am sure the book will be very interesting and valuable. The histories we sent for to America for the school, have not come yet, so I am using Myer's Medieval and Modern History as an outline and supplementing it more or less with Mackenzie and other borrowed books. There is no Armenian text-book and we couldn't afford it if there were, so I have to give almost everything in lectures helped out by special topics translated by the girls now and then from books which I give them. They would find it hard to get everything from an English text-book. I have to speak rather slowly in my Armenian lectures and they have to take notes, so we don't get on very fast.

We expected to use the new building for the lower schools by the 1st of November but it isn't ready yet and we have been obliged to rent the old houses for two weeks longer. The building work goes more slowly now that Dr. Gates has gone. He was the best hustler of all the missionaries.

Last Friday afternoon I took a good ride with the Knapps. Mrs. K pattered on behind on a white donkey but Mr. Knapp and I cantered most of the way riding back to meet her when necessary. That evening we had a station meeting at the Barnums in the old-time way. First we had refreshments—sliced raw pears, cake with whipped cream in the middle, and a kind of sour drink, also some chocolate candies from America (pretty hard). The Barnums have made the house look cosier than it did when the Gateses lived there. After this most of us were armed with scissors and cut out stamped dogs and cats and dolls (to be stuffed later) while others basted the same. Meanwhile we talked business—Dr. Atkinson's plans etc. Then there was a little guessing contest, very easy, one copy of which I will enclose, you may be able to use it at home sometime—the part written in pencil is of course to be guessed—the answers. (Letter too heavy. Will send next week)

Saturday morning Miriam and I spent a long time in the attic, clearing up, and especially putting away Ada's and Ellsworth's things. In the afternoon Miriam and I took a long walk with the Knapps to the Bennyan garden. It is a good scramble down the mountain and up again.

Harpoot
Nov. 5, 1901

Dear old Kindie,

You can't imagine how pleased I was with those pictures of home. They are lovely. I just had to kiss them and then I showed them to Miriam and the others because I was so fond and proud of them. They are beautifully taken and I do enjoy looking at them. It makes home seem more near and real. When I first looked at them, I thought, "Why, the house isn't changed at all." But after reading, I found out why it was not. It is a little mysterious to me why you kept them nearly two years before sending them. Did you want to wait till I had no brother left to comfort and cheer me?

Nov. 6th

I wrote so much while I was waiting for the water to heat for a bath last night. Did I ever tell you what a nice big round bath-tub Ada and I had made. It is of zinc and was and is a great comfort after washing in a bowl for over a year. I rarely go to the Turkish bath, because I don't believe it is good for me. I always feel so tired and dragged out the next day, even if I go to bed as soon as possible after returning home.

The thing which we are all thinking about the most just now is little Winifred's sickness. For nearly two weeks she has not been well, and five days ago she was so poorly that her mother began to keep her in bed. The Armenian doctor whom they call from Mezereh didn't really know what it was but called it malarial fever and gave her quinine. She grew steadily worse and yesterday they decided that it is typhoid fever. Today she is worse than yesterday, showing some very serious symptoms, her teeth and lips being black. She is in a stupor most of the time. They telegraphed this morning for Dr. Shepherd to come from Diarbekir, if possible and if he is not there for Dr. Thom from Mardin. Even if they have not serious cases on hand, it must be several days before either of them could arrive. Sister Laura, the German nurse consented to come up from Mezereh to nurse her and is here now. The other children were not separated from her till yesterday.

Another unusual thing is that Mary has gone away for a little vacation. Last Monday morning the Senior girls went to Dr. Barnum and said that they thought Miss Daniels was tired and ought to have a vacation. The Barnums had been thinking the same thing, so put their heads together and the outcome was that the very next day Mary set off for Malatia in a spring araba with only the arabagi and Stephan, the old school-factotum for company. She expects to be two days on the road and to stay one day there at Miss Daniels. If the Careys arrive on time, they will all start the next day for Harpoot and reach here next Saturday afternoon. If they come late they may spend Sunday there and she will wait and come with them. Miriam just told me that when Avedis, our man, made the bargain with the arabaji, he took his (the arabaji's) coat as a pledge that he would come the next day. Just think of calling an expressman and taking his coat overnight to make sure of him! Mary has been having cold and stormy weather ever since she left. She can't have had much comfort except in the fact of being alone and having no work.

Harpoot
Nov. 11, 1901

Dear Ones All, including George,

I have just been writing to Ada a little about what happens here and it seems as if I couldn't write it over twice more, so I will make this one letter serve for all.

Last Saturday Mary returned from Malatia, bringing the Careys with her, or vice versa they brought her. They were well, but tired after travelling in this country for over three weeks and getting up anywhere from one to three o'clock in the morning. I think they take discomforts in a very sensible, cheerful way.

You doubtless want to know how I like them. Of course I can't judge fairly yet. Mrs. C. is a very sweet, almost pretty young woman of about my height, tho' slighter than I. She seems rather shy and quiet at first. I think she is very much of a homebody and may be lonesome and homesick at first, in spite of her husband. She already knows how to ride and says she isn't at all afraid. I like her.

About Mr. Carey I am not so sure. You all have met him, except Ellsworth. I think his manners rather peculiar. I don't admire the way he pulls up his trouser above his shoe-tops, leans back in his chair and crosses his legs. He talks very confidently. He led the meeting Sunday evening and it was a good meeting, too. He reads the Bible with a great deal of expression—almost too dramatically. I have seen so little of him that I really don't know yet what I do think of him. I think all the missionaries here are not impressed entirely favorably and yet remembering that he is young, are reserving their judgment. He and his wife are going at the language with the greatest energy. Today they have received 79 callers and deserve to sleep the sleep of the just. Miriam and I took a little walk in the rain with Mrs. C. this afternoon. She is a good walker. There are four of us now who are twenty-six years old. I think the dates are like this.

Mr. Carey born February 1875.
Mrs. " " March "
Miriam " April "
T.L.H. " May "

So I am still the youngest missionary. Mr. Carey, by the way, has a smooth face and so seems younger than he is. I like it, but I imagine that he will soon raise a beard.

You wonder doubtless that I do not speak of Winifred. Her fever has not turned yet, but for the last few days she has seemed a little brighter and better. It is probably the result of good nursing. As no telegram came from Dr. Thom, we had decided that the telegram from here had failed to reach him. This afternoon Mr. and Mrs. Knapp were talking about sending another telegram and Mrs. K. had her pen in hand to write down the proper wording of it, when there was a knock at the outside door and there stood Dr. Thom. He had left Mardin last Friday and came on from Diarbekir by araba. He is a kindly, good man, whom one cannot help liking and trusting. His hair and beard are perfectly white. He must be six feet or over in height and limps somewhat having had part of his foot frozen in a storm. He says that Winifred's symptoms are not so bad as we had thought and seems to think the case very hopeful. He must go back to Diarbekir day after tomorrow before the crisis comes. That will be next Saturday or Sunday. Schwester Laura is an invaluable aid to Mrs. Knapp in her care of Winifred.

I must away to bed now, and finish my letter later in the week.

Theresa seems rather pleased to find that even after the arrival of the Careys, she was still the youngest missionary. Edward Carey was a mid-westerner, loud and self-assured, whose manners do not quite seem to have passed muster with Theresa. He was a graduate of the University of Michigan and had graduated from Andover Theological Seminary just before he came out to Harpoot. His wife Lora, who like her husband was born in Illinois, was a sweet-tempered and cheerful but sickly woman and the hardships of Harpoot took a great toll on her from the beginning. Despite this, she managed to make herself useful. She organized a group of Armenian women to make needlework and sold it in England and the United States, and she instructed women in how to take care of their homes.

Nov. 22, 1901

As I said, Mary came back from Malatia with the Careys. She enjoyed her trip very much and was anxious to stay longer at Malatia. Nothing unusual happened in the school while she was gone, except that the girls seemed to me to be unusually good.

I am in despair over our unfinished school building. Dr. Barnum asked Miriam yesterday if she could manage to put up with the old room a little longer. I don't know whether that means two weeks or a month. The last time I went over there the carpenters were all working on tables and benches for the boys and there were not more than two or three men at work on the building. Two or three days ago, a bad accident happened to the painters of the boys' dormitory. Three of them and a woman were on a high scaffolding. It was recess and the school-boys were playing about. Several of them crawled out of the windows onto the scaffolding, tho' the workmen told them to get off because the thing was weak. They all felt it going, then, and the boys scrambled in at the windows but it was too late for the others and they went crashing down. No one was killed but they were badly injured, especially the woman, whose head was cut. She lives in a miserable dark room, with an earth floor and lies on a heap of rags. Fifteen people live in that same room.

One of the men, Ellsworth, was Hagop, that nice plasterer or white-washer who fell from Dr. Gates' roof.

Mrs. Barnum is expecting to invite us all to dinner there on Thanksgiving unless the Nortons invite us there as they have rather hinted that they intend to. However they are always talking of things which they intend to do, long before they do them. Dr. N. has had a telegram saying that his exequatur papers have actually been sent from Con'ple, and he expects them next week. He plans to have his boy, Harold and Addison raise the flag over the consulate on Thanksgiving Day.

We are having a good deal of rain this week, but still there is not enough to effect our water-supply and we continue to have our water for washing, drinking and everything brought in goat-skins from a fountain just outside the city. It has been so dry that most of the chrysanthemums out in the yard have dried up wholly or partly.

Last week again my Outlook did not come. All of the papers are becoming more or less irregular. We have thought it might be on account of the news about Miss Stone (see below) that the papers were taken out lately, but that looks very suspicious for Turkey.

Mr. Browne and Aunt Caro are in Arabkir, I suppose just now, and will not come home for two or more weeks.

This afternoon we have a C.E. meeting to learn about the history, purpose etc. of the society.

I see that my pen is giving out. Love to each one of you, you dear, dear people.

Theresa L.H.

Theresa's reference to Miss Stone refers to an incident in the Balkans—still under Ottoman rule—that rocked the missionary enterprise. In September of 1901, a band of brigands had captured an American missionary, Miss Ellen Stone, and the wife of a Bulgarian preacher in the mountains of Macedonia. The two women were held for 172 days and released only after the United States government got involved and a large ransom was paid.

Theresa's tender thoughts were often with her mother, who was in Galesburg visiting her Aunt Theresa who was seriously ill:

Harpoot
Nov. 13, 1901

Dearest Mamma,

I think you must be at home by this time and dear Aunt Theresa is either better or done with pain forever. I hardly know what to write while I am still so uncertain about the results of the operation. I wanted to write her this week but I can only tell her about my love for her and my prayers and that is so little to write. If God has spared her to us will you please give her my message, and I will wait for news before writing to her.

Dear little mother, what a long, hard journey! I somehow feel farther away from home when you are in trouble and I cannot talk with you or see you. You don't know how dearly I love you all. It brings a sort of pain to think of it, so I don't let myself think too much.

Dr. Thom went this morning after a stay of less than two days. Since he came Winifred's temperature has gone down one degree and she is really better. He says that she will improve now without any marked crisis. We are very glad.

Yesterday evening Mrs. Browne invited Dr. Thom and the Careys to dinner. Mrs. B. has been making some of those stamped, stuffed doll-babies to send to the orphans at Diarbekir and she was in a great hurry to finish them and send them by Dr. Thom, so we all pitched in after dinner and helped. Dr. Thom and Harold pulled bastings and dressed the dolls when they were not romping and playing tricks on each other. The rest, Mr. Carey included, basted and sewed. Mr. C. is very skilful with a needle. He says he made a shirt for himself last summer all alone. He knows how to cook, too. We had a very merry, jokey time together.

I had good home letters last week—one from Ruth, one from Cornelia and some forwarded ones from George. I never seem to have time for comments upon letters. Did I ever tell you how much I enjoyed the letter written at Xmas Cove in which you told me of the changes of furniture etc. in the house? I shall want to know where you put the new rugs.

Always your loving daughter,
Theresa

Chapter Twenty: Dr. Shepard Pays a Visit and Mr. Carey Plays a Wild Gig

There is more of a tinge of homesickness in Theresa's letters of this period: this was going to be her third Christmas in Harpoot; both her brothers had left, and she herself still had at least three or four years left before she would go on furlough. Adding to her unease was the fact that there were rumors among the Armenians of new massacres, and although Theresa makes light of them in her home letters the missionaries in the Eastern Turkey field were apprehensive. "The Armenian people about us are a good deal afraid just now of some disturbances here such as there have been at Moosh," she writes in a February letter. "There are various rumors and reports in the market most of which are false."

In a letter to Ellsworth, however, she is less sanguine: "I heard today a report that two hundred & fifty Armenians had been killed in a village near Chermoog, but I don't believe it. There is no doubt that the Turks are more irritable & the Armenians more frightened. A great many troops have been sent down to Moosh."

In general, there was a great deal of malaise in the land. The memory of the massacres remained and produced a wave of emigration to the United States as conditions continued to deteriorate in the interior of Turkey. The *Missionary Herald* wrote: "Economic conditions in this land continue to grow worse and worse. The torpor produced by the events of 1895 still remains like a dead weight on the hearts of the people, and neither prayer nor faith can yet remove it. Periods of fear still periodically occur, followed by longer or shorter seasons of paralysis of effort. Then there seems an increasing stagnation of trade, in general caused by the partial, or entire, crippling of certain industries."[56]

Theresa's letters, however, continue to chronicle the everyday life of the Harpoot station and its inhabitants, although from this point on, there are gaps of several months in the letters that have come down to us. The station had its usual share of comings and going during 1902: in late spring Harpoot

56. *Missionary Herald*, 1902, p. 64.

finally got a station physician, Dr. Herbert Atkinson, who with his wife Tacy had to spend several months in Constantinople studying French in order to pass the government examinations required to get a licence to practice medicine. Theresa's good friend Miriam Platt had to have surgery and then returned to the United States for several months of convalescence. In the fall, Miss Bertha Wilson, a thirty-one year old graduate of Syracuse University, arrived to shore up the teaching staff. And the search continued for a permanent replacement for Dr. Gates.

Harpoot
Dec. 22, '01

Dear Cornelia,

It is Sunday morning and about half-past eleven o'clock. I'm afraid that if I don't write a home letter today you will get almost nothing this week, because I know I shall be uncommonly busy. You see we have only Christmas Day itself as a holiday, so as we teach the day before Xmas and the day after, we have to be pretty lively about making our preparations for the day. I think the "Xmas feeling" that we used to talk about comes from the fact that everybody is having vacation from the beaming faces of all the people we meet in the streets and the happy crowds in the stores. Twenty busy people can't get up an atmosphere like that. I don't think we could even if the day came in the middle of vacation. It is when rich and poor and all are happy together that you feel it. I never have the "Christmas feeling" here, tho' I enjoy the day. Our vacation begins on the twelfth of January, I think, and lasts two days more than two weeks.

Mrs. Browne has asked Miriam and me to plan for the giving of the presents next Wednesday. We are going to have a hearth and stockings and a Santa Claus instead of a tree. I prefer the latter, because of home. That reminds me that last Thursday as Miriam and I were coming through the market we saw two hamals [porters] coming down a cross-street, each bent over under the weight of a great Xmas tree. It gave me a sudden thrill of pleasure to see them. They had been brought for our school Xmas celebration from a place a day's journey from here. There are no evergreens about us.

Last Wednesday the C.E. Society had a social. There was nothing unusual about it, except that Mr. Carey played his violin for the girls to march. He plays with a good deal of dash and spirit and we all enjoy it. The next afternoon Miriam and I went to the first meeting for girls and young women on the other side of the city. It was held in a pleasant room of the school. About thirty women and more girls were present, which of course was encouraging, tho' we don't build our hopes on numbers. They were mostly Gregorians, handsomely dressed in silk and jewelry. There are very few Christians among them. I led the meeting, but don't expect to every week.

That evening Mary dined with us and after dinner we all did Xmas work. Mrs. Browne stuffed rag-babies (you know those stamped dolls). Mary dressed those already stuffed, Miriam made candy-bags for our own celebration, Aunt Hattie sewed on the dolls clothes and I embroidered a bureau-scarf for Mrs. Barnum. We worked for about an hour together. Friday was another ordinary day. In the afternoon the Badveli (minister) of Husenik gave another lecture on gardening. It wasn't very practical, at least only a little of it was. That evening the boys of Br. Melcone's orphanage had a hantess. The invitations came at the last minute as is generally the case when Armenians get up things. I stayed at home from pure laziness, but I was sorry when the others came home, for they said it was a real lark—very amusing and interesting.

Later

Miriam and I determined beforehand to devote Saturday to our private Xmas preparations. We are giving all our presents together. It is easier and pleasanter. Of course the weekly cleaning was being done, and I don't know how many people came in on errands. We had our little girls (who do our housework) prepare some wool for a pillow for Mrs. Knapp's couch. We always stuff pillows and mattresses with wool here, because we can't get feathers. In the afternoon we had a woman, Tervanda, sew for us and make the pillow. She used to work for Mrs. Gates, sewing, taking care of the children etc. Now she does similar work for Mrs. Knapps she is a treasure. There is not another Armenian woman in the city who can sew as well, only she is not common property and it was only as a special favor that we had her. Just before dark Miriam, Harold and I went out for a half-hour run on the water-course. We have been in thick fog now for nearly a week. That made our exercise, at least outwardly rather uninteresting.

Mr. Barnum's knee is still causing him trouble. Winifred came to our meeting tonight at the Barnums', clothed and in her right mind, but she looks—poor little one—like a newly hatched robin, with her closely-cropped head, thin neck and cheeks and large mouth.

Miriam is writing now in my room, which reminds me of her children. She is having a dreadfully hard time with them, they are so lawless and undisciplined at home. Last Friday she washed out the mouths of seventeen of them with soap and water plus a little salt and vinegar, because they talked so much. She has tried sending them home and every known form of punishment as well as encouragement. She hasn't lost hope yet. She reminds me now to tell Ellsworth about Sateneg, the littlest orphan in Pompish Hripsime's orphanage. She is a sweet, wilful, half-spoiled little thing. The other day I went thro' the yard at recess and she ran up to me, grabbed my dress and said, "Did your brother reach America safely?" I thought she was a little rude, so I didn't answer her question. Afterward she asked Miriam the same question and said she had been praying for him on his journey and so wanted to know about him. Isn't that funny, for that tiny little mite? I don't believe Ellsworth even remembers who she is.

You asked if I don't want a wash flannel blouse. I don't want any new woolen clothes till next year. Toward spring I am going to sit down and think of my clothes and see what is left. Then I can tell what I need and what colors I want to go with the things which I have.

This week no letter came from home, though I am sure you wrote. A letter did come from Ellsworth in the southern mail. It ought to have come the week before, but he didn't put via Con'ple on the address. Seal your letters tightly.

I thank you all for all the lovely letters you have written lately. You have been uncommonly good. I like to hear every detail—about E's homecoming from his side and the other. You don't know how many times I have reread your letters. I am sorry for you and for her that dear Mumsie can't be at home on Christmas, but ever so glad that Aunt Theresa has that comfort.

Dear old Kindie, I thank you for your sweet letters, written, I'm afraid in the long hours of the night. Ellsworth has already written of your sins in that direction—How can you preach effectively?

I am going to send this to George first, if you don't mind, because I am too busy to write this week a special letter. I love him and every one of you more than I can tell.

Affectionately,
Theresa

I have bo't a pretty rug made by our orphans for a lira. I wish it could have been sent by Ellsworth.

Harpoot
Feb. 15, 1902

Dear little Mummy,

You haven't had a respectable letter from me in a long time. In these days there always seems to be a special reason for writing to each member of the family every week. You all write so faithfully and regularly that I hate to send only one letter for all.

My next home letters will tell of your home-coming. What a jubilee it will be, or rather was! I imagine that the fiery steed and the coach went all the way to the station for you, instead of you being allowed to go by electric cars like ordinary people. I know just how the Deacon and Miss B. welcomed you and all the commotion there was in church the next Sunday.

It is Saturday morning now, just before luncheon-time. I have spent the time till now in doing odds and ends. For one thing I went over my letters and picked out those which must be answered. There are about twenty of them to cheer my spirits. I have spent a good deal of time in caring for Miriam who is sick in bed. Today she has moved into her sitting room, that is we put her bed there, and I shall sleep in her bedroom on a camp-bed so that she may not be alone on this floor. Today Dr. Barnum telegraphed to Diarbekir for Dr. Shepard to come here for Miriam. Tho' she is not critically ill, I mean, has no acute sickness, apparently there is no use in her keeping on in this way half of the time in bed and all of the time half-sick. The Barnums will be glad to see him too on account of Dr. B's knee. Miriam is very cheerful all the time.

Evening

I have been out riding this afternoon with Mr. and Mrs. Knapp. I used Dost, Emma's horse. There is still some snow in patches and it was very muddy. I do love a good canter. Dost is a pretty horse, with three white feet and a wavy tail and mane. He paces well but sometimes he has a queer gait—a cross between a pace and a canter, which I don't like. He is best at a dead run.

I took dinner with the Barnums, as usual on Saturday evening. You know that household consists of the three Barnums, Mary, and the Careys. The Barnums use part of the Gates' furniture with their own. The G's left most of their pictures. The Barnums haven't quite as much taste as Mrs. Gates but the house is more homey. Do you want to know what we had for dinner? Roast beef, mashed potato, beets, dried stringed beans cooked in milk, madzoon and bread; for dessert a sort of bread and pudding with lemon sauce, and native cheese, pears, dates, figs and walnuts. The latter three they always have. They are very cheap in this country, so that even the poor eat walnuts. The figs and dates are of a poor quality. I know you will say, "That is pretty good for a missionary."

Two days later, Theresa dashes off a letter to Ellsworth, telling him that the same Turkish official who had been touring the villages "before the events" (i.e. the massacres) was making tours among the villages now, "giving directions to the Turks. The Armenians are much troubled over this."

In her letters to the Milton home she keeps quiet about this.

Wed. eve. Feb. 19

Dr. Shepard reached here yesterday between six and seven. He is a good traveller and came through in two days, tho' it is called a four-days journey. He came entirely alone without even a zabtieh. He is a very genial man and one to inspire confidence. The people here, Turks and Armenians have the highest idea of his skill and flocked to him this time as they did last spring. Of course he is an excellent surgeon and physician. He is very short and his head is set down low between his shoulders. He is very fond of hunting and out-of-door life. Just now he is in Miriam's room, next to me and I hear them laughing and joking. He is full of stories and incidents. He has just told how he and Miss Mellinger were coming up here from Aintab some eight or nine years ago. The weather was very hot and they spent the heat of the day—many hours, near a ruined mosque in a Turkish village. Some storks had a nest there with several little ones in it. All that hot day the mother stork stood over the nest with her wings outspread, changing her position as the sun changed. The people here call the stork legleg. They pronounce it almost like laglag. It is a Turkish word but the Armenians use it too.

Dr. Shepard has decided that Miriam has appendicitis with some complications. An operation is necessary but it is a question whether it shall be performed here or at the hospital at Marsovan or Caesarea. He went to Mezereh to see the Danish nurse Sister Christiana today. I don't know what the decision is, tho' I believe he came to tell her (Miriam) tonight. Miriam is very bright and cheerful. She suffers pain constantly, but usually it is not severe.

The Armenian people about us are a good deal afraid just now of some disturbances here such as there have been at Moosh. There are various rumors and reports in the market most of which are false.

Our Vali here is a comparatively good one. He declares that nothing will happen within his jurisdiction and Dr. Norton pooh-poohs at the thought of any trouble. We were talking about the subject today and Dr. Shepard said he thought the possibility extremely slight of new disturbance here, because the central gov't is opposed. The massacres were the work of the government, but the present restlessness seems due rather to lawless Koords. This is not the first time that the Armenians have been especially frightened since I came. Indeed they are never wholly free from fear.

Mr. Browne and Miss Bush have come up from Hooiloo where they had just gone because the former wanted to see the Doctor. They found the work very encouraging. Aunt Caro said it was like a bit of heaven down there. Almost all their tours this winter have had hopeful results, especially in Peri and Ichmeh.

I had no letters from home last week except Cornelia's but hope to have a double mail day after tomorrow. I think I wrote that once before.

Mr. Knapp, Mr. and Mrs. Carey and I went out about three-quarters of an hour to meet Dr. Shepard but failed to find him. It was dark when he reached here. He thinks Dr. B. probably has a "button" on his knee.

Tell Ellsworth that Mr. Carey rides something like Herbert Gates and his admiration for his horse is almost equal to Herbert's.

Do you want to know about my clothes? Harootoune, the orphan-tailor, alias "Harry" has made my jacket and it looks pretty well. The material is slightly rough and brown. He finishes his work beautifully. I suppose the cut, in spite of the pattern is not quite so stylish as it might be. For the whole thing—materials and making, I paid almost exactly a lira. That is about four and a half dollars. Did I tell you that I sent to Germany for some Jaeger flannels? They cost less for us than in America, partly on account of duty I suppose. My old ones were worn out. My winter dresses are something of a wreck but the season is almost gone.

Harpoot
June 17, 1902

Dear Mamma,

I am too lazy to go upstairs and get my own pen, so use Ada's which I don't like.

Our hot weather is really beginning now and I am glad that school is almost over. This week in all the lower schools we are having visitors' days and exhibitions and expect to finish up with the lower grades and devote ourselves to the upper classes next week. Today the Primary Schools have had visitors and tomorrow the kindergarten has its hantess. (My pen bro't in by Ada at this point) They have a may-pole which they are going to wind with green and red (not, ribbon, but strips of cotton cloth). After that I expect to go to the rehearsal for the Primary School exhibition and then to give an English and a History lesson. After luncheon comes the King's Daughters meeting in the other quarter and then a rehearsal for the little boys' hantess. My evenings are not full, altho' my days are because we are only rehearsing now. The diplomas and certificates are already written and tied up.

I have just come in from a good walk with Mr. Knapp and Ada. Mr. K carried the baby. We went by the upper road, which is not much frequented, but came back by the water course which has become a most popular promenade for Armenians from five o'clock till eight in the evening. We made haste slowly there for every group of people we met had to have a peep at the baby, especially the women crowded around. The older ones wanted to know which was its mother, Ada or I. The younger women all knew us however and explained indignantly. Mrs. Knapp isn't very well known because she doesn't go out much on account of the children and her deafness. The Knapps and Ada will go out to the garden house tomorrow.

Miriam has sent out notices of the Kindergarten Training Class which she will have next year, to the other stations of the mission. Several want to send girls here to study. The Germans expect to have two of their orphan girls join the class.

By the way, Miriam wore a nicely starched dress to school yesterday. The children crowded around to feel of it especially to touch the cuff. One said, "Varzhoo (baby-talk for teacher) is it paper?" A little later another little boy touched the cuff gently and whispered, "Varzhoo, is it wood?" Still later in the day Miriam heard two of the smaller girls talking together and one was saying, "Truly Miss Platt has on a paper dress today."

Margaret is not at all well, (Perhaps I told you last week) and the doctors can't find out what the matter is. She constantly complains that her legs ache. She cries half of the day and has no appetite. She looks sick altho' she is not thin. They have put her to bed, but it is hard to keep her there. She wanders around from bed to bed.

Miriam has just told me that when she went to school today a whole crowd of the little ones gathered around her and said, "Varzhoo, you have a dress which is just exactly like paper, but it really is calico." They had evidently come to this conclusion after much thinking.

...

Later

Aunt Caro called our attention tonight to the fact that the Armenian word for godliness means God-worshipping, the English means God-likeness. There is just that difference in their idea of religion and ours; worship being used with its formal, outward significance.

Emma has just told me something rather trying. Complaints have been coming for months to Dr. Barnum, through Turkish officials, that our school-boys, orphans etc, throw stones at Turkish boys, frighten horses on the road etc. Dr. Barnum has told the boys to keep off the lower road to the garden (Ellsworth knows which) and has restricted them in other ways, tho' he felt that the Turks were generally the ones to blame. Tonight the police commissioner came to say that so many complaints had been made that the Vali had given these orders. Our boys are not to go below the lower garden road or above the Turkish graveyard, and between those limits they cannot go out of sight of the college buildings unless with Shaban or one of the missionaries. Police are to be stationed here and there to see that this is carried out. Vice-versa the Turkish boys are not to come into the Armenian boys' territory. That makes our boys practically prisoners. Of course they won't always keep within these limits and some day a grand explosion will come and some Armenian boys will suffer for it. The Armenian boys are injudicious and headstrong. The other day one of the older orphan boys stabbed with a knife a Turkish boy who was molesting him. Of course it was inexcusable, tho' the Turk was not seriously injured, but we are held responsible for all such things. Some time ago a Turk dropped a great stone upon the head of one of our orphan boys. He seemed to recover, but lately his hands have slowly become paralyzed, the brain evidently injured somehow. Of course the Turks don't consider such a thing as that. No more time tonight,

Most lovingly,

Theresa

The Garden, Harpoot
July 15, 1902

Dear old Ellsworth,

I wonder in what sort of a wild place this will find you. I look forward very eagerly to getting your letters. (If dear Papa should read this, he would be sure to comment unfavorably upon my use of "getting") I received by the last post your card written about a week before starting for the west. How do you enjoy speaking upon scientific subjects in public? Do you find it hard? Does your college work in English help at all in speaking?

I am sitting just now under the trees at the bottom of the garden. I fled down here from Margaret's swinging in the hammock and singing on the aivan, but this place seems to be rather too popular. Three different sets of people have come down, the last being a lot of Turkish women and girl to shake toot [mulberry] trees. I really can't stand the racket and am going home.

Cap't Anderson started off yesterday for the Dersim. He means to go thro' that pass which you wanted to see so much. You know, that great valley where there used to be a Roman road, next to the fourth or fifth peak from the Egin Mt. He took Badveli Tomas (the dragoman), a cavass, a zabtieh and a cook, I believe. Laura wanted dreadfully to go with him, but couldn't on account of the baby. They travel very comfortably, taking one or two tents.

Mr. Stephanides has not been well, and was advised by Dr. Shepard to spend his nights high up on the hills, perhaps at our garden. Accordingly he made his request to Dr. Barnum and has pitched his tent close to the willow trees at the south end of the house. I'm afraid that none of us have received him as cordially as we ought. Our garden, anyway, is too much public property for unalloyed enjoyment on our part. I know that is a selfish remark, but imagine what it would be to always have people from outside loafing about our garden at home and eating the fruit.

I told you that the orphans have been sent away temporarily. About ninety-three are left and those eat from the same kitchen, tho' the boys and girls eat at different times. The others have been sent to friends who may be very poor, but who can keep them for two months and to almost any Protestants in the villages and city who are willing to take them. Mr. Knapp sent them even as far as Egin and Arabkir but not to Diarbekir. Mr. Knapp's idea is that he will save some money in this way; it will do the children good to rough it a little; he will find out where the children can really be supported by relatives and friends and expects that many will not be received back again. Then all this will prepare the way for changes which he wishes to make in the fall in hairigs and mairigs—the 'fathers' and 'mothers' who are in charge of the orphanages. I think he means to close at least two orphanages.

Mr. Knapp really carries things with too high a hand. He began on his own account without consulting the station, a building for industrial purposes. Of course he got into a fuss with the government, not having the proper permission and not being quite square with them, and we of necessity all share in his humiliation before the government and the people. He also fixed up the lower house in the garden so that his cook and family could live there, this, too, without consulting the station. Of course Dr. B. and Mr. Browne were annoyed, as he used station money and the other servants naturally complain that they do not receive favours. Indeed none of us approved of what he did, excepting Mr. Carey.

I have written a good deal, I think, about the Theological class. Baghdasar of Ichmeh, Bedros of Koordistan, Br. Krekor, the hairig who came from Diarbekir, Hampartsoom who was at Haboosi, Harootune of Houlakegh (?), the lame teacher from Garmuri, and several others are in it. I think Mr. Browne takes great pleasure in the class. They have all their lessons in the College building.

[...]

Ashodian was married on Commencement Day to Aghavni Boghosian. We were invited to the bride's house and it seemed to me one of the most heathenish affairs I ever saw—so noisy and coarse. Br. Aram was married about two weeks ago and has taken a house in the city. All the missionaries old and new were invited, except Ada, Miriam and me. Next year Badv. Bedros will have entire charge of the dormitory. Last year he shared the responsibility with Aram and one-eyed Garabed (who by the way, is to teach in Mezereh next year) and things didn't go at all well.

There is a good deal of enthusiasm over tennis this year, but I haven't played much, because everyone is either too good or too bad for me. The lower court has been enlarged and a nice double court marked out. Dr. Shepard comes up to play frequently in the evening and Capt' Anderson who plays the best game of all sometimes comes over. Bathing in the pool is not a very popular amusement this summer. The servants do too much of their washing down there. I think that Mr. Carey and the doctor have been in once in the evening.

Do you hear directly from Dr. Gates? According to our last letters, he and Mrs. Gates do not seem to be much better nervously. The boys are very well and were happy in school. Now they have gone up to their old summer home in Michigan.

This letter is really too long. I believe I will send home first for them to read it there, altho' all will not interest them.

Lots and lots of love, dear brother,
from,
Theresa

The summer also included a camping trip to the lake. Ellsworth, who of course knew the area well, got a lively description of the lighter side of missionary life:

August 16, 1902

Dear Ellsworth,

Here I am sitting under the same old trees by the same old water. We came up on Wednesday—we meaning Mr. Knapp and his three children, Miriam, Ada, Mary, Mr. and Mrs. Carey & I. As William is not well she & Ada & the little girls came by araba over the Diarbekir road and from the end of the lake came by boat to the camp. They were ten hours in the araba and three and a half in the boat. The rest of us started from the garden at five in the morning. We were about six hours on the way. We fell in with the others between Vartateel and Kiloo and ate luncheon together. We have three tents. Two were borrowed from the Andersons. The Knapps have one, Mary and Mrs. Carey another, and we three girls the third. Mr. Carey sleeps out of doors. Sarkis, the Gates' cook, does our cooking this summer and he is a jewel. Kevork does the trotting to and fro the city & in his vague rather heavy way assists Sarkis. Shaban gets the water & protects us by his uniform, which is somewhat shabby. This year the men are providing their own food. Mr. Knapp made an agreement with the Koord who owns the place, by which we buy all our necessary supplies through him, that is, wood, barley, madzoun, milk, etc. and he lets us have the place free. ...

Mr. Knapp has found a little spring up in a valley & nearer to our camp than the spring where we have always gotten our water. He has a scheme now for bringing the water down close to us through pipes next spring. He has another scheme for rigging a sail on the boat which we hire. This year he brought along a shovel & pick axe & has made some fine level places for the tents, & for us to eat. He is certainly better than sitting on pointed rocks or rolling down hill.

We have a good deal of music this year, as Mr. Carey brought along his guitar, mandolin & harmonicum. It's a pity he can't play them all together. He is very jolly, but I don't exactly like his way of joking. It comes very near to being vulgar & is often rude. Yesterday he behaved rather like a lunatic with some Koordish women who came along. Sometimes I have to laugh in spite of myself & sometimes he makes me feel ashamed and wish I weren't there. I am probably very provincial but I do prefer people from the east to westerners, ordinarily.

Last Thursday we went rowing in the moonlight. Tonight we expect to go again and have the boatmen catch fish in their nets....

Do you remember Ajemian who studied agriculture in America and instituted a model farm here under Dr. Norton's direction, with some American machinery? A little while ago some Koords and Turks tore up his gardens, broke his machinery & tried to burn his house. They said that if things were done in Adjemian's way there would be no work for the people....

Chapter Twenty-One: Henry Riggs Becomes President, and Theresa Goes on Vacation; Geragos the Wagoner

Despite the fears and the rumors of impending massacres, the fall of 1902 passed without any earthshaking events. Theresa continued to enjoy her teaching and reported with justified pride that her girls were reading Drummond's *Pax Vobiscum*, "which is really pretty hard English," and that "for composition they are translating the Gospel of John into English." In January, 1903 she wrote another one of her lively reports to the women's auxiliary:

> January 15, 1903
>
> My dear Friends of the Norfolk and Pilgrim Branch,
>
> This is the second day of our Christmas vacation, for the Armenian Christmas is the 19th of January this year, and our school terms have to be planned according to that. Of our ninety or more boarders, about thirty are left, most of whom are orphans. The others went off as joyfully as school-girls go home for the holidays in America, although, instead of walking decorously to the train, they scrambled upon mules or donkeys and put their calico-covered bundles in front of them. None of them went more than a six- or seven-hour's journey, but they often walk half of the way, it is so cold riding in the frosty fog which we always have at this season.
>
> Yesterday was the Armenian New Year, which comes before their Christmas and, in manner of celebration corresponds to our Christmas, being the home festival, while on Christmas Day they make a round of calls. The orphans had their Christmas treat yesterday—a tree and a Santa Claus, who, by the way, had seen Santa so few times in his life that he didn't understand our American conception of him at all and made himself more of a clown than a Santa Claus. Still he amused the children.
>
> At noon all the missionaries and orphan-workers of every description dined together in the orphanage dining-room and were served by the orphan girls who had cooked the dinner. We should have preferred to eat with the orphans but there was not

room for all at once. We sat down before long tables, about two feet wide and a foot high. We ate from individual bowls, or rather tin pans, as the orphans do, which is a great improvement upon the native custom of having ten or twelve eat from one dish. The men all sat on one side of the room and the women on the other, though the missionaries were an exception to this arrangement. When I was a little girl, I always wanted to know, "What did you have to eat?" and perhaps you wonder what sort of food we have here, and whether we Americans find it hard to eat it. Some of the food I had to learn to like, but now I thoroughly enjoy a well-cooked native meal. The menu was rice pilaff (that is, rice cooked with butter), stewed raisins and dried apricots, and roast mutton, with native bread and tahn (a poor sort of butter milk). For dessert we had a sort of pastry cooked with honey and nuts, oranges and candy. The orphans ate a similar meal afterward, and thoroughly enjoyed it, I have no doubt, for it is their one feast in the year. Usually their food is of the simplest sort. Bread with one or sometimes two other dishes is all that they have for one meal.

Some weeks ago I made a little trip with Mr. Knapp to Chemeshgezék, one of our out-stations among the mountains, a two-day's journey from here. We spent the first night in a little village close to the Euphrates River, at the house of an Armenian who has lived for many years in Constantinople and America. He is a graduate of Robert College and the Amherst Agricultural School and is trying to introduce farming machinery and new methods of agriculture into the country, but he is discouraged and almost ready to give it all up and go back to America. The government is very suspicious of him, and the villages, especially the Turks, who have been put out of work by his machinery are openly hostile to him, tearing up his planted fields and trying to destroy his machinery. The Koords from across the river have made several raids upon him and carried off what fruit, vegetables and grain they could lay hands on. He has no redress for this sort of thing and simply has to endure it. Our American consul here has protected him somewhat by his influence.

At Chemeshgezék we were welcomed warmly and kindly, though we were both strangers to the place, for the sake of the missionaries who had been there before us. We stayed at the house of the teacher, who with his young bride, one of our school-girls, has just begun work there. They have only two rooms, so Aghavni (or Dove, if that is easier to say) and I slept in the sitting-room and her husband and Mr. Knapp slept in the kitchen. The latter caught cold, because there was no glass or anything else in the windows, while I found it hard to sleep for lack of air, because the sitting-room windows had all been covered with oiled paper for the winter in place of glass, and could not possibly be opened. There were some tiny holes which the birds had pecked and we persuaded them to enlarge these somewhat for the sake of hygiene.

Aghavni teaches a school for the girls, which is a typical village school. She has twenty-seven scholars, from five years old up to seventeen. She has the usual difficulty in persuading them to comb their hair every morning. The mothers insist that combing the hair so frequently makes it fall out, takes far too much time and is unnecessary. They think that once in a week or two is often enough. When Aghavni sends the girls home for coming with uncombed hair, it makes trouble with the parents, so she was in real distress over the matter. As the coarse wooden combs used here cost only a cent apiece, I suggested that she might keep some combs, which I would give, at school and send the tangle-haired girls outside to comb their hair every morning, scrubbing the comb up carefully after each girl's turn. I gave her some colored Sunday School cards, such as are given every Sunday to the little ones in our home Sunday Schools, and she was greatly delighted. If any of you who hear this letter could collect such cards or any colored picture cards and send them to Mr. Charles E. Swett (Congregational House, Boston) marked for me, I could use them in many such places where they are greatly appreciated. If you would send a note to me, too, so that I might acknowledge your kindness, I should be glad.

I think I wrote to you before that a class of young men had been taking some Bible study and Theological Training here in the spring and summer. In November they scattered, and each went to some place, most of them villages, to work. One young man who ran away from Koordistan secretly, because of the Turks, in order to come and study here, has gone now to the city of Choonkoosh. When Mr. Browne called him to talk over the matter with him, he explained all the difficulties and then said, "Are you willing to go?" "Mr. Browne," said the young man straightening himself up in his energetic way, "If you missionaries wanted me to go and persuade Satan himself, I would say, 'God's will be done.'" I think most of the young men started out with that same spirit.

I hope you often pray for the spiritual growth of our school—teachers and girls. We depend greatly upon your prayers.
Faithfully yours,
Theresa L. Huntington

Just before Theresa wrote this letter—which is also addressed to Miriam Platt who was still convalescing in the United States—a truly compelling figure entered the Harpoot scene to take up the Presidency of Euphrates College: the Rev. Henry Riggs. He was the grandson of the remarkable linguist Elias Riggs whom we encountered in Constantinople in the 1830'ies, one of the founders of the American missionary enterprise in Turkey and a scholar whose translations of Biblical texts into the native languages provided the means for the evangelical and educational work of the missionaries.

There was a great deal of rejoicing at the Harpoot station when the news came that Henry Riggs had accepted the Presidency: the Riggs family had been at the center of the missionary enterprise in Turkey ever since the days of Elias Riggs. Elias and his wife Martha Jane Dalzell had eight children; four lived into adulthood. One of their sons, Edward, was part of the American Board station at Marsovan—Theresa mentions them as she passed through there on her way to Harpoot. Edward and his wife Sarah Hinsdale had 5 children and Henry was born while the family was at Marsovan. Like his grandfather, Henry was a talented linguist: he grew up speaking Turkish and Armenian; he spoke Kurdish fluently as well.

As was the custom with the missionaries, Henry was sent back to the United States for his schooling and graduated with honors from Carleton College in 1896. This tall and handsome young man—Theresa's age—had a clear scientific bent and at some point confessed that he would have liked to become an engineer. But the Middle East and family tradition had a strong hold on him, and after college, 'Harry' Riggs returned to Marsovan as a teacher at Anatolia college, also a Board school. He taught there for three years before entering Auburn Theological Seminary, and after graduating in 1902 he was immediately sent to the Turkey field as a missionary.

Theresa took an immediate liking to the new President:

Harpoot, Jan. 28, 1903

My dear ones,

This is the end of the first day of school or rather the first half day, for school opened at noon. I have enjoyed this vacation more than usual. I have been thoroughly well, for one thing, and most of the time have gone to bed in good season. Then I have enjoyed seeing so much of the girls—the few boarders who were left. I feel as if I knew them all better and they cared for me more than before. I have paid them many hasty visits, in the kitchen, dining-room, and anywhere. Anybody is loveable if you have time enough to get at the loveableness.

Last Monday Ada and I invited the girls to spend the evening here and I think every one enjoyed it. It was exactly a year before, Miriam, that you and I invited them and we washed the grapes on the floor, making some awful spots. On Monday we played passing the key to wear off the bashfulness. After that we had some charades in Armenian. Ada and I had gathered together a lot of garments, Armenian and American, men's (but not trousers) and women's and the combinations were very funny. It was the first time the girls had ever played this and they enjoyed it hugely. Afterward we sat at native tables and ate some fruit, native-fashion,—oranges, apples, grapes, dried figs and leblebs. Then came prayers and they went home.

I really have begun with the most unimportant news. Of course the great event of the week was the arrival of Mr. Browne, Aunt Caro, and Mr. Riggs last Thursday noon. They had a very hard journey on account of the deep snow and the bitter cold. Mr. Browne has been in bed most of the time since he returned, suffering with malaria and tooth-ache as well as his old and more serious trouble. In the last two days his only food has been a cup of tea and an orange. Tonight I believe he intends to try some toasted crackers. Aunt Caro seems well. Of course you want to know what I think of Mr. Riggs. I like him. He seems manly and boyish too, strong and dignified. He is all ready for his work and he takes right hold of it. I should say he was not much of a student, tho' an intelligent thinking man. He seems to have an earnest Christian spirit and I think all who have met him like him. As to appearance, he is over six feet tall and wears a full beard. Mrs. Browne said tonight that he will be twenty-eight next March which adds a fifth to our group of twenty-eight year olds. (Mrs. Atkinson, Miriam, Mr. & Mrs Carey.)

We have been having an uncommonly cold week. The water pipes have frozen up and the plants in our sitting room have been frost-bitten at night. In Mezereh two days ago the thermometer was 29 below zero, Fahrenheit. The river has been half frozen over and our mail, already long-delayed was kept two or three days on that account at Malatia. It is now a week behind time, but we look

for it tomorrow. We hear on every side stories of wolves attacking men and beasts on the roads and I suppose much is true.
Very lovingly, Theresa

In Harpoot, Henry Riggs found plenty of opportunity to put his scientific and practical talents to good use. He was determined to use the station as an example of the good that modern technology could bring and set an astounding number of projects in motion. The Ottoman government had finally paid the much fought-over indemnity—whether pressure from President Roosevelt had anything to do with it we do not know—and Riggs felt the time had come to embark on new projects at Harpoot. These included the construction of a new auditorium, Wheeler Hall, that would accommodate all of the station's 1700 students, and the construction of a well. Riggs also procured a new printing-press; he installed a heliograph in Harpoot which could flash messages up to twenty miles. He set up a seismograph, invented a wind-gauge, obtained patents for a self-winding clock, a wind indicator, a "pocket-size type-writing machine." He installed a clock that chimed on the hour—and which caused a certain amount of merriment and frustration before it was finally made to work right; once, Theresa tells us, it chimed eighty-eight times in succession. He started a "Self-help Department" where the orphans were taught canning, locksmithing, and stove-making. In addition to these activities and his administrative duties, Riggs taught fourteen hours a week (Introduction to the New Testament; Systematic Theology) in the Theological Seminary at Harpoot which was re-opened soon after his arrival.[57]

A year after Henry Riggs arrived, he left the station for the United States on a lightning visit—to marry. His bride, Mt. Holyoke graduate Annie Tracy Riggs, was born in Marsovan and the couple had known each other since childhood: her father was the Rev. Charles Tracy, a Board missionary. "She was a woman of high character, unassuming, and the friend of all," wrote the *Missionary Herald*.[58] "She was always cheerful, always helpful. She understood the responsibility of the wife of a college president, and tried faithfully to meet it. She interested herself in the women about the city, and in the poor; she attended the women's meetings, and interested herself in the orphans; was a member of the Orphan Committee, and in every way made herself an important member of the Harpoot missionary circle."

We meet Annie Tracy Riggs briefly in Theresa's letters. She last mentions her in connection with the missionary Christmas celebrations of 1904, There-

57. All Riggs, ABC 50:24

58. *Missionary Herald,* 1905, p. 494.

sa's last in Harpoot. A few months later, on July 23—exactly one year to the date that she had left the United States with as a new bride—she died in Harpoot. There is no mention of this calamity in the letters; Theresa had left the station five weeks earlier. Fate was not kind to Henry Riggs: within the span of a few years, he lost another wife and their child there. In addition, as President of the College he was also destined to repeat the ordeal that Dr. Gates had been through: to be responsible for the entire station during another massacre of the Armenians in 1915 which reached genocidal proportions.

But in 1903, all of this was still ahead for Henry Riggs. He threw himself into his work, according to the *Missionary Herald*, "with earnestness and enthusiasm." The beginning of his tenure seems to have cranked up the pace of everybody a few notches. Dr. Atkinson, who had been away for a time learning Turkish, was now "besieged with patients" and, as always, we are given quantitative information: "In five months he performed 125 operations, made 302 bedside visits, and gave at his office 861 treatments."

Theresa, too, wrote home about illness:

> Harpoot, Turkey
> April 1, 1903
>
> Dearest Mother,
>
> That date reminds me how near your birthday is. You know there is a little song which says—
>
> Ah, could I once but see her,
> One single time again!
> But if I once could see her
> Still would I wish to see her
> A thousand times again!
>
> Ah, if I once could kiss her,
> How could my heart refrain?
> For if I once should kiss her
> Still would I wish to kiss her
> A million times again.
>
> That is the way I feel about you. But if I go on talking this way, I shall be home-sick and then there will be another one of my blue Wednesday letters.
>
> I'll tell you my "dids", as the girls say, beginning from last Friday. That afternoon was a half-holiday, and the Armenian teachers wanted to go to Mezereh in a body to see one of our old teachers whose mother has just died. That is their idea of comforting people and doing them special honor—to go in a great crowd. Mary

and I went with them. She got a market-horse, who moved like Jake Slocum, but I preferred my own feet, as all the teachers walked. We were about an hour and a half on the way.

How would you have liked it for three days after your mother died to have the room where you sat full of people, looking at you pityingly, frequently giving very long sighs, talking to you at intervals, probably questions about your mother's last hours, or pious platitudes about the will of God? And then to have the people go away after sitting with you for several hours and discuss your behavior and how much you cried? That is the regular program here, and people think that their friends don't care for them unless they come and sit in this way. After staying nearly an hour at the house of the teacher, some of us went to the German hospital to see one of our little school-girls who is probably dying there. The place was overflowing with opthalmia patients from the German orphanage. Fifty or more of them have the disease, tho' only the most serious cases are in the hospital. The disease is a prevalent one in this country. If the people would only keep clean!

Harpoot
May 6, 1903

Dearest Mother,

What a kind, careful little mother you are and how much you do for me! This week the January shipment came and the box just as your dear hands or Cornelia's tied it up. It was among Dr. Norton's things and so was untouched in the custom-houses.

Everything is nice and right so far as I have seen. Both skirts are sensible and pretty. I should say that they were a trifle long, but a tuck is easily taken and the cotton one may shrink. I feel rich in skirts now, and can go to Con'ple feeling quite respectable. The gray is strong and nice-looking and indeed so is the other too—equally so.

I am just delighted at the accession in handkerchiefs, for all my old ones are giving out at once. And I love to have your dear writing on my clothes. I have one of those handkerchiefs in my pocket at this moment. The gloves are an exact fit and a very pretty shade. Ada has some of just the same kind, only black. They look to me more English than American, but that is because I am getting away behind American things and ways.

I thank you, dear Mamma, from a heart full of love, and I thank the dear father who sent the buttons, in the same way. They are quite stunning and I always did like mother-of-pearl things. Perhaps these are manufactured and not real mother-of-pearl, but they are just as pretty.

A week ago yesterday the Atkinsons arrived after comparatively comfortable journey. They reached here late because one of their horses was lame. They seem much as before, tho' I believe both have grown in Christian character. Especially Mrs. Atkinson has had a deep experience, which makes her sweeter and more eager to help in direct missionary work. I regret to say that the Doctor is no more particular than before as to whether his boots are blacked or whether he has on a necktie.

I'm sorry that I sent such a miserable scrap last week. By the time this reaches you, I suppose you will have been sending my letters to Con'ple for two or three weeks. We still plan to start the first of June, being two and a half or three weeks on the way. I am afraid Ada and I will have to go alone which in some respects will be a little hard. Mr. Carey may not be able to go to Van on account of Mrs. Carey's sickness and that may possibly leave Mr. Knapp a little more free to go to Con'ple.

With dearest love to all,
Theresa

Harpoot, Turkey
May 28, 1903

My dear Ones All,

I had such beautiful letters from some of you today, but I really cannot answer them this week, because I am uncommonly busy and I want to answer in detail. Next week at post-time I expect to be travelling but I hope that I shall be able to write a little each day on the way and so have something to send ready. I mean to take your dear letters along with me. For one thing I shall have to study Cornelia's letter about collars and hair-arrangement and such. One can't grasp all of such a subject at one reading.

I must speak of the pictures. Of course I was just delighted with them. Taking all in all I like the smaller one best, tho' Cornelia has just a little too much smile. I like her best in the other one. In the smaller picture Harry looks thin but otherwise I like it (his picture) *very much*. Dear little Ruthie—how she has changed. I certainly think the nose-pinchers improve her appearance much. She really looks almost as old as Cornelia. Or rather Cornelia looks almost as young as she. What pretty hair Ruthie has! Her cheeks are just as plump as they used to be—just like her second-best sister's. Cornelia's face isn't a rounded-off square like ours. Finally, my sisters, it is a very sweet picture. I meant to say more about Harry. He has a good, strong face that I am proud of. In the smiling picture he doesn't look so thin and on that account or rather in that respect I like it. He really doesn't seem to me to be half so much changed outwardly as Ruth. In the long picture, Ruth is a little stiffer and soberer, so I don't like it quite as well as the other. But I should think it very good nevertheless, if the other were not better.

Proceeding to Kindie she looks just as she used to, only I am glad to see that she is not so thin. Her hair is very pretty, as always. The smiling one I like less than the other. But both are sweet and dear.

As for Ellsworth's pictures, again I like the smaller one better, and I call them all—in the group and outside good, only I still think that our dear old Ellsworth is a little better-looking. He has a sweet, honest expression. (I hope he would not object to that word *sweet*) You girls have on lovely dresses. Ada comments upon that every time she picks up the pictures. In general I am very contented from the pictures, as the girls here insist upon saying. I would write more about them but I am uncommonly tired and sleepy.

Ada and I had our pictures taken yesterday. I would give a good deal to have time to tell you all about it—there was so much to make Ada and me laugh within. We let everything be their way—so we all sat or stood in three beautiful stiff rows. There was almost a bit of a grievance about seats of honor, but it finally passed off smoothly. Three separate men, photographers and assistants waved and shouted at us and all took a long peek through the camera. The women and girls did their best to be prim and stiff and what was lacking in this direction was made up for by sundry pokes and straightenings from the photographer in chief. I appeared to be standing in a safe place, but was really just in front of a bottomless abyss. The thing hasn't been developed yet. I almost wish you could see it and have an excuse for smiling but I fear that pleasure will never be yours.

Ada and I expect now to start for Con'ple Mon. June 1, without the Nortons, spending June 7 at Sivas, June 14 at Marsovan and the next Sunday with George or else on the Black Sea. We plan to take only a zabtieh, beside our trusty arabagi Geragos, and to do our own cooking on the way. I almost dread the journey now that it is so near—the khans are so horrible in summer, and having no man with us, we cannot sleep in a tent.

There is so much to tell this week, but the only sensible thing for me to do now is to go to bed.

Always most lovingly,

Theresa

I sat up till 12 o'clock with Emma last night, taking to pieces and repairing a school organ, for a concert which passed off quite successfully today.

In May, Theresa set out on her trip. She needed to see a dentist. In addition, she had been working in Harpoot for five years by then. It was time for a break. June 1, she and Ada Hall left Harpoot for Sivas; then followed a stop at Marsovan with the parents of Henry Riggs ("Dr. Riggs is a broad-minded, practical, noble man. Mrs. Riggs is lovely in face and character—a perfect mother") and some dental work with Dr. Carrington. From there, they went to the Black Sea, in three stages, and then by steamer to Constantinople where she met up with her brother George, teaching now at Robert College, who came along to Sinaia in Roumania where they spent a relaxing ten days resting, sight-seeing and taking walks in the mountains. "I can't describe the beauty of the fir and beech-woods, the views from one or two high pinnacles of rock and finally emerging upon a beautiful mountain pasture, brimming over with grass and exquisite flowers. The cows with their tinkling bells wandered about, nibbling here and there. Far below us beyond the woods was the river valley and far above the peaks and rocks of the mountain. We climbed on and on among such flowers as I have never seen elsewhere, now and then going through strips of wood and then coming out upon still more lovely views. The path was plain and well-made. It was hard to turn to come down. We followed a different path back and reached the hotel soon after seven. I wish I could describe the flowers to you. Even the familiar ones were brighter and deeper in color than anywhere else. I have never seen such rich clover or such enormous, brilliant butter-cups. There were great, purple Canterbury bells; deep, velvety lady's delights, which looked almost like pansies, and numberless other flowers, whose names I don't know—purple, yellow, orange, blue, pink or white. I have pressed a few and I hope the colors will not fade out."

This trip also inspired Theresa to write a piece for *Life and Light for Women* about their "trusty arabagi Geragos," a humble and profoundly religious man who earned Theresa's deep admiration during the two-week journey through the wilds of Anatolia. The article is reproduced here in full:

Story of one Greek in Turkey
by
Miss Theresa Huntington

I wonder whether you would be interested to know a little about our arabaji (wagoner), a thoroughly sincere Christian man in whom I feel a deep interest. Geragos is a Greek, who lives in Sivas. He is thirty years old, and has been an araba driver for fifteen years. He never went to school, but when he was a little boy, and was learning the tailor's trade, someone taught him to read in the evenings. Turkish is the language which he knows best, and he reads it in the Greek characters. He also knows Armenian well; but Greek, which he spoke as a child, he has almost forgotten. Since the massacres of 1895 he has been the arabaji whom we in Harpoot have usually called when we have wished to make a long journey, because we can trust him. So it came that when Miss Hall and I wished to go to Samsoun we summoned Geragos to come on for us from Sivas with his wagon. We were about two and a half weeks on our journey to Samsoun; that meant that we spent fourteen long traveling days with Geragos, and came to know him well. He is tall, with stooping shoulders, deep-set eyes, hollow cheeks, and very black hair. The hard life which he has led has told upon him, and he hardly looks like a young man. He sat cross-legged on the seat in front, while we sat in similar Oriental positions on our mattress and cushions behind; and sometimes after a silence of an hour or two on his part, except for occasional expostulatory words to his horses, he would warm up to a desire to talk, and then a few questions would bring out some of his experiences.

One day, soon after we left Sivas, I saw a book wrapped in paper on the seat beside him, and he explained that he was taking it to a Circassian hoja (teacher) in a village a day or two farther on. It happened that two or three weeks before Geragos was spending the night at the khan in that village, and was reading the Bible. The hoja, who was of course a Mohammedan, came into the khan, which is the general loafing place of the village, and after a time he asked Geragos what he was reading. Geragos offered to read aloud, and explained what he read. The man was much interested, and said: "Joy to the Armenians that they have such a book." He wanted Geragos to give him his copy, but Geragos said he couldn't then, but promised to bring another copy when he passed that way again. After hearing so much I was anxious to see the hoja. At noon we stopped at the village before the khan door. The horses were taken out to be watered and fed, and Geragos went into the khan. After a time the Circassian came up, wearing flowing black robe and an enormous white turban, as is the custom of hojas. Through the khan door I saw the two sitting side by side. Geragos was reading aloud, and eagerly explaining, while the hoja nodded at intervals, and the ever-present crowd looked and listened. The Greek would not let the Circassian take the Bible till he promised to read it.

Geragos told me that a few weeks before he was traveling alone when he overtook a dervish. The man asked for a ride, and was taken in. The arabaji asked the dervish where he was going, and the latter explained that he had just begun a pilgrimage to Mecca. Geragos asked why he went. "Oh," said the dervish, "to seek God and get to heaven." "You can find God and heaven here without making any pilgrimage at all," said Geragos. Then he pulled out his Bible, and asked the dervish if he would like to hear a little from a book. He read the fifth chapter of Matthew, especially the parts about the kingdom of heaven. The dervish said, "These are beautiful words," and wanted to hear more. Geragos found that the man knew how to read, and the dervish said, "Our Holy Book teaches some of the same things; for example, when a man is struck on one cheek he must turn the other."

It interests me to think of those two riding along among the mountains in the old black-covered wagon, sitting cross-legged side by side, and talking about the Bible,—Geragos, with his deep-set eyes, short cropped black hair, red fez and dingy brown arabaji clothes, driving with his Bible on his knee, and beside him the dervish, a middle-aged man with his long black hair braided and untidy, his matted beard, great green turban, dirty white clothes, and bare feet. It reminds me of Philip and the eunuch. Geragos did not tell me these details of the conversation and dress until I questioned him closely.

The two parted after a time, but when the dervish reached Sivas he immediately hunted up Geragos and claimed his promise. Geragos asked him two or three times whether he would surely read the book if it were given to him, and the man promised. "But," said Geragos, "if you read it only once you will not understand it, and perhaps if you read it twice you will not understand. You must read it several times, and think as you read." The dervish agreed to do so, took his New Testament, and went on toward Mecca.

Few Christians let their light shine so naturally and fearlessly and quietly as Geragos. He almost invariably finds a chance to read his Bible aloud in khans in the evening to other arabajis, Turkish soldiers, villagers, and other travellers. They like to hear something new, and to discuss it. One morning very early I wanted some water, and went to call Geragos. A man volunteered to look for him for me, and came back to tell me that he was in his araba in the khan yard praying, so he didn't interrupt him. He doesn't make a parade of his religion, but he isn't the least bit ashamed of it.

Little by little he told me a good deal about his wife, Marie, and his three little boys. "Our wife," he said, apologetically, "is a little 'lacking' in the matter of patience, but she is learning." She is evidently rather an ignorant woman, but he is fond of her, and eager to have her understand the truth and become a real Christian. He teaches her as he would a child, and tries to have her make the children obey. We saw their home at Sivas. The wife grows discouraged when he is away, and when he is at home doesn't want him to go even so far as the market place. The other women say: "Why are you sorry? We are glad when our husbands go away." She wants to enter the church now, but Geragos says, "You must control your temper or I can't testify that you are ready." He is a kind husband, and she is proud of him. He loved to talk to us about his boys, and how he means to send them to college at Marsovan or Harpoot.

He is very particular about the observance of the Sabbath, which is a difficult thing for an arabaji. I know he has lost many travellers as passengers because when the bargain was being made he stipulated that they should rest on Sunday. Once he had a chance to carry the governor of the province from Sivas to Diarbekir for an unusually large sum, but he refused, to the disgust of the governor, because Sunday traveling was involved; he found other work for which he received about half as much money. He asked me once whether I thought it possible for a man to be a Christian and keep a khan. It came out later that he wanted to be a khan-keeper, and thought he could succeed in the business, but he had decided that a man could not do that work and keep Sunday as it ought to be kept, so that a Christian ought not to do it. The life of Geragos preaches as few do in Turkey, or anywhere, and I know it has helped me.

Chapter Twenty-Two: Pantomimes at Christmas, Ominous Signs, and Theresa Plans Her Return

When Theresa got back to Harpoot in August, refreshed and ready to resume her work, she was greeted with the news that there was a new Vali—Governor General of the Vilayet or Province—who according to U.S. Consul Norton was a man of "energy and refinement." His daughter had a German governess; he himself had studied abroad and spoke French and German. Politically, things had quieted down, and Theresa found both the Armenians and the missionaries at the station more relaxed and optimistic than when she had left. In November, there was welcome news of the imminent arrival of a new missionary to help out with the girls's school. Miss Bertha Wilson, from Syracuse—four years older than Theresa—had already arrived in Constantinople and was reportedly on her way to Harpoot. At the Harpoot station, plans were being made for her reception: the younger missionaries were going to ride out to a khan four hours away to greet the arriving party; Mr. Carey planned to go all the way to Malatia.

Theresa wasted no time to report on the newest member in her home letter:

> Harpoot, Dec. 9, 1903
>
> Dear Mumsie,
>
> According to my record I haven't written to you for a month and more, that is, to you personally. I'm afraid I have been bad about answering your questions lately. You wanted to know what I think of Miss Wilson. Of course first opinions are superficial, I thoroughly like her, but she isn't one of those people whom I love from the first. She takes hold of work very willingly, brightly and competently and I like the spirit she shows all through. In time I suppose we shall be dear friends, but she is a little more—what can I say? co-educational than I like, that is I like a little more gentleness and modesty. I don't mean by that, that she is rude and immodest at all, but she is so full of talk and praise of Syracuse, and a little too ready to talk about her "big" friends. Then every-

thing is "perfectly fine" and "perfectly lovely" and "perfectly great." But, dear me, how foolish I am to pick flaws in a very nice girl whom I have only begun to know. She is very independent and self-confident, which, I think, makes me a little more reserved with her than I should be if she wanted my help in anything. I remember I was a long time in really getting acquainted with Miriam and it wasn't till she began to be sick and I took care of her that we became such dear friends.

Miss Wilson has brought a very pretty and satisfactory black horse and loves to use him. I think I told you that she shares Ada's sitting-room, and has Miriam's bed-room. I don't see her nearly as much as I should if we lived in the same house.

Harpoot, Turkey
December 29, 1903

My dearly beloved Family,

Because I haven't time this week for a separate, special letter to each, I will send one to all. Firstly, to begin with, dear Papa's book arrived safely and in good condition. It looks very interesting. I have read one story already. It is certainly broadening and refreshing to read about a land and people so different from one's own. Thank you many times.

Mamma, I think all your bundles have come because all the articles you mention seem to have appeared, though I should say that there were four packages instead of five. The collars are very pretty and ministerial. I suppose your dear hands made them all. I distributed according to directions, giving books to Mrs. Barnum and Aunt Hattie and collars to the three younger ladies. One collar I keep for myself, thanking you muchly and loving it because it is from you; the other collar I save for future use. The other book I want very much to give to one of the Armenians. I shall write to Miss Merriam about the nice bag. I am not quite sure whether the fine lot of cards were in three packages or two. I am very grateful for them, and never have too many. Just today I have two requests for some—one from the S.S. in the other quarter, and one from someone who will send them to a village.

Kindie's books were among the earliest arrivals and I thank my precious sister with all my heart. Several of Paul Lawrence Dunbar's poems I am already familiar with, but I never have seen the complete volume before. "The Warrior's Prayer," which Cornelia speaks of as the best is an old friend of mine. I found it once in a magazine and cut it out sticking it, with various other clippings, into the blank pages in the back of my Armenian hymn book, to learn in the ten or fifteen minute waits which frequently occur before meetings. So I know the poem by heart now. Miss Peabody's poems I have enjoyed very much. There is a sort of refreshing, inexplicable charm about them. I have picked the book up two or three times and found it hard to stop reading. I think I must have nearly read it through by this time. It was too much to send two books. One of the two had suffered a little from water, but not very badly—the other is all right. It is queer that the Xmas mail is very often partially soaked. One of Mamma's packages of cards had to be spread out to dry, but the damage was not great.

Aunt Hattie sends Mamma her love and thanks her heartily. I think she will not write herself. I am not sure whether the others will thank you themselves or whether they expect me to write their thanks.

Christmas eve we had our entertainment for the girls—shadow pantomimes and they were delighted, it being the first time they had ever seen anything of the sort. We hung up the sheet in the dining-room and the Americans came in to see, too. The first and most elaborate thing was Little Red Riding Hood. Then we had various other scenes—a barber shaves a man with a tremendous head of hair (wool) and beard (snipping off bit of his paper nose now and then); an impolite guest comes and shows herself to be very ill-mannered at the table; a woman goes to bed and is disturbed by her crying baby, by mice, by fighting cats, by an enormous spider descending upon her, etc. The final scene was Santa Claus filling a row of stockings. It was really very amusing and successful. Miss Wilson, Ada and two Armenian teachers did most of the acting. Winifred and I each came in once, but for most of the time I was stage-manager, lady's maid etc.

After all this Mr. Riggs gave a very clever sort of side-show. He was concealed under something which appeared to be a grave, with white stones at head and feet and covered with white. From this two ghosts arise (one on each side) who have quarreled on earth and want to have it out here. Mr. Riggs' two arms were dressed up as puppets and these had a good time thwacking each other till one finally beat. This sounds much more gruesome and rough than I meant to make it for it was really very bright and clever.

After this the girls sat down at their round, low tables and had their Xmas treat—oranges, pears, apples, figs, nuts, raisins, candy, leb-lebs and bastegh. Most of them didn't want to eat it all then, but it was divided up and each carried off her share to nibble on our Xmas day, which was a holiday for them.

In the morning the girls sang carols bright and early, as they always do Xmas morning. We had breakfast at 7.30 and prayers after instead of before as usual. The children found it fearfully trying to have prayers and begged for a short hymn and a very small portion of a chapter. After that we had a jolly time looking at the contents of our stockings.

I was lazy most of the day. Indeed after luncheon I slept for nearly two hours. I had a sore throat—the beginning of a hard cold and finally I decided not to go to dinner or to the Careys in the evening. It wasn't hard to know my own preference, for I much preferred to go to bed. Only I hesitated because I hated to have any fuss made over me. I practically cured my cold by so doing and I really didn't seem to care at all for missing the merrymaking. Mrs. Carey had the three older children dressed up as brownies, who sang and brought the gifts. This evening the children repeated it all for the teachers of the girls' school, so I missed little. Only one important thing I didn't hear and that was Mr. Riggs' announcement of his own engagement to Miss Annie Tracy of Marsovan. The affair has been going on for a long, long time, but finally on Xmas day, he rec'd a cablegram which sent him up into seventh heaven. He hopes that she can come on to Marsovan next summer and that he and his sister can have a double wedding at that time. Everyone calls Miss Tracey a very lovely girl.

I have had two good rides this week. Once I went in a snowstorm with Mr. Knapp and Miss Wilson. When we were going at a good canter, Miss W. went over on her head just between her horse's feet. She does not seem to have been hurt at all. This is the second or third time that she has been off so far. She is a fearless rider, but not a very skilful one yet.

There are many more things to tell, but I am awfully sleepy and it is late. I did mean to tell you about our school-cats. Now and then a stranger gets in with our two and some door is left open by accident and we have a great row in the small hours of the night, a racing up and down the stairs and in the hall by my room and fearful yowlings and spittings. I always endure it till one of the teachers gets up and scares them off, being too lazy myself, you see, to do the work. Yester, a teacher whose room is just opposite mine made me laugh one morning after such a rumpus, by asking me

Right, Laura Ellsworth (Sept. 1898). *Below,* Dr. Caleb Gates, Mrs. Gates, Herbert and Moore Gates

Dildilian Bros
(Art Photographers)
MERZIFOUN
ANATOLIA-COLLEGE
TURKEY IN ASIA

Facing: Top left, Henry Harrison Riggs and Annie Tracie Riggs, Summer 1904, Harpoot. *Top right,* Mary Daniels, 1885. *Lower right,* Henry H. Riggs, 1903–4. *Lower right,* Annie Tracy Riggs, 1904. *This page: Right,* Dr. Clarence Ussher. *Below left,* Caroline Bush, 1905. *Below right,* Rev. Egbert S. Ellis

Top left, Mrs. Lora G. Carey.
Top right, Harriet Seymour.
Left, The Rev. George P. Knapp and Mrs. Anna Knapp.

(in Armenian) if I heard the cats weeping and shouting in the night. That is the Armenian idiom, but it gives you a queer impression of the cats' performance.

Because I am too lazy to write all this over again for George, I send this via him, tho' it will delay it a few days in reaching America. My dearest love to you all.

With a hug and kiss all around,

Theresa

But all was not well at the station for very long. Theresa's letters from early 1904 hint at an ominous development for the college, although it would have been impossible for her or anyone else at the Harpoot station to see, at this point, that this was a rehearsal of events that a mere decade later would close down the college completely. In a letter of Jan. 28 she writes; "The Professor and all the other prisoners are still waiting in prison and the trial has come to an end for the present, with no decision. The prisoners have to provide their own food, except I believe one or two "breads" a day are given to each."

During the first part of his imprisonment, Professor Tenekejian had been tortured but since he would not confess to anything, the torture ceased. Day after day, Theresa reports, the trial dragged on; day after day, old Dr. Barnum attended it and kept note of the proceedings. "Much of it," writes Theresa, "is a mere farce."

In a letter, Henry Riggs elaborated on the trial and provided a chilling insight into what passed for as legal proceedings for Armenians in that time and place. He wrote:

> Almost if not quite all of the professors, including professor T., testified to having been beaten, tortured, threatened with death and other nameless horrors to make them testify to the propositions which were presented to them. One favorite method of torture was for days together to keep the prisoners awake constantly. This was what drove pr. T. into temporary insanity. He testified that for some days the men who guarded him would not let him sleep, threatening him with loaded guns when he got drowsy. Then when the prisoner was worn almost to madness he was urged to sign the desired testimony. The man who was first arrested, and was the principal witness in the case told a story that would make a pretty good story for a dime novel. He was threatened, beaten, abused and tortured, and then his wife was beaten almost to death before him, to get him to give evidence against various prominent individuals, among them the professor, to the effect that they were

> members of a revolutionary committee. At last the man was so used up by the torture that he went into a sort of fit, and the police thought he was going to die on their hands; so they threw him out of a window, thinking to get rid of the results of their misdeeds. When they brought him up and found him not be dead, but only had two legs broken, they told him he must corroborate their story that he jumped from the window trying to escape; that if he did they would see to it that he was handsomely pensioned, but if he would not they would kill him. All the testimony in the case seems to be of the same sort, all secured under torture.[59]

Eventually, the charges were dropped and the Professor was released. Using back streets, under the cover of darkness, the professor quietly walked back to his house and soon resumed his academic teaching. In a letter of February 18, 1904 Theresa writes:

> The best news of the week is that Prof. Tenekejian has been released from prison with twenty-nine others. Two of the twenty-nine were sentenced to seven month imprisonment each, but as they had already been kept in prison eight months, they had served out their sentence and were released with the others. Some fifteen or sixteen men were sentenced to imprisonment anywhere from two to fifteen years and two who killed a Turk in defence of their own lives and property are to be hanged. I suppose most of the men who were punished are not guilty. One of them was thrown out of a window by Turks at the time of his capture last summer and both of his legs broken. He has not had proper care in prison and his legs are in a terrible condition. I suppose he will not live out his sentence.
>
> There is a great rejoicing over the release of so many, but it is all in fear and trembling. This afternoon we give a reception to the teachers of both departments in honor of the professor's return.
>
> Some houses have been searched again this week and papers and letters collected. Several men were put into prison, but all except one have been released.

The *Missionary Herald* summarized:

> Information has recently been received from the State Department at Washington that a dispatch from the United States Legation at

59. ABC.16.9.7 vol. 24.

> Constantinople reports the termination of the trial of Prof. Nicholos Tenekejian, of Euphrates College, at Harpoot, followed by his release. This professor was thrown into prison last May upon a charge that he was an active member of a revolutionary organization. The trial was greatly delayed, and in the meantime effort was made by force to compel him to confess to the crime. Some thirty members were arrested at the same time. As he was an employee in an American college, our government requested that an early trial be had, and that a representative from the United States consulate be present to see that justice was done. The English consulate at Harpoot was also represented at the trial. No condemning or even compromising testimony was presented, while it was clearly shown that the professor on trial had been among the foremost to discountenance any revolutionary ideas among students in the college and elsewhere.[60]

Tenekeijan himself made only a few comments on his release: "This college has made me what I am; it has given me whatever there is in me of good; during my imprisonment the teachers, students and missionaries have shown me their deepest love and sympathy. I owe everything to this institution, so here is my life from now on, a gift to the College."

It is a comment of chilling literality. During the First World War, due to his affiliation with Euphrates College, Professor Tenekijan, along with all the other male professors, was imprisoned and later murdered.[61]

Theresa owed a letter to the ladies auxiliary of the Norfolk and Pilgrim Branch which includes more details about the imprisonment:

> March 3, 1904
>
> Dear Friends,
>
> I wrote you in my last letter, I think, about the long-continued imprisonment of our Professor, who with many others was arrested upon the charge of having conspired against the government. Almost everyone knew that the charge was groundless and that they were entirely innocent. After the trial had dragged along for eight months a decision was reached last month and twenty-eight of the prisoners including the Professor were declared innocent. If the government could possibly have made them out to be guilty, it would have done so, I do not doubt, but they could not concoct

60. *Missionary Herald*, 1904, vol. C, p. 130.
61. ABC 16.9.7, vol. 24.

anything at all from the testimony given. Two other men were condemned to seven months imprisonment but as they had already more than served out their sentence, they were acquitted with the others. There were still other men who received sentences of imprisonment for various periods. Most of them, I suppose from what I have heard, were guilty more of indiscretion than anything else—of speaking against the government, singing Armenian national airs etc.

There was a good deal of excitement over the freeing of the prisoners, but the Armenians were afraid to make any public demonstration. Professor Tenekejian entered the city and went to his home by unfrequented by-streets, so that no crowd or noise might attend his return. Of course there was great relief and joy among all the teachers and students.

The Professor looks a little worn and thin, and has not yet taken up all his regular work. I wish there were time to tell of some of the details of his prison life, which he has described to us. At the beginning he was kept awake for thirteen consecutive days and nights (with the exception of two hours), a really horrible form of torture—so that he might be compelled, when his mind was somewhat unbalanced by sleeplessness to give evidence against himself. Whenever he began to yield to sleep the guards with him pointed their revolvers at him and threatened to shoot. He was not beaten as were many of the prisoners. The place where they were imprisoned, though a comparatively new building, was too horrible to describe—filled with filth and vermin. After the first few months of their imprisonment, owing largely to the efforts of our consul and the work of the American and British representatives in Constantinople, and also to the attention given to the matter in American newspapers, the prisoners were transferred to somewhat better quarters.

I am sure that this unusual justice on the part of the Turkish government was an answer to many prayers.

My reference to Armenian national airs above reminds me of a naive remark which one of our girls made not long ago. She was invited to one of the missionary houses where she heard several of our American national songs. With some surprise she said to me, "Do you have national songs? Why should you have any? You are a free people."

Just now there is a small-pox scare in the city and we are having our teachers and girls vaccinated. In this land small-pox is regarded much as scarlet fever (or even measles) is with us—as a children's disease. Many cases of weak eyes and blindness are due to it. Miss Barnum asked the girls this week who had already had the disease and found that there were about twenty out of eighty-three girls. I was surprised that the proportion was not greater. The Armenian word for small-pox is "flowers" and the question as to whether one has had the disease is put thus, "Have you flowered?" It is almost impossible to keep the school wholly free from the danger of contagion, for the people make light of the sickness and conceal it if they know that it will prevent the well children of the family from going to school.

Last Sunday I went to one of our villages, a two hours' ride away. We lost our way in the fog on the hills, and so reached our destination late. The women were singing in the chapel already when we reached the door, but it wasn't too late for me to lead their meeting. They gave my muddy, muddy overshoes a place of honor in the corner of the chapel and led me up to the red gingham cushion in front where the leader sits. I enjoyed the meeting thoroughly, as I always do when I go to a village, because the women are so attentive and serious. Sometimes while I was speaking I was startled by a sudden rush of wings as a little flock of sparrows alighted on the floor or suddenly took flight from there to sit on the rafters.

Between the women's meeting and the general preaching service which Mr. Knapp conducted I went to the house of one of the chief "brethren" and sat with half a dozen women and "brides", (the two kinds are carefully distinguished here) around the cursie. This is a deep hole in the earthen floor in which cakes of dried manure are burned to heat the room. The heat is rather damp and ill-smelling and personally I prefer to be cold. We pulled a piece of fearfully dirty cloth over our knees and while our toes were warming, talked about Miss Seymour and Miss Bush, whom all the village women love dearly; about their prospects of finding a new pastor, about the work of their Bible woman, the condition of their school, the climate of America etc.

I had brought a few colored Sunday School lesson cards with me which had been sent me from America, and was surprised and touched to see that the older women were as pleased with them as the children, and asked as eagerly what they represented.

In the shipment which arrived from America soon after Christmas a box came to me containing ten delightful little dolls. I have no idea by whom it was sent as there was no name or address upon it, but I think it must have come from some one or some society in our Branch. So I want to give my warmest thanks to the senders and the thanks, too, of the little girls who are going to receive the dolls in the future. I am keeping them now for next Christmas. One doll I have already given to a little orphan who was hungering for one.

Several times I have received picture cards from unknown senders and if any of you are among that number, will you please receive my thank also. We never have too many cards, especially the little colored Sunday School lesson cards.

With cordial greetings to all,
Sincerely,
Theresa L. Huntington

After this distressing episode, Theresa turned her attention to lighter things and writes to her sister Ruth, who at this time was in her last semester at Wellesley:

Harpoot, Turkey
March 3, 1904

Dearest Ruthie,

I should make it your turn to receive a letter oftener, if it didn't mean no letter for Milton and I know that they expect one there always and are disappointed if it doesn't come regularly. Will you forward this to them as soon as you can?

This week there have been two rather unusual events. One is that Mr. Riggs has connected the large school-bell with the clocks in the school so that it strikes the hours. It is very convenient to have it so. He hasn't gotten it quite properly regulated yet so that it runs straight. Night before last it struck fifteen at midnight and at about three o'clock Mr. Riggs had to get out of bed and shut off the electric current, the thing was acting so queerly. Last night it struck one at three successive hours. In the day time when it knows that Mr. Riggs' eye is upon it, it is all right.

I wrote before, I think, that Mr. Riggs and Mr. Carey have gone to Diarbekir and Mardin. The care of the clock he, Mr. R., has intrusted to Emma. You know he has fixed up an electrical arrangement by which the bell on the school strikes the hours. It is a rather uncertain, flighty bell and sometimes strikes several successive hours at the same time. We call it Mr. Riggs' baby because he has to get up in the night so often to attend to it. This morning it struck forty-six at six o'clock. Emma went over and straighted it out and it is quiet and obedient now for a while.

Harpoot, Turkey
May 4, 1904

Dear Mamma,

I was very glad to hear by the last post that Harry's operation was successful. It rather troubled me to think about it. Is it this operation on his throat which is to help his ears, or is something more necessary?

There seems to be nothing to tell this week except that there is an epidemic of mumps in the city. We have several cases in the school and today it is plain that Mrs. Knapp is a victim, too, which of course means that all the little Knappkins will have their turn. I cannot remember whether I have had it on only one side or both.

We have had a very cold spring and everything is a month or so behind, i.e. the trees and flowers. One year on the 21st of May there were cherries in the market. This year at this time the trees are hardly through blooming. Yesterday, or rather the day before the little Knapps hung some May-baskets at our doors. I was trying to catch Winifred in the dark and hid by the dormitory door to wait for her to come out. When I heard a step I jumped and caught our fat startled old matron in my arms. It took her dignified soul some time to grasp the situation. By the next morning she was ready to have a good laugh over it.

We had a hard thunder shower two or three days ago in the midst of which came one clap which was enough to make one's hair stand on end. The lightening struck a house near by where two of our girls live. Fortunately no one was at home. A box of clothing etc. was destroyed and some spoons and forks which were in it were melted into shapeless lumps.

Ada and Mrs. Knapp came back from their eight days' trip last Friday. They enjoyed it but had rather a hard time of it coming home because of the down-pour of rain and their losing their path in the dark. Their muleteer was an ex-robber and they had the excitement of being followed by three armed robbers for some distance. There were five men in their party, including a zabtieh. The condition of this vilayet is safer and quieter than at any time before since I came, thanks to a Vali with a strong hand. There is permission now for any Armenian to go to America or elsewhere, if he pays the gov't 15 £, disposes of all his property and renounces his Turkish citizenship. I don't know when this emigration is going to stop.

Love to each dear one,
Theresa

At the end of term, the Armenian teachers sat for a group picture. The picture hasn't survived, but Theresa's comments have, and they are worth saving for the light they throw on her as a judge of character and on the expectations of the American missionaries of their 'native' teachers in general:

Harpoot
July 12, 1904

Dear, dear Papa,

I am sending by this post the pictures of the girls and teachers, taken several weeks ago. The picture of the College girls is pretty bad. They really do look better than that. I have written the names of the Seniors on the back. The girls in the front row are Juniors; those in the third row, and a few in the second, Sophomores and the back row are Freshmen. They did not know before hand that it was to be taken and so all had on their everyday school-clothes. Several needed to fix up their hair a little, but didn't have the chance.

The teachers' picture is a little better, but not really good. The arrangement is stiff, but we let the photographer have his own way entirely in it, because he blamed us for the failure of the first attempt. Ada's picture is miserable and mine looks rather cross. I'll tell you just a bit about some of the teachers. You know Varzhoohee means teacher and is used as a title after the first name, just as we say Miss. Degen means Mrs.

Yester V. teaches in the College. The other College instructors are the Professors from the Boys Department and the American teachers. Yester V. is a widow with a daughter in the Junior class. I forgot, she has a husband living in America, but he does not support her. She is a strong, capable teacher, but a little too sharp and severe.

Markarid V., who is likewise a grass widow, with a husband in Hungary, teaches in the High School. She is good but a little queer and tiresome. Anna V. Der Ghagarian is a protege of Mr. Browne's. She has a very sweet face which you would not guess from the picture. Her specialties are History and Embroidery. Anna V. Avakian is a lively young teacher who has done excellent work in the two years since her graduation. She is the one who is to study at Con'ple next year, if the government gives her her teskereh. This is a miserable picture of her. Deeroohi V. is a faithful old Puritan who is one of the chief pillars of the school. When she was a child she fell from a roof and her arm and jaw were injured. A good surgeon could probably have set things straight at the time but there was no one to do it. Her eyes are weak, but in spite of her misfortunes she does good work and is really a noble woman. Takoohi V. is a pretty young teacher—daughter of the leading Armenian Doctor here. She is a little too giddy. Aroosiag V. is the daughter of the Barnum's old cook. She is energetic and capable, tho' not so refined as some of the others. All these teach in the High School and Grammar School.

Anna V. Gelgelian is the head of the Primary School. She supports her widowed mother and sister. She is a thorough teacher, but has grown rather sharp and severe and fallen into ruts. As she has taught ten years without a break, we proposed to send her to Marsovan for a year of study and change, but tho' we would support her, we could not take the whole family upon us, so she felt that she must stay and care for them. Vartoohi V. and Aghavni V. Yeshilian are her assistants. The former is good in some ways, though not wholly reliable, the latter is a complete failure in discipline and not very good in anything. Anna V. Bonapartian is a sweet girl of only one year's experience. She and Varseneg have the smallest girls. Varseneg V. is rather sentimental and dreamy. She has sweet ways with the children, but little force and system. Degen Mariam is the kindergarten teacher who has just left us to join her husband in Bulgaria. She has done much good work and it will be very hard to fill her place. Pariz V. rules her little boys with a rod of iron, but she is kind and they love her. She is strong and coarse-grained outwardly, but has succeeded well. Aghavni is her assistant.

I forgot to mention Mariam V. Apkarian who teaches in the Grammar School. She is very homely, but always bright and cheery and true—a genuine Christian. We shall miss her next year, for she will probably leave us to be married.

I am afraid you have wearied of this long-drawn-out account. If the picture had been taken by a good photographer, you would think that both teachers and girls had much more attractive faces.

> Since vacation began, I have spent most of my days in the city. Books and other school supplies have to be looked over. I give English lessons to a girl who is trying to make up back work and to Markarid V. who is ambitious to teach English better. I also take Armenian lessons myself. I find it a real pleasure after two years without lessons. My Turkish I have dropped temporarily. There is really no one who can take Gulzar's place. Next year we expect a new girl from Aintab and perhaps she will teach me.

Theresa's colleague and head of the Girl's Department, the problematic Miss Daniels, wrote a similar letter in a report to the Woman's Board which also sheds an interesting light on the Armenian teachers at the school and the missionaries' expectations of them:

> We have now in the school six teachers of experience and the four post-graduates; most of whom are doing satisfactory work. The Woman's Board has endowed one chair, which is now occupied by Miss Nazloo Nemejenian. In the class-room, she is quiet and dignified, uses a well-modulated voice. With her leading the unruly and disobedient girls become quiet and orderly, and in love with the lessons she teaches. Among other lessons she has taught Natural Theology and Mental Philosophy. She is a real student. Outside the class-room she is faithfulness itself. Such a load of responsibility as she takes from me. Miss Mariam Enfiajian has the same rank and honor, although the chair she fills is not endowed. But we are expecting that the Lord will give us the money in His time. Mariam is quick, energetic and just the opposite of quiet Nazloo. She is very mathematical, and it is a pleasure to watch her examine a class in Trigonometry, Geometry, or Algebra in her self-possessed way, although the room be filled with guests. I must write a word about our sweet-voiced singer, Rebecca. She has been teaching four or five years. Most of her time has been given to music—vocal and instrumental—and the burden has been heavy, as the care has been wholly here. But she has done wonderfully and is constantly improving. Our Yester deserves a word. She is the head of our primary school. Such a large heart as she has, it seems to take in all her scholars. Love is the ruling spirit in her room. And so I might continue to sound the praises of each teacher. You know a mother is never tired of talking about her children.[62]

62. ABC 16.9.9, Eastern Turkey Supplementary (2).

Theresa spent part of her summer vacation that year in "the garden" as usual, and also made another excursion to the lake. By September, she was back in Harpoot, rejoicing in the fact that her dear friend Miriam Platt had returned from her sick-leave in the United States, looking very well. Henry Riggs' brother Ernest, who was married to Alice Shepard, daughter of the legendary Doctor, had joined the College as an instructor.

Harpoot, Turkey
Oct. 6, 1904

My dearly-beloved Family

I suppose you are more or less scattered now, and this bit of a letter is hardly worth sending around to the absent ones. Still I address it to all. About half an hour ago the mail came. I was very eager for it today, because I knew it would bring news of the boys. I was very grateful to Mamma for the card telling about it, and I thank Ellsworth too for his letter written on the steamer. I heard in some round-about way that George had the mumps in Paris. Why didn't he want to tell me? I received such a dear letter from Aunt Caro today, telling about the boys and all the family. She admires you all. She says, "All take me into the home as if I belonged there."

The most exciting event since I wrote last is Miriam's arrival. She came on Saturday with Br. Melcone. The Knapp family, Ada and I went to the khan four hours from here to meet them. The others also rode out but not so far. Miriam looks *very* well. I think I have never seen her so fat and rosy before, and I am astonished that she was so little tired by the long journey. It is nice to have her in the house again—she is so sweet and "homey." She has all the housekeeper's instinct and is always thinking of ways to make the house more convenient, comfortable and pretty. Bertha is just the opposite. Ada and I are between. Mr. Ernest Riggs and Bertha are nearly well now, but still very weak. Perhaps I did not tell you that those two and Mr. Dinglian, the Marsovan teacher who came with them, all began to be ill at the same time—apparently a sort of gastric fever with malaria. The Doctor does not know exactly what it was, but there was plainly some common cause, which they met with on the journey. They had high fever and were at one time very ill. I think all have lost ten pounds or more in weight.

Miriam brought me your dear, lovely gifts, but I have not time to speak of each separately now. I will do so next week, but till then, know that you have a heartful of thanks from me.

It is recess just now and the little yard is full of shouting, laughing girls. This is one of the days when they are supposed to speak English. It is a very hard rule to enforce.

Has Markarid V.'s gift of silk reached you yet, Mamma? It is rather gaudy and I don't suppose you will like it, but still I hope it won't be lost, for it will grieve the giver's heart. I know you have ever so many letters to write, but I hope you can write a little note to her.

Most lovingly,
Theresa

Harpoot, Turkey
Oct. 19, 1904

My Dearly-beloved and Longed-for,

This is a letter full of gratitude for the beautiful things which your loving hearts and hands prepared for Miriam to bring to me. It hadn't occurred to me that you might send anything by her, so I was properly surprised, as Ada says. Everything is *very* useful, as well as nice. I had three hair-brushes before, all of them mere wrecks, not fit for polite society. My combs were in the same condition, and I was planning to order one from America "to travel home in." I like both comb and brush very much, they are so sensible and *nice*-looking, and they match so well. I would much rather have these than more showy white ones. My two belts are the envy of the ladies of the station. Everybody likes them and I have been very hard up for belts all summer till now. They are a great comfort after the narrow belts which I have been using so long. I suspect that they were Cornelia's choice. I certainly approve of her taste. The soap-box, the drinking-cup and the tooth-brush holder are all a great comfort, simple, convenient, and exactly what I needed. I am afraid that the list which I sent of the things I lost on the way from Egin last spring, seemed rather like an appeal for assistance. The last of all the appear was Mamma's gift which Miriam produced some four days ago. It surprised me even more than the other things, and gave me that sort of pain in my heart for a minute, which your gifts often do. Miriam said that Mamma had given her some money telling her to buy "something to eat" for me. So she invested in about a dozen cakes of "Swiss milk chocolate" and a box of crackers. The chocolate is the nicest kind. When I saw the things, I just had to kiss them, to think how you had thought of giving your little girl on the other side of the world something to eat and such a lot!

And now I thank all you dear ones, Papa, Mamma, Cornelia, Harry and Ruth, and I kiss your hands, as the Armenians do. These are my Christmas presents, so you must not send me anything more.

My letters last week were a regular feast. Papa, Mamma, Harry and Ruth all wrote about the boys' home-coming and George a little, too, though more about other things. I read the letters most greedily. All were interesting and dear, but I think Harry's was the best this time, because it was so long, and he told such funny, interesting little details. It really isn't fair to compare, though, because each letter had its own especially nice little parts. Did Ellsworth speak at the Geographical Meeting in New York? And what was his subject, if he did? How soon he goes! I can address his letters to America only two months more. I want to hear what pretty things the boys brought home. Do you use them in the house? Mamma advises me not to bring things on account of the duties. I really have very little. I think everything I have, except two or three rugs, will go into my two trunks.

Chapter Twenty-Three:
Theresa Needs a Traveling Hat; Complains About Garrulous Armenians, and Asks: "Was it worth it?"

When 1904 was drawing to a close, Theresa decided to take a furlough. She had been working hard for six years and she was tired. Unbeknownst to her, her fatigue had not gone unobserved. Dr. Atkinson, the station doctor, was keeping an eye on Theresa and her colleagues in the Female Department and in a letter to Dr. Barton, observed that this year, her fatigue was different from previous years. The reason, wrote the perceptive Dr. Atkinson, was the absence of Mary Daniels. "Miss Huntington," wrote Dr. Atkinson, "has had more responsibilities this year than ever before, she has also worked harder and done more than ever before. She ends up the year tired but not nervously exhausted or on the verge of prostration as she has each previous year. This is simply due to the fact that she has worked *with* miss Barnum instead of *under* Miss Daniels.

> Miss Daniels has no close friend in the circle, Dr. Atkinson continued. "Perhaps you at the rooms should understand the reason for this state of things. First Miss Daniels lacks self-control. She quickly gets into a passion, screaming at and scolding both teachers and pupils. She rules the school, but through fear. Second, she is selfish and babyish. She controls everything and wishes to have credit of everything. She arranges everything then asks the opinion of others and if they make a suggestion or differ in opinion Miss D. would go off in tears accusing her colleagues of various things. She carried this to such an extent that she tried to forbid Miss Huntingon to have talks with the scholars....Third, she is of a jealous disposition. I have said enough for you to infer that. She endeavours to shut out and belittle her colleagues. It is this constant strained condition, this constantly being the object of jealousy and its attacks that has used Miss Huntington up in previous years. Both Miss Huntington and Miss Platt have been subject to this, and they are both too noble to utter a word of complaint about their own troubles, and they will say nothing but kind words

> for her though I know that the young ladies are praying that something may occur to prevent Miss Daniels from returning, that she may find a lover and get married or something like that."[63]

Mary Daniels did return to Harpoot, but not before it had been pointed out to her that she needed to change her ways. She seems to have accepted the criticism graciously, and matters improved greatly.

Around the time that Theresa was planning her furlough, the Woman's Board journal *Life and Light* published an up-beat overview of the extensive work of the female missionaries of the Harpoot station:

> When we realize that the course of study in Euphrates College extends from the kindergarten through primary, grammar and preparatory schools to real college work, and that more than a thousand pupils are studying in the various departments, we shall see how great is its opportunity, how important that its wide influence should be truly Christian. The college provides teachers not only for our village schools, but for Gregorian, Catholic and German schools, and even for other mission stations. Miss Daniels is principal of the girl's department, over five hundred girls being under her oversight. She has just been at their home in Franklin, Mass., for her year of furlough, and sailed May 10, returning to Harpoot. Miss Barnum is an efficient teacher in the college, and has taken Miss Daniels' work during her absence. Miss Huntington, Miss Platt, and Miss Wilson are a strong and happy partnership, working zealously together to make intelligent Christian women of the girls under their care. Miss Huntington plans to take her furlough after Miss Daniels is back at her post. The kindergarten grows apace under the care of Miss Platt. One little lad told his mother, "When I do wrong Miss Platt does not scold me as you do, but just whispers in my ear, and it makes me feel awfully."
>
> Miss Seymour, greatly beloved, has returned to this country to make her home after many years of most faithful and fruitful service. Miss Bush, for more than thirty years the companion of Miss Seymour in touring and evangelistic work, is now in America on furlough. She does not take her rest in idleness, however, but has made many addresses, and has stirred many hearts with a new sense of the needs of Turkey, and of our own slothful and sinful falling short of duty that we do not meet that need. She expects to

63. ABC 16.9.7, vol. 3.

> return to Harpoot next autumn, taking with her a young woman as associate and helper. Mrs. Barnum, who makes very many calls, has grown to have a place of much influence among the women of the city, who come to her in great numbers for help in all kinds of need. After more than a quarter century of service in Turkey Mrs. Browne feels that the needs of her children will detain her in this country. Mrs. Knapp finds most of her time and thought taken by her own children. When is the work of a mother done? As the wife of the President of the college, Mrs. Riggs, daughter of Dr. C.C. Tracy, of Marsovan, finds endless opportunities for helping both teachers and students. She helps in the "brides' meetings" for young married women, and also in oversight of the orphanages. Mrs. Carey has introduced lace making among the needy women, and the steady employment and the wages it brings are both a blessing. Mrs. Atkinson, wife of the physician in charge of the medical work in the city, herself a trained nurse, is rejoicing in the advent of a little one into her own home.[64]

But Theresa was not just tired; she was also homesick, and her homesickness was beginning to show in her correspondence. Thrifty and careful as ever, she instructs her 'Dearest Mamma' to begin preparations for a shipment of traveling clothes:

> Now for clothes. First I need a lot of under-clothing, I am sorry to say. What I have I can make last till early summer, by patching, but they positively are not respectable for traveling, so I need the following things:
>
> I. 2 equipoise waists—low neck or rather, medium, for I believe there is a very low kind, which I don't care for. But I don't want the high ones. You already know my style. I believe my bust measure is 36 in. and my waist 26 in. The last ones sent were right and you may have kept a record of measurements.
>
> II. 3 prs of drawers—open at sides, tucked but untrimmed otherwise. I have lace of edging here to use.
>
> III. 6 prs of summer stockings—cotton, of course. I wear 4 1/2 shoe.
>
> IV. 3 night-dresses.
>
> I hadn't been expecting to get any under-clothing before going home, but I saw that I must and it costs no more at one time than

64. *Life and Light*, 1905, vol. 35.

another. Even if anything should hinder my coming this year, it would be well to have the things. If you go to the rooms, I think Mr. Hosmer will give you some sort of discount book to use at the shops. I will write to him about it.

Now for outside raiment. I need one good cotton shirt-waist to wear for travelling etc. To begin at the beginning, I have decided not to let you send me a travelling suit, for I should spoil a pretty new dress with dust and dirt. Miriam thinks, as you said, that my grey suit will do, so I am going to keep it and wear it very little. The inside satin lining is a little worn, so I will send you a bit that you may match it and send me the piece to patch with. I think half a yard would be enough. I send you a piece of the dress, that you may get a cotton blouse which goes well with it.

I also want a grey flannel blouse which suits it—not too dark—just medium. I don't want it to be elaborate, but just sensible for travelling on a cool day or on the steamer.

There is just one more need—a travelling hat for summer. I know this is a miserable time to get straw. My thought was not a grey straw (that isn't becoming to me and it fades), but perhaps a small white sailor with a soft grey silk scarf twisted around it—something suiting the dress. I leave it all to you, only I would like it rather small (the brim not over four inches wide) and round. However I trust your judgement in it all. You know the sort of simple thing I like.

Harpoot, Turkey
Dec. 28, 1904

My dear Everybody,

I feel rather uncertain as to where you all are, though I suppose you are together. When does Ellsworth start? It is three weeks tomorrow since I have received a letter from Milton, tho' I have heard from George and Harry in that interval. My Christmas is over, but I am still wondering what you did on Thanksgiving Day.

Christmas itself was a snowy day and very much like other Sundays externally, except for our Christmas meeting in the evening. Monday morning I was wakened before five by the girls' carols. We had breakfast at seven and the stockings afterward. It is fun to watch the children. Little Katherine was bewildered and didn't get so much pleasure out of her gifts as the older children. At about nine o'clock I went up to school and till 1.40 did my work as usual. From then till dinner time I did up a few bundles which had been belated. We dined at 4.30, the Careys, Mr. Margot, and Bertha being our guests. I am sure you did not have any better turkeys than we. At 6.30 we all went up to the "White House." Everyone was present, including Baby Henry. Mrs. Atkinson, who is still very delicate and weak, was carried up in a chair and I think it did her good to be with the crowd. The room was beautifully decorated with greens. First there were songs and recitations by the children and the older people helped out, too, in that. It was all very sweetly and graciously planned and done. I wish you could have seen Katharine singing "Jolly Old St. Nicholas" with the other children, coming in like a sweet little echo at the end of each line. They sang it twice by special request and then the baby inquired whether they were to "do Jolly" again.

There was no tree, but a great Noah's ark was revealed at one end of the room, when the screens were taken away. Mr. and Mrs. Noah, that is, Mr. and Mrs. Riggs were seen within, looking anxiously out of the windows through a paper telescope. It seems that the flood was just abating. Mrs. Noah was eager to get out on account of the noise of the animals, the prevalence of measles in the ark etc, but Mr. Noah insisted that it was too muddy. Finally she prevailed upon him to send out a cotton dove, which flew out with wonderful naturalness, being assisted by a thread from above. Then the gang-plank was let down and all the animals came out, one at a time—a frog, a giraffe, a cat, three rats, an enormous crab, a squirrel, a goose etc—all made of wires tied over with cotton and the faces fixed up with black ink and buttons. They were very clever and funny. There was one for each person. Later we all found gifts tied up inside the animals. When the family began to disembark, there was a great commotion and shouting of, "Porter," as the mail-bag, several suit-cases, satchels and a big laundry-bag were thrown out. These contained our gifts for each other which were distributed. It was all very jolly and bright.

For refreshments we had the remains of the Riggs' wedding cake and wedding-rice (gathered from among their possessions on their wedding-trip). Some of that rice was what was poured over Ruth. Perhaps I ate a grain that had been on her head. Properly washed up and made into "Glorified Rice" (see cook-book) it was delicious. I never enjoyed rice more. Later we had lemon ice, cake and beautiful home-made candy.

It was a pleasant day in every way and yet I am always thankful when Xmas is over here—it is such a scramble to get ready, there being no vacation. I had some very nice, useful gifts. Perhaps I will write of them later when I make out the list.

Please excuse me for sending such a short letter this week and know that I love you all most dearly,
Theresa

Harpoot, Turkey
February 3, 1905

My dearest Kindie,

Last week I received letters from Papa, George and you and a note from Mamma, giving accounts of Christmas which I was delighted to hear. I hope dear Mumsie's eye was quite well long ago. What a beautiful plan for a vacation for Papa and Mamma! If it was carried into effect they are not at home now. I wish I knew surely. As for you, darling sister, I suppose you will say that the suggestion of your going abroad is a mere day-dream at present, but I just wish you could go with that party of which you spoke, next summer. If Papa and Mamma are having a vacation, will that preclude your going? If you could travel in Europe it would give me a hundred times more pleasure than to go myself. Just now especially, home seems to me the most interesting and much-to-be-desired place on earth. As for your ever paying any travelling expenses for me, as you remotely suggested, you well know that I would not listen to such a thing for an instant. I have written to Harry and Mamma lately about my own journey. It seems still very unreal to me and I have little time to think of it at all. When the weather warms up a little and spring seems nearer, it will begin to seem nearer.

We have been having a long stretch of very cold, cloudy or foggy weather and long for a change. That is one of the things I look forward to at home—a house that is more or less warmed all over. I wear a sweater or jacket and gaiters all the time in the house now and at night have six blankets and "comforters" over my bed, to say nothing of a hot-water bag within. I often wash my hands in water in which pieces of ice are floating around. Of course if I had time enough I could go to somebody's kitchen and hunt up some hot water, but I can't waste the time. The weather here is really less cold on the whole than at home, but our buildings are not well heated and fuel is expensive. At least I have fewer colds than at home.

Harpoot
March 1, 1905

My dear Kindie,

I usually begin my home letter in these days late in the evening when I am sleepy and stupid and can't think of anything to tell.

Do you know, dearie, I think I never thanked you for sending that money for Elva's wedding-present, partly in my name. You were ever so sweet and kind to do it, and it wasn't fair for me to have the credit. Have you heard what was bought?

Do you ever go to Wellesley now that Ruth is not there? I shall feel like a cat in a strange garret when I go back—a ten years' graduate.

Just now there are eight or ten girls sitting in my room on the floor, studying. Bed time was half-an-hour ago, but this class begged to sit up later so I granted them forty-five minutes grace on the condition that they shall not make a bit of noise when they go to bed, and not expect the same permission again this term. The girls are in the first class in the High School, and nice, bright girls. I teach them in Sunday School, and they are "quick as a wink" as Miriam say,—not all, but the majority.

Last Friday afternoon, Mr. Riggs gave a lecture on steam-boats which interested everyone very much. That same day Miriam and I went calling, but succeeded in going to only four houses, all on our own street. They represented every station in life. At the first was a sweet woman with three little children, one of whom is in our Kindergarten and the other, two classes above. They have a kitchen and one living-room. I think the father and mother are both Christians. They certainly train their little ones well, according to their light.

The mother is taking daily lessons in reading from a Bible woman. She read a little from the Bible to us very falteringly, but she evidently has set her heart on learning.

At the second house was a tired mother who had just finished the family washing. The family is not poor, but they have to economize a little, I think. The woman is about forty and has had twelve children. Four boys have died and eight girls are living. Several are in our school. She came in as she was in her old working "bloomers". She is a bright, thoughtful woman but worn out by hard work.

The next house was that of a sick furrier. There are half-a-dozen lively, mischievous children—three of whom are in school. There was a dear little boy, three years old, who kept saying, "I know a lot," "I can say a piece," etc. but he could not be prevailed upon to say what he knew. He told us he had a new dress and offered to bring it and show it to us. When we went, he called after us, "Good-bye" which his older sisters had taught him to say in English. His name, by the way, was Reuben.

The family had any number of brothers, cousins, uncles etc, in America. Indeed what family about here has not? Before they brought us coffee to drink, they offered us a confection made of roses and sugar, which is considered a special delicacy here.

The fourth house was that of our hostler. The mother is a stout jolly village-woman, with a little flock of four clinging about her skirts. It pays to make calls, even tho' it is hard to manufacture time.

Everything is still covered with snow here. I enclose a picture of a little orphan with his sled. It is an unusually good specimen of a sled. The boy wrote a letter about sliding which I may copy and send some day. He is really a very little lad.

Will you please send this letter such as it is to the others?

Most lovingly,
Theresa

Harpoot, Turkey
March 8, 1905

Dear little Mother,

In these days I usually begin my letters late in the evening and consequently write rather stupidly and solemnly. I have just come home from Winifred's birthday party. She is thirteen today and is a tall, healthy-looking girl. She is not exactly pretty, but her hair and skin are beautiful.

... Miss Bushnell of Erzroom with whom I came out is to go to America in the summer, and she wrote to me in the fall suggesting that we travel together. I, personally, am disappointed that I must return as I came, only in the company of women and those, too, wholly inexperienced in travel. It is so much easier and pleasanter to have a man in the company. As far as sight-seeing goes, my journey here was a failure. We just got over the ground and arrived. If I go with Miss B. and Winifred, we shall probably come by way of the Mediterranean, taking a North German-Lloyd steamer from

Italy. I don't remember whether they leave Genoa or Naples. Little by little I suppose plans will shape themselves. Perhaps by July we shall know of other people who are travelling. I never care to go from Vienna to Con'ple again by train, unless I have to. Perhaps it is not so bad on the Oriental Express, but that is very expensive.

As to Miss Bushnell, perhaps it is not quite kind or Christian to say it, but tho' she is a nice girl, I don't really want to travel with her at all, because she isn't very cultivated or dainty in her ways. I honor and respect her character, but she isn't the sort of girl whom I enjoy being with very much. I suppose I ought to be ashamed to write this, but this letter is only for you at home.

I wish I knew where you are at this minute—still in Southern California, I suppose. I had no letter from Milton last week again, but I assume that you left, as you planned. I hope you are having the best time of your lives.

I am "going to go" as the deaf and dumb boy said. It is the same thing over and over. The same kinds of work and the same difficulties. The Armenians, here at least, never have learned to pull together. It is so from the Primary School to the "Union" of the pastors of our field. I think it is a national characteristic and one which is a fearful obstacle to progress. Jealousy is the chief cause. There is always a division or quarrel somewhere. The gates of the temple of Janus could never be closed in this region.

Our new Vali is expected this week. We hear only vague and rather unsatisfactory things about him. Doubtless he is just the opposite of the old one, and we feel a little anxious about the possible political situation in the future. They have been searching some houses again lately.

We don't know when to expect Dr. Norton. We hear that he came by a northern route and the strike on the Batoom railway probably has hindered him. I think one reason for his choosing this route was to avoid the cholera. It is very prevalent in Van just now. It seemed to flourish even in the coldest winter weather. I think there has never been a case in Harpoot, but Malatia and other places north of us have often suffered.

Next week the "Great Fast" begins, that is, Lent, and just before comes Parée Gentáhn; the last feast, before the fast begins. It corresponds to the Carnival in Catholic countries. We usually have a holiday at that time, because there are many Gregorians in the school. This year we have a day and a half as holidays—next Friday afternoon and all the following Monday. I plan to spend much of my extra time in making calls.

We still have snow and fog and cold weather. I have never before seen such a late spring here.

Now good-night, with my dearest love,
Theresa

March 15, 1905

Yesterday the new Vali arrived. Almost all Mezereh went to meet him—some a whole day's journey. The municipality appropriated 20£ for a feast at the khan where he spent the last night. What a lot of the money was wasted! The new man is not known and understood yet, but he is supposed to be a contrast to our former free-minded, progressive Vali. The Armenians wait with a good deal of fear to see how he turns out. The taxes already are about all they can bear. People are selling their beds and kitchen utensils to pay the required sums. Even we who live here can't appreciate what our freedom and safety are. For example on Monday we went to the house of the pastor in the "other quarter". His brother from Bitlis has been living with him for a year and studying. The young man's wife three years ago was imprisoned at Moosh because a copy of a revolutionary song was found in the school where she was teaching. Her baby was born in prison. A week ago the young man received a telegram saying that she had been set free. The gov't was so suspicious about the message that they sent zabtiehs to take the young man to Mezereh to be examined. They caught first another young man of the same name and carried him off. The one they were seeking was sick at the German hospital at the time, but he had a relative who was a man of importance in the Armenian community. This man went before the gov't succeeded in satisfactorily explaining the matter. At the same time that the wife was released her father was put into prison because of some letter which he had received from his son-in-law here, which was thought to be suspicious. Aren't you glad you are a safe American citizen?

To Ellsworth she wrote: "We are fearful lest the new man be of the wrong sort. I think I wrote our good Vali was removed. He was too progressive and made too many enemies. The new man is conservative and I fear worse."[65]

Dr. Peet, the American Board Treasurer in Constantinople, sounded the same note in his letter to Dr. Barnum:

> He is said to be a strong Moslem and an earnest man in his anti-Christian views, but the Grand Vizier has been strongly warned both by the British and French Embassies of the consequences which may follow if this man is allowed to carry out his anti-Christian views in that province. The Grand Vizier has given promises that he will be restrained and guided aright. How much this will amount to in practical working may well be questioned. However, this may be said; that the embassies are not going to sleep over the promises given by the Grand Vizier.
>
> There are other things I would tell you if I could meet you face to face. I do not like to put them upon paper. I may say, however, that both our own legation and the British Embassy have reason to feel that a careful watch of the situation all along the line where our people are situated will be expected by the home Governments. Whatever may be the outcome of affairs in the spring, this much is certain; a very careful attention is being given to the situation in the Turkish Empire. The weakening of the great power to the north of you has been a signal for calling into most vigilant exercise a degree of carefulness and watchfulness on the part of the remaining Christian powers, our own included, which heretofore has not been exercised by them.[66]

Some news got out. In August, 1904, the *Missionary Herald* published the following report:

> The London Times reports, on information received from Constantinople, that no fewer than 3,000 Armenians, men, women, and children, were killed in the district of Sassoun between April 25 and May 29, and that fifty Armenian villages were destroyed. Thirty-one shops in the town of Moosh belonging to Armenians were said to have been demolished, and nothing but the intervention of the French consul at Moosh prevented a big massacre near that town.[...] The situation is indeed very grave, yet, so far as we have information, our own missionaries in Eastern Turkey are not molested in their work.[67]

---

65. Yale University Archives, Ellsworth Huntington Papers, Theresa Huntington Ziegler file.
66. William Peet to Dr. Barnum, 3 March, 1905. Yale University Archives, Ellsworth Huntington Papers.
67. *Missionary Herald*, vol. 100, August, 1904.

The reality of her leaving was beginning to dawn on Theresa. In April, she wrote to her sister:

> My blessed Ruth,
>
> In some ways it is really hard to think of going, dear as the thought of being at home is. It seems to me that I never really have gotten near to the girls, have gotten hold of them till the last six months. The first two or three years that I was here, while my work was comparatively easy, it was rather unsatisfactory to me, and as I look at Bertha now and see how little she understands the people (comparatively) and how her slight knowledge of the language hampers her, I feel thankful that I am through with that period. And I suppose that the stage which I have reached seems to Emma, in turn, very elementary.

> Harpoot, Turkey
> May 3, 1905
>
> My dear Mamma,
>
> It is the middle of vacation and my going seems near. I have spent practically all the last week in looking over my things and sorting them, preparatory to packing. It is astonishing how much has accumulated and of course the things to be left have to be packed as well as the things to go. I keep thinking of the verse, "A man's life consisteth not in the abundance of things which he possesseth." It wastes life to own too many things. [...]It is a tremendous problem how to live comfortably without seeming to the people to live luxuriously. To them $300 a year is an enormous salary. I often feel ashamed of having so much.
>
> Dr. Norton expects to leave for Smyrna next week, passing thro' Ourfa, Aintab and Marash. I am much disappointed that he goes so soon for I had a lingering hope that I might go with him and see the southern mission, but I cannot leave my work so soon. Indeed if it were not for Mr. Knapp's company, I should feel that I ought not to go before school closes. Mr. K—is still a little uncertain, but will probably start June 5th, and Winifred and I, of course, with him. I am so glad that I shall see some different people. The missionaries are all dear, nice people, but sometime I hunger and thirst for a change. It seems like a dream to me to think of going home. I often think how disappointed you will all be in me. Distance and time lend a sort of halo, but you will find me not nearly so good as

you think and not at all good-looking. I want to warn you beforehand so that you may not expect more than you will find.

The government is coming down on us on all sides just now. At least we have just begun to feel their work, tho' it was begun several months ago. For one thing an order has come that all boxes which come into the Vilayet for Americans or Armenians must be opened before government officials, the reason being presumably their fear that fire-arms may be brought in. It seems very unreasonable since everything is opened at Samsoon in the Custom-House. The February shipment came last week and we were notified nothing must be opened except before an officer.

Last Thursday Mr. Carey and Prof. Tenekejian started for Egin and Arabkir. On Sunday, Dr. Norton received a telegram from Mr. Carey saying that the "government' at Egin was sending him home because he had no teskereh and asking Dr. N. to get the Vali's permission for him to stay. It came out that some months ago orders had come from Con'ple that no American missionary was to travel about in the vilayet without a teskereh. Of course we have used teskerehs heretofore when we have been to our stations in other vilayets, but Egin is in our own province. I don't know how Mr. Carey's case has been settled, but he has not reached home yet.

A third difficulty is one which can put an end practically to all our educational work, unless our Minister protests at Con'ple and the restrictions are removed. The law is that no teacher can take charge of a school or in fact teach at all unless he has a diploma, certified by the government. When our pupils go out to teach whether from the High School or College they always have paid something to have their diplomas certified, but now the government absolutely refuses to certify them. They have begun to have similar trouble in the Marsovan field, but the crisis will come after this year's Commencement, and I suppose there will be a long quarrel over the question at Con'ple.

Ripples from Turkey's war troubles reach us here. A few days ago 3000 troops were sent from the barracks at Mezereh down to Arabia where there is beginning to be trouble. That leaves only 1000 soldiers here, but they are gathering in new recruits now. From Trebizond and the provinces to the north of us they are sending troops to Macedonia.

I told you that the February shipment came last week. I like all the under-clothing very much and think it fits, tho' I haven't tried everything on as yet. The nightdresses are especially pretty and I was pretty hard up in that line, that is, most of my old ones, all except one, are ragged. Thank you for all your trouble and love. The satin lining for the jacket I shall not use now for the old lining does not begin to be bad enough to be ripped out. Perhaps I can find some bits of ribbon of the same color somewhere to mend it. The satin is beautiful.

May 17, 1905

My very dear Father,

Have you been reading anything about the rebellion in Arabia? They are calling out the "Redeefs" (i.e. Reserves) here now. I believe 5000 more men have been mustered in from this region. We hear the bugles here in the city daily. It is a horrible sound to the Armenians, for they always remember how the soldiers were called out to massacre them. I often see the girls shrink when they hear that sound. The Turks are persecuting the Armenians more than usual just now, for they always feel that the A's are partially or wholly responsible for whatever goes wrong. The A's, you know, are exempt from military service, but pay a military tax. I suppose that will be increased soon. The soldiers probably leave tomorrow and we hope the city will quiet down somewhat.

Did I tell you last week of the order from Con'ple, forbidding missionaries to travel about in their vilayets. That will prevent the Annual Meeting of the Eastern Turkish Mission which there was a little hope of holding in July in Van. I hope our gov't will interfere. That order will not prevent our going to Con'ple. In fact we have already gotten our teskerehs.

Mr. Knapp is just opening a sort of farm for orphan boys an hour and a half from here. He wants to make it a kind of colony under the charge of an Armenian who graduated from the Amherst Agric. School. I hope it will succeed, but I don't believe the man is the one to win the boys and help them spiritually. The first lot started today.

The summer exodus to the garden has begun. The Careys and Ada went out today. The Atkinsons and Bertha go on Saturday and the Riggs family soon after. Of course the workers among them come in to the city daily. That is, the married ladies stay there and the others come. During the summer Mrs. Carey gives up the lacework and her "brides" meetings. This winter Mrs. Atkinson has been talking to the "brides" every other week about the care of children, the care of the sick etc. You know here, by the way, a woman is a bride as long as her mother-in-law is alive or as long as she has any small children. Yesterday, according to a previous invitation, they brought their babies with them for the Doctor to examine and to tell what their weaknesses were, how their diet ought to be changed, etc. Forty mothers came, bringing forty-five babies. The doctor asked the age of each, weighed it, measured the back, chest, etc, explained what was wrong and how it was to be remedied. The first baby was frightened and cried. Whereupon the other forty-four moved by one impulse of sympathy, all lifted up their voices and wept, too, so that there was a regular pow-wow for a while. Emma who translated for the Doctor, said she thought it was very helpful, but she found her part rather exhausting.

I'm afraid my letters will be shorter every week now till I start. The letters from California have been very interesting.

Much love to each of you.

Your affectionate daughter,

Theresa

As Theresa prepared to leave Harpoot, it was to Ellsworth, as always, that she wrote most openly and honestly. Was her innermost person fit for this work? Or was she, as a missionary, somehow lacking—"a round peg in a square hole." And underneath that lurked a fear: having spent this much of her youth in Harpoot, did she have any alternative but to continue with the work after her furlough?

My dearest Ellsworth,

Last week I received your letter mailed at Liverpool and was most glad to know definitely about your plans. I wonder whether you had time while at Liverpool to look up Ada's friends again. So you mean to enter Tibet after all. I feel rather scared when I think of all the dangers of many kinds which you will meet, but my worrying will never make you any safer.

...You are a funny boy, dear brother, you like such a lot of girls and yet no one is the one. And George is just he opposite. Looking at you two, one would suppose that it would be the other way about. But truly, dearie, I know very well that you will be happiest when you have a home and in time I believe God will give you one....Yes, it is true that the happiest life for most women and I think the ideal for most is a home of their own. But as for me, I was never the sort of girl that men care for—never pretty enough nor gay enough, and now I have ceased to be young enough. I have

> never loved any man nor do I think that God intends the happiness of a home for me. When I find myself longing for things I can't have, and envying others their happiness, it makes me better to think of those words of Carlyle: "Foolish soul. What act of legislature was there that thou shouldst be happy? There is in man a higher than love of happiness: he can do without happiness, and instead thereof find blessedness."
>
> But one would think from this that I am discontented, and really I don't think I am.
>
> I don't know what to write about work here. Emigration constantly increases and so do jealousy and quarrels. Sometimes I am horribly discouraged about all this work. There aren't the results which we ought to see, and the people don't appreciate it at all. I should like to run away like a coward. I think I am a round peg in a square hole or vice versa.[68]

There were, in fact rumblings of discontent among the Armenians. Some felt that they were not given enough voice in the running of the college; others disagreed with the efforts of the missionaries to spread their faith to the outlying villages; they wanted to concentrate more on the towns. There was disagreement on religious grounds as well; Henry Riggs commented that "there seems to be a smack of the spirit of the good old days when a heretic was burned at the stake, and anyone who does not believe in the literal and verbal inspiration of the Bible is a heretic."

As Theresa was preparing to leave, the missionaries were ready to welcome two new persons into their midst: both Annie Riggs and Lorna Carey were pregnant. Annie, robust and healthy, was due about one month after Theresa's departure. There were no signs of trouble ahead, and the shock of what followed was all the more profound. The details of what happened are somewhat sketchy but even in their brevity, they offer an insight into the kind of tragedy that occurred all too often in missionary life: the death of women in childbirth.

We know little about how Annie Tracy Riggs lost her baby, but we do have a description of what happened a few days after this tragedy, in her husband's writing:

> She seemed so like herself Sunday morning that we all felt lighthearted. One of the friends sent in a beautiful pomegranate blos-

68. Yale University Archives, Ellsworth Huntington Papaer, Theresa Huntington Ziegler file.

som. Annie held it and looked at it, and when we were alone she said, "It reminds me of the song

Oh cross, that liftest up my head
I dare not ask to fly from thee
I lay in dust life's glories dead
and from the ground there blossoms red
life that shall endless be."

After noon she was very tired, tried to sleep but was restless. About three o'clock she said, "How I would like a breath from the sea." Then she asked me to read from Sidney Lanier's Hymn of the Marshes, which she loved dearly. I read "Sunrise" while she lay listening and breathing in, it seemed the spirit of the sea, and as I finished, smiling peacefully she said, "Isn't that beautiful." Then she thought she could sleep so I stepped out. When I returned Annie was restless, said she could not breathe. We called the doctor, and he did what he could, but gave little relief. She was quiet for a time, and then she said in an earnest tone, "Jesus," and after a pause again, "Jesus." She spoke incoherently now, and did not know anyone; after a time she dropped into a quiet sleep, then she opened her eyes, spoke to us, said she was tired, could not talk, had been dreaming—soon she fell into a peaceful sleep, from which she never awoke. For what seemed hours I fanned her and she breathed as if in a natural sleep. Then her breath began to come harder. Again the doctor tried to give the tired heart some strength, but to no purpose. The dear spirit had already begun to slip from its prison—the twilight was just fading from the sky as she passed from the Sabbath evening here to the Sabbath morning of her new home.[69]

The body of Annie Tracy Riggs was dressed in the wedding gown she had worn only a little over one year ago. Flowers were heaped about her casket and on her heart, Henry Riggs laid one single pomegranate blossom. The small circle of missionaries gathered for the internment. A native pastor offered a prayer, and Dr. Barnum spoke a few words. "Later in the evening," wrote Henry Riggs, "in the glorious sunset light, under the trees she loved so well the precious casket was lowered into its last resting place, with the little casket that had been laid there only a few days before laid over her heart."

---

69. ABC 16.9.7, vol. 24.

Dr. Atkinson was distraught:

> What was the cause of her death? It is not clear to me. I think heart failure, or more strictly speaking general collapse brought on by the depression caused by the grief over the loss of her child. Her husband says she died of a broken heart.
> Never has the death of a patient of mine so discouraged and disheartened me as this one has. It is one of the saddest cases I have ever seen. A beautiful happy young bride one day, and now a mother dead with her child. Poor Harry Riggs, how our hearts aches for him. He has lasped into silent grief.[70]

Dr. Atkinson himself had a hard time accepting the death of Annie Riggs. He writes that he would gladly have given his life to save hers; he thought of giving up medicine altogether.

As if this was not enough, another tragedy lay in store for the station.

For several years, the Careys had been hoping and praying for a child, and Mrs. Carey had become pregnant at last. But from the beginning, there were ominous signs: Dr. Atkinson reports that albumin was discovered in her urine. Lorna Carey, this delicate and amiable woman who was hard of hearing, was not feeling well. In December, Emma Barnum wrote the following account. Her delicate language almost manages to hide what must have been a harrowing end for Lorna:

> For over a week the doctor felt that her condition was very serious, and on Sunday he felt convinced that the only hope for her was an operation, for she was growing steadily worse. She herself felt this, so Mr. Carey was spared the pain of telling her. Dr. Michael, and one of the German nurses came up to help, and on Christmas morning there was a slight operation with the hope that nature would do the rest, but no relief came, and on Tuesday the dear baby girl for whom she had been praying for so long, had to be taken away. An incubator had been prepared in the hope of saving this little life, but it had already ended it was found, so the whole effort was mostly to save the mother's life. Five long hours did they wait and fight for that life, but as she came out of the chloroform we saw at once that she was leaving us. Her mind was very clear, and although her sufferings were heartrending, her death was most triumphant. She knew she was going, and said goodbye. When

70. ABC 16.9.7, vol 3.

> Mr. Carey begged her to stay with him, she would say, "I'll try," but add almost immediately, "I can't."
>
> Mr. Carey's faith and courage have been wonderful from the very beginning, and yet I don't see how he could have endured it without Mr. Riggs. He has clung to him and both men have been drawn very close together. It seems as if these two men were preaching such a sermon on Christian faith and peace as must make a lasting impression on many lives.[71]

It certainly did on Emma's. Two years later, she and Henry Riggs were married in Harpoot.

71. ABC 16.9.7, vol. 20.

Chapter Twenty-Four:
Theresa Divulges a Secret and Asks: "Will You Be Wonderfully Surprised?"

The Harpoot summer was at its glorious best when Theresa and her party set out from Harpoot, the same way she had come seven years earlier: down the hill to the plain, over the plain, over the mountains, to Samsoun on the Black Sea and from there, by steamer, to Constantinople. Her travel companion included Dr. and Mrs. Barnum, on their way to the United States on furlough.

After a few days in Constantinople Theresa and the Barnums caught a steamer to Naples. From Naples, Theresa expected to travel by herself to Rome to meet up with her sister Cornelia and her traveling party. But there was a surprise for her. Waiting for the tug boat in Naples harbor to take her ashore, she caught sight of two figures in a small row-boat alongside the steamer. To Ellsworth:

> ...after two or three minutes I turned my head and saw thro' the crowd on the other side of our boat a small row-boat and in it a young man who I knew must be John and in an instant I saw Cornelia beside him. They didn't see me till I went to their side.[...] Cornelia looks and acts just as of old. I see practically no difference. I think I am more changed. I like "John" very much, but more anon. (I don't call him that yet.)

That letter is the last one Theresa's eldest daughter found in the attic of the New Hampshire family summer house. On her return, we know that she resigned from the Woman's Board as a missionary and married Charles Ziegler a year and a half later.

But a mystery persisted: had she met him before she left for Harpoot? Was there an agreement that he would wait for her? Were there, perhaps, letters somewhere that she had written to him from that far-off place?

Theresa's eldest daughter Carol Peck and I speculated about this many times. Mrs. Peck knew that her father's sister and Theresa were classmates at

Wellesley. Maybe she had met Elizabeth Ziegler's brother then? What, if anything, had transpired between them?

In an attempt to cast some light on this, I decided to take a look at Theresa's brother's, Ellsworth Huntington's, papers at Yale. This is a vast collection that in addition to the scientific materials—including many notebooks of field notes from his three years in Harpoot—includes letters he wrote and received from a vast number of correspondents. In a file labeled: 'Personal correspondence; Theresa Huntington Ziegler,' I found several letters from Theresa written during the time she and her sister Cornelia were travelling in Europe on their way home. They contained page after page of misgivings on Theresa's part about Cornelia's friend "John" and what he was up to. Cornelia, Theresa claimed, was blindly in love, and John in turn did not look as if he had serious intentions. We don't know the details of how this story ended, but John was not the man Cornelia eventually married.

Later in the collection, I came across this letter from Theresa to Ellsworth, written from Milton:

> March 16, 1906
>
> My dearly-beloved Ellsworth,
>
> How joyful the thought is that you will be at home before long! I was very grateful to you for your letter which reached me last week, dated Nov. 13 and Nov. 27. We enjoy every bit of your journal and nibble away at it for days.
>
> There is a good deal of general news to write—George's and my delightful trip to Nashville to the Student Volunteer Convention, coming home via Mammoth Cave (disappointing) and Washington (wholly satisfactory), the plans for Ruth's wedding to come off in June; Cornelia's plan to take four girls abroad (chiefly to England) in the summer; George's final decision to go to Robert College for his life-work; dear Harry's stay in Utah; various church functions and entertainments etc. etc. But after all there is just one thing which I can write of fully today, and that is the question of my return to Turkey, which you brought up. You said, "I only wonder whether you feel that you ought to go back no matter what else may open before you. Whatever comes to you, I hope it will be a work into which your whole life can enter, a work that you can love as I love mine." Dear lad, were you thinking of marriage when you wrote that? Will you be wonderfully surprised if I tell you that two days ago I promised to marry Charles Ziegler, Elizabeth's older brother? Of course you remember him more or less well. He began to care for me before I went to Turkey, but I

did not know it then. It is simply wonderful to me that he loves me, but I can't help loving him in return. I hope God will make me more worthy as the days go by. And I wish you would add to your prayer for me, dear, that Charles may never be disappointed in me or in anything. It takes more faith than I have yet to believe that.

I hardly feel as yet that I am "engaged,"—that it is real and true. Charles' business is very exacting, so I cannot see him often. I expect to spend next Sunday there—and rather dread it, as it is the first time with the family in this new relation. I don't know when I shall be married. You doubtless think first of dear Harpoot. I believe someone will be found soon to take my place. Just as I felt sure the first time that it was God's will for me to go there, I feel now that this new life is God's will for me. Only it is such a beautiful, happy thing for Him to give me that I find it hard to believe that it will not all turn out to have been a mistake, and my face be set toward Turkey again.

I suppose you want to ask a great many questions. He is eleven years older than I—for which I, at least, am not sorry. His family were completely taken by surprise and are quite dazed; mine only a little less so, because they naturally knew a little of his letters, etc. It isn't announced yet, but I can imagine that some people will be amazed and the Woman's Board will be just a bit mad with me. I shan't visit Miss Stanwood for some time.

Now I must write this same news to Grandma and Aunt Theresa. It is going to cause me a deal of trouble in the correspondence line!

Dearie, won't you write the best kind of letter that you can to Charles? He is your brother, you see. His address is Mr. Charles Ziegler, 1 Ellis St., Roxbury, Mass.[72]

Theresa did write many letters during that week. Another one she wrote must have been addressed to the American Board of Commissioners for Foreign Missions at Beacon Street in Boston. On March 24, James L. Barton—who had spent a year as a missionary in Harpoot himself and who was now Board Secretary—wrote in reply:

72. Yale University Artchives, Ellsworth Huntington Papers. Personal Correspondence; Theresa Huntington Ziegler.

Miss Theresa L. Huntington
Milton, Mass.

My dear Miss Huntington,

Your note was received this morning giving the information that circumstances are such that you cannot return to Harpoot. While this brings a sense of most keen disappointment, yet I want to say frankly that I believe you have made the right decision and that the Lord will bless you in it. I do not say this from the Harpoot side for the gain of Mr. Ziegler is the supreme loss of Harpoot and the American Board. Your work at Harpoot was worthy of all praise and the memory of your years there among the people and your associates will always be precious. I say this after constant correspondence with the station and knowing as I do how fully you were respected and loved. We can never fill your place, although we shall hope to find someone who will go out to work in the college. I am sure we can depend upon you to co-operate with us in finding your successor.

I wish to send my hearty congratulations to Mr. Ziegler. I hope I shall have the privilege of meeting him and of expressing in person the congratulations which I deeply feel are due him. We shall always remember you as a member of the Harpoot circle. You know the statement, the truth of which you will realize more and more I am sure, that when one has been a missionary of the American Board, he never ceases to be such wherever he may go and whatever he may do. I feel sure that your interest in the work of the Board and especially at Harpoot, will never slacken and that we shall always have in you a coadjutor and friend.

I suppose it will be necessary to take the matter to our Prudential Committee and ask them to accept your resignation. This is a formality which will need to be gone through with for the use of our records. With cordial greetings and best wishes for all your future plans and life, I remain,

Faithfully yours,
James L. Barton

P.S. You understand, of course, that you are entitled to an allowance while on furlough here for the full 12 months, since your return from Turkey. The fact that your resignation is accepted does

not at all vitiate your right to this furlough with allowance continued.
Faithfully yours,
JLB[73]

We can well imagine Theresa's relief on reading this warm-hearted and generous response by Secretary Barton. As Theresa's and Charles's plans for an October wedding were beginning to take shape, there was another response—this time in the form of a moving letter from one of her Armenian women friends in Harpoot. It must have been written very soon after the news of her engagement had been received. The penmanship is excellent and careful.

Harpoot, 1906. May 1.

My dear Miss Huntington

When I heard the news of your engagement I was sorry much for my part and for the school to lose such a useful worker but on the contrary I wish you gladly to have a good fortune for the future. I congratulate you for your new friend. May God keep both of you and bless you in every case. I hope you shall find much comfort and enjoyment in your new life. Till now I had expected to see your dear aspect but now in one moment every hope was lost and I can not make me believe that truly I shall not see you in this world. "As Ephesians wept and fell on Paul's neck sorrowing most of all for the words which he spoke, that they should see his face no more." I am glad that at least I could come and see you in the last evening before you have gone and I could help you a little.

I will never forget those kind deeds which you have done for me. It was good for me to have such a compassionate friend as you but as it is pleasing to God to be separated from you what can I say? Only here after I will remember you lovingly...

Mariam my niece wanted to send me some things with you perhaps she has written you about it, but now I will write her telling your circumstances. I hope some day you shall have the chance to see her. She is uncomfortable I try to make her encourage with my letters and pray for her. These days we are obliged to change our house again because of the owner who wishes to come and live in it. In this Easter vacation I looked for a suitable house but I could not find.

73. ABC 16.9.16.

I hope God will show us His will in it. My parents are in the same condition. Our great trouble is my father's illness which causes us much distress. In every vacation it seems to me unendurable thing to bear such a condition but always I ask strength from my Lord and He grants me. Glory for His name that in Him I can find rest and comfort.

I read a book lately which is called "The Christians secret of a Happy Life." I was helped much by reading it. I will buy one if I can find.

Hereafter I can not expect a long letter from you but I hope you will be so kind to remember me by short letters and would you please to give informations about your new companion?

Please give my love to your mother and tell her that I keep her letter as a remembrance from her.

(in Armenian): Please permit me to add a few lines in Armenian so that I can finish my letter quickly. Dear Miss Huntington, I hope I have not bored you with my words and you will forgive me if there are mistakes in what I wrote since it was not corrected.

Please also convey my loving greetings to your new groom and wish him joy. I congratulate him for associating himself to such a noble wife and let me say according to our custom, "May the Lord give joy to both of you." I would be very happy and grateful if you will write to me. And if it will please you, may I also ask that you send me your picture for me to keep as a memory with me.

I remain your sister who remembers you lovingly and your sincere friend,
Markarid B.

p.s. I wish I were able to write about happier things, but unfortunately I could not.
My mother was very sorry when she heard that you will no longer be returning to us. She always remembers you lovingly.

Theresa Lyman Huntington and Charles Lincoln Ziegler were married on October 18, 1906, in Milton, Mass. The couple spent their first married years living with Charles's family in Roxbury where they had their four children: Constance Herbert Ziegler was born in 1907, followed by Caroline Durant Ziegler in 1909. Their son, Lyman Huntington Ziegler was born in 1912 and in 1919, when Theresa was 45, came their youngest daughter, Miriam Huntington Ziegler.

After the death of Grandpa Ziegler, Theresa and Charles moved to a charming and spacious house in Waban, part of Newton. There were to be no other moves; this was the house the family lived in until both Theresa, and later Charles, died.

James Barton was right when he said that there would always be a missionary side to Theresa's life. She gave frequent talks on her experiences in Harpoot. From 1926 to her death in 1945, she was a member of the Board of Managers of the Walker Home—a boarding house for missionary children whose parents were overseas, and also a retirement home for missionaries—in nearby Auburndale.[74] This was the place to which the first President of Euphrates College in Harpoot, Crosby Wheeler, and his wife, had come to spend their final days, and along with them many others of "the Harpoot circle" as well. Ada Hall, back in England, and Miriam Platt remained good friends and she kept in touch with many of her Armenian friends as well; her daughters Caroline and Miriam remember Armenian dishes these women would bring when they visited. Theresa was active in the Women's Association of very same Congregational church in Waban that I had called out of the blue when I sought some more information about her, and where her daughter had happened to answer the phone. She was a loyal Wellesley alumna as well and often went to meetings and reunions there.

There was a severe side to Theresa as a mother, quite in keeping with the prevalent child-rearing theories of the time. "None of us felt that we ever measured up to her expectations," one of her daughters said. There was even a puritan streak in her: on Sundays, there was to be no play for children and no work for adults. That day was reserved for Sunday school and church and family hymn-singing in the afternoons with an occasional walk. There was to be no make-up, no shaving of legs, no frivolity on the part of her daughters.

But if Theresa was a perfectionist—"the word 'ought' came up an awful lot" said her daughter Miriam—she was also hard on herself. "She wore the same drab dress, day after day after day—and it wasn't until she found she had cancer that she went out and bought a lot of beautiful clothes, including a bright red dress," Miriam remembers.

But there was a light side to Theresa as well. She loved to laugh. She was generous with her time and became like a second mother to some of her nieces and nephews. She was vigorous and energetic. And—she was devoted to her husband. "I never heard them argue or fight; they were totally devoted to each other," Miriam said, and added that Theresa and Charles never tried to hide

---

74. Edith G. Field, *A History of the Walker Missionary Homes,* Auburndale, MA, Unpublished Manuscript.

their affection for each other. They would snuggle, and hug, and the undercurrent of physical attraction between them was not lost on the children.

Harpoot came up frequently in stories and conversations, and Waban is not far from the missionary cemetery in Newton she must have visited many times. We do not know her own final appraisal of the work that she and the other missionaries had done in Turkey, but we can imagine with what anguish she must have received the news that kept coming from there in the years after she returned, when the work of the American Board was swept away in the horrors of the Armenian genocide of 1915.

Theresa Huntington Ziegler died in 1945 at age 70. On hearing the news, her brother Ellsworth, already a Professor at Yale, wrote to Charles Ziegler:

> Dear Charles:
>
> When I came home last night Rachel met me with the news about Theresa. Of course I am not surprised, but even the final coming of death is a shock. I knew that to you and the children it must be even more so.
>
> Our George's death has for the first time given me a full appreciation of what death means. Even when Father and Mother died it was not so great a blow. I think I see now how lonely one must feel to lose the closest of all companions.
>
> I know the serene spirit and the faith with which you take whatever comes, and I glory in it. Life will go on and there will still be pleasant things in it—your children, your home, your friends, and tender memories of the many hours, days, months, and years that you have spent with Theresa. The more you remember, the better.
>
> Since Theresa was ill, and now more than ever, I enjoy especially the thought of the three years we spent together in Harpoot. We had been very close before—studying the same lessons, slumping at a signal into a big chair to study from the same book. And then, after college was over and she taught two years, we had a marvelous time together [in Harpoot]. I remember best our horseback rides over brown mountains just touched with green in spring or white with snow in winter. How she loved it, and how we laughed when her horse rolled in the snow or in the brook. And how mad I was when her horse threw her and a stupid Turk would not catch the animal.
>
> I remember, too, how thoughtful of others she was in school at Harpoot and in the home there.

I did not fully appreciate her then. When one is young one takes these fine traits of character for granted. As the years went on and I saw her with her husband and children I sized her up as better than I had realized. One of the things that impressed me most was the way people relied on her advice when she became a Director of the Home at Auburndale.

She is gone from us now, Charles, but not lost. We have been very fortunate to have her all these years—you for near forty, I near seventy. There is little more that we could ask Heaven for as far as she is concerned. I am sure your loneliness will be comforted.

Your affectionate brother, Ellsworth.

March 23, 1945

Afterword

What happened to the people in Theresa's 'Harpoot circle'? Some of her friends and colleagues remained missionaries of the American Board to the end of their days; most of them, even if they had gone on to do other things with their lives, appear in the obituary pages of The Missionary Herald. These are the ones whose lives we have glimpsed through Theresa's letters:

Laura Ellsworth, as we have seen, did not last long as a missionary and was, in fact, not deemed very suitable missionary material by some in the 'circle.' She stayed in Harpoot for a year and then went on to Sivas, where she married a Mr. Anderson at the British Consulate there. She eventually moved to Scotland with him and two daughters. *Dr. Ussher* was transferred to Van and married Elizabeth Freeman Barrows there; she died at Van during the massacres of 1915. After her death, Dr. Ussher returned to the United States but came back to Turkey for another stint 1919-1922; he lived in California after his retirement and died in Santa Monica in 1955. *"Aunt Hattie" Seymour* returned to the United States in 1905 after almost forty years in Harpoot; she died in Philadelphia in 1912. "Aunt Caro," her friend and fellow touring missionary with an equally long stint in Harpoot, stayed on in Harpoot one year after Theresa and died, after several years of being an invalid, in the Auburndale Walker Home in 1919. *Ada Hall* went back to her native Liverpool when Theresa left in 1905, and the two friends corresponded for years after that. *Dr. Caleb Gates* assumed the Presidency of Robert College where he stayed until 1932. In the aftermath of World War I he was a major actor in behalf of the Armenians as Chairman of Near East Relief from 1917 to 1919. *Mrs. Mary Ellen Gates* died in 1937 in Brattleboro, Vermont; Dr. Gates died in Denver in 1946. *Lora Carey,* who was in poor health most of her time in Harpoot and who had been praying for a child ever since she and her husband arrived there in 1901, met a tragic fate. She died in childbirth in 1905, along with the newborn baby. Both were buried in Harpoot. Two years later, the Rev. Edward Carey married *Miriam Platt.* The wedding was held in Constantinople in the home of Dr. Gates. The Careys returned to the United States in 1910; for many years, Mr. Carey was vice-President of a department store in Poughkeepsie. Edward Carey died in 1952, Miriam, who remained active in many civic causes, died in 1958. *The Barnums* stayed on in Harpoot, which for them was home. After fifty years there, Dr. Barnum died in 1910. His wife, Mary Barnum, survived him by five years and both were buried in the Harpoot missionary cemetery. *Dr. Atkinson* finally got his hospital in Mezereh and did heroic work there during the war until he himself succumbed to typhus on Christmas Day, 1916. His wife, *Tacy Atkinson,* returned to the U.S. in 1917; she died in Philadelphia in 1937. *Mrs. Anna Knapp* and all the 'Knapkins' were home on furlough when *George Knapp* died in Diarbekir in 1915, under suspicious circumstances. Mrs. Knapp died in a nursing home in Walkham, Mass. in 1954. *Bertha Wilson,* the newest of Theresa's woman colleagues, stayed in Harpoot until 1907, whereas old-timer *Mary Daniels* stayed on through World War I and the massacres of 1915 and returned in 1917. Mary continued working in the home offices of the Woman's Board and died in 1923 in Franklin, Mass. *The Brownes,* another long-time Harpoot family, retired in 1912 after 37 years of missionary work when Dr. Browne was seventy years old. *Leila Browne* died in California in 1923 and the Rev. *John Browne* spent his years of widowhood at the Walker Home in Auburndale where he died in his early nineties in 1939. A sad fate awaited the newly married *Annie Tracy Riggs.* A year after her arrival in Harpoot, she died there in childbirth along with her baby. Her husband Henry Riggs claimed that she died "of a broken heart." He nearly did, too, on losing Annie who had been his childhood companion in Marsovan and to whom he had been married for only a little over a year. In May, 1907, the Harpoot missionary circle that had been so hard hit by the deaths of Mrs. Riggs and Mrs. Carey, had a happy event to celebrate: the wedding of *Emma Barnum* and Henry Riggs. Their daughter, Annie, a lovely, blonde girl, was born in Harpoot. In 1916, little Annie Riggs died of typhus and a year later Emma succumbed to the same disease. One of the most poignant discoveries I made in the Houghton archives was Emma Barnum's will, dictated on her deathbed to her husband. "It is my desire and request that a part or all of this bequest be used in establishing, preferably at or near Harpoot, a memorial to my little daughter Annie Barnum Riggs, in the form of an orphanage, children's hospital ward, or some other work for suffering children that may fittingly commemorate her spirit of loving, sympathetic service." Emma, calm, patient, and always a tower of strength in the Harpoot station, did not have enough strength left to sign her full name. The signature is a shaky capital E and half a shaky m. After this crushing blow, *Henry Riggs* spent the rest of the war years in Harpoot performing heroic deeds in order to alleviate the suffering of the Armenians. His own words written about that time will provide the epilogue to the story of the work at Harpoot. Henry Riggs got married for the third time in 1920 to Annie Denison who came as a missionary to Harpoot. In 1923, they were expelled from Harpoot and the station was closed. They moved to Beirut where they lived until 1940. As WW II broke out, Mrs. Riggs and their two daughters returned to the U.S. Henry Riggs, grandson of missionaries, a man who could preach a sermon in six languages, died in Jerusalem on his way to Beirut in 1943 and is buried there together with his third wife.

And the "dear home people"? Theresa's father, the Reverend Henry Strong Huntington, retired from the active ministry of the Congregational church in Milton in 1907 and devoted himself to historical research and writing. In 1914, he published a book about the life of Samuel Huntington, signer of the Declaration of Independence and President of the Continental Congress. Henry Huntington died in 1920; his wife Mary, in 1924.

Cornelia, who sometimes is called 'Kindie' in the letters and who according to her niece Carol Peck was "a delightful, warm-hearted and capable manager in whatever situation she found herself," eventually joined the faculty at Robert College in Constantinople where she met her husband, Theron Damon. The Damons, who had two children, lived in Turkey until 1941 and remained closely associated with Robert College all their lives. Cornelia, a vital, aristocratic-looking world traveler with many interests and an active Wellesley alumna, died in 1960.

Ellsworth, who according to a Time Magazine obituary was "an expert on everything human," was a favorite of his nieces and nephews. "We kids loved being with him," writes Theresa's daughter Miriam, "because of the wonderful stories he could tell, his curiosity about the world, and his boundless energy, enthusiasm and good humor." Ellsworth met his wife Rachel Brewer when he was past 35; they had three children. At his death in x he was a distinguished scientist and Professor of Geography at Yale University. He wrote copiously on the topic of race and climate; today many of his ideas could only be called racist. *George*, who graduated from Auburn Theological Seminary, spent all of his active life at Robert College. He married Elizabeth Dodge and might well have become President of the college. But in early middle age, he contracted polio and spent the rest of his life in a wheel-chair. They had no children but became marvelous 'second' parents to their nieces and nephews. "Uncle George never gave in to self-pity," wrote Miriam, "and was always mentally alert and socially involved until his death in the early fifties." *Harry* graduated from Yale and Auburn Theological Seminary; the early part of his life was conventional enough with marriage to Edith Morrell and six children. Gradually, however, Harry's life took a decidedly unconventional turn. To quote his daughter, Alice Allen: "He left the ministry, became what we would now call a secular humanist, and founded the American Sunbathing Society. He was convinced that nudism could transform society into a saner place, and devoted the rest of his life to that belief." This put too much of a strain on the marriage to Edith; they divorced. The family, however, kept in touch. Miriam: "We used to love it when Uncle Harry came to visit, with his sandals, reddish beard, twinkling eyes and delicious sense of humor. He invited us to visit his nudist camp--Burgoyne Trail in western MA--which we all did, fully dressed! He eventually married a nudist sympathizer, Aunt Pat, and they lived a useful life for many years in Philadelphia. He was over 100 when he died." Harry, too, had an obituary in Time Magazine. *Ruth* was the youngest of the Huntington children and she, too, was a Wellesley graduate. She married Sam Fletcher, an engineer, and settled in Birmingham, Alabama. They had six children. Miriam remembers Ruth as a "small, motherly, gentle person, easy to talk to." Ruth and Theresa were very close, and Ruth's daughter Mary Hunt remembers that the Ziegler home in Waban was like a second home for her during the years that she continued the family tradition on the female side by attending Wellesley College.

Epilogue

One hundred years after Theresa Huntington, my Armenian husband and I are crossing the Harpoot plain. No missionary party has set out from Harpoot to meet us. A crowded minibus makes the run from Malatia to Elazig—Theresa's Mezereh—in an hour and a half, several times a day. For one brief moment, just before we reach our destination, there is a clear view across the plain to the north: a dark clump of houses in the saddle of a high mountain: Harpoot.

We get off the bus without a clear idea of how to get up there. A man offers us directions to the only hotel in town but insists that we first join him in his office for a cup of tea. He turns out to be an accountant, and he is clearly wondering what brings us to Elazig. This is no tourist town: it is on the edges of the Kurdish area and our minibus has passed through several army checkpoints on the way from Malatia.

I have a friend whose mother used to work in Harpoot, I say, being careful not the use the Armenian version of the name. We would like to go up and see the place so we can tell her about it.

This is all in Turkish, with my husband translating for me. His Turkish is good; he spoke it with his grandmother who came from Aintab and spoke nothing else. The accountant is mystified: how come my husband speaks such good Turkish? He has probably figured it out, I think to myself. Armenians, he is thinking. Come back to see the old country.

The accountant's name is Ali. He seems to be a big man about town. Has other foreign friends, he says. A German came through last year and sends him postcards now and then. Another American couple. From Detroit. He took them to see the big Euphrates dam. Would we like to see the big Euphrates dam?

By the second cup of sweet tea, Ali has persuaded us to let him take us to Harpoot. It will be a pleasure for him, he says. He will be only too happy to take the rest of the day off. A few minutes later we sit in his red Mazda, heading up the mountain, past another checkpoint.

Theresa galloping through a blizzard on her way to Mezereh, her veil plastered to her face. Armenian children walking up the steep road to school. Consul Norton, on his way up for a Thanksgiving dinner. Crosby Wheeler and Susan Wheeler, eyeing the town for the first time, wondering if they'll be greeted by a shower of rocks. Henry Riggs, on his way down to the Mezereh bank with money for the American relatives of an Armenian family about to be massacred. *This is the mountain.*

We drive around, asking old people: American school? Christian cemetery? The slopes of the mountain dip in undulating valleys towards the plain. Here and there on the wide brown slopes, like mushrooms out of the ground, stand clusters of tombstones.

But they are Moslem tombstones.

The fortress is still there, making it possible to see where the buildings of the Harpoot station must have stood. Wheeler Auditorium, large enough to hold one thousand seven hundred students. The four-story college building. The Girls' school. The Boys' dormitory. The Kindergarten. Twenty-four buildings, all made of stone, all gone.

The war; then a severe earthquake in 1939. I feel an aching need to find something to touch, but there is nothing left to touch.

"Do you suppose Theresa ever asked herself, after what happened in 1915, if it would have been better if the missionaries had never come here?" I wonder. "Do you think there might have been Armenians left here then, without the provocation of all that Western influence?"

My husband shrugs his shoulders. Who can know?

"Yes, I've heard there were some Americans here a long time ago," Ali says. "I think they had a school, for Armenians. But then the Armenians all got rich and left the country. So they closed the school."

Bibliography

Anderson, Rufus. *History of the Missions of the American Board of Commissioners for Foreign Missions to the Oriental Churches*. 2 vols., Boston: Congregational Publishing Society, 1873.

Bartlett Samuel C. *Historical Sketches of the Missions of the American Board.* Boston, 1876; repr. New York: Arno Press, 1972.

Beaver, R. Pierce. *American Protestant Women in World Mission. A History of the Feminist Movement in North America*. Grand Rapids, MI: William B. Edermans Publishing Company, 1980.

Bowie, Fiona, Deborah Kirkwood, and Shirley Ardener, eds. *Women and Missions: Past and Present.* Anthropological and Historical Perceptions. Providence/Oxford: Berg, 1993.

Davis, Leslie A. *The Slaughterhouse Province. An American Diplomat's Report on the Armenian Genocide, 1915-1917*. Edited by Susan K. Blair. New Rochelle, NY: Aristide D. Caratzas, 1989.

Centennial of Constantinople Station: 1831-1931, Constantinople: Near East Mission of the American Board, 1931.

Eddy, David Brewer. *What Next in Turkey: Glimpses of the American Board's Work in the Near East*. Boston: The Taylor Press, 1913.

Euphrates College, *Historical Statement and Report for 1903*. Boston: Trustees of Euphrates College,1903.

Field, Edith G., *A History of the Walker Missionary Homes*. Auburndale, MA, 1964. Unpublished Manuscript.

Flemming, Leslie A., ed. *Women's Work for Women*. Boulder, Colorado, 1989.

Gates, Caleb F. *Not To Me Only*. Princeton: Princeton University Press, 1940.

Grabill, Joseph L. *Protestant Diplomacy and the Near East, 1810-1927*. Minneapolis: University of Minnesota Press, 1971.

Haig, Vahe. *Kharpert and Her Golden Plain*. New York, 1959.

Hepworth, George H. *Through Armenia on Horseback*, New Yorl: E. P. Dutton & Co., 1898.

Hill, Patricia R. *The World Their Household. The American Woman's Foreign Mission Movement and Cultural Transformation, 1870-1920*. Ann Arbor: The University of Michigan Press, 1985.

Hovannisian, Richard, ed. *The Armenian Genocide in Perspective*. New Brunswick, N.J.: Transaction Books, 1986.

Hunter, Jane. *The Gospel of Gentility*. New Haven: Yale University Press, 1984.

Kinross, Lord, *The Ottoman Centuries. The Rise and Fall of the Turkish Empire*. New York: Morrow Quill Paperbacks, 1977.

Lynch, H.F.B. *Armenia, Travels and Studies*. 2 vols. London, 1901; repr. Beirut: Khayats, 1965.

Manwell, Reginald D, and Sophia Lyon Fahs, *The Church Across the Street*. Boston: The Beacon Press, 1947.

Melson, Robert F. *Revolution and Genocide*. Chicago: University of Chicago Press, 1992.

Merguerian, Barbara J. "The American Response to the 1895 Massacres," in *Genocide and Human Rights, Journal of Armenian Studies*, Volume IV, Nos. 1 and 2, Belmont, MA: NAASR, Armenian Heritage Press, 1992.

Mirak, Robert. *Torn Between Two Lands*. Cambridge, MA: Harvard University Press, 1983.

A Modern Crusade in the Turkish Empire. Chicago: Woman's Board of Missions of the Interior, 1908.

Müller, Mrs. Max. *Letters from Constantinople*. London: Longmans, Green, and Co.

Palmer, Alan. *The Decline and Fall of the Ottoman Empire*. New York: M. Evans and Company, 1992.

Pears, Sir Edwin. *Life of Abdul Hamid*. London: Constable & Co., 1917.

Philibosian, Hapet M., ed. *Memoranda of Euphrates College. (Formerly Armenia College) 1878-1915*. Boston: Euphrates College Alumni Association, 1942.

Richter, Julius. *A History of Protestant Missions in the Near East. 1910*, repr. New York: AMS Press, 1970.

Riggs, Henry H. "Personal Experiences in Karput (Harput), 1915-1917." Inquiry Document 482, Records of the American Commission to Negotiate Peace, N.A., D.S., R.G., 256.

Riggs, Henry H. *A.B.C.F.M. History 1910-1942. Section on the Turkey Missions*. Unpublished Monograph, Harvard University Library, 1942.

Scott, Anne Firor. *Natural Allies*. Women's Associations in American History. Urbana and Chicago: University of Illinois Press, 1991.

Stone, Frank Andrews. *Academies for Anatolia*. Lanham: University Press of America, 1984.

The Missionary History of Congregationalism. New York: The National Council of Congregational Churches, 1920.

Ussher, Clarence D. and Grace H. Knapp, *An American Physician In Turkey*. Boston: Houghton Mifflin Co., 1917.

West, Maria A. *The Romance of Missions or Inside Views of Life and Labor in the Land of Ararat*. New York: Randolph and Company, 1875.

Wheeler, C. H. *Ten Years on the Euphrates*. Boston: American Tract Society, 1868.

Wheeler, Mrs. Crosby H. *Missions in Eden*. New York: Fleming H. Revell Company, 1899.

Wheeler, S. A. (Mrs. Crosby). *Daughters of Armenia*. New York: American Tract Society, 1877.

Woman's Board of Missions of the Interior. Annual Reports, 1896-1910.

JOURNALS

Missionary Herald.

Life and Light for Women.

MANUSCRIPT COLLECTIONS

The American Board of Commissioners for Foreign Missions, Houghton Library, Harvard University, Cambridge, MA.

General Records of the Department of State, Record Group 59, National Archives, Washington, D.C.

Despatches from U.S. Consuls in Harput, Turkey, 1895-1906, T579 (microfilm), National Archives, Washington, D.C.

Index